D1228193

1951-

BASIC INCOME

BASIC INCOME

A Radical Proposal for a Free Society and a Sane Economy

PHILIPPE VAN PARIJS

YANNICK VANDERBORGHT

HARVARD UNIVERSITY PRESS

Cambridge, Massachusetts

London, England

2017

Copyright © 2017 by the President and Fellows of Harvard College
All rights reserved
Printed in the United States of America
First printing

LIBRARY OF CONGRESS CATALOGING-IN-PUBLICATION DATA

Names: Parijs, Philippe van, 1951– author. | Vanderborght, Yannick, author.
Title: Basic income : a radical proposal for a free society and a sane
economy / Philippe Van Parijs and Yannick Vanderborght.
Description: Cambridge, Massachusetts : Harvard University Press, 2017. |
Includes bibliographical references and index.
Identifiers: LCCN 2016045726 | ISBN 9780674052284 (alk. paper)
Subjects: LCSH: Guaranteed annual income. | Public welfare. |
Basic needs. | Economics—Sociological aspects.
Classification: LCC HB846 .P37 2017 | DDC 362.5/82—dc23
LC record available at https://lccn.loc.gov/2016045726

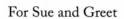

For Sue and Greet

Contents

BASIC INCOME

Prologue

"The money that one possesses is the instrument of freedom;
that which one strives to obtain is the instrument of slavery."

—JEAN-JACQUES ROUSSEAU, *Confessions*

To REBUILD CONFIDENCE and hope in the future of our societies, in the future of our world, we shall need to subvert received wisdom, shake our prejudices, and learn to embrace radical ideas. One of these, simple but crucial, is that of an unconditional basic income: a regular cash income paid to all, on an individual basis, without means test or work requirement.

The idea is not new. Since the end of the eighteenth century, it has occurred to any number of bold minds. Today, however, the conjunction of growing inequality, a new wave of automation, and a more acute awareness of the ecological limits to growth has made it the object of unprecedented interest throughout the world. Anyone looking into the fate of our developed welfare states can safely be expected to encounter it, as is anyone trying to figure out how to design basic economic security in the less developed parts of our finite planet. The idea of an unconditional basic income is bound to intrigue, and quite often to thrill, those who want tomorrow's world to be a world of freedom—of real freedom, not mere formal freedom, and for all, not just for the happy few.

In chapter 1, we present the central case for an unconditional basic income: how it addresses the problems of poverty and unemployment, lousy jobs, and crazy growth; and how it can claim to provide an instrument of freedom and an essential ingredient of a sustainable emancipatory institutional framework. In chapter 2, we discuss a number of alternative proposals for which people attracted to the basic income concept, including ourselves, tend to feel some sympathy, and indicate why we believe basic income is to be preferred. In chapter 3, we sketch the intellectual and institutional fate, from the sixteenth century onwards, of the two established models of social protection: public assistance and social insurance. In chapter 4, we retrace, from the end of the eighteenth century onwards, the fascinating history of the idea of a radically distinct third model: basic income. Chapter 5 starts with the moral case against basic income. In response, we present what we believe to be its fundamental ethical justification, invoked only elliptically in chapter 1, and discuss a number of alternative philosophical approaches. Chapter 6 asks whether a substantial basic income is affordable and discusses the many ways of funding it that have been proposed. Against this background, chapter 7 assesses the political prospects for basic income by surveying the attitudes towards it adopted by political and social forces around the world and exploring ways of avoiding a possible backlash. Finally, chapter 8 considers the specific challenges that basic income faces in the context of globalization. Throughout the book, the primary focus is on proposals for affluent societies, but their increasing relevance for less-developed countries is also discussed in many places.

After scrutinizing the idea of an unconditional basic income, one may choose to endorse it or to reject it. This book explains why we believe it should be endorsed. But this is not a partisan tract. It is in large part a comprehensive, critical synthesis of the fast-expanding multidisciplinary and multilingual literature on the subject. As such, it hopes to provide a depository of reliable information and illuminating insights that should be useful to people arguing for but also against basic income, helping to correct factual errors and conceptual confusions often found in arguments on either side. It also aims to address head-on the most serious objections to the desirability and feasibility of a basic income. Dodging these objections may help one win a televised debate, but it cannot secure the lasting victory of a just proposal— quite the contrary. Yes, a better world *is* possible, and in order to achieve it, it is necessary to be imaginative and enthusiastic. But intellectually honest discussion that does not elude inconvenient facts and embarrassing difficulties is just as indispensable. This is the collective effort this book invites you to join.

A basic income is not just a clever measure that may help alleviate urgent problems. It is a central pillar of a free society, in which the real freedom to flourish, through work and outside work, will be fairly distributed. It is an essential element of a radical alternative to both old socialism and neoliberalism, of a realistic utopia that offers far more than the defense of past achievements or resistance to the dictates of the global market. It is a crucial part of the sort of vision needed to turn threats into opportunities, resignation into resolution, anguish into hope.

1

The Instrument of Freedom

WE LIVE IN A NEW WORLD, remade by many forces: the disruptive technological revolution brought about by the computer and the internet; the globalization of trade, migration, and communication; a fast-growing worldwide demand running up against the limits imposed by a shrinking pool of natural resources and the saturation of our atmosphere; the dislocation of traditional protective institutions, from the family to labor unions, state monopolies, and welfare states; and the explosive interactions of these various trends.

This creates unprecedented threats, but also unprecedented opportunities. In order to evaluate these threats and these opportunities, one needs a normative standard. Throughout this book, ours will be the standard of freedom—more precisely, of real freedom for all and not just for the rich. This normative perspective will be spelled out and discussed in chapter 5. For the moment, this rough characterization will suffice. It is this normative commitment that makes us passionately want to prevent the developments listed above from igniting sharp conflicts and breeding new forms of slavery. It makes us want to use them instead as levers for emancipation. For this purpose, action is urgently needed on many fronts, from the dramatic improvement of our cities' public spaces to the transformation of education into a lifelong activity to the redefinition of intellectual property rights. More than on any other front, action is needed to restructure radically the way in which economic security is pursued in our societies and in our world. In each of our societies and beyond, we need a sturdy floor on which we can stand as individuals and as communities. If we are to stem our anxieties and strengthen our hopes, we must dare to introduce what is now commonly called a *basic income:* a regular income paid in cash to every individual member of a society, irrespective of income from other sources and with no strings attached.

A New World

What makes such a radical reform today more relevant, indeed more urgent, than ever? Among the record number of people who come out in favor of it publicly, many invoke the new wave of automation already on the way and predicted to keep swelling in coming years: robotization, self-driving vehicles, a massive replacement of human-brain workers by computers.[1] It will enable the wealth and earning power of some—those who design, control, and are in the best position to exploit the new technologies—to reach new heights, while that of many more plummets. However, technological change, recent and predicted, is only one of the factors that can be expected to drive the polarization of earning power within countries.[2] It interacts to different extents in different places and at different times with other factors, in sufficiently complex ways that ascribing a precise weight to any of them is impossible. Globalization amplifies this polarization by offering a worldwide market to those with scarce skills and other valuable assets, while those with widely held qualifications must compete with each other worldwide via trade and migration. The shrinking, weakening, or dismantling of public and private monopolies reduces the extent to which the earning power of poorly productive workers can be boosted through implicit intrafirm subsidies. At the same time, dwindling loyalty feelings among the firms' most valued employees force wages to track productivity differences more closely. And inequalities in earnings are amplified by differences in saving capacity and inheritance, which are in turn amplified by returns on capital.[3]

The upshot of these various trends is already visible in the distribution of earnings. If a parade of people of increasing heights is used to represent the distribution of earnings, the giants at the end get taller from decade to decade, the walkers of average height come later and later in the procession, and there are more and more dwarfs whose earnings do not reach the level of what is regarded as a decent income, or are at risk of falling under it.[4] Such a polarization of earning power can be expected to manifest itself in different ways, depending on the institutional context. Where the level of remuneration is and remains firmly protected by minimum-wage legislation, collective bargaining, and generous unemployment insurance, the result tends to be massive losses of jobs. Where such protections are or become weaker, the results tend to be dramatic increases in the numbers of people having to scrape by, doing precarious jobs that pay miserable wages.[5] Such trends are already visible, but if the predicted effects of the new wave of automation materialize, they will get much worse.

Some argue that these effects will create only a short-term problem. After all, this is not the first time that the imminence of automation is being invoked to create urgency around introducing some sort of guaranteed income.[6] In the past, while some jobs were lost, others were created. The fact that goods could be produced with less work was offset by the increase in the amount of goods produced; an automaker, having found a way to make cars with only a fourth of the workers required before, simply made four times more cars. Labor-saving technical change, it is argued, is not a calamity but a blessing if higher productivity shows up in economic growth. Rising production levels can be relied on to keep providing good jobs and thereby decent incomes to the bulk of the population, whether directly through their wages or indirectly through the social benefits to which they are entitled by virtue of these wages. In the past, a broad consensus existed between the right and the left that continued growth would keep unemployment and precariousness in check. Today's unprecedented interest in basic income in the more affluent parts of the world is evidence that this consensus has ended.

Belief in the cure-all of growth is being undermined from three sides. First, there are doubts about the desirability of further growth. Concerns about the ecological limits to growth have been voiced since the 1970s. These are now amplified by awareness of irreversible and largely unpredictable impacts on climate. Second, even among those who do not question the desirability of sustained growth, there are doubts about its very possibility. Particularly with regard to Europe and North America, they anticipate what Larry Summers diagnosed as "secular stagnation." Third, even those who believe growth to be both desirable and possible have grounds to question the belief that growth offers a structural solution to unemployment and precariousness. True, there is a neat negative correlation between growth and unemployment rates. But after all, we have had massive growth since the beginning of the golden sixties—GDP per capita has doubled or trebled since then—and we have not exactly seen the end of joblessness and job insecurity.[7] Each of these doubts about growth as a solution to unemployment and precariousness in the context of further automation could be challenged in various ways. But together they suffice to explain and justify growing calls for a more credible response to the impending challenge. Even NSA whistleblower Edward Snowden has reached this conclusion. He told *The Nation* in 2014: "As a technologist, I see the trends, and I see that automation inevitably is going to mean fewer and fewer jobs. And if we do not find a way to provide a basic income for people who have no work, or no meaningful work, we're going to have social unrest that could get people killed."[8]

Basic Income

Thus, the expectation that meaningful work will be lacking easily leads to the conviction that the growing jobless population must be provided with some means of livelihood. But there are two very different ways of fleshing out this conviction, and one of them is very unattractive. It consists of expanding the old model of public assistance first born in the sixteenth century and instantiated by today's guaranteed-minimum-income schemes of a conditional sort. Typically, such programs supplement the income, if any, that poor households gain directly or indirectly from work up to the point that those households reach some socially defined threshold.

Whether comprehensive or restricted to some sections of the poor population, these schemes make major contributions to eliminating extreme poverty. But due to their conditionality, they have an intrinsic tendency to turn their beneficiaries into a class of permanent welfare claimants. People are entitled to continuing handouts on the condition that they remain destitute, and can prove it is involuntary. They are also subjected to more or less intrusive and humiliating procedures. In countries with developed work-related social insurance systems (where people's eligibility to collect pensions and other periodic payments is based on their having been employed or self-employed for some amount of time), these effects have been confined to relatively small minorities. As the trends mentioned above persist, however, growing shares of populations will be affected. Indeed, the numbers of the precarious will be further swollen as many sources of informal safety, resting on personal ties, continue to weaken: households fall apart in ever greater proportions, nuclear families become smaller, and worker mobility disperses extended families across wide geographies and erodes local communities. Thus, if conditional minimum-income schemes are the only way of addressing the expected lack of meaningful jobs, it seems that the technological progress that is meant to liberate us is going to enslave a growing part of the population instead.

Is there another option? For people committed to freedom for all, the proper way of addressing today's unprecedented challenges and of mobilizing today's unprecedented opportunities does require a minimum-income scheme,

but of an unconditional sort. Brazil's basic income champion Eduardo Suplicy popularized the phrase "the way out is through the door." By this he
meant to say that the provision of a basic income is the most obvious and also
the best way out of poverty—just as the door is the most obvious and best way
out of one's house. It is crucial, however, that this scheme should be unconditional in a strong interpretation of this adjective.[9] Existing schemes can already be called "unconditional" in a number of weaker senses. Being a form of
public assistance rather than social insurance, they are not restricted to people
who paid enough social contributions to qualify for social insurance benefits;
they are usually not restricted to citizens of the country that provides them,
but also cover other legal residents; and they are paid *in cash* rather than in
kind. But a basic income is unconditional in additional ways. It is strictly an
individual entitlement, as opposed to linked to the household situation; it is
what is commonly called *universal,* as opposed to subjected to an income or
means test; and it is *obligation free,* as opposed to tied to an obligation to work
or prove willingness to work. Throughout this book, when we use the term
"basic income" we mean an income that is unconditional in these three additional ways.

We are far from being the first to use "basic income" in this sense or a
sense close to it. The first occurrences of the expression understood in this
way are to be found in a passage of a 1953 book by Oxford political economist
George D. H. Cole laying out John Stuart Mill's discussion of socialism,
and in a 1956 textbook on economic policy by Dutch economist Jan Tinbergen. In 1986, a similar definition was adopted (under Dutch and British
influence) by the newly founded Basic Income European Network (BIEN),
and it was preserved when BIEN became the Basic Income Earth Network
in 2004.[10] Several national networks, including the United States Basic Income Guarantee network (USBIG), have since adopted the equivalent expression in their names, thereby spreading its use. In the United States, the most
common expression was for a long time "demogrant," although "basic income"
was also occasionally used in the late 1960s.[11] Other terms that are or were
used to refer to the same concept include state bonus, social dividend, universal dividend, universal grant, universal income, citizen's income, citizenship
income, citizen's wage, and existence income (along with corresponding expressions in other languages).

By way of further clarification it is important to note that, while it is unconditional in the various senses mentioned above—and to be taken up again
shortly—a basic income remains conditional in one important sense. Recipients

of it must be members of a particular, territorially defined community. In our interpretation, this condition must mean fiscal residence rather than permanent residence or citizenship. This excludes tourists and other travelers, undocumented migrants, and also diplomats and employees of supranational organizations, whose earnings are not subjected to the local personal income tax. It also excludes people serving prison sentences, whose upkeep costs more than a basic income, but who should be entitled to it from the minute they get out.

Should the amount of the basic income be, by definition, uniform? Not necessarily. First, it could vary with age. Some basic-income proposals are explicitly restricted to adults, and have then a universal child-benefit scheme as their logical complement. Usually, however, a basic income is conceived as an entitlement from birth. In this case, its amount is usually, though not in all proposals, set at a lower level for minors.[12] Second, it could vary with geography. Within countries, a basic income is generally conceived as being uniform, irrespective of measurable differences in cost of living (most notably, housing costs). This makes it function as a powerful redistributive instrument in favor of the "peripheries." It could, however, be modulated to take such differences into account, especially if it were to operate on a supranational level (a possibility to be discussed in chapter 8). This would reduce, though not cancel, the redistributive impact in favor of poorer areas.

Third, even if it remained invariable through space, a basic income could be variable across time. To play the role it is intended to play, it would certainly need to be paid on a regular basis rather than just once or at unpredictable intervals. As we'll see in chapter 4, the very first basic-income proposals (Thomas Spence's in 1797 and Joseph Charlier's in 1848) called for payments once a quarter. The state bonus scheme imagined by Mabel and Dennis Milner in 1918 had it paid once a week. At the other extreme, the Alaska dividend is paid once a year. Most proposals since Joseph Charlier's final version, however, specify payment once a month.[13]

A basic income does not only need to be paid regularly. Its amount must also be stable enough and, in particular, immune to sudden declines. This does not mean that it should be fixed. Once in place, it can meaningfully be linked to a price index or, even more meaningfully, to GDP per capita. The latter idea was defended, for example, by Dennis Milner in the first developed basic income plan for the United Kingdom in 1920 and quite recently by labor leader Andy Stern, who likes the idea "because it will mean that the gains of society will accrue more widely for every American

9

citizen, and not just the few."[14] To cushion possible downward shocks, however, linking the amount to an average index over several years is wiser than linking it just to the current year.

Finally, is a basic income mortgageable and taxable? It makes most sense to set the rules so that a basic income cannot be mortgaged; its beneficiaries must not be allowed to use its future stream as a guarantee for loans. This requirement flows naturally from viewing basic income not as a top-up on other incomes but rather as the bottom layer for every person's income, which current legislation usually protects against seizure. That a basic income is also best conceived as income-tax-free is less obvious. There are tax systems in which this makes a difference. For example, if the unit of personal income taxation is the household and if a progressive tax schedule is applied to the total income of all households, including basic incomes in tax bases amounts to giving smaller basic incomes to members of larger households. By contrast, if personal income taxation takes the form of a flat tax or is strictly individual, subjecting the basic income to income taxation is equivalent to reducing it by a fixed amount—and in that case, it is more simple administratively just to set it a lower level and make it tax free.

In light of these various clarifications, it should be clear that the word "basic" in basic income is meant to convey the idea of a floor on which one can stand because of its very unconditionality. It is a foundation on which people can build their lives in various ways, including by topping it up with income from other sources. Nothing in the definition entails a specific amount. For example, a basic income is not by definition sufficient to cover what could be regarded as basic needs. The level of the basic income is of course very relevant in discussions of the merits of particular proposals, and various people have argued that some minimum level should be required for a scheme to deserve the label "basic income." The advantage of the definition we adopt, following common usage, is that it enables us to conveniently separate these two big questions: whether a scheme is unconditional enough for it to qualify as a basic income and whether it is pitched at the right level. We shall therefore stick to this definition, while understanding that there are circumstances in which deviating from it may make strategic sense.

Nonetheless, in developing the argument for basic income in the context of a particular country, it is convenient to have an amount in mind that is both modest enough for us to dare to assume that it is sustainable and generous enough for it to be plausible that it will make a big difference. Whatever the country concerned, we suggest picking an amount on the order of one fourth of its current GDP per capita. In places where payments are modulated according to age or place, this would be an average rather than a uniform amount. Expressing all following amounts in US dollar equivalents (as we will throughout this book), this would come out, in 2015, at $1,163 per month in the United States, $1,670 in Switzerland, $910 in the United Kingdom, $180 in Brazil, $33 in India, and $9.50 in the Democratic Republic of the Congo. Correcting for purchasing power parity, these figures become $1,260 for Switzerland, $860 for the United Kingdom, $320 for Brazil, $130 for India, $16 for the Congo. A worldwide basic income funded with a quarter of world GDP would come to about $210 per month or $7 per day in nominal terms.[15] These figures provide us with a handy benchmark that will enable us to put specific schemes and proposals into perspective throughout the book.[16]

No claim is being made here that an individual basic income of one fourth of GNP per capita suffices to get every household out of poverty. Whether it does depends on the poverty criterion chosen and the country considered, and also on the composition of the household and the part of the country in which it is situated. In the United States, for example, a basic income at 25 percent of GDP per capita ($1,163) exceeds the 2015 official poverty lines of $1,028 and $661 for single people and cohabiting adults, respectively.[17] In most but not all countries, an individual amount of 25 percent of GDP per capita lies above the World Bank's absolute poverty line of $38 (or $1.25 a day), but, at least for single people, below the European Union's criterion of "risk of poverty" which is 60 percent of median disposable income in the country concerned.[18]

There is, therefore, nothing profound, let alone sacrosanct, about the choice of 25 percent of GDP per capita. Perhaps it can plausibly be sold as sitting on the border between "modest" and "generous" versions of the idea. But the specific amount should not be given too much importance at this stage. As we have already seen and shall see further (in chapter 4), very different amounts have been proposed by advocates of the idea. We shall argue ourselves that higher levels can be ethically justified (in chapter 5) and that lower levels are politically expedient (in chapter 7). These lower levels will be lower than what many households are entitled to under existing regimes of public assistance and social insurance in countries with developed welfare states. It is important to keep in mind that basic income should substitute only for existing benefits that are lower than it. In the case of individuals currently receiving higher benefits, the basic income is best thought of as an unconditional floor that must be topped up by conditional supplements, with the existing conditionalities maintained and the post-tax levels adjusted downward without lowering the total disposable incomes of poor households. Contrary to the way in which it is sometimes characterized and to the chagrin of those among its advocates who want to sell it as a radical simplification, a basic income should not be understood as being, by definition, a full substitute for all existing transfers, much less a substitute for the public funding of quality education, quality health care, and other services.[19]

Our claim is that, under twenty-first-century conditions, there is a fundamental difference between an unconditional basic income as we have characterized it and public assistance as exemplified by existing conditional minimum-income schemes. Both are relevant to the alleviation of poverty, but an unconditional basic income means far more. It does not operate at the margin of society but affects power relations at its very core. Its point is not just to soothe misery but to liberate us all. It is not simply a way of making life on earth tolerable for the destitute but a key ingredient of a transformed society and a world we can look forward to. To show why, we shall focus in turn on each of the three unconditionalities noted above as distinguishing basic income from existing minimum-income schemes—its provision of entitlements that are individual, universal, and obligation free. Before doing so, however, we shall briefly discuss a feature that it shares with most of these but that remains nonetheless controversial.

A Cash Income

Fundamental to the concept of a basic income is that it is paid in cash and not in the form of food, shelter, clothes, and other consumer goods. This is in sharp contrast to the earliest forms of guaranteed minimum income instituted in Europe from the sixteenth century onwards and also to food-distribution programs put in place more recently in less-developed countries. The main argument in favor of in-kind provision is that it increases the likelihood that resources will provide for basic necessities for all members of the household rather than be wasted on luxuries or worse. The same argument is the motivation behind the special forms of currency often used to provide minimum income, such as food stamps and other earmarked vouchers.[20] The fact that there is greater public support for in-kind poor relief focused on health and the necessaries of life than for blank checks reflects widespread concern that money will not be spent responsibly.

On the other side of the argument, there is first of all the fact that a fair and efficient distribution of cash, especially in an era of electronic payments, requires far less bureaucracy than a fair and efficient distribution of food or housing. Cash distribution is also less prone to clientelistic pressures, lobbying of all types, and waste through misallocation.[21] Furthermore, when cash is distributed rather than food it creates purchasing power in the areas where poor people live, boosting local economies rather than depressing them, as the distribution of imported free food tends to do.[22] Such advantages become more salient when one recognizes that secondary markets can readily spring up for in-kind transfers, making the argument that they will provide first and foremost for necessities more theoretical than real. Most fundamentally, a priority placed on achieving greater freedom for all carries with it a general presumption in favor of cash distribution, with no restriction as to the object or timing of its spending. This leaves the beneficiary free to decide how to use it, thus allowing individual preferences to prevail among the various options available even with a modest budget.[23] It is no coincidence that the clearest and most general form of minimum income provided in kind is to be found in prisons.

This presumption in favor of cash on grounds of freedom should not be embraced dogmatically, however. First, its advantage depends on the existence of a sufficiently open and transparent market: discrimination annihilates or curtails for its victims the purchasing power a cash income is supposed to give them. Second, in emergency or temporary situations, there might be no time to wait for a market to develop and the only way to save people from starvation might be to provide food and shelter.[24] Third, as mentioned before, a basic income is not meant to replace all services provided or funded by the state. A combination of mild paternalism, awareness of positive and negative externalities, and concern for the preconditions of competent citizenship can easily override the argument for cash in the case of some specific goods such as basic health insurance and education at the preschool, primary, and secondary levels. Such provisions in kind can be defended in terms of the long-term interests of the individuals concerned, and also in terms of societies' interests in maintaining the healthy and well-educated workforces and citizenry that are crucial to well-functioning economies and democracies. Analogous arguments can be made for provisions of safe and enjoyable public spaces, and some other public goods and services.[25] For all these reasons, making a strong case for a basic income paid in cash is consistent with supporting public provision of various services in kind.

An Individual Income

Like most conditional forms of minimum income, a basic income is paid in cash. But unlike them, it is also unconditional in the sense that it is strictly individual. "Strictly individual" refers to both of two logically independent features: it is paid to each individual, and at a level independent of that individual's household situation.[26] Let us consider each in turn.

A basic income is not paid to one person, the "head of the household," for the benefit of all the household's members. It is given individually to each adult member of the household. If minors are included in the scheme, possibly with a reduced amount, their basic incomes will need to be given to one adult member of the household, presumptively their mothers.[27] The chief argument against individualization and in favor of a single payment to the head of the household is simplicity. This advantage holds particularly if the basic income is allowed to take the form of a tax credit—that is, of a reduction of the tax liability of the household by as many times the level of the basic income as there are members in the household entitled to it. If there is a single breadwinner in the household, there may then be no need for any transfer at all: the tax bill of the breadwinner is simply reduced and his or her net earnings accordingly increased. For anyone committed to freedom for all, however, direct payment to all individual members of the basic income to which they are entitled can make a big difference insofar as it affects the distribution of power within the household. For a woman with low or no earnings, control over the household's expenditures will tend to be greater and exit options will tend to be less forbidding if she receives a regular income as an individual entitlement for herself and her children than if her existence and that of her children entail a higher net income for her partner.

A basic income is also strictly individual in a second, more controversial sense.[28] Under existing, conditional minimum-income schemes, how much an individual is entitled to depends on the composition of the household. Typically, adults are entitled to significantly higher benefits if they live alone than if they live in a household with one or more other adults.[29] The argument behind this widespread feature is straightforward: when addressing poverty, one needs to pay attention to economies of scale in consumption. The per-capita cost of satisfying basic needs is higher for people who do not share their housing costs with others, or therefore such associated costs as heating, furniture, and kitchen and laundry equipment. Consequently, single people need more to be lifted out of poverty, and it makes sense to differentiate entitlement according to household composition.

Despite these scale economies, there is a strong case for a basic income that is strictly individual in this second sense, too. There are two reasons why the amount to which an individual is entitled should be independent of the size of the household to which he or she belongs. The first is that cohabitation is hard to confirm. There used to be a time when it was easy to check, because cohabitation was nearly synonymous with marriage. Confirming whether two people are married is straightforward, and in the past that meant that checking whether two people formed a single household could be dispensed with. Today, marriages don't last as long, and are often de facto dissolved long before they are formally dissolved. Above all, unregistered cohabitation has become far more prevalent. These changes all make it trickier and more invasive to check for cohabitation than it used to be. Control is less expensive and privacy is less threatened by consulting municipal records than by checking the sharing of a washbasin or fluctuations in electricity or water consumption.[30] The more general the trend towards informality and volatility in the formation, decomposition, and recomposition of households, the more that competent authorities are stuck in a dilemma between arbitrariness and unfairness on one side and intrusiveness and high monitoring costs on the other, and consequently the stronger the case for a strictly individual transfer in this second sense.

Second, and more fundamentally, differentiating according to household composition has the effect of discouraging people from living together. While it might seem paradoxical, a more strictly individual tax or benefit scheme is a more community-friendly one. The degressive profile of a household-based scheme creates a loneliness trap: people who decide to live together are penalized through a reduction in benefits.[31] Other negative effects follow. The mutual support and sharing of information and networks stemming from cohabitation is weakened. Scarce material resources—space and energy, fridges and washing machines—are underutilized. And the number of housing units for a given population increases, leading to less dense habitats and hence greater mobility challenges. As concern for the strengthening of social bonds and the saving of material resources intensifies, the argument against household differentiation grows stronger by the day. In the pursuit of sustainable freedom for all, cohabitation should be encouraged, not penalized.

Thus, a basic income differs from conditional minimum-income schemes by virtue of being paid on an individual basis. It also differs from them by virtue of being unconditional in two further senses which are more central to our case for the urgency of a basic income. It is unconditional in the sense of being *universal,* not subjected to a means test. The rich are entitled to it just as much as the poor. And it is unconditional in the sense of being *obligation free,* and not being subjected to a willingness-to-work test. The voluntarily unemployed are no less entitled to it than the employed and the involuntarily unemployed. As we will show, the combination of these two unconditionalities is crucial. The former frees people from the unemployment trap, the latter from the employment trap. The former facilitates saying yes to a job offer, while the latter facilitates saying no. The former creates possibilities, while the latter lifts obligations and thereby enhances those possibilities. Without the former, the latter could easily foster exclusion. Without the latter, the former could easily foster exploitation. It is the joint operation of these two features that turns basic income into a paramount instrument of freedom.

A Universal Income

Existing minimum-income schemes all involve some kind of means test. The benefit received typically amounts to the difference between the household's total income from other sources (earnings, interest on savings, contributory pensions, and so forth) and the stipulated minimum income for that particular category of household. Consequently, its level is at its highest when income from other sources is zero, and it falls as income from other sources increases, dropping by one unit for every unit of income gained from other sources. Some schemes have been reformed so as to allow for the possibility of earning without incurring an equivalent reduction in benefit over a limited income range or for a limited time. However, even in those cases, the reduction in benefit tends to combine with the loss of means-tested fee exemptions or discounts so as to generate an outcome close to the unit-by-unit reduction that defines the pure case. (Indeed, sometimes the outcome is worse, or at least is perceived to be worse by people often ill-equipped to collect and process scattered, changing, and complex information.) Apart from income, some schemes also take other "means" into account, such as the value of any property one owns or the resources of close relatives not belonging to one's household. Whether or not the means deemed relevant to the means test extend beyond the beneficiaries' income, any such scheme needs to operate *ex post*—that is, on the basis of some prior assessment, reliable or not, of the beneficiaries' material resources.

A basic income, by contrast, operates *ex ante,* with no means test involved. It is paid upfront to rich and poor alike, regardless of the income they derive from other sources, the property they own, or the income of their relatives. Consequently, if it is funded exogenously—for example, by revenues from publicly owned natural resources or by transfers from another geographical area—the introduction of a basic income increases everyone's income by the same amount. If instead it is funded through the taxation of income or consumption within the population concerned, high earners and big spenders will fund their own benefit (and more). The key difference between a basic income and an income-tested scheme is therefore not that a basic income would make everyone richer, and even less that it is better for the rich. Paradoxically, the key difference is instead that it is better for the poor.

How can one make sense of this counterintuitive claim? If the aim is the eradication of poverty, the universal character of basic income, added to its individual nature, might make it look at first glance like a pathetic waste of resources. To understand the strength of this objection, define the "poverty gap" as the volume of transfers required to lift the income of poor households up to the poverty line. The "target efficiency" of an anti-poverty program is commonly measured by the proportion of the program's expenditure that contributes to closing this gap. A conditional minimum-income scheme that strictly targets the poorest by making up the difference between their income and the poverty line is bound to be more efficient in this sense than a basic income, which seemingly wastes valuable resources by distributing them to countless households above the poverty line. Yet there are three distinct reasons for preferring a universal income.[32]

The first reason has to do with universality as such, the fact that the benefit is paid to all, not only to those identified as poor. Many studies comparing the effectiveness of universal versus targeted benefits schemes in reaching the poorest members of society have shown the superiority, in this respect, of the universal systems.[33] In order to access benefits targeted at the poor, people who are eligible for them have to take steps that they may fail to take, whether out of ignorance, shyness, or shame. With a means-tested scheme, the information campaign required to achieve the same take-up rate among net beneficiaries that would be achieved by a universal scheme entails considerable human and administrative costs. Even with a scheme that relies on nothing but income as the relevant criterion, decisions to include or exclude leave a lot of room for arbitrariness and clientelism. With a basic income paid automatically to all legal residents, access to benefits does not require any particular administrative steps. Moreover, society is then no longer visibly divided between the needy and the others, those who need help and those who can manage on their own. There is nothing humiliating about receiving a basic income granted to all members of society. This does not only matter in itself for the dignity of the people involved. It also enhances effectiveness in terms of poverty alleviation.[34] Thus, by avoiding complication and stigmatization, a universal scheme can achieve a high rate of take-up at a low information cost.

The objection might be raised that, while a basic income would admittedly reduce the administrative cost of informing, monitoring, and sanctioning, it would involve a much higher administrative cost of distributing benefits and collecting the resources required to fund them. There is no question that the total volume of transfers is much higher when payments are made to all, not just to the poor. But we are not talking about postmen delivering monthly cash installments from door to door. In an era of pay-as-you-go taxation and automatic electronic transfers, this part of the administrative cost amounts to little, relative to the cost of ensuring that all and only those who satisfy a means test will receive benefits. At least in sufficiently formalized economies with tax systems that work reasonably well, the overall administrative cost of achieving any given rate of take-up among net beneficiaries can safely be expected to be less for a universal scheme than for a means-tested one. In this sense, freedom from want is cheaper to achieve with a basic income than with a conditional scheme.

Second, universality as such, the fact that one remains entitled to the basic income irrespective of any other income one may be earning, is important not only for freeing people from a lack of money. It also matters for freeing them from exclusion from work. Under a means-tested scheme, even precarious earnings cancel the entitlement to part or all of the benefits. Rational avoidance of uncertainty contributes to trapping welfare recipients in situations of unemployment. The risk is compounded by the very nature of many of the jobs the most disadvantaged would qualify for: jobs with precarious contracts, unscrupulous employers, and unpredictable earnings. If they are unsure about how much they will earn when they start working, about whether they will be able to cope, or about how quickly they might lose the work and then have to face more or less complex administrative procedures in order to reestablish their entitlement to benefits, the idea of giving up means-tested transfers holds less appeal. As Thomas Piketty notes, it can take several months to establish a benefit entitlement that depends on one's economic situation, and "these few months can be very important for households whose everyday economic balance is very fragile." He goes on to pose the obvious question: "As working for a few months might make me lose the benefit of the minimum-income scheme for several terms at the end of this period of activity, then why take such a risk?"[35] Even when the probabilities of problems occurring are relatively low, the prospect of triggering off a spiral of debt is likely to be perceived as a major threat by people who are ill-equipped to know, understand, and *a fortiori* appeal to rules that can often be changing and opaque. By contrast, with a universal basic income, people can take jobs or create their own jobs with less fear.

This advantage of universality as regards access to employment is strongly reinforced by the effect of a feature closely associated with it, which provides a third reason to favor universality: the fact that any earnings people do produce go to increase their net incomes. This feature is not a logically necessary corollary of universality, as one could in theory tax an income at 100 percent, but it can be regarded as a natural corollary because, in practice, it is hard to imagine an explicit taxation of low earnings of this confiscatory sort. (Note that this feature does not entail universality either; as will be explained in chapter 2, it is also present in so-called negative-income-tax schemes, which involve no universal payments.) Why does this feature matter? Consider a typical public assistance scheme. In its attempt to be as target-efficient as possible, it uses available funds to make up the difference between poor households' incomes from other sources and the income level which it aims to guarantee to all households of a particular type. As mentioned above, this entails clawing back one unit of benefit for each unit earned by the poor through their own efforts. Thus, the concern not to waste any money on the non-poor amounts to imposing an implicit marginal tax rate of 100 percent on any income the poor earn through labor. This situation is commonly called a poverty trap or unemployment trap: the earnings people receive for a low-paid job are offset, or even more than offset, owing to work-related expenses, by the corresponding reduction or suppression of the means-tested benefit.[36] Under the mild assumption that no explicit tax rate will ever reach 100 percent, a basic income, being universal, creates no such trap. It is not withdrawn or reduced but kept in full when people earn a low income. Note that this facilitation of access to

low-paid employment operates also in the presence of minimum wage legislation, not only because employment can take the form of self-employment
or work in a cooperative, but also because waged labor can be part-time or
discontinuous and can take the form of apprenticeships or internships commonly exempted from minimum-wage provisions. As these forms of more
casual work gain in potential importance, so does the trap created by the
means test, even in the presence of strict minimum wage provisions.[37]

In light of these three considerations, the contrast between a means-tested
minimum-income scheme and a basic income should be clear. The former provides a safety net that fails to catch a great many people it should catch, and in
which many others get trapped; the latter provides a floor on which they can
all safely stand. This difference may be of little significance as long as the trap
catches only a small minority of people suffering from various handicaps. It
becomes of central importance when, for the reasons sketched above, a large
and growing proportion of the population is at risk of getting trapped. One
reason often given for not raising the level of means-tested benefits is precisely
that it would catch even more people in the unemployment trap.

It is true, indeed self-evident, that universality is achieved at a far higher
level of public expenditure. Paying a given sum of money to all costs far more
money than paying it only to the poor. But there is cost and there is cost.
Much of the cost, if the scheme is funded by taxation, consists in taking money
with one hand and giving it back with the other hand to the same households.
The rest simply represents a redistribution of private spending between different categories of the population. This is quite different from a budgetary
cost that involves the use of real resources, such as to build infrastructure or
employ civil servants, and that represents *ipso facto* an opportunity cost (because
there are other things that could be done with the material and human resources on which public money is being spent). Abstracting from possible administrative gains and losses and from positive or negative behavioral responses,
a shift from a means-tested to a universal scheme does not make the population
as a whole either richer or poorer. It is, in this sense, costless.

Obviously, this conclusion holds only in a static perspective—that is, assuming that the behavior of economic actors remains unchanged. But this
cannot be assumed. Indeed, a change in behavior is what the proposal is all
about: thanks to basic income's being universal, we have just argued, people
currently trapped in unemployment will have a greater incentive to work, and
employers will have a greater incentive to hire them. But one cannot look only
at the impact on behavior in the lower segment of the income distribution.

Considering the impact that a shift to universality might have on incentives in the rest of the distribution does raise a genuine cost issue, to which we shall turn after discussing basic income's third distinctive (and most controversial) feature.

An Obligation-Free Income

As discussed so far, a basic income is a regular cash income that is individual and universal. It further differs from conditional minimum-income schemes in having no strings attached; it carries no obligation for its beneficiaries to work or be available on the labor market. In this precise sense, we shall say that a basic income is *obligation free*.[38] In existing, conditional schemes, the exact extent of the obligation of being available for work varies considerably from one country to another—indeed, sometimes from one local authority to another within the same country.[39] Typically denied the right to the benefit are those who give up a job at their own initiative, those who are unable to prove that they are actively looking for a job, and those who decline to accept jobs or other forms of "insertion" deemed suitable by their local public assistance office given their content, location, and schedule. What such a system can lead to is vividly depicted by sociologist Bill Jordan in *Paupers: The Making of the New Claiming Class*. Describing the context that prompted a group of welfare claimants to articulate the case for an unconditional basic income, he writes: "The cornerstone of that system was the regulations under which state benefits were provided or withheld. It was these regulations which gave the employer his power, for they allowed the authorities to force someone into a job, however rotten or badly paid it might be." These regulations "ensure that the meanest employer, paying the worst wages for the filthiest jobs, is not kept out of a worker while there is one able-bodied unemployed man available."[40] A basic income, by contrast, is paid without any such conditions. Homemakers, students, and tramps are entitled to it no less than waged workers and the self-employed, and those who decided to quit no less than those who were sacked. No one needs to check whether its beneficiaries are genuine job seekers or shirkers.

Thus, while universality addresses the unemployment trap, freedom from obligation addresses the employment trap. Without universality, freedom from obligation could easily prove a recipe for exclusion: an obligation-free, means-tested benefit would amount to hush money for those hopelessly stuck in the unemployment trap. But without freedom from obligation, universality would prove a recipe for exploitation: work-conditional universal benefits would amount to subsidies to the employers. The latter could get away with paying lower wages to workers obliged to accept and stay in jobs if they wanted to retain their benefits. By contrast, the universality of basic income admittedly constitutes a potential subsidy for jobs that are poorly productive in an immediate economic sense, but its freedom from obligation prevents it from subsidizing those that are lousy or degrading. The conjunction of these two unconditionalities enables us to see why there is plausibility both in the claim that a basic income would depress wages and in the opposite claim that it would boost them.

Universality facilitates saying yes to jobs that pay little, even so little or so unreliably that they do not yet exist. The lower limit set by means-tested minimum-income schemes is switched off. People with low immediate earning power are no longer priced out of jobs. Average earnings, for this reason, may diminish.[41] However, because the benefit is obligation-free, the "yes" will be forthcoming only if the job is attractive enough, whether in itself or thanks to the useful training, gratifying contacts, or promotion prospects it provides, irrespective of how little it is paid. An obligation-free income facilitates saying "no" to jobs that pay little and are unattractive. If, as a result of this enhanced freedom to say no, lousy jobs fail to attract or retain enough takers, employers might choose to automate the work. Where machine replacements are impossible or too expensive, jobs will need to be made more attractive. And where this, too, proves impossible or too expensive, pay for jobs will need to go up. Yes, those lousy, poorly-paid jobs which you would not dream of doing will need to be paid better—perhaps even better than yours (and ours), and this is a good thing.[42] Average earnings, therefore, might well go up.

The net effects of these opposing forces on the average level of labor compensation and on the overall employment rate cannot be predicted.[43] How they turn out will be affected by the balance of market forces and social norms—and by such institutional factors as the regulation of part-time work and self-employment, and the presence and scope of minimum wage arrangements, whether imposed by law or negotiated by social partners. One thing is certain, however: the combination of the two unconditionalities gives more options to the people who have least of them. A basic income may add little to the bargaining power of those with valuable talents, education, or experience; with strong insider status, influential connections, or strong union backing; or with few family constraints. But it will empower those without such advantages to be choosier among possible occupations. Only the workers themselves are able to compare alternative jobs' intrinsic qualities—far better than any expert, legislator, or bureaucrat—as they take into full account what they like to do, what they need to learn, whom they get on with, and where they wish to live.[44] The extent to which this will happen obviously depends on how high the basic income is. But it need not be set at a level that allows someone to live a decent life without doing any work for it to enable that person to choose, temporarily or permanently, a more attractive occupation (and thus for it to boost the wages needed to keep people in lousy jobs). Work quality can be expected to get a big boost as a result of both today's existing jobs' being improved and many non-existing jobs' becoming viable. In particular, the average quality of the jobs performed by the most vulnerable can safely be expected to increase.[45] This is why so many people committed to freedom for all like the combination of universality and freedom from obligation. This is why they want a basic income.

An Active Welfare State

Given the foregoing, it seems hard to deny that basic income, owing to its multidimensional unconditionality, constitutes a powerful instrument of freedom. But is it sustainable? Using Anthony Atkinson and Joseph Stiglitz's terminology, it could be said that an expected—and intended—effect of basic income is a replacement of "production within the firm" by "production within the household" (that is, unpaid productive activities at home and in the community) and by "consumption within the firm" (meaning a higher quality of work).[46] But it is only production within the firm (the paid activities in the private and public sector that register in a country's GDP) that can provide a basic income with the tax base it needs. We shall discuss at length (in chapter 6) the various ways in which a basic income can be funded and the impacts to be expected on behaviors of economic agents and hence on the sustainability of the scheme. In particular, we shall consider a number of experiments and econometric exercises aimed at shedding light on these questions. At this point, we want to highlight just a few considerations too often overlooked in the discussion of the economic impact and economic sustainability of a basic income.

A common worry is that the supply of labor will be badly affected by the combination of an obligation-free minimum income and increased taxation of the productive activities required to fund it. A preliminary point worth making is that an important function of providing people with at least a modest income is that it enables them to work. As the Namibian bishop and basic-income advocate Zephania Kameeta remarked, "the people of Israel in the long journey out of slavery received manna from heaven. But it did not make them lazy; instead, it enabled them to be on the move."[47] This observation holds fully in the context of less-developed countries where a basic income would provide means of subsistence to many, in the absence of any preexisting form of minimum income protection. But it also holds against the background of existing means-tested schemes, to the extent that a basic income improves the take-up rate among the poor and thereby reduces extreme poverty.

As we turn to the impact on material incentives, it is worth observing first that even with a much increased marginal tax rate on the earnings of many workers, the marginal return to work could still remain considerably higher than it was decades ago when much lower marginal tax rates prevailed, simply because real wages have risen.[48] Second, as it is the relative level of remuneration that determines social pecking orders and access to prestige-yielding consumption, a reduction in the absolute level of the marginal gain might do little to reduce workers' interest in economic advancement. "The incentive to production depends in the main, not on the absolute magnitude of the rewards offered, but on their relation one to another," notes G. D. H. Cole, one of the earliest academic advocates of basic income. And thus: "The more nearly a community approaches the conditions of social equality, the smaller are the differences of income which will suffice to provide strong incentives to effort."[49] Third, there are many and varied motives for working and for working well apart from either absolute or relative earnings, all of which can be given more traction under a basic income system. In his discussion of guaranteed income proposals, Peter Townsend spells them out as follows: "A man works to preserve the respect of his wife, children, friends and neighbours, to fulfill the psychological needs induced by the customs and expectations of a lifetime and to . . . replenish the stock of information, cautionary tales and anecdotes which he requires to maintain his participation in the web of social relations."[50]

It would be wrong, however, to reduce the economic impact of a basic income to its immediate impact on the supply side of the labor market. By providing an unconditional floor, a basic income can be expected to help unleash entrepreneurship by better buffering the self-employed, worker cooperatives, and capital-labor partnerships against the risk of uncertain and fluctuating incomes.[51] Even more important is the expected longer-term effect on human capital. Concerns are sometimes expressed that rising marginal tax rates will reduce the incentive to invest in further education and training, and also that young people enjoying the lives a basic income enables them to afford will neglect the education which would enable them to feed families later in their lives.[52] Such effects cannot be ruled out but should be largely offset by a number of other ways in which a basic income can be expected to affect a society's human capital.

First of all, getting rid of the unemployment trap by providing a firm floor instead of a net is not only a way of recruiting into the workforce some people whose immediate productivity is low. It also helps to prevent unemployed workers from sinking into unemployability through the mutual reinforcement of the obsolescence of their productive skills and the lowering of their professional aspirations.

Second, the combination of the last two unconditionalities—universality and freedom from obligation—generates a systematic bias in favor of the creation and survival of jobs with high training content. One aspect of this is that a basic income helps give all young people access to unpaid or low-paid internships, otherwise monopolized by the privileged whose parents are able and willing to provide them with what amounts to privately funded basic incomes. This effect can be expected to be particularly strong in those countries where apprenticeships and internships are not heavily subsidized by governments or by agreements between labor unions and employer federations, and where, therefore, individual employers are weary of investing in human capital only to lose many people once they are properly trained.

Third, a basic income makes it easier for anyone to work part-time or to interrupt work altogether in order to acquire further skills, to look for a more suitable job, to engage in voluntary activities, or simply to take a badly needed break. This reduces the risk of ending up with a skilled labor force that is irreparably burned out or obsolete well before retirement age. Coupled with a redirection of the educational system towards lifelong learning, such a more flexible and relaxed labor market should be far better suited to the development of twenty-first-century human capital than a market that makes a rigid division between young students and mature workers.

Finally, this positive impact concerns not only the human capital of the present working population, but also that of their children. Like other ways of making family income more secure, basic income can be expected to have a beneficial effect on children's health and education.[53] To the extent that it addresses the unemployment trap, it reduces the number of children whose eagerness to work is negatively affected by their growing up in households without anyone employed. Above all, by facilitating chosen part-time work and promoting a smoother conciliation of work and family life, it enables parents to devote more attention to their children when this is most needed.

The underlying, general point is that the efficient working of an economy does not require pushing up the employment rate, maximizing the labor supply in a shortsighted fashion. Making an economy more productive (sensibly interpreted) in a sustainable fashion is not best served by obsessively activating people and locking them in jobs that they hate doing and from which they learn nothing. As the poet Kahlil Gibran put it in 1923, "if you cannot work with love but only with distaste, it is better that you should leave your work. . . . For if you bake bread with indifference, you bake a bitter bread that feeds but half man's hunger." It is not only poets who believe such things. In the same vein, Götz Werner, the boss of a firm with over twenty thousand employees (whom we'll meet again in chapter 7), claims that his business would do better, not worse, if an unconditional basic income gave all his employees a real option not to work.

For these reasons, it is arguably not only fair but also economically clever to give all, not just the better endowed, greater freedom to move easily among paid work, education, caring, and volunteering. This intimate connection between the greater security provided by a basic income and the expansion of a desirable form of flexibility makes basic income an investment rather than a cost.[54] It also explains why a basic income can be viewed as an intelligent, emancipatory form of "active welfare state." The latter expression is most commonly used to refer to so-called "active labor-market policies" and the more or less meddlesome activation machinery usually implied by that label. Interpreted in this repressive way, the active (or activating) welfare state tracks the beneficiaries of existing schemes to check whether they are either really unfit for work or really looking for a job. In line with this project, the level of benefits is reduced, eligibility conditions are restricted, and enforcement is tightened. The British and German reforms initiated at the turn of the century under Tony Blair and Gerhardt Schröder, respectively, and pursued by their conservative successors, illustrate what this can lead to in practice. Workfare programs in North America provide other examples.

In contrast to this repressive interpretation, however, there can also be an emancipatory interpretation of what an active welfare state could be. In this case, activation is a matter of removing obstacles such as the unemployment and isolation traps, and empowering people with easier access to education and training, in order to give them a wider spectrum of options for paid or unpaid activities. It consists of freeing them to work rather than forcing them to work. It forms the core of an emancipatory active welfare state, in sharp contrast also to the means-tested minimum-income schemes typical of "passive" welfare states that focus their transfers on the inactive and thereby keep them inactive. True, by providing an obligation-free income, a basic-income scheme can be viewed as desacralizing paid work: it legitimizes pay without work for all, not just for the disabled and the rentiers able to live on income from property or securities. But by providing a universal floor to which income from other sources can be added, it can nonetheless also be viewed as an instrument of activation that will help other instruments, such as retraining or social work, do a better job. Being obligation-free, basic income can help to "de-commodify" human labor; but being universal, it also helps to "commodify" the labor of people who would otherwise remain excluded.[55] There is therefore no need for basic-income supporters to reject as a matter of principle all the rhetoric and the policies that go by the name of the active welfare state. There is even less of a need to try to sell the basic income by invoking the necessity of a passive welfare state owing to the alleged rarefication of paid work.

In particular, a basic income is fully compatible with the view that recognition and esteem are not earned by self-indulgence, but by service to others. A basic income is there to facilitate the search by all of us for something we like to do and do well, whether or not in the form of paid employment. Many at some stages in their lives might best contribute to the well-being of those close to them or of the human community as a whole through unpaid activities, from running voluntary childcare initiatives to contributing to Wikipedia. However, most people at the "working age" stages in their lives will best contribute through some sort of paid work, whether or not within a firm, whether or not on a full-time basis. A social norm that values this—a work ethic in this sense—is consistent with a basic income, indeed contributes to its sustainability, without cancelling the liberating impact associated with the expansion of the range of ways in which this social norm can be met.[56]

A Sane Economy

These remarks should suffice to allay the suspicion that a substantial basic income would trigger a fatal collapse. Do they suffice to establish that basic income is needed for the sake of maximal economic growth? Certainly not.

And fortunately so. Involuntary unemployment is a major issue for people committed to freedom for all. Growth has routinely been offered as the self-evident remedy for unemployment. But, as mentioned above, strong doubts have emerged as to the possibility and desirability of sustained growth in rich countries and about its ability to provide a solution to unemployment. A basic income offers an alternative solution that does not rely on an insane rush to keep pace with productivity growth. The time will come, John Maynard Keynes wrote, when growth will no longer be the path to follow, when "our discovery of means of economizing the use of labour" will be "outrunning the pace at which we can find new uses for labour." And then "we shall endeavour to spread the bread thin on the butter—to make what work there is still to be done to be as widely shared as possible."[57]

A basic income is a smooth and smart way of moving in this direction. It does not impose a maximum limit on everyone's working time but it makes it easier for people to reduce their working time, both because it reduces what they lose if they do and because it gives them a firm income on which they can rely. It thereby attacks the root cause of troubles for both those who get sick by working too much and those who get sick because they cannot find jobs.[58] It does not amount to giving up the objective of full employment sensibly interpreted. For full employment can mean two things: full-time paid work for the entire able-bodied part of the population of working age, or the real possibility of getting meaningful paid work for all those who want it. As an objective, the basic income strategy rejects the former but embraces the latter.[59] And it pursues it both by subsidizing low-paid work with low immediate productivity and by making it easier for people to choose to work less at any given point in their lives. At the expense of material consumption? In developed countries, certainly. And deliberately so—because our economy not only needs to be efficient. It must also be sane.[60] And sanity requires us to find not only a way of organizing our economy that does not make people sick but also a way of living that is sustainably generalizable. An unconditional basic income is a precondition for both.

2

Basic Income and Its Cousins

FOR MANY OF OUR READERS, this chapter is unnecessary. But for some, at least one section of it is absolutely essential. They are the readers who found the diagnosis of the previous chapter compelling enough but could easily think, and kept thinking while reading, of one or more far better solutions than the one we propose. In this chapter, we briefly present and discuss the main alternatives to an unconditional basic income. For most of these alternatives we ourselves have more than a modicum of sympathy. Some of them can be usefully combined, albeit to a modest degree, with a basic income. And in the absence of a basic income we would readily concede that their implementation would, in many circumstances, greatly improve the status quo. Yet there is no doubt in our minds that an unconditional basic income, rather than these alternatives, is most capable of creating the institutional conditions for a free society and a sane economy—along with reforms in other areas outside the scope of this book.[1] We shall briefly explain why.

Basic Income Versus Basic Endowment

A basic income is a regular income, paid at intervals that may vary from one version to another. Why not instead pay a basic endowment to all at the start of adult life? That has been proposed, for example, by Thomas Paine (1796), Thomas Skidmore (1829), and François Huet (1853).[2] Versions of the same idea have been developed subsequently under other labels. Thus, James Tobin (in 1968) advocated a "national youth endowment"; William Klein (1977) and Robert Haveman (1988) a "universal personal capital account"; and most systematically and ambitiously, Bruce Ackerman and Anne Alstott (1999), a "stakeholder grant."

Basic income and basic endowment have much in common. Both are paid in cash, on an individual basis, without means test or work test. Moreover, a basic endowment could easily be converted into a basic income. It would only need be invested in such a way as to generate an actuarially equivalent annuity up to the recipient's death, thus generating a regular flow of income. Conversely, if a basic income could be mortgaged, as a concern for freedom would seem to recommend, it would provide an equivalent endowment.[3] Given this, there might seem to be no significant difference between the two proposals. Yet there is one, and one that justifies in our eyes a resolute preference for an unconditional basic income.

To see this, it is important to specify versions of the two ideas that lend themselves to a fair comparison. Universal basic endowments in cash already exist or have existed in a number of countries, but they are tiny relative to the volume of regular transfer payments.[4] Bruce Ackerman and Anne Alstott's proposal is far more generous: a grant of $80,000, possibly handed out in four installments of $20,000, and an unconditional basic pension from age 65. If this grant were spread evenly in 528 monthly payments between the ages of 21 and 65, this would amount to about $150 per month (abstracting from inflation). But account obviously needs to be taken of two facts: some people die before reaching 65 and, above all, the grant can yield interest. Ackerman and Alstott calculate that a grant of $80,000 at age 21 would be approximately equivalent to a monthly basic income of $400 from age 21 to age 65. But because their assumption of a real rate of interest of 5 percent is rather optimistic, let us take $300 as a more realistic approximation.[5]

There is, however, no need to quibble about the fine details of the reasoning leading up to such an estimate. To get an idea of the amounts involved, let us take as a relevant baseline a monthly basic income of $1,000—that is, 25 percent of GDP per capita in a country somewhat less wealthy than the United States. An "equivalent" basic endowment would amount to some $250,000 per person. For a fair comparison, further complications would need to be introduced, especially regarding the different types of savings that would naturally be coupled with each proposal and would help to fund them.[6] For present purposes, however, we can set aside these complications and compare two roughly equivalent schemes funded in roughly the same way: a basic income of $1,000 between the ages of 21 and 65 versus a basic endowment of $250,000 at age 21. We can leave aside people aged less than 21, about whom the Ackerman-Alstott proposal says nothing, and those aged over 65, for whom their proposal amounts to a basic income restricted to the elderly.

Despite their similarities, basic endowment and basic income seem to belong to very different normative perspectives. The basic endowment is about equalizing opportunities at the start of adult life, while basic income is about providing economic security throughout life. Which one is to be preferred by people committed to freedom for all?[7] At first sight, it seems obvious. The basic endowment offers all the possibilities offered by a basic income, since it can be turned into an annuity. But the converse is not true if the basic income is not mortgageable, as most basic income advocates insist it should not be. The additional possibilities associated with a basic endowment include the possibility of "stake blowing," whether deliberately for consumption purposes or involuntarily through bad investments, such as buying the wrong house, opting for the wrong study program, or starting the wrong business. As Ackerman and Alstott note, once a young citizen has collected the money, it "is hers to spend or invest. She may go to college, or not. She may save for a house or a rainy day—or blow her money in Las Vegas."[8] Freedom, after all, is also the freedom to make mistakes.

Nonetheless, there is no doubt in our minds that a concern for the freedom of all, for the real opportunities given to all, should make us prefer a monthly basic income of $1,000 to an "equivalent" one-off stake of $250,000. Why? Lifetime opportunities are determined only to a very limited extent by the endowment received at 21. They are powerfully affected by intellectual abilities, parental attention, school quality, social networks, and many other factors. On average, those young people who are already favored along these various dimensions are precisely those who are most likely to make the best possible use of their endowment. The real possibilities associated with the same nominal amount will therefore be considerably less for those who lack the intelligence, guidance, education, and connections that would enable them, at the beginning of their adult lives, to competently select, in light of what they care about upon reflection, what is best for themselves.[9]

An unconditional lifelong basic security does not only protect the freedom of all of us against our own freedom in our youth. It also ends up spreading freedom, in the form of real possibilities, far more widely, including the possibility of making investments and taking risks throughout life. If there is a choice to be made between a basic-income scheme at a significant level and an "equivalent" basic-endowment scheme, those committed to freedom for all should therefore opt without hesitation for the former. However, this choice need not be incompatible with supporting a supplementary "capital endowment," providing the latter is modest enough not to jeopardize the sustainable funding of a significant level of basic income.[10]

Basic Income Versus Negative Income Tax

Conceptually more remote than basic endowment but in many ways the closest competitor to basic income is a scheme most commonly known as a "negative income tax." The concept of negative income tax can be traced back to Augustin Cournot, one of the founding fathers of mathematical economics. He wrote: "The bonus, an invention of modern times, is the opposite of an income tax; to use algebraic language, it is a negative income tax."[11] The idea recurs in writings of Abba Lerner and George Stigler.[12] And it was popularized by Milton Friedman in his *Capitalism and Freedom* and several other writings and interviews.[13] It is often asserted, including by Friedman himself, that a basic income funded by personal income taxation and a negative income tax are equivalent.[14] Moreover, many of the arguments used in favor of basic income as opposed to means-tested minimum-income schemes are also used in favor of negative-income-tax proposals. Yet there is a crucial difference between a basic income and a negative income tax, and, for people committed to freedom for all, this difference matters greatly.

To understand the appeal of the equivalence claim, some will find it sufficient to have a quick look at stylized representations of a means-tested minimum-income scheme (see Figure 2.1), a basic income (Figure 2.2), and a negative income tax (Figure 2.3), assuming that there is no other public expenditure. Others may find it more intuitive to consider a simple numerical example. Take again the case of a basic income of $1,000 per month paid individually to each adult and funded by an income tax of 25 percent from the first dollar earned, abstracting from any other public expenditure. Instead of paying to all and taking from all, the government could net the transfers—that is, make payments and require no taxes from some while requiring taxes and making no payments to the others. This would amount to transforming the basic income of $1,000 into a uniform and individual refundable tax credit of $1,000. One would thereby achieve the same profile of effective marginal tax rates and the same distribution of post-tax-and-transfer incomes. Thus:

- Someone with no earnings receives a $1,000 benefit in both cases.
- Someone who earns $2,000 ends up with $2,500: in one case through a basic income of $1,000 plus net earnings of $1,500 (75 percent of $2,000), in the other case through gross earnings of $2,000 plus a negative tax of $500 corresponding to the difference between a tax credit of $1,000 and a tax liability of $500 (25 percent of $2,000).

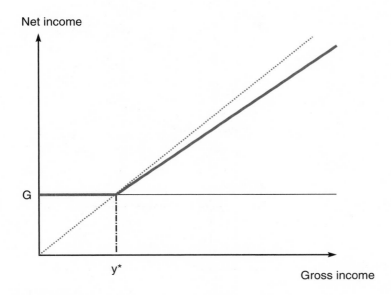

Figure 2.1 Net income with a means-tested minimum-income scheme

The horizontal axis represents gross income, before taxes and transfers. The vertical axis represents net income, after tax and transfers. The 45° line represents what net income would amount to with zero taxation and no guaranteed minimum income: gross and net incomes are the same. G represents the level of the minimum income.

In standard means-tested minimum-income schemes, transfers make up the difference between the beneficiary's gross income and the minimum level of income (G) below which no household is allowed to fall. The bold line represents net incomes, taking into account both these transfers and the taxation required to fund them, here supposed to be linear. People with a gross income above y* are net contributors to the funding of the minimum-income scheme. Those with a gross income below y* are net beneficiaries of the scheme.

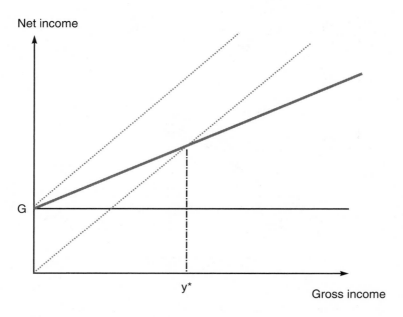

Figure 2.2 Net income with a basic income

The tax-free basic income G is paid to each citizen irrespective of his or her gross income. The second dotted line, starting at G and parallel to the 45° line, represents gross income plus basic income. The bold line represents net income, taking into account both taxation and basic income. The breakeven point y* corresponds to the intersection of the bold line representing net income and the 45° line corresponding to gross income. People with a gross income above y* are net contributors to the funding of the basic income. Those with a gross income below y* are net beneficiaries of the scheme.

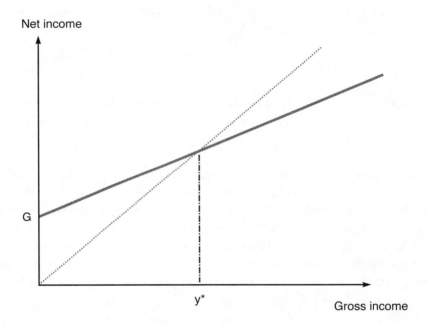

Figure 2.3 Net income with a negative income tax

The bold line represents net income, taking into account both positive and negative taxation at the same rate. In this linear version, the benefit (or negative tax) shrinks in the range under the breakeven point (y*) at the same rate (expressed as a percentage of each additional unit of gross income) as the tax rises in the range above it. The benefit (or negative tax) paid to a household is gradually reduced as its income increases, and is equal to zero at the breakeven point y*, the level of gross income at which the negative income tax turns into a positive income tax on the contributors. This breakeven point is the same as in the basic-income scheme.

- Someone who earns $4,000 ends up with $4,000 (her income level corresponds to the so-called breakeven point): in one case through a basic income of $1,000 plus net earnings of $3,000 (75 percent of $4,000), in the other case through gross earnings of $4,000 plus nothing, since the tax credit of $1,000 is equal to the tax liability of $1,000 (25 percent of $4,000).
- Someone who earns $8,000 ends up with $7,000: in one case through a basic income of $1,000 plus net earnings of $6,000 (75 percent of $8,000), in the other case through gross earnings of $8,000 minus a positive tax of $1,000 corresponding to the difference between a tax liability of $2,000 (25 percent of $8,000) and a tax credit of $1,000.[15]

The alleged equivalence thus illustrated must now be qualified. First of all, in the example above, taxation is linear: the marginal rate of tax is the same for all levels of earnings. Unlike the notion of basic income, the notion of negative income tax is sometimes restricted to this special case, which was Friedman's preference. But it can easily be used in a broader sense, consistent with progressive or regressive taxation. However, it does assume that the transfers are funded by personal income taxation, whereas the definition of basic income allows for many other sources of funding to be discussed in chapter 6.

Second, in the example above, the unit of distribution is taken to be the individual. This is so by definition for basic income. But it is not for the negative income tax. Indeed, in line with common fiscal practice, most negative income tax proposals and all negative income tax experiments take the household as the relevant unit for both positive and negative transfers, thereby raising the various difficulties that support the case for individualization. However, a negative income tax is in principle compatible with taking the individual as the unit both for entitlement to benefit and for tax liability. It is only if this is done that equivalence can be claimed between basic income and negative income tax.

Third, in the example above, the income base is defined in the same way for the sake of negative and positive taxation. Some advocates of the negative income tax, however, see one of its advantages being the ability to use a broader base for the assessment of the negative tax, by including in it the income of relatives who are not members of the household. The German economist Hans-Georg Petersen, for example, saw in this possibility of making room for "the important role of self-responsibility in the family" a major advantage of a negative income tax over a basic income.[16] Obviously, an equivalence with basic income is only possible if the same income base is adopted for the negative and positive part of the tax schedule, as is the case in most negative-income-tax proposals.

Fourth, in the example above, it is taken for granted that entitlement to the negative income tax, like entitlement to the basic income, is unconditional in the sense of not being predicated on availability for work. This condition is generally fulfilled by negative income tax proposals, including Friedman's, but not by all. In particular, the most famous among the proposals often granted this label, President Nixon's Family Assistance Plan (to which we will return in chapter 4), granted transfers to able-bodied adults only providing they were willing to work. If the refundable tax credit is not obligation-free, obviously, no equivalence can be claimed.

This being clarified, we can now focus on the essential difference between basic income and negative income tax by considering the case most favorable to the equivalence. In this case, the unit is the individual, there is no work test, and the funding is secured by a personal income tax with the same linear profile. This forces us to scrutinize the two features discussed in chapter 1 under the heading of universality. One of them is shared by both schemes. The other is the key difference.

The feature that is shared by both and distinguishes them both from means-tested schemes of the standard sort is that they get rid of the prohibitive 100 percent effective rate of taxation on the lowest earnings.[17] Both schemes can guarantee the same level of minimum income with the same profile of marginal tax rates. The budget constraints can therefore be regarded as identical. The range of choices between different bundles of consumption and leisure faced by workers is the same and so is, it seems, the behavior they are expected to adopt as rational economic agents.

It is important, however, also to pay attention to the second feature: universality as such, or the fact that the basic income is paid upfront at the same level to all, irrespective of income from other sources. At first sight, this is just a secondary administrative difference that should count in favor of a negative income scheme: to reach the same final result, the latter avoids a wasteful back-and-forth between taxpayers and the government. However, poor people cannot wait until the end of the tax year before receiving the transfer that will enable them not to starve, and it is therefore self-evident that a negative income tax scheme must include a procedure of advance payments. All those who expect to have an income lower than the breakeven point (not only the subset of those who expect to earn a gross income lower than the guaranteed minimum) must have access to this procedure.[18] In an era of electronic benefit delivery and pay-as-you-go taxation, the administrative cost of the information and control aspects of this additional procedure required by a negative income tax scheme would easily outweigh the administrative cost of the back-and-forth required by a basic-income scheme. At the same time, for the familiar reasons of complication and stigmatization, the rate of take-up among beneficiaries would remain well below what can be easily achieved by a universal scheme. While equivalent on paper to a basic income as a tool for reducing poverty, therefore, a negative income tax suffers from a defect as regards this objective, closely analogous to one of the objections to standard means-tested schemes.

The upfront nature of payments matters for making basic income an effective tool against not only poverty but also unemployment. This is due to the fact that the unemployment trap is not only a matter of the difference in income between being in or out of work—by hypothesis identical in both cases—but also a matter of avoiding the risks associated with precarious employment and its administrative consequences. In this respect, some negative-income-tax advocates believe that their scheme can improve on current welfare arrangements.[19] But because of the need to switch back and forth between different administrative statuses of claimant or worker, a negative-income-tax scheme presents the same intrinsic defect as standard means-tested schemes. Only the upfront payment associated with a basic income can get rid of it altogether.[20]

Consequently, even when it operates at an individual level and corresponds on paper to an identical net income profile, a negative-income-tax scheme is by no means equivalent to the closest possible basic-income scheme and does not present the same advantages as regards both poverty and unemployment. The basic reason, stressed by philosopher Michel Foucault in his discussion of the negative income tax (to which we will return in chapter 4), is that it remains a policy targeting the poor. The welfare states that developed in Europe since the end of the nineteenth century all "wanted to ensure that economic interventions were such that the population was not divided between the poor and the less poor." By contrast, according to Foucault, the negative income tax, like the Poor Laws of another age, "distinguishes between the poor and those who are not poor, between those who are receiving assistance and those who are not."[21] What our societies need for the sake of freeing everyone from poverty and unemployment, and what those committed to freedom for all should fight for, is a floor on which all can stand, not just another, more sophisticated policy targeted at the poor.

While this principled superiority of a universal basic income should be clear, it is true that how much difference it makes is partly a matter of economic and administrative circumstances. To start with, the upfront payment of the basic income could be made the default option rather than compulsory for all. This is actually the way in which James Tobin imagined his "demogrant" would best be administered.[22] People with stable employment could request receiving their basic income in the form of a tax credit, and if all were in a position to do so, the difference between it and a negative income tax would vanish. Indeed, imagine that every adult member of a society had one and only one employer. All employers could then pay every month to the government a given percentage of the wage bill, while being credited for as many times the basic income as they had employees. All employees would receive every month a net wage that took both the tax and the basic income into account, including the basic income of children for which they were primary caretakers. Employees on unpaid leave could still receive a basic income through their employers. In this imaginary situation, arguably, the uniform refundable tax credit that constitutes a negative income tax provides as firm a floor as would a basic income paid upfront. Things get more complicated when some people are students or unemployed, others have customers but no employers, and others again have several employers—and when, moreover, people keep moving in and out of these various positions. In this more realistic situation, a monthly income declaration, if administratively manageable, could still reduce the disadvantage of a negative income tax by accelerating the refund of the tax credit to those entitled to it. Yet, the twofold advantage of a basic income paid upfront to all would remain obvious, though not for those with a good and regular income as much as for many others, including in their own households.

It is fair to concede, however, that negative-income-tax schemes may offer significant advantages in terms of political feasibility. First, even when marginal tax rates and net taxation of the various types of households are exactly the same, a negative-income-tax scheme involves a gross volume of taxes and expenditure that is far smaller than the corresponding basic-income scheme. This makes it look much cheaper, and hence more palatable, in the illusion-prone court of public opinion.[23] Second, unlike a basic income, a tax credit of the same amount that increases the worker's net wage preserves the impression that the source of the corresponding income entitlement is labor performed.

This makes it more congenial to labor organizations, whose power base is in the firm (that pays the wages) rather than in the government (that pays the benefits). Third, the administrative transition from a standard conditional scheme to a negative income tax can be smoother: all existing social insurance transfers can be kept as they are and simply taken into account when determining whether a negative or positive tax applies, whereas the introduction of a basic income would require a downward adjustment of the net amounts of all other benefits. These political advantages may provide good reasons for settling for a negative income tax as the best achievable outcome under some circumstances, or for adopting a negative income tax as part of a promising transition path. (In chapters 6 and 7, transition paths will be further explored.) But they do nothing to undermine the principled preference for an unconditional basic income which anyone committed to freedom for all should share.

Basic Income Versus Earned Income Tax Credit

A negative income tax can be viewed as a uniform refundable tax credit. Other forms of refundable tax credit have been proposed or are in place, and some would argue they have decisive advantages over the negative income tax. The best-known among them is the Earned Income Tax Credit (EITC), a refundable tax credit restricted to low-paid workers currently in place in the United States. Initially proposed in the early 1970s as an alternative to Nixon's Family Assistance Plan by senator Russell B. Long (a conservative democrat from Louisiana like his father Huey Long, the leader of the "Share Our Wealth" movement in the 1930s, to which we return in chapter 4), the EITC was enacted in 1975 under President Gerald Ford.[24] It was massively expanded in 1993 under the Clinton administration and has become the main program for poverty alleviation in the United States, covering nearly twenty-seven million recipients in 2013. Most OECD countries have introduced similar in-work tax credits schemes from the 1990s onward.

Like a negative income tax, the EITC takes the form of a tax reduction for some and a payment of benefits by the tax administration for others. But the tax credit is not uniform, and it is a function of earnings only—that is, of labor income, not of total income. The EITC increases as earnings increase, remains constant over some range, and then is gradually phased out.[25] Whereas an increase in the lowest earnings leads to a reduction in benefits under a negative income tax scheme and even more under a means-tested

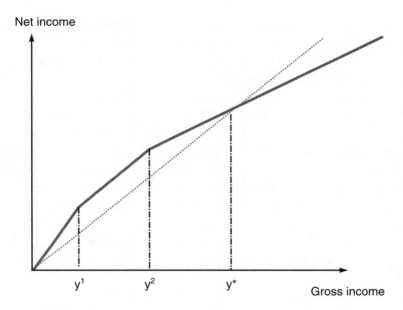

Figure 2.4 Net income with an earned income tax credit

The 45° dotted line represents net income in the absence of any taxation or transfer. The bold line shows how net income is affected by an EITC scheme. The amount of the credit to which a worker is entitled first increases (phase-in segment) up to earnings level y^1, then remains constant (plateau) up to earnings level y^2, and finally decreases (phase-out segment) up to a breakeven point y^*, which is the border between earnings levels that trigger a credit and earnings levels that trigger a tax.

minimum-income scheme (see Figures 2.2 and 2.3), it leads to a rise in benefits under an EITC scheme in the lowest earnings bracket (see Figure 2.4).

As is the case with most negative income tax proposals, under the EITC currently in place in the United States the household is taken as the relevant unit for calculating the amount of the transfer. In the case of married taxpayers, for instance, the earnings of both spouses are taken into account in order to check whether they qualify for a refundable credit, which creates disincentives to work for secondary earners within married couples. Although also present in similar schemes elsewhere, such as the British Working Tax Credit or France's *Prime d'Activité*, for example, this is not a defining feature of the earnings tax credit; eligibility could in principle be made dependent on each individual's earnings.

One advantage claimed for the EITC is that its take-up rate of about 80 percent is high relative to existing means-tested schemes such as Temporary Assistance to Needy Families (TANF) and Food Stamps (both to be discussed in chapter 3). However, this high rate is achieved only because many beneficiaries rely on costly tax preparers, and the rate is lower among poorer workers in the phase-in range of the scheme and in some ethnic groups. Moreover, the EITC check is often not paid until many months after the period during which qualifying wages were earned. Like the negative income tax, the EITC operates *ex post*, a key feature that, as one study observes, is "surely an important brake on the credit's ability to cushion families against income shocks."[26] As with the negative income tax, an obvious solution would be to incorporate advance payments into the scheme. A mechanism that allowed recipients to claim a portion of their EITC in advance through their paychecks was in place from 1979 to 2010, but was cancelled due to a very low take-up rate. Many claimants did not want to run the risk of owing money back at the end of the fiscal year.[27] The advantage universal schemes possess in this respect over means-tested guaranteed income schemes easily generalizes to the comparison with refundable credit schemes targeted at workers with low earnings.

Yet the main difference between a basic income or negative income tax and the EITC is obviously that the latter focuses exclusively on the working poor. This is no doubt why it enjoys a wider appeal than means-tested public assistance. The operation of such schemes, as Jennifer Sykes and her colleagues put it, "shows that government programs aimed at assisting families do not need to be universal to avoid stigma, as long as they are associated with behaviors most Americans condone, such as work."[28] This key difference explains, for example, why the EITC has benefited from bipartisan support in the United States, and seems to remain one of the least controversial components of the American welfare state.

However, compared to basic income or negative income tax, it has the obvious disadvantage of doing nothing for the jobless. As a result, it "serves as a boon to low-wage employers," labor leader Andy Stern notes. "If the EITC did not exist, theoretically people would be less willing to take low wage jobs."[29] This is a fatal defect for people committed, as we are, to freedom for all. However, if EITC-like measures are introduced against the background of a means-tested minimum income, they amount to pulling the distribution of net income in the direction of what would result from a negative income tax or basic income (see Figure 2.5). The introduction of EITC

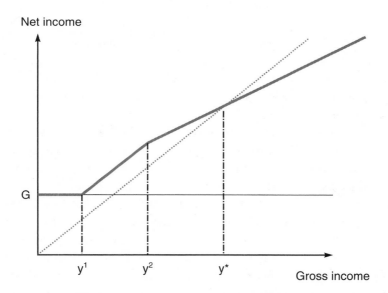

Figure 2.5 Net income with an earned income tax credit combined with a means-tested minimum-income scheme

The 45° dotted line represents net income in the absence of any taxation or transfer. The bold line shows how net income is affected by the combination of an EITC scheme (see figure 2.4) and a means-tested minimum-income scheme (see figure 2.1). In this example, when earnings are between 0 and y¹, the net income is lifted to the minimum-income level G. This makes the phase-in segment of EITC invisible. However, the refundable tax credit makes it possible for net earnings to exceed G at a level of gross earnings lower than G. And in the whole of the plateau range of the credit (up to y²), the incentive to work more is high because the marginal tax rate is zero. It falls in the range in which the credit is being phased out (y*).

as a complement, not as a substitute, for means-tested minimum-income schemes can therefore be viewed as a step in the direction of a basic income.[30] But such a move has the disadvantage of juxtaposing two conditional schemes, which is unavoidably less legible for the least well-off than an integrated scheme would be. And people's freedom is not simply defined by the set of options they have, but rather by the set of options they understand they have. From our standpoint, therefore, there is nothing that could make us prefer such a hybrid scheme to a negative income tax, let alone to a basic income.

Basic Income Versus Wage Subsidies

Basic income, the negative income tax, and the earned income tax credit can all be viewed as subsidizing work for which the pay is little, either because it is part-time or because it is not very productive in an immediate sense. This is what enables them all to address the unemployment trap and give more people access to jobs. But if making work pay is the real focus, why not go for what would seem to be a more straightforward strategy? Wage subsidies to low-paid workers are direct public contributions that either increase workers' pay or reduce its cost to their employers or do both.

Many such schemes, whether temporary or permanent, targeted or general, have been proposed and many have been implemented—for example, in the form of reductions of social insurance contributions on low wages. A particularly ambitious wage-subsidy scheme is the one advocated by Edmund Phelps, a past winner of Nobel Memorial Prize in Economic Sciences. He calls for an employment subsidy unlimited in time, paid directly to the employer, pitched at three-quarters of the cost to the employer of the lowest hourly wages, phased out gradually as the hourly wage increases, and restricted to private-sector full-time workers.[31]

Why not instead propose subsidies of limited duration? Basically, because that would cause employers and workers to invest less in their relationship, since the cost of turnover would be (more than) covered by the subsidy, with damaging effects on productivity. Why not propose a flat employment subsidy, irrespective of the wage level? Because that would require a significant rise in tax rates, with consequences for both political feasibility and economic desirability. Why does Phelps restrict his scheme to full-time workers? Above all, because he wants to draw the unemployed "into a life of full-time job holding and career building, so that they become self-supporting and have a better chance of realizing their abilities." And why only the private sector? Because "the purpose of the subsidies is to permit the broadest possible integration of disadvantaged workers into the business of society, which is the activity of the private sector."[32]

What about the earned income tax credit discussed above? Its most fundamental defect, in Phelps's opinion, is that it focuses on households with low annual earnings, not on workers with low hourly wage rates. It therefore induces reductions by some workers of their working time.[33] Unsurprisingly, his verdict is even more negative for "a flat lump-sum entitlement payable to every adult and child in the country, regardless of current work status or work history," as exemplified by Friedman's "negative income tax" and Mc-Govern's "demogrant." Phelps remembers "being part of a group advising Senator Robert Kennedy, all of whom, from James Tobin to the young Martin Feldstein, were supporters of the scheme. None of us saw the importance of tying such support to work." But eventually he came to believe that, in the absence of such a link, "all too many young people would lack the vision and the will to resist yet another year of avoiding life's challenges and risks." Phelps concedes that, relative to standard public assistance, a negative income tax would "temper the tendency of welfare to keep people away from jobs," but insists it "would do nothing to restore job holding as the means of self-support and the vehicle for personal growth and the sense of belonging and being needed."[34]

In response to the fear that his scheme would "doom the disadvantaged to an eternity of dead-end jobs," Phelps recognizes that it would reduce the return to education. But his main concern is to provide incentives to get into employment and stay in it: "Once the bourgeois repast is sweetened and made more widely available, more people will respond with bourgeois behavior."[35] Phelps also concedes that only a tiny reduction in inequality can be expected from the operation of his scheme. Too bad: "In a society dedicated to broad opportunity for human liberation and development, equality often has to take the back seat."[36]

One may wonder, however, whether "broad opportunity for human liberation and development" is really what is being pursued by and can be expected from Phelps's employment subsidy proposal. The first chapter of his *Rewarding Work* begins by quoting US president Calvin Coolidge's famous assertion that "the business of America is business" and the epilogue concludes with an echo of it: "We need to return to the founders' thinking. The business of government is fundamentally business, to paraphrase Smith and Coolidge."[37] Phelps strongly suggests that the ultimate goal of social and economic policy should not be freedom, but simply business—indeed, busy-ness, or busy lives rather than free people. Phelps's factual diagnosis does not differ greatly from ours. But next to this analysis, his response is guided by normative considerations. It would be unfair to reduce these to what has just been suggested.[38] But they are crucially different from ours. If busy-ness is all that matters, wage subsidies are definitely superior to an unconditional basic income. For those committed to freedom for all, however, the opposite is clearly the case.

Basic Income Versus Guaranteed Employment

Another measure sometimes proposed as an alternative to an unconditional basic income is a legal entitlement to a job: guaranteed employment rather than guaranteed income, a right to work with an income rather than a right to an income without work. Many of the early public-assistance schemes from the sixteenth century onwards can be construed as measures of this type, in that assistance was restricted, among the able-bodied, to the inmates of workhouses or at least to those agreeing to perform a job assigned to them by municipal authorities. But guaranteed employment, as an alternative to a guaranteed income for those able to work, still has advocates today who say the government should not operate as a distributor of handouts to people in or out of work but as an employer of last resort. In the case of the United States, one such scheme has been elaborated and forcefully advocated by Rutgers law professor Philip Harvey. The basic idea is that every resident should be entitled to a job. This entitlement would be enforced through a job-creation program administered by public authorities at the federal, state, or local level. The jobs offered would need to match the qualifications and aspirations of the unemployed and pay wages similar to those paid for comparable work in the private and public sectors. Jobs would be created mainly in community services, such as childcare or the improvement of public spaces. Means-tested income support would be restricted to those considered unable to work.[39]

One appealing argument in favor of such a scheme is that its net cost would be less than an equivalent guaranteed income scheme, since its beneficiaries would be expected to work for their income. But if there is no other way of getting an income for the able-bodied unemployed, such a scheme amounts to a combination of forced hiring and forced labor. Given the costs of equipment, training, supervision, and litigation, the conscription of the least skilled and the least motivated would have every chance of resulting in negative net productivity. As Bill Jordan puts it: "If we know anything about forced labour schemes, it is that they are monstrously inefficient: this is as true of the Gulags as it is of the inter-war concentration camps, the make-work schemes that proliferated in Thatcher's Britain and prison labour. Enforcement costs—staff administering tests and conducting surveillance—are enormous and work effort is abysmal."[40] Depending on how strict governments want to be about providing everyone with an income and yet not providing any income to able-bodied people who don't work, the net cost of such a workfare regime could well be close to the cost of incarcerating real convicts. Like many critics of such a workfare regime, its more lucid advocates are under no illusion: once generalized beyond the cherry-picking of the most employable, the practice of forcing people to work for their income is expensive.[41] If such an obligation can be justified, it should certainly not be out of a concern for cost containment—unless the jobs on offer are made so unattractive that some people will prefer to starve or beg than take them, with savings then resulting from a low rate of take-up.

Suppose, however, that the fallback option for those considered fit to work is not so awful that the guaranteed employment scheme is a form of forced labor. In this case, should people committed to freedom for all not welcome the idea of a government as employer of last resort? This possibility should not be cheaply dismissed by evoking the "Arbeit macht frei" that used to welcome those entering Nazi concentration camps. Guaranteeing to all the real possibility of access to paid work is an important objective—indeed, one that is central to our plea for an unconditional basic income. Even so, there are two considerations that make this avenue unpromising.

One of them is well formulated by labor leader Andy Stern. Because of the importance he attaches to work in giving purpose to our lives, he writes, "it was only natural that my initial thought for a solution to the coming tsunami of technological unemployment would be to guarantee a job for every American who wants one." However, further reflection made him change his mind: "Inevitably, a handful of people in a government agency would end up deciding the value of a particular job or category of work for the entire country at the expense of individual differences and choice. Also, a guaranteed jobs program would require a huge government bureaucracy." Thus he concluded: "It'd be a lot easier and more efficient just to give people cash."[42]

The second consideration was well expressed by philosopher Jon Elster. One important reason and often the chief reason why access to a paid job matters to people over and above the income it yields is the recognition it gives to the incumbent. It provides evidence that her time, effort, and skills are valuable to society.[43] If the job is given to people as a matter of legal right within the framework of a guaranteed employment scheme, however, this function is lost. There is thus something self-defeating in making the government the employer of last resort. There is nothing analogously self-defeating in enabling people to price themselves into a job sufficiently meaningful to them, thanks to a universal benefit they do not lose when taking the job. Nor is there self-defeat in encouraging work-sharing, by facilitating voluntary working-time reduction, as an unconditional basic income does.

Consequently, as with Edmund Phelps's wage-subsidy proposal, one needs to assume an intrinsic value of something like "busy-ness," understood as paid employment, to establish the superiority of a public-employment guarantee over an unconditional basic income. Those committed to freedom for all, in all its dimensions, will wisely stick to the latter. But they do not need to rule out guaranteed employment schemes, along with guaranteed training schemes, that operate as modest complements rather than alternatives to an unconditional basic income.[44]

Basic Income Versus Working-Time Reduction

Suppose that there is far from enough work for all those who would like to work, and that faith in growth as the solution has, for whatever reason, been given up. It is then tempting to advocate reducing significantly the working hours of those who work full-time (or more) and redistribute these hours among the unemployed. There have been a long string of proposals of this sort, ranging from a 1977 call by a French collective called Adret for working just two hours a day to a 2010 argument for a twenty-one-hour workweek by the New Economics Foundation.[45] Note that there is only a superficial continuity between these proposals and the old fight for the shortening of the working day and of the working week, as eloquently described by, among others, Karl Marx.[46] The central motivation of the struggle is no longer to reduce a burden but to share a privilege. However well intentioned and prima facie plausible, contemporary proposals for a reduction of the length of the working week necessarily face three serious dilemmas between unacceptability and counterproductivity.

First, if the reduction in working hours is matched by a corresponding reduction in pay, the worst-paid workers are likely to be driven below the poverty line—clearly an unwelcome, indeed unacceptable, outcome. If, instead, the monthly pay is maintained despite the drop in working hours, the hourly labor cost increases. Either this matches an increase in productivity, in which case there are no working hours up for redistribution, or it does not, in which case a lower demand for labor can be expected in response to higher unit-labor costs. Instead of shrinking as hoped, unemployment will tend to swell.[47]

Second, if hours are reduced only for those jobs for which there is an excess supply of labor, an unacceptably unfair privilege is bestowed upon the others, who can keep working as many hours as before. If, instead, the reduction applies across the board, onerous bottlenecks are created, willing scarce talent remains underused, and expensive training is wasted—again, quite possibly at the expense of total employment.

Third, if the compulsory reduction in working time were meant to apply to all workers, whether waged or self-employed, a nightmarishly expensive and intrusive bureaucracy would be required to achieve anything approaching a fair implementation. If, instead, the measure were restricted to waged workers, then the self-employed, both real and fake, would proliferate. Employers would rather hire the services of self-employed workers—highly skilled or not—who could work without time limit than have employees on their payrolls with tightly limited hours. As a result, an unhealthy bubble of pseudo-self-employed, precarious workers would develop and the expected impact on job-sharing would fail to materialize.

The combination of these three dilemmas makes for a formidable, even decisive, objection to a significant top-down reduction of the working week.[48] But this should not make us give up altogether the idea of reducing the working week's average length. Rather, we should aim to accomplish that in a form that is softer, more flexible, more efficient, more freedom-friendly, and more bottom-up—a form more suited to an increasingly diverse and fast-changing labor market, more respectful of the variety in people's preferences at different stages of their lives, and more liberated from the ideal of lifelong full-time employment for all women and all men. This form is the unconditional basic income.

Given that the right to a basic income is not subjected to the condition of being involuntarily unemployed, workers can give up their jobs without ceasing to be entitled to their unconditional basic income. And given that the level of the basic-income component of a household's income remains unaffected when its members decide to reduce their working time, the cost to them of doing so is reduced and their propensity to do so accordingly increased. The employment capacity thereby freed up by current incumbents can be occupied by those currently unemployed, especially as basic income's universality enables the unemployed to start off with part-time jobs or to accept low pay for jobs with significant training components. As discussed in chapter 1, basic income is a job-sharing device that makes it easier to cure both those who are sick because they work too much and those who are sick because they cannot find work. It makes it easier for all workers to spread their work as best suits them over longer segments of their adult lives.

Instead of forcing people into involuntary leisure by imposing tighter limits on their working weeks or their working lives, a basic income facilitates voluntary leisure for those most deprived of it, with those choosing to work longer contributing to the funding of what enables others to work less.[49] For people committed to freedom for all, there is no doubt as to which of the two formulas is preferable, even irrespective of the three dilemmas that undermine the effectiveness of any acceptable version of a significant top-down reduction of the maximum length of the working week.

3

Prehistory: Public Assistance
and Social Insurance

THE IDEA OF AN UNCONDITIONAL BASIC INCOME started making furtive
appearances in Europe only at the end of the eighteenth century. It became
the subject of short-lived public debates in the United Kingdom soon after
World War I, and in North America in the late 1960s and early 1970s. It
surfaced in various European countries in the early 1980s and, from then on,
grew step by step into a subject of international debate and worldwide activism. Chapter 4 will tell this fascinating story. But the story cannot be
properly understood without talking first about two other models of social
protection: public assistance and social insurance. Their gradual implementation has deeply shaped the context in which interest for basic income has
developed and into which it will need to be fitted in due course.

Public Assistance Conceived: Vives's *De Subventione Pauperum*

In Thomas More's *Utopia* (1516), the fictional Portuguese traveler Raphael
Hythlodaeus, who allegedly visited the island of Utopia, tells of a conversation he had in England with the Archbishop of Canterbury. "Petty larceny
isn't bad enough to deserve the death penalty," he told the Archbishop. "And
no penalty on earth will stop people from stealing, if it's their only way of
getting food." He suggested an alternative to the gallows: "Instead of in-
flicting these horrible punishments, it would be far more to the point to
provide everyone with some means of livelihood, so that nobody is under the
frightful necessity of becoming, first a thief, and then a corpse."[1] When the
conversation was suddenly interrupted, he had just started sketching how
this objective might be achieved: "Revive agriculture and the wool industry,

so that there is plenty of honest, useful work for the great army of unemployed."[2]

An economic revival might do the trick, but More might well have had in mind another, more direct way of "providing everyone with some means of livelihood." It was articulated for the first time just a few years later by one of his close friends and fellow humanists. In 1517, one year after having arranged for the publication of *Utopia* in the university town of Louvain, Desiderius Erasmus founded there the *Collegium Trilingue* and recruited in this connection a young scholar called Juan Luis Vives (1492–1540). Born in Valencia, Spain, to a family of converted Jews, Vives studied at the Sorbonne in Paris and was then living in the booming harbor city of Bruges. In a letter to More, Erasmus described him as someone who "despite his youth, has a knowledge of all branches of philosophy far above the bulk of the scholars." In the spring of 1525, on his way back from a teaching stint at Oxford, Vives was hosted in More's house in London. He was then working on a book which he believed could get him into trouble. Even just the title and the outline had to be kept under wraps. Vives wrote to his friend Francis Craneveldt in October 1525, "I do not dare entrust them to a letter, even to a dearest friend, for fear that it would fall in the wrong hands."[3] The book was published in Antwerp the following year under the title *De Subventione Pauperum*.

What was so new in Vives's book and what was so subversive about it? *De Subventione Pauperum* was the first developed plea for a scheme of public assistance, the first form taken by what is now called the welfare state. The first half of the book consists of a theological discussion that anchors the scheme in the Christian duty of charity. The obligation to help the poor is an old theme in the Christian tradition, sometimes expressed with great vigor. Thus, Vives appeals to a famous statement by Saint Ambrose (340–397), bishop of Milan, to the effect that refusing to succor the needy when one is well-off is on a par with stealing: "It is the hungry man's bread you withhold, the naked man's cloak that you store away, and the money that you bury in the earth is the price of the poor man's ransom and freedom."[4] Vives agrees: "If it is a crime to take something from a rich person, how much more wicked is it to take it from the poor? From the rich person one is only taking money, but from the poor person one is taking life itself."[5]

It is in the second half of *De Subventione Pauperum* that novelty shows up. There, Vives argues for a direct involvement of civil authorities in poor relief, using, among others, arguments reminiscent of More's Raphael: "When people's generosity is at an end, those in need do not have anything to eat. Some of them will find themselves virtually obliged to become thieves in the town or on the roads." Once his scheme is in place, "there will be fewer thefts, crimes, robberies, murders, and capital offences."[6] Vives does not only argue for the principle of public assistance. He spells out the form it should take: unambiguously a scheme strongly conditional in the sense of targeting the poor, taking their household situation into account, requiring willingness to work, and preferring kind over cash. "Above all, we must recognize the law imposed by the Lord on all humankind: that is, that each person should eat bread got through his own work. When I use the words 'eat', 'feed' or 'subsistence' I understand them to mean not just food, but also clothing, shelter, fuel, light and everything that is needed to keep the human body. No poor person who can work, according to his age and his health, should remain idle."[7]

The work condition, in particular, is stressed with great force. For every poor, there will be something to do:

> For example, someone who cannot sew clothes can sew stockings. If he is of an advanced age, or slow in thinking, he should be taught an easier trade, which can be taught in a few days, like digging earth, drawing water, carrying a load, pushing a cart. . . . Even blind people should not remain idle. There are many things they can do. . . . Sick and old people should be given easy things to work on, according to their age and their health. No one is so ill that he lacks the strength to do anything at all. In this way, occupied and focused on their work, the thoughts and bad practices which would otherwise be born in them will be restrained.[8]

The scheme does aim to cover all the poor, whatever the source of the poverty, but the work condition can be differentiated accordingly: "Those who waste their fortune in bad and stupid ways, like gaming, whoring, by luxury or on gluttony, still have to be fed because people cannot be left to starve. For those, however, the most unpleasant work should be reserved. . . . They must not die of hunger, but they should be limited by a frugal diet and hard work."[9]

The objective of the scheme is to reach all the poor and only the poor. As some who have been "honorably educated" may be reluctant to reveal their neediness, "they need to be traced with care and relieved discreetly." On the other hand "special care must be taken to protect against fraud by idle people and malingerers, so that they do not have the chance to cheat." The level of subsistence guarantee to the poor must remain frugal: "they should not receive any luxuries, because they could easily form bad habits." But a top-up may be required over and above what they earn through their work: "For the poor who live at home, it is necessary to procure work or employment in public works; other citizens have no shortage of work to give them. If it turns out that their needs are greater than what they happen to earn by work, one can add what is judged they lack."[10]

How is all this supposed to be funded? Partly from the product of the work performed by those conscripted as part of the scheme, but above all from voluntary donations by the better off. "People cannot be forced to do good, because otherwise the very idea of charity and welfare will perish." But people will give generously if they know the money is well used. Indeed, "it is to be hoped that in other towns, where the same care is not taken for poor people as it is here, many rich people will send their money, because they know it will be well distributed to help those most in need."[11] Crowd-funding for charitable purposes, one might call this today.

Public Assistance Implemented:
The Poor Laws from Ypres to Locke

The public assistance scheme thus delineated and advocated by Vives was not entirely new. At the beginning of the sixteenth century, towns started attracting growing numbers of beggars. As individual charity, whether or not coordinated by parishes and religious congregations, proved increasingly unable to cope, municipal authorities in several places felt they needed to step in. Municipal schemes of poor relief are known to have existed since the 1520s in several European towns.[12] Vives's book can be viewed as a systematic justification of such publicly organized assistance and as an elaboration of what he believed to be its best version.

Several of these schemes, however, and most directly the one in the small German town of Leisnig, were inspired by protestant doctrine. In 1520, just three years after posting his theses in Wittenberg, Martin Luther (1483–1546) wrote this in an "open letter to the Christian nobility of the German nation": "One of our greatest necessities is the abolition of all begging throughout Christendom. Among Christians no one ought to go begging! It would also be easy to make a law, if only we had the courage and the serious intention, to the effect that every city should provide for its own poor, and admit no foreign beggars by whatever name they might be called, whether pilgrims or mendicant monks."[13] The Church establishment did not like this, for two reasons: it infringed on the monopoly of the Church over the care of the poor; and, by banning begging, it threatened the livelihood of the Franciscans and Dominicans. (By then, these mendicant orders, founded three centuries earlier, represented a powerful force.) Unsurprisingly, therefore, Vives feared that his book might be accused of dangerous heretic leanings.[14]

This very accusation was leveled at another scheme which closely matched Vives's blueprint, introduced by the magistrates of the Flemish town of Ypres in 1525. Mendicant monks accused it of contradicting the doctrine of the Church. The magistrates were summoned to justify their scheme before the Faculty of Theology of the Sorbonne. They did so in 1531 in *Forma Subventionis Pauperum*, a sophisticated document that did not quote Vives explicitly but most likely found inspiration in his *De Subventione Pauperum*.[15] Like Vives, its authors insisted that "sturdy beggars, who do not want to work for their living, will be set to work with their hands, because otherwise, to their own detriment and that of the community, they will sinfully feed their idleness through the charity of good people, and take advantage from the work of others." In light of the explanation provided, the Ypres scheme was approved with a number of provisos.[16]

"We have shown the advantages of our policy more widely here, so that they can be better known," says the Ypres report. "It is in the nature of a good thing that the broader it is spread, the more good comes of it."[17] And indeed, it did not take long for this sort of scheme to spread. In 1531, following the favorable judgment by the Sorbonne theologians, Emperor Charles V promulgated an edict that regulated begging and put poor relief under civil authority throughout his Empire, while more cities introduced similar schemes.[18] Vives's *De Subventione Pauperum* was published in Spanish in 1531, in Dutch and German in 1533, in Italian in 1545, and in French in 1583.[19] Both in Spain and in the Low Countries, it gave rise to fierce disputes.[20] The trend was set, however, and the generalization of public assistance to the poor by municipal authorities proved irreversible.

This holds especially for England. Vives had regular direct contact with the Court of Henry VIII before the latter's divorce from Catherine of Aragon. England's first attempt to regulate begging, by a statute of 1531, bears resemblance to his scheme. The Ypres report was published in English in 1535, and its translator is believed to have been involved in drafting Thomas Cromwell's 1536 legislation, which further developed public assistance.[21] This was the beginning of a process that was strengthened by the dissolution of the monasteries under Henry VIII and led to the Elizabethan Poor Laws of 1597–1601. These laws of unprecedented coverage forced municipal authorities throughout the kingdom to give assistance in kind to the needy while requiring work from all the able-bodied, if necessary in workhouses set up for this purpose.[22] The funding came from "poor rates," a tax levied on all parishioners with a wealth exceeding some threshold that developed imperceptibly out of the medieval practice of charitable donations volunteered under religious and social pressure.[23] This model ruled unchallenged in England for the next two centuries or so, and was copied elsewhere. From the end of the seventeenth century, it was exported across the Atlantic, first to New England and later to other North American colonies, where municipal schemes for assistance to the poor were set up and where poor-relief legislation emulated the model of England's Poor Laws.[24]

When criticism came, for example in John Locke's *On the Poor Laws and Working Schools* (1697), it was mainly in the form of a complaint to the effect that the enforcement of the legislation was too lax. According to Locke (1632–1704), "Every one must have meat, drink, clothing, and firing. So much goes out of the stock of the kingdom, whether they work or not." Indeed, he recommended that "if any person die for want of due relief in any parish in which he ought to be relieved, the said parish be fined according to the circumstances of the fact and the heinousness of the crime." However, "the true and proper relief of the poor . . . consists in finding work for them, and taking care they do not live like drones upon the labour of others. And in order to this end we find the laws made for the relief of the poor were intended; however, by an ignorance of their intention or a neglect of their due execution, they are turned only to the maintenance of people in idleness, without at all examining into the lives, abilities, or industry of those who seek for relief."

In Locke's scheme, idle vagabonds older than fourteen are to be sentenced to three years of forced labor, either on ships or in houses of correction. If younger, they will have to attend a "working school," with the great advantage that "computing all the earnings of a child from three to fourteen years of age, the nourishment and teaching of such a child during that whole time will cost the parish nothing" and the additional advantage that "they may be obliged to come constantly to church every Sunday, along with their schoolmasters or dames, whereby they may be brought into some sense of religion." To make sure the law is enforced, Locke recommends the appointment of "beadles of beggars." And if these beadles repeatedly "neglect their said duty, so that strangers, or other beggars . . . be found frequenting the streets," they must themselves be sentenced to three years in houses of correction or on ships.

In 1723, the Workhouse Test Act restricted "outdoor relief" to those unable to work, and generalized "indoor relief"—that is, the workhouse system—for all the able-bodied poor. Two centuries after Vives, this was just a slight variant of what he was advocating. It was nonetheless in England, towards the end of the century, that real novelty occurred, with what looked at first sight like a major step towards a genuine minimum-income system.

Public Assistance Threatened:
Speenhamland and the Backlash

Dating back to the origin of the Poor Laws, assistance in cash occasionally emerged in England, especially in years of exceptionally high food prices. Its various forms included payments to unemployed agricultural workers, allowances to large families, and even wage supplements. In May 1795, the magistrates of the district of Speenhamland, in the South of England, passed a resolution that amounted to a systematization of such occasional measures. It required parishes to pay a cash benefit that would complement the earnings of poor workers. This complement was calculated so as to enable each household to reach a threshold linked to family size and the price of wheat. This scheme, soon known as the "Speenhamland system," entitled the poor residing officially within the borders of a municipality to a cash benefit that supplemented whatever they earned, while still requiring them to "provide for themselves." In 1796, the British prime minister William Pitt tried but failed to generalize this system throughout England. The effects the scheme produced on poverty, unemployment, and economic growth wherever it was implemented quickly became the subject of intense controversies.[25]

Unsurprisingly, this move met with the opprobrium of the conservative camp. Thus Edmund Burke (1729–1797), in a memorandum addressed to William Pitt in November 1795, stated bluntly: "To provide for us in our necessities is not in the power of government." Hence, whenever a man cannot find work that could provide for his necessary subsistence, he "comes within the jurisdiction of mercy. In that province the magistrate has nothing at all to do: his interference is a violation of the property it is in his office to protect. Without all doubt, charity to the poor is a direct and obligatory duty upon all Christians, next in order after the payment of debts, full and strong, and by nature made infinitely more delightful to us." Burke therefore invited the government "manfully to resist the very first idea, speculative or practical, that it is within the competence of Government, taken as Government, or even of the rich, as rich, to supply to the poor, those necessaries which it has pleased the Divine Providence for a while to withhold from them." He concluded: "My opinion is against an over-doing of any sort of administration, and more especially against this most momentous of all meddling on the part of authority; the meddling with the subsistence of the people."[26]

By far the most detailed and influential critique of public assistance to the poor, the *Essay on the Principle of Population* (1798) penned by Thomas Malthus (1766–1834), was published just two years after Pitt's attempt to generalize Speenhamland. Its empirical basis was largely drawn from Frederic Morton Eden's *State of the Poor* (1797), a lengthy history and critique of the Poor Laws that came to the conclusion that a legal provision for the poor "checks that emulative spirit of exertion, which the want of the necessaries, or the no less powerful demand for the superfluities of life, gives birth to: for it assures a man, that, whether he may have been indolent, improvident, prodigal, or vicious, he shall never suffer want."[27] Malthus's essay developed this analysis, arguing that the generalization of public aid to the poor causes them to work and save less, encourages them to marry younger and have more children, and pushes up the price of the goods they consume, thereby reducing their real wages. He therefore recommended abandoning public relief altogether. Pitt's Poor Bill, he wrote, will "tend to increase the population without increasing the produce" and "the poor therefore in general will be more distressed."[28]

Later editions of his *Essay* included a "plan of the gradual abolition of the poor law." We must acknowledge, Malthus wrote, that "we are bound in justice and honour formally to disclaim the *right* of the poor to support" and this should be clearly notified to the rising generation.[29] Hence, if a man marries without the prospect of being able to support a family,

> [A]ll parish assistance should be denied him; and he should be left to the uncertain support of private charity. He should be taught to know, that the laws of nature, which are the laws of God, had doomed him and his family to suffer for disobeying their repeated admonitions; that he had no claim of right on society for the smallest portion of food, beyond that which his labour would fairly purchase; and that if he and his family were saved from feeling the natural

consequences of his imprudence, he would owe it to the pity of some kind benefactor, to whom, therefore, he ought to be bound by the strongest ties of gratitude.[30]

This view that the English Poor Laws, the most systematic form of public assistance so far, were a big mistake was widely shared by other major thinkers in England and beyond.[31] Thus, in his *Principles of Political Economy and Taxation* (1817), David Ricardo (1772–1823), one of the founding fathers of modern economics, states squarely that the "pernicious tendency" of the Poor Laws "is no longer a mystery, since it has been fully developed by the able hand of Mr Malthus; and every friend to the poor must ardently wish for their abolition." For what is the tendency of these laws?

[I]t is not, as the legislature benevolently intended, to amend the condition of the poor, but to deteriorate the condition of both poor and rich; instead of making the poor rich, they are calculated to make the rich poor; and whilst the present laws are in force, it is quite in the natural order of things that the fund for the maintenance of the poor should progressively increase, till it has absorbed all the net revenue of the country, or at least so much of it as the state shall leave to us, after satisfying its own never failing demands for the public expenditure.[32]

In the same vein, Georg Wilhelm Friedrich Hegel (1770–1831), possibly Germany's most influential philosopher, discussed the English Poor Laws in his *Elements of Philosophy of Right* (1820). Ensuring the livelihood of the needy without the mediation of work, he wrote, "would be contrary to the principle of civil society and the feeling of self-sufficiency and honor among its individual members." From his examination of the Poor Laws, he concluded that "the most direct means of dealing with poverty, and particularly with the renunciation to shame and honor as the subjective bases of society and with the laziness and extravagance which give rise to a rabble, is to leave the poor to their fate and to direct them to beg from the public."[33]

Alexis de Tocqueville (1805–1859) was no more indulgent. In his notes on the trip he made to England in 1833, he cited the complaint of a certain Lord Radnor that "public charity has lost its degrading character" and his anecdotal account of the various forms of abuse that plague the operation of the Poor Laws: the old man who hides some of his resources, the young woman who would otherwise have been helped by her stepfather, the young people who waste their earnings in the pub.[34] And two years later, in his *Memoir on Pauperism*, he summarized in one long sentence his assessment of the Poor Laws:

> I am deeply convinced that any permanent, regular, administrative system whose aim will be to provide for the needs of the poor, will breed more miseries than it can cure, will deprave the population that it wants to help and comfort, will in time reduce the rich to being no more than the tenant-farmers of the poor, will dry up the sources of savings, will stop the accumulation of capital, will retard the development of trade, will benumb human industry and activity, and will culminate by bringing about a violent revolution in the State, when the number of those who receive alms will have become as large as those who give it, and the indigent, no longer being able to take from the impoverished rich the means of providing for his needs, will find it easier to plunder them of all their property at one stroke than to ask for their help.[35]

Public assistance, therefore, "is a very dangerous expedient. It affords only a false and momentary stop to individual suffering, and however used it inflames society's sores." What is the alternative? Individual charity. "It can produce only useful results. Its very weakness is a guarantee against dangerous consequences. It alleviates many miseries and breeds none."[36]

A somewhat less radical position was defended by the social reformer and founding father of utilitarian philosophy Jeremy Bentham (1748–1832). In his *Second Essay on the Poor Laws* (1796), he did support help to the indigent, mainly out of consideration for the security of property holders, but also expressed strong opposition to any relaxation of the compulsion to work:

> individuals destitute of property would be continually withdrawing themselves from the class of persons maintained by their own labour, to the class of persons maintained by the labour of others; and the sort of idleness which at present is more or less confined to persons of independent fortunes, would thus extend itself, sooner or later, to every individual of the number of those on whose labour, the perpetual reproduction of the perpetually consuming stock of subsis-

tence depends; till at last there would be nobody left, to labour at all for anybody.[37]

Consequently, "To a person possessed of adequate ability, no relief ought to be administered, but on condition of his performing work: to wit such a measure of work as, if employed to an ordinary degree of advantage will yield a return, adequate to the expense of relief."[38] Bentham advocated the development of "Industry Houses" aimed at providing the indigent with the basic necessities of life while forcing them and their children to work in exchange for shelter. In his plan, a privately owned "National Charity Company" would be entrusted with the management of publicly subsidized workhouses throughout England.[39]

In 1832, a Royal Commission was set up to investigate the Poor Laws, with Bentham's former secretary Edwin Chadwick and Oxford economist Nassau Senior as its most influential members. The final report, published and widely disseminated in 1834, shared much of Malthus's grim diagnosis: the effect of the Speenhamland system and other forms of public assistance was to "diminish, we might almost say to destroy, all . . . qualities in the labourer. What motives has the man who . . . knows that his income will be increased by nothing but by an increase in his family, and diminished by nothing but a diminution of his family, that it has no reference to his skill, his honesty, or his diligence,—what motive has he to acquire or to preserve any of these merits? Unhappily, the evidence shows, not only that these virtues are rapidly wearing out, but that their place is assumed by the opposite vices."[40]

The report did not conclude that all forms of public relief should be abolished, however. It only concluded, once again, that all forms of "outdoor relief" should be restricted to the sick and the old, while the able-bodied could only rely on "indoor relief"—that is, relief within regulated workhouses under conditions sufficiently unattractive that the poor would want to escape from relief altogether. The 1834 Poor Law Amendment Act (known as the "New Poor Law") was enacted by the British parliament along these lines, and put an end to all poor relief outside the workhouse, despite the fact that indoor relief proved much more expensive than the outdoor relief it replaced, and despite opposition from the nascent working-class movement.[41] Pitt's attempt to generalize the Speenhamland system had thus led to a major backlash. England was not back to private charity, as Burke, Malthus, Ricardo, Hegel, and Tocqueville would have liked. But it was back to Vives.

Bold Declarations: Enlightenment and Revolution

Was there nothing more promising in all these years—nothing that pointed in the direction of a genuine guaranteed income without ending up collapsing into forced labor? In some brief passages in the writings of a handful of Enlightenment thinkers, assertions can arguably be found for the first time that governments have a duty to guarantee the subsistence of all citizens, completely aside from the Christian duty of charity.[42] According to Montesquieu's *Esprit des Lois* (1748), for example, alms do not suffice and the state "owes all its citizens a secure subsistence, food, suitable clothes and a way of life that does not damage their health." However, Montesquieu (1689–1755) also congratulated Henry VIII on having contributed to England's industrial development by destroying religious charitable institutions that fostered laziness, and suggested that temporary assistance linked to particular accidents is much better than "permanent establishments."[43]

Jean-Jacques Rousseau (1712–1778) was less ambivalent, but quite elliptical. He closed his *Discourse on Inequality* with the statement that "it is manifestly against the law of nature . . . that a handful of people should be overfilled with superfluities, while the hungry multitude lacks the necessaries," but stopped short of indicating how this situation was to be redressed.[44] In *The Social Contract,* he wrote that "every man has naturally a right to everything he needs" and that "no citizen shall ever be wealthy enough to buy another, and none poor enough to be forced to sell himself," but it is most unlikely that he was thinking of an income untied to a duty to work: "In a country that is truly free, the citizens do everything with their own arms and nothing by means of money; so far from paying to be exempted from their duties, they would even pay for the privilege of fulfilling them themselves. I am far from taking the common view: I hold enforced labor to be less opposed to liberty than taxes."[45] In his *Confessions,* he would later write: "The money that one possesses is the instrument of freedom, that which one strives to obtain is the instrument of slavery."[46] But that was not the appropriate place for him to explore institutional consequences.

However vaguely formulated, these new ideas were soon to find political echoes in the aftermath of the French Revolution. Far more than in England, poor relief in the kingdom of France, as in most of Catholic Europe, had remained until then the preserve of the church and of private charity out of Christian duty. But the presence of the church was shrinking, especially in cities, the way it dealt with poverty came under growing criticism, and some *depôts de mendicité*, the French equivalent of workhouses, had been established from 1767 onwards.[47] A *comité de mendicité* (committee on beggary) was set up in 1790. In a report presented on its behalf to the *Assemblée Nationale* in July 1790, the extinction of begging was presented as "a duty for a wise and enlightened nation" by author François de Larochefoucault-Liancourt (1747–1827). The committee further argued: "One has always thought of practicing charity towards the poor and never of asserting the rights of the poor man on society and of society on him: this is the great duty which the French constitution must fulfill, since no other constitution so far has acknowledged and respected the rights of man."[48]

In September 1792, France's constitutional assembly elected a committee in charge of preparing a new constitution under the leadership of one of its members, the philosopher, mathematician, and political activist Antoine Caritat, Marquis de Condorcet (1743–1794). While the committee was carrying out its work in the midst of a chaotic situation (King Louis XVI was guillotined in January 1793), the Jacobin left, then in a minority position, lobbied for the inclusion of social rights. In a speech of December 1792, its leader, Maximilien de Robespierre (1758–1794), forcefully asserted that "the first right is the right to exist. Hence, society's first law is the one that guarantees to all its members the means of existence."[49] In April 1793, he spelled this out in the draft of a new declaration of human rights: "Society is obliged to secure the subsistence of all its members, either by providing them with work or by guaranteeing means of subsistence to those unable to work. The assistance indispensable to those who lack the necessary is a duty for those who possess the superfluous."[50] The text adopted by the constitutional assembly in June 1793 was a compromise between the less radical proposal that had emerged from Condorcet's constitutional committee and the demands of the Jacobins, who wanted Robespierre's draft incorporated in the new constitution. It was approved by a large majority in a referendum held in July-August 1793. Its article 21, following closely Robespierre's proposal, included the first-ever constitutional assertion of social rights: "Public assistance is a sacred debt. Society owes subsistence to the unfortunate citizens, either by providing them with work or by securing means of existence to those unable to work."[51]

This was a major new step on paper, but the bold declarations led to nothing on the ground. After gaining the upper hand for a short while, the Jacobins were kicked out of power. Robespierre was guillotined in July 1794; the 1793 constitution was never implemented; and the content of article 21 did not reappear in subsequent French constitutions. This does not mean that this episode left no durable trace. It did, for example, in the writings of two German philosophers who followed the Paris events with great attention and enthusiasm. Immanuel Kant (1724–1804), in his *Metaphysics of Morals* (1797), defended the view that a government is "authorized to constrain the wealthy to provide the means of sustenance to those who are unable to provide for even their most necessary natural needs."[52] And Johann Gottlied Fichte (1762–1814), in his *Commercial State* (1800), argues that "there ought to be no poor people in a rational state."[53]

However, something more significant happened that was barely noticed in the middle of the revolutionary chaos: something that was going to give social protection a powerful new departure, first in continental Europe and later throughout the world.

Social Insurance: From Condorcet to Bismarck

In July 1793, while the constitutional referendum was still being carried out, an order of arrest was issued against Condorcet, former leader of the constitutional committee, at the Jacobins' initiative. To avoid incarceration and a likely death sentence, Condorcet went into hiding in Paris. He left his hiding place in March 1794, was soon arrested, and died mysteriously in his cell. During those nine months in hiding, he wrote his most famous book. *Esquisse d'un Tableau Historique des Progrès de l'Esprit Humain* was published one year later, in the same year that the Speenhamland system was instituted. Its last chapter contains a short passage in which Condorcet offers the first general formulation of an idea destined for a rich future, the idea of social insurance:

> There is therefore a necessary cause of inequality, of dependency and even of misery, which constantly threatens the most numerous and most active class of our societies. We shall show that we can to a large extent remove it, by opposing luck to itself, by securing to those who reach old age a relief that is the product of what they saved, but increased by the savings of those individuals who made the same sacrifice but died before the time came for them to need to collect its fruit. . . . It is to the application of calculus to the probabilities of life and to the investment of money that one owes the idea of this method. The latter has already been successfully used, but never on

the scale and with the variety of forms that would make it really useful, not merely to a handful of individuals, but to the entire mass of society. It would free the latter from the periodic bankruptcy of a large number of families, that inexhaustible source of corruption and misery.[54]

This idea of contribution-based social insurance for all workers and their families is fundamentally different from the guiding idea behind public assistance. Crucial is that the "periodic bankruptcy of a large number of families" is no longer going to be prevented by the rich helping the poor, but by workers helping each other.[55] Condorcet's idea had no immediate impact at the time, but it found fertile ground in the nineteenth century.[56] The Industrial Revolution and the rapid disintegration of traditional solidarity systems made it increasingly urgent to find forms of social protection that went beyond the narrow framework of public assistance. Voluntary associations for mutual aid sprang up in many European cities, often in connection with the emergence of the labor movement. And the creation of state-organized social insurance started being advocated by some socialist movement leaders as an alternative both to Marx's socialist revolution and to Proudhon's non-state mutualism.[57] In Germany, the idea of publicly organized compulsory social insurance was first proposed by Leopold Krug (1810) and later developed by the so-called *Kathedersozialisten*, a group of socialist academics led by Adolf Wagner (in 1881) and Gustav von Schmoller (in 1890) that had a decisive influence on the birth of the modern social insurance system. In an attempt to counter the rise of the socialist movement and to strengthen German unification, the German chancellor Otto von Bismarck set up, between 1883 and 1889, the first comprehensive system of compulsory workers' insurance covering illness, invalidity, and old age, with an active involvement of employers and trade unions in its management.[58]

Bismarck's pioneering schemes were not immediately copied in the rest of Europe. On the left, they had to face the resistance not only of the revolutionaries who saw them as an attempt to reconcile the proletariat with capitalism, but also of some reformists who were putting all their hope in a more generous and comprehensive public assistance system. Yet they ended up prevailing. Speaking in 1905, the French socialist leader Jean Jaurès (1859–1914), for example, criticized means-tested public assistance for leaving too much room for administrative discretion: "Once you start speaking about a 'lack of resources,' you introduce an element of appreciation, of discussion, an element of uncertainty." By contrast, he argued, eligibility to social insurance is based on past contributions, and can therefore be seen as a true entitlement—which makes a "real, substantial difference." People reaching retirement age will get their pension "without any discussion, with an absolute certainty." Jaurès, therefore, was "sure that one day it is the general and systematic organization of insurance extended to all risks that will replace assistance."[59]

Compulsory insurance against work accidents was adopted in France in 1898, and the public old-age pension system in 1910.[60] Many other countries in Europe and beyond introduced similar models around the same time. In such a model, workers and/or their employers pay compulsory contributions, typically in the form of some fixed percentage of gross wages, and in exchange they or their families are entitled to retain part of a breadwinner's income in the event of illness, unemployment, disability, old age, or death. From Bismarck onwards, social protection ceased to be a relatively marginal activity of modern governments and was gradually recognized as one of their core tasks, often executed in collaboration with so-called "social partners"—that is, employers' and workers' representatives. This marked the birth of the modern welfare state, with social insurance at its core. Today, social insurance schemes play a major role in all welfare states, and an overwhelming role in the so-called "Bismarckian" welfare states of continental Europe. In the United States, they include unemployment insurance, Medicare, and "Social Security" (Old-Age, Survivors, and Disability Insurance).

Though these schemes are not targeted at the poor, and involve massive transfers to the non-poor, they soon had huge impacts on poverty. Part of their impact was the direct consequence of covering insurable risks. But another, growing part of the impact was the incorporation by the insurance schemes, in more or less unintended and untransparent fashion, of a growing component of *ex ante* redistribution or genuine solidarity—that is, an increasing amount of redistribution from more advantaged to less advantaged categories of the population that is largely predictable and hence cannot be justified by the insurance motive alone.[61] This took the form, for example, of uniform health coverage, family allowances, and minimum and maximum levels of retirement pensions, all funded by proportional social security contributions. Disguised as social insurance, this genuine solidarity between high-paid and low-paid, and low-risk and high-risk, workers could perform a large part of the job performed in the past by private charity and public assistance.

As they developed along these lines, social insurance schemes quickly dwarfed public assistance schemes and relegated them to a secondary role in the fight against poverty. Social insurance schemes were also generally regarded as superior to public assistance schemes because of their inclusive, "universal" nature. A scheme that covers all workers, rich and poor, is more respectful of the dignity of the poor than one that identifies the poor and targets them. This argument works quite well in contexts where most in a population qualify as workers or dependents of workers who paid (or whose employers paid) the relevant insurance contributions to entitle them to the full range of social benefits. It fails, however, when this condition is not satisfied. Many young people may not manage to enter the labor market. Many workers may prove unable to find another job before the end of the period during which they qualify for unemployment insurance. The dislocation of households may produce multitudes of single parents with no work records. Moreover, in many contexts worldwide, most work is not even performed within the formal sphere. In such contexts, public assistance makes no less sense than at the time of Vives and Speenhamland. But it now has to operate as a more or less significant complement to the more or less comprehensive social insurance schemes that have developed since then.

Public Assistance After Social Insurance:
From Roosevelt to Lula

Countries with firmly entrenched social insurance systems saw the emergence of modernized public assistance systems. Those play marginal yet important roles by providing ultimate safety nets to the residual population that is not covered at all, or not sufficiently, by the social insurance system. In the United States, Franklin D. Roosevelt's Social Security Act of 1935, generally considered the founding moment of America's modern welfare state, included, next to a bulky social insurance component made up of old-age insurance and unemployment insurance, a noncontributory public assistance program called Aid to Dependent Children (ADC), renamed Aid to Families with Dependent Children (AFDC) in 1962 and transformed into Temporary Assistance to Needy Families (TANF) in 1996. This program, restricted to households with children, was funded at the federal level and implemented at state level, with a degree of state autonomy that was significantly increased in 1996.[62] Besides this minimum-income program for families, a food stamps program, now known as the Supplemental Nutrition Assistance Program, was initiated in 1964 within the framework of President Lyndon B. Johnson's "War on

Poverty." It gives vouchers to low-income adults who are available on the labor market but unable to find a job, allowing them to purchase food in accredited stores.[63]

A decade after Roosevelt's legislation, the United Kingdom passed a more comprehensive National Assistance Act (in 1948), itself based on Sir William Beveridge's wartime report "Social Insurance and Allied Services." The act provided for "assistance grants" payable in cash to all poor households for an unlimited period of time and at a level meant to be sufficient "to meet their requirements," subject to the able-bodied's being "registered for employment in such manner as may be prescribed by the Board." This scheme, still essentially in place today, complemented a reinforced and unified national system of social insurance. It explicitly marked the definitive abolition of the Poor Law system.

During the second half of the twentieth century, schemes broadly similar to the British public assistance program were introduced elsewhere in Europe, often building on and integrating preexisting local schemes, in an attempt to address systematically the gaps in social insurance. Sweden (in 1957) was the first country to adopt a public assistance law aimed at turning previous forms of poor relief into a genuine countrywide minimum-income scheme. Denmark and Germany followed suit in 1961, the Netherlands in 1963, Norway in 1964, Belgium in 1974, and Ireland in 1975. France introduced its own scheme only in 1988, when the government headed by Michel Rocard launched the *revenu minimum d'insertion* (minimum integration income), reformed and relabeled in 2009 as *revenu de solidarité active* (active solidarity income). Today, most member states of the European Union have implemented some form of national minimum-income scheme, which often relies on subnational authorities for implementation and administration. The main exceptions are Italy and Greece. Besides Europe and North America, such schemes have also been introduced in other OECD countries in the second half of the twentieth century. Japan, for instance, adopted its Livelihood Protection Law in 1950. According to this law, still effective today, all needy individuals are entitled to receive public assistance, provided they meet a very strict means test and stringent availability-for-work requirements.[64]

While generosity level, degree of centralization, and detailed conditions vary considerably across countries and sometimes even within countries, all such schemes aim to create a safety net for households without adequate incomes from work, savings, or social insurance, by guaranteeing them conditional access to a minimum income, most often pitched below the poverty line. Public assistance operates as the ultimate safety net for people in need: it involves a means test, requires willingness to work from the able-bodied, and operates at the level of the household as a whole. Such guaranteed-minimum-income schemes play a relatively marginal role in countries where a developed system of social insurance manages to cover the bulk of the population (often thanks to major yet hidden deviations from the strict insurance principle).

By contrast, they have come to play a far more important role in less-developed countries with large informal economies. One early example is South Africa's "old-age grant," a noncontributory pension scheme created in the 1920s for whites only and extended to the whole population towards the end of the Apartheid regime.[65] Recent years have witnessed growing interest throughout the so-called developing countries in similar sorts of conditional cash-transfer schemes. Brazil's *bolsa família* (family grant) is the most massive example. It was created in 2003 as part of President Luiz Inácio Lula da Silva's *fome zero* (zero hunger) program through the amalgamation of the means-tested child-benefit system *bolsa escola* (school grant), introduced at the federal level in 2001 under President Fernando Enrique Cardoso, and various other means-tested programs. It allocates benefits to households with an income below some threshold that varies with household composition, on condition that young children are subjected to health checkups and older children attend school. By 2014, it covered about 14 million families, more than a quarter of Brazil's population. Other well-known programs of the same sort include Mexico's *Progresa*, started in 1997 and later relabeled *Oportunidades,* and Chile's *Chile Solidario,* created in 2002.[66] Supported by international organizations and many impact studies, they are now spreading far beyond Latin America. Nationally organized conditional minimum-income schemes are thereby becoming a worldwide phenomenon, including in countries where the relative modesty of social-insurance systems gives them far more than a marginal role in the distribution of income. This is all still a long way from an unconditional basic income, but it completes the historical sketch of the context in which the idea has emerged and into which it will have to fit if it is ever to be realized.

4

History: From Utopian Dream
to Worldwide Movement

THE YEAR 1795 was when the magistrates of Speenhamland set up a means-tested cash benefit scheme that started looking like a genuine minimum-income scheme, but soon led to a backlash. It was also when the book in which Condorcet first formulated the general idea of social insurance, much later to become the main principle of our welfare states, was published. And it was the year when one of Condorcet's closest friends started writing a short piece that, while it was barely noticed at the time and soon forgotten, would be rediscovered and recognized two centuries later as the first proposal of something quite close to a genuine unconditional basic income.[1]

Basic Income Imagined: Thomas Spence versus Thomas Paine

In a pamphlet entitled *Agrarian Justice* (1796) and addressed "to the Legislature and the Executive Directory of the French Republic," Thomas Paine (1737–1809), by then a prominent figure in the American and French revolutionary movements, put forward a scheme radically different from both public assistance and social insurance.[2] In it, he proposed to "create a national fund, out of which there shall be paid to every person, when arrived at the age of twenty-one years, the sum of fifteen pounds sterling, as a compensation in part, for the loss of his or her inheritance, by the introduction of the system of landed property. And also, the sum of ten pounds per annum, during life, to every person now living, of the age of fifty years, and to all others as they shall arrive at that age."[3]

What did these sums represent at the time? With their fifteen pounds per capita, a young couple "could buy a cow, and implements to cultivate a few acres of land."[4] However, even with the low life expectancy prevailing at the time, the bulk of the fund—close to 80 percent according to Paine's own calculations—would finance the payment of a strictly individual, universal, unconditional basic income to every man and woman aged fifty or more.[5]

Paine's moral justification for this proposal is reminiscent of an idea that can be found in the Christian tradition—namely, that the earth is the common property of mankind. A version of this idea had been expressed in the fourth century by Saint Ambrose: "The earth has been created in common for all, rich and poor: why do you claim for yourselves the right to own the land?"[6] It was echoed in Vives's *De Subventione Pauperum:* "He [God] has put everything which He has brought into existence into the great realm of the world, without barriers or locks, so that they can be common to all He has created."[7] And it was famously rearticulated in John Locke's *Treatises of Government* (1689). Even for Locke, however, this common ownership remains explicitly linked to the Christian duty of charity. According to Locke, "it would always be a sin, in any man of estate, to let his brother perish for want of affording him relief out of his plenty. As justice gives every man a title to the product of his honest industry, and the fair acquisitions of his ancestors descended to him; so charity gives every man a title to so much out of another's plenty, as will keep him from extreme want, where he has no means to subsist otherwise."[8] Moreover, the gift of the earth is linked to the imposition of labor: "God, when he gave the world in common to all mankind, commanded man also to labour, and the penury of his condition required it of him." He gave the world "to the use of the industrious and rational (and labour was to be his title to it) not to the fancy or covetousness of the quarrelsome and contentious."[9]

In sharp contrast, Paine asserts: "It is not charity but a right, not bounty but justice, that I am pleading for." And from the "position not to be controverted that the earth, in its natural, uncultivated state was, and ever would have continued to be, the common property of the human race," he derives a new and radical conclusion: as the land gets cultivated, "it is the value of the improvement only, and not the earth itself, that is in individual property. Every proprietor, therefore, of cultivated lands, owes to the community a ground-rent (for I know of no better term to express the idea) for the land which he holds; and it is from this ground-rent that the fund proposed in this plan is to issue." The universal nature of the scheme he proposes follows directly from this justification: "It is proposed that the payments, as already stated, be made to every person, rich or poor. It is best to make it so, to prevent invidious distinctions. It is also right it should be so, because it is in lieu of the natural inheritance, which, as a right, belongs to every man, over and above property he may have created, or inherited from those who did. Such persons as do not choose to receive it can throw it into the common fund."[10]

Thus, what Paine proposed was a universal, obligation-free, individual cash payment, but not throughout adult life. It did not take long, however, before his proposal was radicalized into a genuine lifelong basic income. In *The Rights of Infants,* a pamphlet published in London in 1797, the English schoolteacher and activist Thomas Spence (1750–1814) started off attacking Paine's *Agrarian Justice* for having constructed on the basis of a "great fundamental truth" only "an execrable fabric of compromissory expediency."[11] Next he formulated the proposal he claimed he had tirelessly defended since his youth.[12] All land and houses of each municipality should be entrusted to a committee of women, their use should be auctioned off, and part of the proceeds should be used to cover all public expenditures, including for the construction and maintenance of buildings, and the taxes owed to the government. "And as to the overplus, after all public expences are defrayed, we shall divide it fairly and equally among all the living souls in the parish, whether male or female; married or single; legitimate or illegitimate; from a day old to the extremest age; making no distinction between the families of rich farmers and merchants . . . and the families of poor labourers and mechanics."[13]

Spence's justification for his basic income plan is fundamentally the same as Paine's: "such share of the surplus rents is the imprescriptible right of every human being in civilized society, as an equivalent for the natural materials of their common estate, which by letting to rent, for the sake of cultivation and improvement, they are deprived of." According to Spence, however, the effect of Paine's plan would be that "multitudes of the people will be poor and beggarly, and unable to purchase numberless articles of use and luxury that their wants and inclinations would prompt them to wish for," whereas his own scheme would provide all with "inexhaustible means of comfortable subsistence." The more generous level of the dividends paid under his scheme would then boost the general level of economic activity: "Domestic trade would be at amazing pitch, because there would be no poor; none but would be well clothed, lodged, and fed: and the whole mass of rents, except a trifle to the government, being circulated at home, in every parish, every quarter, would cause such universal prosperity as would enable every body to purchase not only the necessities of life, but many elegancies and luxuries."[14]

The root of the difference must be that the funding of Paine's scheme is re-stricted to the value of land in its unimproved state, whereas Spence's scheme relies on all real estate, buildings, and other improvements included. Note, however, that Paine also hints at another ethical foundation for his scheme—closer to the one we shall defend ourselves in chapter 5—that could justify a level of benefit far more generous than Spence's:

> Personal property is the effect of society; and it is as impossible for an individual to acquire personal property without the aid of society, as it is for him to make land originally. Separate an individual from society, and give him an island or a continent to possess, and he cannot acquire personal property. He cannot be rich. . . . All accumulation, therefore, of personal property, beyond what a man's own hands pro-duce, is derived to him by living in society; and he owes on every principle of justice, of gratitude, and of civilization, a part of that ac-cumulation back again to society from whence the whole came.[15]

Whether or not Spence was right in seeing himself as more generous than Paine, his plan was debated by some radical English reformers in the 1820s, before sinking, along with Paine's, into oblivion.

Basic Income on a National Scale: Joseph Charlier

In London on February 21, 1848, the Communist League published a little book that the young German Karl Marx had finished writing in Brussels, in a great hurry, the previous month: the *Manifesto of the Communist Party*. A few days later, on February 24, King Louis Philippe of France was forced to abdicate following the revolutionary events in Paris. On March 4, Marx was arrested in Brussels and expelled from Belgium. On March 28, a document was seized by the police at the house of Joseph Kats, brother of the Jacob Kats (1804–1886) who was a writer and prominent member of Brussels's *Asso-ciation Démocratique*, of which Marx was vice chairman. Written in Flemish and titled *Project of a New Social Constitution*, this document stipulates that "the earth is the universal heritage of the people" and that "its fruits must be equally distributed among all of them" (article 4); that "all personal property rights over real estate are abolished" (article 5); and that all land, whether built on or not, will be rented out by the state with their revenues "regarded as the fruits of nature in order to be distributed equally among all members of society in as many equal parts as there are people, no one excluded" (article 6). This is clearly an unconditional basic income justified unwittingly in fundamentally the same way as the schemes proposed half a century earlier by Paine and Spence. But the short document is not more specific. Nor is its author known.[16] Nor is there any known connection with a book-length development of the same idea published in Brussels later that same year.

Compared to Marx's *Manifesto,* its contemporary, *Solution du Problème Social,* is equally ambitious and no less original. But it is less engagingly written, and little is known about its author—a certain Joseph Charlier (1816–1896). It had no noticeable impact at the time or indeed at any later point. Thomas Paine had advocated a basic endowment for the young and a basic pension for the elderly. Thomas Spence had advocated a genuine basic income at a municipal level. Charlier's book offers the first developed plea for a genuine basic income on a national scale: a uniform "territorial dividend" to be paid every quarter to each "indigenous" resident of the country, whether male or female, whether adult or child, and to be funded by rents on all properties, whether built or not.[17] There is nothing to suggest that Charlier knew either Paine's *Agrarian Justice* or Spence's *Rights of Infants*—or even the *Project of a New Social Constitution,* which was seized, while he was writing his book, less than a mile from his home. His point of departure, however, was the same as theirs: nature was created for the sake of meeting everyone's needs.[18] Therefore, he argued, private land ownership is incompatible with justice, and the state must ultimately become the sole owner of all land and all buildings on the land. Being a reformist, he proposed a transitional regime that would expropriate land, while granting lifelong annuities to current landowners and expropriating some proportion of the value of each new building with each inheritance. The revenues from this rent would provide all households with an income sufficient to cover their "absolute needs" and thereby provide "a sovereign remedy for the plague of pauperism."[19]

In this book and others he published on the subject up to the end of his life, Charlier refined his proposal and defended it against all sort of objections.[20] Yes, the level of the dividend will be such that "the state will secure bread to all but truffles to no one," he argued. "Too bad for the lazy; they will have to get by with the minimum allowance. The duty of society does not go beyond this: to assure to everyone his fair share in the enjoyment of the elements that nature has put at his disposal, without usurpation by some people to the detriment of others." Nonetheless, the distribution of bargaining power will be deeply altered: "It is no longer the worker who will have to bow before capital, it is capital, reduced to its true role of collaborating agent, that will have to negotiate with labor on an equal footing." Consequently, repugnant jobs will have greater difficulty being filled: "Undoubtedly, by raising and improving the material condition of the masses, the implementation of a guaranteed minimum income will make them choosier in the choice of their occupations; but as this choice is usually determined by the price of manpower, the industries concerned will need to offer their workers a salary high enough to compensate for the inconveniences involved." Therefore, the proposed scheme "will have as an immediate consequence a reparatory remuneration for this class of pariahs presently condemned to misery by way of reward for their irksome and useful labor."[21]

Towards the end of his long life, Charlier wrote a letter to the rector of the University of Brussels along with a copy of his last book, a briefer restatement meant to popularize his message. In this letter, Charlier reiterated his conviction that his proposal "is the only rational and just solution that should be given to the social question, no offense to my more or less self-interested contradictors. There are truths which one neither wants nor dares to face."[22] He probably received no more answer to this letter than to his previous ones. The world was not ready to hear his passionate plea. His 1848 book seems to have been barely read at the time and his subsequent writings seem to have been just as quickly forgotten.[23]

Basic Income Taken Seriously:
John Stuart Mill's Fourierism

This cannot be said of another, far more authoritative author who joined the tiny team of isolated early basic income supporters at about the same time. The year 1848 not only saw the publication of Marx's *Manifesto* and Charlier's *Solution*. It was also the year that John Stuart Mill (1806–1873) published the first edition of his *Principles of Political Economy,* one of the founding classics of modern economics. Unsurprisingly, the book included a substantial discussion of the Poor Laws.[24] Like the eminent critics of the Poor Laws quoted in chapter 3, Mill identifies and recognizes the structural problem inherent in public assistance to the poor: while the consequences of assistance itself are beneficial, he writes, the consequences of relying on it "are for the most part injurious." But unlike Ricardo, Hegel, or Tocqueville, this did not make him advocate a return to private charity. Subject to some conditions, he wrote, "I conceive it to be highly desirable that the certainty of subsistence should be held out by law to the destitute able-bodied, rather than that their relief should depend on voluntary charity."[25]

What are these conditions? Essentially that there should remain an incentive to work—that is, that the condition of the person receiving help should not be made as desirable as that of "the labourer who supports himself by his own exertions." If that is the case, there will be no need to set up a system of forced labor for the undeserving poor—that is, "an organized system of compulsion for governing and setting to work like cattle those who had been removed from the influence of the motives that act on human beings." Moreover, "the state must act by general rules. It cannot undertake to discriminate between the deserving and undeserving indigent. . . . The dispensers of public relief have no business to be inquisitors." What is needed, therefore, is neither private charity nor workhouses, but a legal guarantee of subsistence for all the destitute, whether able-bodied or not, whether "deserving or not."[26]

Was Mill more specific? Not in the first edition of his book, but arguably in the second, published as early as the following year with one major addition: "The increased importance which the Socialist controversy has assumed since this work was written has made it desirable to enlarge the chapter which treats of it; the more so, as the objections therein stated to the specific schemes propounded by some Socialists have been erroneously understood as a general condemnation of all that is commonly included under that name."[27] Which "specific scheme" did Mill find worth taking seriously? Undoubtedly Fourierism, which he describes as "the most skillfully combined, and with the greatest foresight of objections, of all the forms of Socialism."[28]

The eccentric and prolific Charles Fourier (1772–1837) was, along with Robert Owen and the Count of Saint-Simon, one of the three "great utopians" whom Engels criticized for viewing socialism as the realization of an ethical ideal rather than the product of historical forces.[29] In *La Fausse Industrie*, Fourier expressed a conception of justice quite close to the one invoked by Paine, Spence, and Charlier: "If the civilized order deprives man of the four branches of natural subsistence, hunting, fishing, picking and grazing, which make up the first right, the class which took the land owes to the frustrated class a minimum of abundant subsistence." And he put great emphasis on the impact of granting this obligation-free "minimum of abundant subsistence" on the quality of work: "As the masses, once an abundant minimum is guaranteed to them, would want to work only a little or not at all, one would need to discover and organize a regime of attractive industry which would guarantee that people would keep working despite their well-being."[30]

However, while the scheme Fourier had in mind in *La Fausse Industrie* was clearly not work-tested, it was just as clearly means-tested, targeting the poor: obligation-free but not universal.[31]

Fourier's chief disciple and the founding father of the Fourierist school was the French philosopher and economist Victor Considerant (1808–1893). He joined his master in advocating a right to an obligation-free minimum income that would both require and generate a dramatic improvement in the attractiveness of work, but his wording suggests that he was thinking of a genuine universal basic income: "Forwarding the minimum [*avancer le minimum*] is the basis of freedom and the guarantee of the emancipation of the proletarian. No freedom without minimum. No minimum without industrial attraction. This is what the emancipation of the masses is all about."[32]

The potential ambiguity is completely lifted in Mill's sympathetic presentation of Fourierism in the second edition of his *Principles:* "This [Fourierist] System does not contemplate the abolition of private property, nor even of inheritance; on the contrary, it avowedly takes into consideration, as elements in the distribution of the produce, capital as well as labour. . . . In the distribution, a certain minimum is first assigned for the subsistence of every member of the community, whether capable or not of labour. The remainder of the produce is shared in certain proportions, to be determined beforehand, among the three elements, Labour, Capital, and Talent."[33]

No wonder Mill found this scheme appealing. As recommended in his discussion of the Poor Laws, the Fourierist scheme guarantees "certainty of subsistence" to all, whether able-bodied or not. No inquisitorial distinction is made between the deserving and the undeserving. Yet incentives are preserved through the remuneration of labor, capital, and talent as a top-up over and above the minimum that has been "first assigned." This must have seemed to Mill an elegant way of addressing what he described in his *Autobiography* as "the social problem of the future," which was "how to unite the greatest individual liberty of action, with a common ownership of the raw materials of the globe, and an equal participation of all in the benefits of combined labour."[34]

A number of other nineteenth-century thinkers defended the idea of a tax that would capture the whole value of land. They include, in particular, the British social philosopher Herbert Spencer (1820–1903), the French economist Leon Walras (1834–1910), and the American social reformer Henry George (1839–1907). However, none of them implied as clearly as Thomas Spence, Joseph Charlier, or John Stuart Mill in his interpretation of Fourierism that the revenues should be spent on the distribution of a cash income to all rather than on other public expenditures.[35]

Basic Income Debated: England after World War I

Something more akin to a real public debate took shape in Britain shortly after the end of World War I. The first to open fire was the mathematician, philosopher, nonconformist political thinker, militant pacifist, and Nobel laureate Bertrand Russell (1872–1970). In *Roads to Freedom*, a short and incisive book first published in 1918, he argues for a social model that combines the advantages of socialism and anarchism:

> Anarchism has the advantage as regards liberty, socialism as regards the inducement to work. Can we not find a method of combining these two advantages? It seems to me that we can. . . . Stated in more familiar terms, the plan we are advocating amounts essentially to this: that a certain small income, sufficient for necessaries, should be secured to all, whether they work or not, and that a larger income, as much larger as might be warranted by the total amount of commodities produced, should be given to those who are willing to engage in some work which the community recognizes as useful.[36]

In particular, Russell says this plan constitutes one of two ways of securing the freedom artists need in order to "keep alive a much-needed element of lightheartedness which our sober, serious civilization tends to kill." One of these ways consists of "doing only a few hours' work a day and receiving proportionately less pay than those who do a full day's work." The other "would be that the necessaries of life should be free, as Anarchists desire, to all equally, regardless of whether they work or not. Under this plan, every man could live without work: there would be what might be called a 'vagabond's wage,' sufficient for existence but not for luxury. The artist who preferred to have his whole time for art and enjoyment might live on the 'vagabond's wage'—traveling on foot when the humor seized him to see foreign countries, enjoying the air and the sun, as free as the birds, and perhaps scarcely less happy."[37]

Like Fourier and Charlier, Russell warned that the provision of this "certain small income, sufficient for necessaries" would affect people's willingness to work. Like them, however, he regarded this as an argument in favor of the proposal, rather than a drawback: "One great advantage of making idleness economically possible is that it would afford a powerful motive for making work not disagreeable; and no community where most work is disagreeable can be said to have found a solution of economic problems."[38] In his later essay *In Praise of Idleness,* Russell returns to this theme: "Modern technique has made it possible for leisure, within limits, to be not the prerogative of small privileged classes, but a right evenly distributed throughout the community. The morality of work is the morality of slaves, and the modern world has no need of slavery."[39] Yet, he also suggests that granting to all the right to idleness may be viable only if there is sufficient social pressure against using it: "When education is finished no one should be compelled to work, and those who choose not to work should receive a bare livelihood, and be left completely free; but probably it would be desirable that there should be a strong public opinion in favor of work, so that only comparatively few should choose idleness."[40]

In the same year as Russell's *Roads to Freedom,* the young engineer, Quaker, and Labour Party member Dennis Milner (1892–1956), published jointly with his first wife, Mabel, a short pamphlet entitled *Scheme for a State Bonus.* Using an eclectic series of arguments, they argued for the introduction of an income paid unconditionally on a weekly basis to all citizens of the United Kingdom. Pitched at 20 percent of GDP per capita, the "state bonus" would be funded by contributions from everyone "with any income at all," and should make it possible to solve the problem of poverty, particularly acute in the aftermath of World War I. As the state bonus scheme is based on the moral right to the means of subsistence, any obligation to work enforced through the threat of a withdrawal of these means is ruled out. "Persuading people to work," the Milners wrote, "is an educational problem. Starvation must not be used as an educative force, for it only makes inefficient workers." Having gained access to the "primal necessities of life," workers will be "in a fairer position for bargaining" about wages. Better wages, in turn, "will mean a greater demand for necessities, and thus a steadier state in all the staple industries."[41]

Dennis Milner subsequently elaborated the proposal in a 1920 book entitled *Higher Production by a Bonus on National Output: A Proposal for a Minimum Income for All Varying with National Productivity*. Many of the arguments that play central roles in later pleas for basic income can be found in this book—from the unemployment trap to labor market flexibility, from low rates of take-up to the ideal complement of profit-sharing. Milner's proposal was enthusiastically endorsed in several publications by Bertram Pickard (1892–1973), a prominent Quaker and United Nations official.[42] It was supported by the short-lived State Bonus League—under whose banner Milner took part in a national election—and discussed at the 1920 British Labour Party conference. In 1921, however, the Labour Party definitively rejected the proposal. In 1927, Milner married the psychoanalyst Marion Blackett. He spent some years in the United States and died in 1954 without ever having returned, it seems, to his State Bonus proposal.[43]

It did not take long, however, for another English engineer to take up the idea again, with significantly greater impact. Clifford H. "Major" Douglas (1879–1952) was struck by how productive British industry had become after World War I and began to wonder about the risks of overproduction. How could a population impoverished by four years of war consume the goods available in abundance, when banks were reticent to give them credit and their purchasing power rose only very slowly? To solve this problem, Douglas proposed, in a series of books and popular lectures and writings, the introduction of "social credit" mechanisms, one of which consisted in paying all households a monthly "national dividend."[44] The social credit movement enjoyed varying fortunes. It failed to establish itself in the United Kingdom but attracted many supporters in several parts of Canada.[45]

While the social credit movement aroused a short-lived enthusiasm in broad layers of the British population, basic income itself was gaining ground in a small circle of intellectuals close to the British Labour Party. One of the most prominent among them was the economist George D. H. Cole (1889–1959), the first holder of Oxford's Chichele Chair of Social and Political Theory. Cole was fully aware of the earlier pleas by the State Bonus League and the social credit movement.[46] In several books, he consistently defended what he seems to have been the first to call a "social dividend" and "basic income."[47] Incomes, he argued in 1935, should "be distributed partly as rewards for work, and partly as direct payments from the State to every citizen as 'social dividends'—a recognition of each citizen's claim as a consumer to share the common heritage of productive power. . . . The aim should be, as speedily as possible, to make the dividend large enough to cover the whole of the minimum needs of every citizen."[48] In Cole's perspective, earnings would eventually be reduced to the status of pocket money, without this needing to shatter work incentives:

> If the maximum a man could earn came to no more than the amount of his social dividend, the incentive to earn it, in a society living nearly at a common standard, would be fully as powerful as the incentive to earn many times as much in the class-ridden society of today. For the demand for little luxuries and larger supply of substitutable necessaries is the keenest of all human demands. . . . Earnings will become, under such a system, more and more of the nature of "pocket money," without any loss of the incentives to effort such as absolute equality of incomes would involve. Work will have its sufficient reward; but the main part of national income will no longer be distributed as a by-product of industry.[49]

Politically less active, but enjoying a stronger international reputation than Cole, another Oxford economist, James Meade (1907–1995), defended the "social dividend" with even greater tenacity. The idea is present in his writings from the 1930s onwards as a central ingredient of a just and efficient economy.[50] And it is still at the core of Meade's *Agathotopia* project, which he advocated with great enthusiasm in the last years of his life: partnerships between capital and labor and a social dividend funded by public assets are there offered together as a solution to the problems of unemployment and poverty.[51]

Against the background of this rich interwar discussion, one might have thought that the soil was ripe for a political breakthrough in the United Kingdom. No such breakthrough occurred, however. As mentioned in chapter 3, the report prepared under the chairmanship of Lord Beveridge and published in 1942 proposed a combination of social insurance and residual public assistance and left no room for an unconditional basic income. Lady Juliet Rhys-Williams (1898–1964), like Beveridge a liberal politician, made a last attempt in 1943 with her "new social contract," which included the payment of a universal and individual benefit to all adults, subject to availability for "suitable employment."[52] Beveridge prevailed, however, and the British discussion on basic income was extinguished for several decades, despite James Meade's attempt to revive it in the 1970s when he was appointed as chair of a committee on "the structure and reform of direct taxation" in the United Kingdom.[53]

Meanwhile, not much was happening on the continent. The closest one could find to the idea of a basic income was in *Die Allgemeine Nährpflicht* (1912), by the Viennese social philosopher and reformer Josef Popper-Lynkeus (1838–1921), "a prophetic and saintly person" according to his friend Albert Einstein: "As an extreme individualist he prized man's freedom from want and dispensable constraint as the highest aim." According to Popper-Lynkeus, "Everyone, without exception—that is, without regard to age, sex, religion, belief, or unbelief, without regard to political opinions or identification with party or no party, without regard to physical and mental capacity, irrespective of one's moral or mental qualifications—should be guaranteed, as of right, a minimum for subsistence, to preserve his physical and moral integrity." However, this "universal duty to feed" should take the form of subsistence goods and services in kind: "not only a minimum of food, basic housing and house furnishings, clothes, medical services, heating, illumination, education, hospitalization, and, if misfortune strikes, also burial to all, but also a basic minimum of entertainment in the form of concerts and theatrical entertainment." And it must be coupled with an "obligatory universal labor service composed of and participated in by every able-bodied man and woman."[54]

Something similar was proposed later by the "French movement for Abundance" set up by Jacques Duboin (1878–1976), a socialist member of France's National Assembly, though with an economic rationale close to the one mobilized by the social credit movement. Duboin advocated a universal "social income" in the form of non-hoardable currency in order to tackle the "great replacement of man by machines," here again in exchange for a lengthy "social service."[55] Though sometimes interpreted as forerunners of contemporary pleas for an unconditional basic income, these proposals are better understood as recommending a uniform basic wage, spread over people's whole working lives, in exchange for several years of conscripted labor.

Guaranteed Income in the Early 1960s: Theobald Versus Friedman

In the United States, a similar scheme, associating universal income and universal social service in the "industrial army," had been vividly described and advocated in *Looking Backward*, an 1888 science-fiction novel by socialist

Edward Bellamy (1850–1898). It was also advocated by Paul and Percival Goodman in their *Communitas,* where the free in-kind provision of subsistence goods is coupled with six or seven years of service in the national economy "spaced out as convenient with a certain choice as to the years in which to serve."[56] However, the most relevant development in the first half of the twentieth century is the movement "Share Our Wealth," launched by Democratic Senator Huey P. Long (1893–1935) of Louisiana in the early 1930s, with the motto "Every Man a King." Long unveiled his plan in a radio address in 1934. His aim was to end the depression by limiting the concentration of wealth at the top and redistributing income on a universal basis. His proposals included granting every family a lump-sum "homestead allowance" of "around $5,000," and ensuring that "no family's annual income would be less than from $2,000 to $2,500."[57] In February 1935, Long claimed that over seven million Americans had joined the twenty-seven thousand Share Our Wealth clubs across the United States. Denounced as a demagogue by his critics, he was assassinated in September 1935 shortly after announcing he would run for president, and his movement fizzled out.[58] It is nonetheless in the United States, but only in the turbulent 1960s, at the peak of the civil rights movement, that a real debate on basic income picked up again, with three distinct sources, which could be labeled "post-industrial," "neoliberal," and "liberal" (in the American sense).

First, from the early 1960s, Robert Theobald (1929–1999) started advocating a "guaranteed income" on the grounds that automation was at the same time making goods abundant and workers redundant.[59] The guaranteed income, he argued, "is essential for both short-run and long-run reasons. In the short run, it is required because an ever-growing number of people—blue-collar, white-collar, middle-management and professional—cannot compete with machines; in the absence of the guaranteed income the number of people in hopeless, extreme poverty will increase. In the long run, we will require a justification for the distribution of resources that is not based on job-holding."[60] Ultimately, as also suggested by the title of one of Theobald's books, *Free Men and Free Markets* (1963), what must guide this distribution is a concern for freedom for all: "A guaranteed income provides the individual with the ability to do what he personally feels to be important. . . . The guaranteed-income proposal is based on the fundamental American belief in the right and the ability of the individual to decide what he wishes and ought to do."[61]

Theobald suggested an annual income entitlement of $1,000 for adults and $600 for children, which would gradually replace the "present mosaic of measures," such as old-age insurance, unemployment compensation, public assistance, food stamps, and housing subsidies. How this "Basic Economic Security" was to be administered he never spelled out very clearly. He was certainly widely understood as proposing a scheme that would just "fill the gap" between the income of a household and the poverty threshold.[62] But some formulations suggest that he might have thought of a universal payment to all: "The need is clear: the principle of an *economic floor* under each individual must be established. The principle would apply equally to every member of society and carry with it no connotation of personal inadequacy or implication that an undeserved income was being received from an over-generous government."[63]

Along with other activists and academics, Theobald was one of the chief authors of a report sent to President Lyndon Johnson in May 1964 that urged the government to address the "cybernation revolution" by guaranteeing an adequate income to all: "We urge, therefore, that society, through its appropriate legal and governmental institutions, undertake an unqualified commitment to provide every individual and every family with an adequate income as a matter of right. . . . The unqualified right to an income would take the place of the patchwork of welfare measures—from unemployment insurance to relief—designed to ensure that no citizen or resident of the United States actually starves."[64]

The second main source of the US debate is a couple of pages in the penultimate chapter of the widely read *Capitalism and Freedom* (1962) by Chicago economist and Nobel Memorial Prize winner Milton Friedman (1912–2006). Friedman never advocated a basic income but he did popularize a proposal that, though different from a basic income, can be partly defended on the same grounds: the negative income tax (see chapter 2).[65] If we want to alleviate poverty, he argues, "the arrangement that recommends itself on purely mechanical grounds is a negative income tax."[66] A negative income tax amounts to a uniform refundable tax credit. Even in the versions closest to a genuine basic income, it lacks one crucial feature of it: its being paid upfront to all. But the two ideas have enough in common for the discussion of one of them to be relevant to the discussion of the other.

The formulation in Friedman's book is not very detailed. In subsequent articles and interviews, however, he spelled out his proposal and the long-term perspective in which it was being made. The negative income tax, in his view, should replace the bulk of America's welfare programs.

> We have a maze of detailed governmental programs that have been justified on welfare grounds—though typically their product is "illfare": public housing, urban renewal, old-age and unemployment insurance, job training, the host of assorted programs under the mislabeled "war on poverty," farm price supports, and so on at incredible length. . . . The Negative Income Tax would be vastly superior to this collection of welfare measures. It would concentrate public funds on supplementing the incomes of the poor—not distribute funds broadside in the hope that some will trickle down to the poor.[67]

Friedman, however, did not favor just any negative income tax. He wanted one that was "low enough so that the public will be willing to pay the bill" and also "low enough to give people a substantial and consistent incentive to earn their way out of the program." Depending on the level of the income guarantee and the corresponding tax rate, the scheme could vary, in his judgment, from the eminently desirable to the irresponsible. "That is why it is possible for persons with so wide a range of political views to support one form or another of a negative income tax."[68]

Moreover, even a low negative income tax remained for him a second best relative to private charity: "If we lived in a hypothetical world in which there were no governmental welfare programs at all and in which all assistance to the destitute was by private charity, the case for introducing a negative income tax would be far weaker than the case for substituting it for present programs. . . . For such a world, I do not know whether I would favor a negative income tax—that would depend on how effectively private charity was in fact providing for the destitute."[69]

In the real world, however, perverse existing arrangements have created public obligations towards welfare recipients that need to be honored:

> I believe that the best, though admittedly imperfect, solution for such residual hardship [once everyone is granted unrestricted access to the labor market] would be voluntary action on the part of the rest of us to assist our less fortunate brethren. But our problem is far

more serious. Restriction of access in the first sense [licenses, minimum wage, and so forth], plus ill-conceived welfare measures, have made millions of people dependent on government for their most elementary needs. . . . I support a negative income tax not because I believe anyone has a "right" to be fed, clothed, and housed at someone else's expense but because I want to join my fellow taxpayers in relieving distress and feel a special compulsion to do so because governmental policies have been responsible for putting so many of our fellow citizens in the demeaning position in which they now find themselves.[70]

Or again: "I see the negative income tax as the only device yet suggested by anybody that would bring us out of the current welfare mess and still meet our responsibilities to the people whom the program has got in trouble."[71]

Thus, what justifies a guaranteed income, in Friedman's view, is only a damage-control argument. This is not the case, it is worth noting at this point, for the other founding father of "neoliberalism," Friedrich Hayek (1899–1992), Friedman's colleague at the University of Chicago and fellow Nobel Memorial Prize winner. From *The Road to Serfdom* (1944) to *Law, Legislation and Liberty* (1979), Hayek unambiguously supported a minimum-income scheme as a permanent feature of a free society. He does reject "the security of the particular income a person is thought to deserve" because "it can be provided only for some and only by controlling or abolishing the market." Instead, "the security of a minimum income," which can be "provided for all outside of and supplementary to the market system," is "an indispensable condition of real liberty": "There is no reason why in a society which has reached the general level of wealth which ours has attained [the security of a minimum income] should not be guaranteed to all without endangering general freedom. There are difficult questions about the precise standard which should thus be assured. . . . but there can be no doubt that some minimum of food, shelter and clothing, sufficient to preserve health and the capacity to work, can be assured to everybody."[72] And even more firmly: "The assurance of a certain minimum income for everyone, or a sort of floor below which nobody need fall even when he is unable to provide for himself, appears not only to be a wholly legitimate protection against a risk common to all, but a necessary part of the Great Society in which the individual no longer has specific claims on the members of the particular small group into which he was born."[73] According to Hayek, no government

is morally entitled to coercively determine relative incomes, but only on condition that one cushions the risk "by providing outside the market a uniform
minimum income for all those who for some reason are unable to earn at
least that much in the market."[74] Unlike Friedman, however, Hayek never
specified the institutional setup most appropriate to secure this "uniform
minimum income."[75]

Basic Income in Liberal America: Tobin and Galbraith

The third and by far the strongest source of the US debate on basic income is
less ambivalent and lies closer to the other end of America's political spectrum. Starting in 1965, the Yale economist and Nobel Memorial Prize winner
James Tobin (1918–2002) published a series of articles in which he defended
what he initially called a "credit income tax."[76] This scheme was not meant
to replace the whole system of public assistance and insurance schemes—let
alone to help extinguish the welfare state altogether—but rather to recon-
figure its lower component so as to make it a more efficient and work-friendly
instrument for improving "the economic status of the Negro" or for "raising
the incomes of the poor," to quote the titles of two of Tobin's articles.[77] With
his colleagues Joseph Pechman and Peter Miezkowski, Tobin published in
1967 what can be regarded as the first technical paper on negative-income-tax
schemes, in a broad sense that covers the upfront-basic-income variant. In the
scheme they proposed and analyzed, each household was to be granted a basic
credit at a level varying with family composition, which each family could
supplement with earnings and other income taxed at a uniform rate. In their
view, this "credit income tax" was preferably to be administered through "automatic payments of full basic allowances to all families, except those who
waive payment in order to avoid withholding of the offsetting tax on other
earnings." It could therefore be regarded as a household-level "demogrant":
universal and obligation-free, though not strictly individual.[78]

In the same period, another influential liberal economist went through a
remarkable change of mind. In the first edition of his best seller *The Affluent
Society* (1958), the Harvard economist John Kenneth Galbraith (1908–2006)
expressed great skepticism as to the possibility of a guaranteed minimum income: "An affluent society, that is also both compassionate and rational,
would no doubt, secure to all who needed it the minimum income essential
for decency and comfort. . . . It can use the forthright remedy of providing for
those in want. Nothing requires it to be compassionate. But it has no high

philosophical justification for callousness. Nonetheless any such forthright remedy for poverty is beyond reasonable hope."[79] The best hope he saw for the reduction of poverty "lies in less direct but, conceivably, almost equally effective means," such as education and slum clearance.

In an article published in 1966, however, he expressed a very different view on what could be reasonably hoped, repudiated the "strongly traditional" approach to poverty he had held until then ("we should help them to help themselves"), and argued:

> We need to consider the one prompt and effective solution for poverty, which is to provide everyone with a minimum income. The arguments against this proposal are numerous, but most of them are excuses for not thinking about a solution, even one that is so exceedingly plausible. It would, it is said, destroy incentives. Yet we now have a welfare system that could not be better designed to destroy incentives if we wanted it that way. We give the needy income, and we take away that income if the recipient gets even the poorest job. Thus we tax the marginal income of the welfare recipient at rates of 100 percent or more. A minimum income, it is said, would keep people out of the labor market. But we do not want all the people with inadequate income to work. . . . And there is no antidote for poverty that is quite so certain in its effects as the provision of income.[80]

The second edition of *The Affluent Society* (1969) reflects this radical change of mind. The passage quoted above remained unchanged up to the sentence "Nonetheless any such forthright remedy for poverty is beyond reasonable hope," but at that point made room for the following paragraph:

> Within the last ten years, the provision of a regular source of income to the poor, as a matter of broad social policy, has come to seem increasingly practical. The notion that income is a remedy for indigency has a certain forthright appeal. As elsewhere argued, it would also ease the problems of economic management by reducing the reliance on production as a source of income. The provision of such a basic source of income must henceforth be the first and the strategic step in the attack on poverty.[81]

The "elsewhere argued" refers to a chapter titled "The Divorce of Production from Security," completely rewritten for the second edition so as to support the following position:

> For those who are unemployable, employable only with difficulty or who should not be working, the immediate solution is a source of income unrelated to production. In recent years, this has come extensively into discussion under various proposals for guaranteed income or a negative income tax. The principle common to these proposals is provision of a basic income as a matter of general right and related in amount to family size but not otherwise to need. If the individual cannot find (or does not seek) employment, he has this income on which to survive.[82]

Galbraith stuck to this position till the end of his life. In his June 1999 lecture at the London School of Economics on "the unfinished business of the century," he put it as follows: "Everybody should be guaranteed a decent basic income. A rich country such as the US can well afford to keep everybody out of poverty. Some, it will be said, will seize upon the income and won't work. So it is now with more limited welfare, as it is called. Let us accept some resort to leisure by the poor as well as by the rich."[83]

In 1968, consistently with his revised conviction, Galbraith supported, along with James Tobin, Paul Samuelson, and Robert J. Lampman, a petition signed by over one thousand economists calling for the US Congress to adopt "a system of income guarantees and supplements."[84] In the meantime, academics had been joined by other components of American civil society. Thus, at its inaugural convention in August 1967, the *National Welfare Rights Organization* (NWRO) adopted as its first goal: "Adequate income: a system that guarantees enough money for all Americans to live dignified lives above the level of poverty."[85] And in his last book, *Where Do We Go From Here?*, published the same year, Martin Luther King, Jr. (1929–1968) wrote: "I am now convinced that the simplest approach will prove to be the most effective—the solution to poverty is to abolish it directly by a now widely discussed measure: the guaranteed income. . . . The dignity of the individual will flourish when the decisions concerning his life are in his own hands, when he has the assurance that his income is stable and certain, and when he knows that he has the means to seek self-improvement."[86]

Short-Lived Climax: McGovern's Demogrant

All this helped create a climate in which public authorities felt they had to move ahead. In January 1968, President Lyndon B. Johnson had already set up a Commission on Income Maintenance Programs which included, along with several businessmen, economists Robert Solow and Otto Eckstein. Johnson insisted: "We must examine any and every plan, however unconventional."[87] Published in November 1969, the final report recommended, as an alternative to the existing welfare system, a "basic income support program" that would take the form of a "direct federal cash transfer program offering payments to all, in proportion to their need." This amounted to a household-based negative income tax without any work requirement: "We do not think it desirable," the authors wrote, "to put the power of determining whether an individual should work in the hands of a Government agency when it can be left to individual choices and market incentives." Under this plan, adults with no other income were to be paid $750 per year (about 15 percent of GDP per capita at the time), while the maximum amount per child would be $450.[88]

Before this report was published, however, Republican Richard Nixon had taken office as president in January 1969 after winning the election against Democrat Hubert Humphrey. He immediately launched the preparation of the Family Assistance Plan, an ambitious public assistance program that would provide for the abolition of the aid program targeting poor families (AFDC), and incorporate a guaranteed income with financial supplements for workers. The plan came close to a household-based negative income tax, but with one major difference: the legislation made provision for a reduction of benefits "if recipients refused to accept suitable employment or register for job training."[89] Indeed, the speech in which President Nixon presented the plan to the nation on August 8, 1969 is the one in which the term "workfare" was coined: "In the final analysis, we cannot talk our way out of poverty; we cannot legislate our way out of poverty; but this Nation can work its way out of poverty. What America needs now is not more welfare, but more 'workfare.'"[90]

The plan was adopted in April 1970 by a large majority in the US House of Representatives, but rejected by the Finance Committee of the US Senate in November 1970. A revised version of the plan, which brought in new distinctions between employable and non-employable recipients, was definitively rejected in October 1972. Opposition to the Family Assistance Plan had been sharp across the political spectrum. Some, like the National Welfare Rights Organization, found it too timid—benefits levels were too low, work requirements too strong—while others, like the US Chamber of Commerce, found it too bold. They feared a guaranteed income scheme would kill off incentives to take low-paid jobs.[91]

Starting in January 1972, however, as the controversy about the Family Assistance Plan reached its height, a considerably more ambitious guaranteed income plan managed to attract much attention. One of the candidates for the Democratic presidential nomination, Senator George McGovern, with Tobin and Galbraith on his campaign team, decided to incorporate a basic-income proposal into his platform. Labeled "minimum income grant," "national income grant," or sometimes "demogrant," it consisted of paying every American a yearly installment of $1,000. "I propose that every man, woman, and child receive from the federal government an annual payment. This payment would not vary in accordance with the wealth of the recipient. For those on public assistance, this income grant would replace the welfare system."[92]

In his explanation of the proposal, McGovern stressed that various methods of implementation could be thought of, that they would "require full examination by the best economic talent available," and that therefore his plan was "not designed for immediate legislative action." However, he pledged that, if elected, he "would prepare a detailed plan and submit it to the Congress." The proposal he mentioned in greatest detail is one by James Tobin, which "calls for the same payment to be made to all Americans": "the payments are made on an individual basis. Thus, there would be no incentive for a family to break up in order to receive higher total benefits." It is Tobin's proposal that suggested to McGovern the figure of $1,000 per capita (about 16 percent of GDP per capita in 1972, while Tobin's proposal corresponded to about 18 percent in 1966): "Using a 1966 base, Professor Tobin suggests a payment of $750 per person. At the present time, a payment of almost $1,000 per person would be required. This would amount to $4,000 for a family of four—just about the official poverty level boundary."

The issue was salient in the Democratic primaries, particularly in California, where Hubert Humphrey, McGovern's main rival, ridiculed the idea of a large handout being given to everyone, rich and poor. After McGovern won the nomination in July 1972, officials from the Nixon administration attacked his proposal, including through aggressive commercials.[93] In an article published that month, Galbraith came to McGovern's rescue by emphasizing the positive impact of a basic income on work incentives.[94] In late August 1972, however, McGovern withdrew his controversial plan and replaced it by a scheme that restricted the income guarantee to the poor unable to work. In his autobiography, McGovern recalled the attacks against his $1,000 plan:

> Although the proposal was not that different from Nixon's own Family Assistance Plan, his commercial pictured it as a scheme to force a working minority of Americans to support a welfare majority too lazy to work. The commercial was absurd on its face, but the anxiety to which it would appeal had to be allayed. . . . As the controversy over the $1,000 plan mounted, I asked some of the leading economists as well as tax and welfare experts in the country to re-examine the whole area and develop an integrated program of tax and welfare reform. . . . [We] determined that instead of implementing the $1,000 plan, direct grants would be paid, at least initially, only to those below the poverty level.[95]

This revision of his basic income plan, McGovern acknowledged, "disappointed some of [his] supporters."[96] The Presidential election took place in November 1972, and Nixon won a landslide victory, just a few weeks after the final demise of his own Family Assistance Plan. These events marked the end of the short but spectacular appearance of basic-income-type ideas in the US debate.

Under subsequent administrations, some modest reforms were made to improve work incentives for welfare recipients—in particular, the creation of the earned income tax credit (see chapter 2).[97] However, the discussion continued in a more academic vein, on the basis of four large-scale experiments that took place in the United States between 1968 and 1980. Initiated by the federal administration in connection with the preparation of Nixon's Family Assistance Plan, these unprecedented experiments were a major landmark in social scientific research. Never had there been a scientifically motivated social experiment on such a scale. Households were randomly assigned to groups enjoying the benefit of a negative-income-tax scheme for a number of years and to control groups that continued living under existing arrangements. The main goal was to establish the effects of the guaranteed-income scheme on various indicators such as weight at birth, school performance, divorce rate, and above all, labor supply. We shall return later (in chapter 6) to the question of what can be learned from these experiments for the introduction of a basic income under present conditions. Let us just note here that among the most discussed effects were an uncontroversial yet relatively modest reduction in the labor supply of secondary earners and an alleged increase in the divorce rate in one of the experiments.[98] Such results contributed to killing for many years the political attraction of basic-income-type proposals in the United States, even among some of their keenest supporters, such as Senator Daniel Patrick Moynihan, one of the inspirers of Nixon's Family Assistance Plan. At a hearing about the results of the experiments organized at the US Senate in 1978, Moynihan exclaimed: "We were wrong about guaranteed income! Seemingly it is calamitous. It increases family dissolution by 70 percent, decreases work, and so forth. Such is now the state of science, and it seems to me we are honor-bound to abide by it at the moment."[99]

Unique Achievement: Alaska's Dividend

Under the influence of the US debate, several official reports discussing a "guaranteed annual income" were published in Canada in the early 1970s.[100] These reports inspired the so-called Mincome negative income tax experiment, conducted in 1975–78 in the city of Winnipeg and in the small town of Dauphin (Manitoba) at the request of Canada's federal government. Data collection was interrupted after two years, however, and the results were never officially published. It was only many years later that they were analyzed (see chapter 6). The very fact that the Canadian government lost interest long before the experiment was completed confirmed that the North America of the 1970s was not ripe for a major new step towards something that would start resembling an unconditional basic income.[101] And yet it was North America that hosted, just a few years later, the most decisive step towards a basic income in the strictest sense of the term. This happened with barely any connection to the big US debate of the late 1960s and early 1970s. Here is the story.[102]

In the mid-1970s, Jay Hammond (1922–2005), the Republican governor of the state of Alaska from 1974 to 1982, secured ownership of the Prudhoe Bay oil field, the largest in North America, for the citizens of Alaska (rather than for all US citizens). However, he was concerned that the huge wealth generated by oil extraction would benefit only the current generation of Alaskans. He therefore proposed setting up a fund to ensure that this wealth would be preserved for future generations, thanks to the investment of part of the oil revenues. In 1976, the *Alaska Permanent Fund* was created by an amendment to the State Constitution. In order to get the current Alaskan population interested in its continuity and growth, Governor Hammond conceived of a dividend paid annually to all residents, at a level that was not equal for all but proportional to the number of years of residence in the state. "The Dividend concept," Hammond explains in his memoirs, was "based on Alaska's Constitution, which holds that Alaska's natural resources are owned, not by the State, but by the Alaskan people themselves."[103]

The initial formulation of the dividend scheme was challenged successfully before the US Supreme Court on the grounds that, owing to the differentiation according to length of residence, it violated the equal protection clause: American citizens immigrating from other states were being discriminated against. Hammond needed to modify the scheme in order to accommodate this objection. For this purpose, he turned it into a genuinely universal basic income paid to all legal residents at the same level, including newcomers and foreign nationals. Though initially disappointed by the Supreme Court decision, Hammond later observed that the modification had "strengthened the constituency" that protects the Permanent Fund against "invasion by politicians who would love to get hands on these dollars."[104] The program was first implemented in 1982. Since then, every official resident of Alaska for at least one year is entitled to an equal annual dividend. Around 637,000 applicants qualified in 2015. This dividend corresponds to some proportion of the average financial return, over the previous five years, of the Alaska Permanent Fund. The fund was initially invested exclusively in the Alaskan economy, but later took the form of a worldwide portfolio, thereby enabling the distribution of the dividend to cushion fluctuations in the local economic situation instead of amplifying them. The dividend stood at around $400 per person per annum in the early years, and reached a first peak of $2,069 in 2008. Due to the financial crisis, it dropped below $900 in 2012, but picked up again to reach $2,072 in 2015 (close to 3 percent of Alaska's GDP per capita).

Although Alaska's oil dividend is by no means sufficient to cover an individual's basic needs—at its maximum, it reached about 20 percent of the official US poverty line for a single person and it never exceeded 4 percent of Alaska's GDP per capita—it is clearly a genuine basic income: it is an obligation-free cash payment made to all on an individual basis. Is it surprising that it should have been introduced by a Republican administration? Not according to its conceiver: "Alaska's dividend program is, of course, anything but socialistic. Socialism is government taking *from* a wealthy few to provide what government thinks is best for all. Permanent Fund Dividends do just the opposite. They take from money which, by constitutional mandate, belongs to *all* and allows each individual to determine how to spend some of his or her share. What could be more capitalistic?"[105]

Is it surprising that the Alaska dividend scheme has not been emulated elsewhere? Perhaps. There are now over fifty countries with sovereign wealth funds similar to the Alaska Permanent Fund. Yet, despite various proposals, Alaska's dividend scheme remains unique so far.

Transnational Network: From Europe to the Earth

What had been happening in Europe in the meanwhile? Not very much. With some delay, the exceptionally lively American debate of the late 1960s and early 1970s did produce a modest echo in some European countries. But to the extent that it did, what percolated across the Atlantic was Friedman's negative income tax, not McGovern's demogrant or Alaska's dividend. This gave the whole set of ideas a neoliberal flavor, which did not facilitate its reception.

In France, for example, the negative income tax was the object of a report commissioned in 1973 by the Planning Bureau.[106] It also inspired a book-length sympathetic analysis by Stanford PhD and then-adviser to President Valéry Giscard d'Estaing, Lionel Stoleru, who would later be put in charge of introducing France's means-tested minimum scheme (in 1988) as a member of Michel Rocard's socialist government.[107] However, it was soon associated with a narrowly market-oriented approach to the fight against poverty. Thus, economist Xavier Greffe, while recognizing that the proposal "rests on justified criticisms of current social policy" and "would increase the effectiveness of social policy," nonetheless found it badly defective: "Located at the heart of liberal discourse, the negative income tax implicitly admits that the market constitutes the privileged mechanism of social integration and that it therefore suffices to help individuals artificially when they access it in order to overcome inequality and the lack of integration."[108]

Similarly, in one of his legendary lectures at the *Collège de France*, Michel Foucault (1926–1984) first presented the negative income tax in a way that sounded sympathetic: "After all, it does not and should not concern us to know why someone falls below the level of the social game; whether he is a drug addict or voluntarily unemployed is not important. . . . The only thing that matters is that the individual has fallen below a given level and, at that point, without looking further, and so without having to make all those bureaucratic, police, or inquisitorial investigations, the problem becomes one of granting him a subsidy. . . ."[109]

Ultimately, however, the negative income tax is for Foucault essentially a tool in the service of "neoliberal" policies. Now that the peasant population no longer provides an "endless fund of manpower," that function is to be served by the population assisted by the negative income tax scheme—admittedly "in a very liberal and much less bureaucratic and disciplinary way than it is by a system focused on full employment": "Ultimately, it is up to people to work if they want or not work if they don't. Above all there is the possibility of not forcing them to work if there is no interest in doing so. They are merely guaranteed the possibility of minimal existence at a given level, and in this way the neoliberal policy can be got to work."[110] For Foucault as for many of those in Europe who cared about the fate of the poor and the unemployed, this association with the functional needs of capitalism and neoliberal thought sufficed to discredit the idea, or at least to discourage active interest in it.

What gradually prompted an unprecedented interest in basic income throughout Europe, however, had very little, if anything, to do with the North American negative-income-tax discussion. Largely unaware of its very existence and indeed unaware of each other, a number of quite different voices started pleading for a universal and unconditional basic income as a better response to the social challenges of the day than full employment through growth.

Thus, in 1973, sociologist Bill Jordan, later to become one of Britain's most vocal basic-income advocates, published a little book in which he described how this idea came up through the struggles of an association of unemployed people in a small English town.[111] Two years later, Jan Pieter Kuiper (1922–1986), a professor of social medicine in Amsterdam, started publishing a series of articles in which he recommended uncoupling employment and income as a way of countering the dehumanizing nature of paid employment: only a "guaranteed income," as he called it, would enable people to develop independently and autonomously.[112] In 1978, in Denmark, a physicist, a philosopher, and a politician joined forces and published, under the title *Revolt from the Center*, a national bestseller that advocated a "citizen's wage."[113] Soon after, the anti-conformist Swedish aristocrat and Capri resident Gunnar Adler-Karlsson published a couple of articles (in 1979 and 1981) in which he attacked the goal of full employment and advocated instead a guaranteed income.

In one country, the Netherlands, these voices were amplified enough to become politically relevant (see chapter 7). In 1977, the *Politieke Partij Radicalen*, a small party born out of a left-wing secession from a Christian democratic party, became the first political party with parliamentary representation anywhere in the world to officially include a basic income *(basisinkomen)* in its electoral platform. The movement in favor of the idea grew quite rapidly, mainly thanks to the involvement of the food-sector trade union *Voedingsbond*, a component of the Netherlands' main Trade Union Confederation FNV. In June 1985, the Dutch Labor Party (PvdA), then in opposition, set up a working group and published the first of four issues of a magazine exclusively devoted to basic income. A few days later, a climax was reached when the prestigious *Scientific Council for Government Policy* (WRR) published its widely discussed report *Safeguarding Social Security*, in which it recommended unambiguously something it had been showing interest in for some years: the introduction of what it proposed calling a "partial basic income"— that is, an individual, universal, and obligation-free basic income, but at a level lower than the poverty line for single-person households (see chapter 6). The WRR report contained other elements, such as the partial privatization of social insurance and moves to render the labor market more flexible, and met with strong opposition—in particular from the Labor Party, which saw it as a threat to the Dutch model of social solidarity.[114]

In his extensive official response to the report, the Dutch prime minister, Christian Democrat Ruud Lubbers, wrote that the government, with the support of social organizations, rejected the WRR proposal on the grounds that "the connection between work and income is excessively weakened."[115] A young member of his party, later to become prime minister in turn, Jan Peter Balkenende, spelled this out more fully: "A guaranteed minimum income for everyone, independently of the duty to work is something we reject: there is not the slightest reason to further hollow the valuable principle that people should as far as possible provide for their own subsistence and that of their dependents."[116] Nonetheless, the government did not want to rule out the possibility that the WRR proposals may become relevant in the middle and long term: "Depending on future developments, for example in matters of working time reduction, technological development, economic growth and workers' participation, but also depending on socio-political conceptions in this area, new policy responses will be sought in coming years."[117]

Nowhere else in Europe was the debate, at the time, this close to the political agenda. But awareness of the idea and the arguments for it was emerging.

Witness the creation, in 1984, of a first national network on basic income, Britain's Basic Income Research Group.[118] Witness also, two years later, the real start of a discussion crossing national borders with the creation of an international network. In September 1986, the *Collectif Charles Fourier*, a small group of academics and trade unionists, organized in the university town of Louvain-la-Neuve in Belgium the first gathering of basic-income supporters from across Europe.[119] Pleasantly surprised to discover how many people were interested in an idea they thought they were almost alone in defending, the participants decided to set up the Basic Income European Network (BIEN) with the aim "to serve as a link between individuals and groups committed to, or interested in, basic income—that is, an income unconditionally granted to all on an individual basis, without means test or work requirement, and to foster informed discussion on this topic throughout Europe." Since then, BIEN has run a regular newsletter and organized a congress every second year. Owing to the growing number of participants from outside Europe—Latin America, North America, South Africa, Asia, Australia—BIEN decided at its 2004 congress in Barcelona to become a worldwide network and to reinterpret its unchanged acronym as Basic Income Earth Network.[120]

Since the mid-1980s, the history of basic income is no longer a set of isolated national developments, completely independent and mostly ignorant of each other. Thanks to the existence of an international network, to the power of the internet, and to the spreading of the idea, new initiatives around basic income are now happening every day and are being echoed worldwide. We shall return to many of them when discussing (in chapters 6 and 7) the economic and political feasibility of a basic income. But before doing so, we need to address the question of its ethical justifiability.

5

Ethically Justifiable?
Free Riding Versus Fair Shares

OF ALL OBJECTIONS TO A BASIC INCOME, one sticks out above all others—
and is more emotional, more principled, and more decisive in the eyes of
many. It relates to its being unconditional in the sense of being obligation-
free, of not requiring its recipients to work or be willing to work. Someone
can concede that a basic income would provide an effective way of reducing
poverty and unemployment while still being fiercely opposed to it on ethical
grounds. This objection comes in two main versions. In one version, the
"perfectionist" one, the underlying principle is that work is part of the good
life and hence that an income granted without some work requirement
amounts to rewarding a vice: idleness. In the other version, the "liberal" one,
the underlying principle is not about virtue but about fairness. As Jon Elster
puts it, an unconditional basic income "goes against a widely accepted notion
of justice: it is unfair for able-bodied people to live off the labor of others."[1]
How can this objection be refuted?

Basic Income and Free Riding

If one adopts the view, as we do, that the shaping of our social institutions
should not be guided by a specific conception of the good life but by a coherent and plausible conception of justice, this second version of the objection is far more serious than the former. We do not mind people adopting a
work ethic in their personal lives. Indeed, we may subscribe to some version
of it ourselves. Moreover, as mentioned in chapter 1, we have no difficulty
admitting that it is through the actions they perform, in particular through
the work they do for others, that human beings earn recognition and esteem.

Besides, a widespread work ethic does not harm the sustainability of a generous basic income—quite the contrary—and some argue that an unconditional basic income would foster an ethos of contribution as a counter-gift.[2] However, none of this justifies making basic material security conditional upon work or willingness to work. The imposition of such a condition would only be legitimate if it could be derived, as implied by the second version of the ethical objection, from a compelling conception of what fairness requires. It is therefore on this second version that we shall focus, even though much of what we say in response to it also applies to the first version.

It is no doubt at least in part because of the appeal of this objection that, from Gracchus Babeuf onwards, many authors advocating a universal income paid to all citizens have also advocated a universal obligation to work. Thus, Babeuf's radical-egalitarian manifesto of 1796, while asserting that "nature gave every man an equal enjoyment of all goods" also asserts that "nature gave man the obligation to work" and that "there is oppression when one exhausts himself and lacks everything while another swims in abundance without doing anything."[3] Similarly, in Edward Bellamy's 1888 socialist utopia *Looking Backward*, the equal income paid to all was coupled with a substantial social service. A wide range of other authors, including Josef Popper-Lynkeus, Jacques Duboin, and Paul Goodman, advocated a more or less rigid version of the same idea.[4] And so did André Gorz before his conversion to an unconditional basic income. The universal right to an equal income was then proposed as the counterpart of a universal duty to perform a social service of twenty to thirty thousand hours to be freely spread, with some quotas, over one's lifetime.[5] The underlying normative intuition, plausibly shared by all these authors, was phrased as follows: "society is a specific and coherent reality to which each is linked by a reciprocal duty: each individual owes society the amount of work society needs to function and to provide all with the necessary, and society owes each what he or she will need to live, throughout his life."[6]

How can the proposal of an unconditional basic income be vindicated against this sort of objection? Let us first accept, for the sake of the arguments of the present section, that enjoying a basic income without doing any work does constitute unfair free riding—that is, that it violates some norm of reciprocity, some conception of justice that stipulates that income should be distributed according to people's productive contributions.[7] There are three reasons why this accusation should be relativized and the accusers should temper their indignation. There are also three further reasons why the introduction of an unconditional basic income, far from increasing injustice as characterized, could reduce it.

The first reason for relativizing the accusation resides in the double standards that are generally at work here. If one is serious about denying an income to those able but unwilling to work, this denial should apply to the rich as well as to the poor. This is not a problem for the likes of Babeuf or Bellamy, since in their schemes all citizens are subjected to the obligation to work.[8] But it is a problem for those who, in today's socioeconomic context, want to refuse to the poor the leisure the rich can get away with. Bertrand Russell stigmatized this asymmetry: "The idea that the poor should have leisure has always been shocking to the rich."[9] And so did John Kenneth Galbraith: "Leisure is very good for the rich, quite good for Harvard professors—and very bad for the poor. The wealthier you are, the more you are thought to be entitled to leisure. For anyone on welfare, leisure is a bad thing."[10] A modest unconditional income that would give to the poor, as well, the option of some chosen leisure would address the unfairness of such double standards.[11]

A second way of relativizing the accusation of free riding directed at idleness in the productive domain rests on the following analogy with idleness in the reproductive domain.[12] It is presumably no accident that a morality that strongly stigmatizes premarital, extramarital, and homosexual sex and thereby tries to restrict sexual gratification to those willing to contribute to society's reproduction has been gradually abandoned as the progress of hygiene and medicine has led to overabundant procreators. Similarly, should a morality that stigmatizes an access to an income without work and thereby tries to restrict material gratification to those willing to contribute to society's production not be abandoned when technological progress is leading to overabundant workers?[13] After all, as a result of a long history of technical progress, division of labor, and capital accumulation—of which the trends mentioned in chapter 1 are only the most recent episode—we have moved from a situation in which, say, 90 percent of the population were required to satisfy everyone's basic needs in food, housing, and clothing, to one in which, say, 10 percent suffice. As pointed out earlier (in chapter 2), those who want to reduce the working week today do not want to do so in order to reduce a burden, but rather in order to share a privilege.[14] In this context, should one still be as outraged as in the past at able-bodied people living off the labor of others?[15]

The third way of relativizing the accusation consists of pointing out that, once the basic-income regime is in place, only a tiny minority will take advantage of it in order to do nothing or very little. This can be expected because the universal nature of a basic income, which makes it combinable with recipients' other income, gets rid of the inactivity trap created by means-tested schemes. Moreover, experiments with basic-income-type schemes suggest that even when freedom from obligation causes a fall in the labor supply, this does not translate into an expansion of leisure as idleness, but rather into an upsurge of productive activities in a broader sense such as education, childcare, and engagement in the community. If one can expect only an insignificant minority of really lazy scroungers, there is no big clash between basic income and justice as reciprocity to get worked up about.

Indeed, there are three reasons why the introduction of an unconditional basic income might even yield progress in terms of justice so conceived. First, any sensible interpretation of the foundation of the reciprocity-based objection to basic income must imply that those unable to work, owing to physical or mental disabilities, should get incomes all the same. Distinguishing such a disability from an unwillingness to work can often be tricky. When information is not readily available or is unreliable, trying to enforce this criterion of justice as strictly as possible can do more harm than good on its own terms, and might moreover prove very expensive. In order to avoid penalizing unfairly people who are sick, and wrongly assumed to be lazy, a modest unconditional income can be justified as the least bad measure.

There is a second, far more general reason why the introduction of an unconditional basic income could help bring about greater justice understood as reciprocity. For those truly concerned about free riding, the main worry about today's situation should not be that some people get away with doing no work, but rather—and this is a central point in the feminist discussion of basic income we will present in chapter 7—that countless people who do a lot of essential work end up with no income of their own. A huge amount of essential, productive work currently goes unpaid, as it is performed at home. As persuasively argued by Nancy Fraser (in 1997) and Carole Pateman (in 2004), if there is massive free riding anywhere, it is within the traditional family structure in the form of men free riding on the unpaid work done by their partners. Some have proposed a direct payment for this work.[16] But such a "household wage" raises serious objections. As it would be withdrawn, unlike a basic income, when "homemakers" opt for paid employment, it would penalize women's participation in the labor market and thereby deepen the "household trap" in which they might get caught (a topic we will take up in chapter 6). Moreover, by constructing household work as a paid job, it would reinforce the gender division of domestic roles and require some bureaucratic monitoring of the work henceforth paid out of the public purse. Given these serious obstacles, an obligation-free basic income may well prove the least bad way of tackling free riding.[17] The best feasible approximation of the principle that income should be distributed according to work does not exclude a basic income. It rather requires one, pitched at such a level that a further increase would worsen the injustice stemming from overpayment of the truly lazy more than it would reduce the injustice stemming from underpaying those who currently care for children, the elderly, or the disabled without any form of payment.

In order to understand the third reason why an unconditional basic income could improve and not worsen the situation in terms of justice as reciprocity, one needs to see that a fair distribution of burdens should also take the irksomeness of work into account. At present, the intrinsic attractiveness of a job and its remuneration are positively correlated. This can be viewed as a form of free riding or exploitation by the better paid: thanks to their bargaining power, they can do jobs they enjoy while benefiting from the toil of people who have no option but to accept low-paid jobs that the better paid would hate doing. A basic income, being obligation-free, would strengthen the bargaining power of the most vulnerable participants in the labor market and would therefore mean that the irksomeness of a job, its lack of intrinsic attractiveness, would be better reflected in the pay it commands. With irksomeness better compensated for, unfair free riding will not expand but shrink.

Real Freedom for All

All the responses presented above accept, for the sake of argument, that it is "unfair for able-bodied people to live off the labor of others" and, underlying this indictment of free riding, embrace some conception of justice as reciprocity. Such a conception is compelling as a conception of *cooperative* justice—that is, as a characterization of the fair allocation of benefits and burdens of cooperation between participants in some cooperative venture. But it is not compelling as a conception of *distributive* justice—that is, as a characterization of the just distribution of entitlements to resources among the members of a society. It is only against the background of such a distribution that people can enter fair cooperative arrangements for mutual benefit, with the cooperative surplus distributed according to some criterion of cooperative justice. And it is to a conception of distributive justice, not of cooperative justice, that one must appeal in order to best defend the fairness of an unconditional basic income.[18]

This is what we did, albeit informally, throughout our first two chapters. An unconditional basic income is what we need, we argued, if what we care about is freedom, not for just a few but for all. We thereby appeal to an egalitarian conception of distributive justice that treats freedom not as a constraint on what justice requires but as the very stuff that justice consists in distributing fairly. This requires that freedom be interpreted as "real freedom," not just "formal freedom"—that is, as involving not only the sheer right but also the genuine capacity to do whatever one might wish to do. Being egalitarian about this real freedom does not imply that one should aim to equalize it at any cost. Inequalities can be regarded as just if they work to the benefit of everyone, even their apparent victims. If we accept this, what we must go for is the greatest real freedom for those with least of it—that is, the maximization of the minimum level of real freedom or, more succinctly, "maximin real freedom" and, less esoterically, "real freedom for all."[19]

Adopting such a conception of distributive justice generates a strong presumption in favor of an income paid to all in cash, on an individual basis, without means test or work test, indeed in favor of such an income paid at the highest sustainable level. For mildly paternalistic reasons touched upon earlier (in chapter 2), it makes sense to distribute this income at short and regular intervals throughout people's lives, possibly at a lower level for children and a higher level for the elderly. And for analogous reasons, it makes sense not to give the whole of this highest sustainable income in cash, but to allocate part of it in particular to free or heavily subsidized education and health care and to the provision of a healthy and enjoyable environment, at the cost of a lower cash basic income. How should the total amount be shared between these various components? There is no neat and general answer to this question, but a simple thought experiment should provide rough guidelines: Suppose we had nothing but the income that can be paid unconditionally to all, and knew nothing about our own life expectancy, health state, and other risks. How would we want it to be spread over our lifetimes, and how much would we want earmarked for specific expenditures?[20]

So far so good. But could it not be objected that we adopt a skewed notion of freedom? An unconditional basic income at the highest sustainable level would suit very well those who care a lot about access to plenty of leisure and enjoyable jobs—call them Lazies—but not quite as well those who care above all about their incomes and associated advantages in terms of consumption, power, and prestige—call them Crazies. For as the basic income needs to be funded, there is bound to be a trade-off between the level at which it is pitched and average post-tax earnings. Maximizing the former does not entail minimizing the latter, but certainly reducing them to less than they could be. This trade-off being inescapable, is our conception of distributive justice not treacherously biased toward favoring the real freedom that matters to the Lazies at the expense of the real freedom that matters to the Crazies?

Answering this challenge requires us to formulate more carefully our conception of distributive justice as real freedom for all, because the Lazies' cherished real freedom to spend their time as they wish and the Crazies' cherished real freedom to purchase whatever they wish pull in different directions. Strictly speaking, what our conception of distributive justice requires is not maximin real freedom—although we shall keep using this expression for convenience—but rather the maximinning of the gifts that form the substratum of this freedom—that is, the maximization of what is received by those who receive least by way of material basis for the exercise of their real freedom. In all sorts of ways, but for most of us primarily as part of our earnings, we benefit very unequally from what was freely given us by nature, technological progress, capital accumulation, social organization, civility rules, and so on. What a basic income does is ensure that everyone receives a fair share of what none of us today did anything for, of the huge present very unequally incorporated in our incomes. And if given to all and pitched at the highest sustainable level, it ensures that those who receive least receive as much as is durably feasible.

The underlying intuition has been well expressed by a number of advocates of basic-income-type ideas. It can be found, for example, in Edward Bellamy's utopian novel *Looking Backward:* "How did you come to be possessors of this knowledge and this machinery, which represents nine parts to one contributed by yourself in the value of your product? You inherited it, did you not? And were not these others, these unfortunate and crippled brothers whom you cast out, joint inheritors, co-heirs with you?"[21]

It was also clearly formulated by the Oxford economist and political theorist George D. H. Cole, one of the very first academics to argue for a basic income: "Current productive power is, in effect, a joint result of current effort and of the social heritage of inventiveness and skill incorporated in the stage of advancement and education reached in the arts of production; and it has always appeared to me only right that all the citizens should share in the yield of this common heritage, and that only the balance of the product after this allocation should be distributed in the form of rewards for, and incentives to, current service in production."[22]

And the same idea underpins the justification of an unconditional basic income by Nobel Memorial Prize winner Herbert A. Simon:

> When we compare average incomes in rich nations with those in Third World countries, we find enormous differences that are surely not due simply to differences in motivations to earn. . . . These differences are not simply a matter of acres of land or tons of coal or iron ore, but, more important, differences in social capital that takes primarily the form of stored knowledge (e.g., technology, and especially organizational and governmental skills). Exactly the same claim can be made about the differences in incomes within any given society.[23]

Consequently, much of what we earn must be ascribed, not to our efforts, but to externalities which owe nothing to them. "How large are these externalities, which must be regarded as owned jointly by members of the whole society?" Simon answers his own question: "When we compare the poorest with the richest nations, it is hard to conclude that social capital can produce less than about 90 percent of income in wealthy societies like those of the US or Northwestern Europe." Hence, if one were to introduce a flat tax of 70 percent to fund an unconditional basic income and all other government expenditures, "this would generously leave with the original recipients of the income about three times what, according to my rough guess, they had earned."[24]

The appeal of the conception of distributive justice on which our principled justification of basic income rests depends on our realizing the extent to which our economy functions as a gift-distribution machine, as an arrangement that enables people to tap—very unequally—our common inheritance.[25] There are other ways of motivating the plausibility of this picture. In actual life, the opportunities we enjoy are fashioned in complex, largely unpredictable ways by the interaction of our innate capacities and dispositions with countless other circumstances such as happening to have a congenial primary school teacher or an inspiring boss, to belong to a lucky generation, to have a native language in high demand, or to get a tip for the right job at the right time. Against this background, justice requires that we should look directly at jobs and other market niches as incorporating very unequal gifts to which we are given very unequal access by a complex, messy combination of factors. All of these gifts, and not only the much smaller amount that takes the form of donations and bequests, are up for fair distribution among all.[26] And note that the correct term is fair distribution and not fair redistribution: the taxes that fund a basic income are not levies on what was created out of nothing by today's producers, but rather fees to be paid by these producers for the privilege of using for their personal benefit what we have collectively received.[27]

Before moving on to other possible philosophical justifications of an unconditional basic income, let us consider three important objections to it. First, can earnings really be assimilated, albeit partly, to gifts? It is true that one generally needs to do something in order to get a job and keep it. However, this undeniable fact does not create a fundamental difference with donations or bequests. Attending politely your aunt's boring tea parties may be one of the necessary conditions for you not to be forgotten in her will. But this investment of yours does not entitle you, ethically speaking, to the whole big chunk of wealth possessed by a person to whom you, unlike us, happen to be related. Similarly, the fact that one needs to go to the office every morning and busy oneself once there does not make one "deserve" the whole of the salary one is able to earn by virtue of a combination of circumstances most of which are no less arbitrary, ethically speaking, than the fact that one happens to have a rich aunt. The granting of a basic income to everyone should therefore not be misunderstood as aiming to equalize outcomes or achievements. Rather, it aims to make less unequal, and distribute more fairly, real freedom, possibilities, and opportunities. Granting a basic income to all helps equalize what people are given—the material substratum of their real freedom—and only as a consequence, indirectly and more roughly, what they achieve with what they are given.

Second, is there a risk of overshooting the mark? How can we be sure that only this gift component of earnings is taxed away? We can ensure that by allowing economic agents to anticipate this taxation and make their decisions accordingly. In order to fund the highest sustainable basic income, any type of taxation can be used—on bequests, donations, labor income, capital income, transactions, consumption, carbon emissions, value added, whatever—and any tax profile can be chosen—linear, progressive, regressive, or any combination—provided they are predictable by those subjected to them. Barring unavoidable mistakes and unlucky gambles, all will then end up with at least the gift incorporated in the basic income they all receive. And because of efficiency considerations under this constraint of predictability, many people will end up with incomes that exceed, and sometimes far exceed, what can pass as compensation for their productive efforts. These people include those endowed with particularly lucrative talents, but also, for example, the entrepreneurs who happen to be in a position to take advantage of unevenly spread information in an economy in permanent flux, or workers who are given more than their reservation wages because this is expected to boost their productivity.[28] Such inequalities can be justified, but only to the extent that they boost the real freedom of those with least of it or, less loosely put, only to the extent that reducing them would shrink the value of what can be sustainably given to those who receive least.

Finally, by giving a key role to a minimal gift expressed in purchasing power, is our conception not giving an unwarranted key role to the market? If what is up for distribution is understood as an inheritance broadly conceived, then a conception of justice as the fair distribution of freedom would seem naturally to lead to the demand that fair claims to this inheritance should be distributed, at least presumptively, in cash form (as discussed in chapter 1). It is, however, important to realize that this gives a crucial role to market prices in determining the fair distribution of budget sets, of the range of choices open to each. In a market that functions well enough, the price of a good is supposed to track its opportunity cost—that is, the cost to others of someone's appropriating that good. This cost is affected by the resources needed to produce the good, given the available technology, and by the demand for these resources, given the preferences of all potential consumers for goods whose production requires these resources. Needless to say, the market can only be given this role to the extent that it is free from discrimination, and to the extent that the prices that form spontaneously are corrected in order to better track opportunity costs unrecorded owing to different types of market failures (not least the fact that tomorrow's generations cannot bid for today's goods).

A defense, on grounds of justice, of an unconditional income paid in cash does not presuppose a blind faith in the perfection of the market, but it does assume sufficient trust in the idea that prices reflect how valuable goods are in a sense that is relevant to determining a fair distribution of access to them. It therefore assumes an economy largely governed by something like a duly regulated market.[29] It seems reasonable enough to suppose that this will remain the case for the foreseeable future. Note, however, that granting to all an unconditional income does not increase dependence on the market. Quite the contrary. As stressed in chapter 1, because of its freedom from obligation, a basic income contributes to weakening the cash nexus, to de-commodifying labor power, to boosting socially useful yet unpaid activities, to protecting our lives against forced mobility and destructive globalization, and to emancipating us from the despotism of the market.

John Rawls Versus the Malibu Surfers

The conception of distributive justice appealed to in the previous section is one that belongs to a family of conceptions commonly labeled liberal-egalitarian. It is liberal in the sense that it does not rest on a particular conception of the good life but instead is committed to respecting equally the various conceptions of the good life that are present in our pluralist societies.[30] It is egalitarian in the sense of taking as a baseline an equal distribution of the resources people have at their disposal in order to try to realize their conceptions of the good life. However, it allows for deviation from strict equality on the condition that it can be justified to people regarded as equal. Such deviation is legitimate if it is required to make room for people's individual responsibility; justice is about equalizing opportunities, capabilities, possibilities, and real freedom rather than outcomes. It can also be legitimate because of efficiency considerations; justice is about sustainably maximizing the prospects of those with the worst prospects, not about equalizing prospects even at everyone's expense. The most influential theory that fits this characterization is the one proposed by John Rawls, founding father of the liberal-egalitarian tradition and of contemporary political philosophy, in his 1971 *A Theory of Justice*. Does Rawls's theory also provide a justification for an unconditional basic income? Yes, no, and perhaps.

At first sight, the answer is an obvious yes. The core of Rawls's theory consists of three principles hierarchically ordered. The *liberty principle* lists a number of fundamental liberties such as freedom of expression, freedom of association, and the right to vote. The *principle of fair equality of opportunity* stipulates that people with the same talents should have equal access to all social positions. Finally, under the constraint of these first two principles, the *difference principle* requires economic and social inequalities to work for the greatest benefit of the worst-off. More precisely, Rawls assumes that with each social position one can associate an index that aggregates the social and economic advantages—income and wealth, powers and prerogatives—enjoyed by people who occupy that position.[31] The difference principle is a maximin principle that requires that the index associated with the worst social position—the position with the lowest index—be as high as possible. Moreover, jointly with the other two principles, it is meant to secure what Rawls calls the social bases of self-respect.

This sounds quite promising for the justification of an unconditional basic income, for the difference principle does not require only that everyone should be guaranteed a minimum level of consumption. In addition to income, it mentions wealth, and an unconditional basic income is tantamount to an endowment spread over people's lifetime. It further mentions powers and prerogatives, and the unconditional nature of a basic income gives power to the weakest in both employment and household contexts. Last but not least, concern for the social bases of self-respect should favor a way of securing a minimum income that both facilitates access to paid activities for everyone (by getting rid of the unemployment trap) and avoids the stigmatization and humiliation that tends to be associated with targeting the needy. The more efficient the targeting, the more the recipients are identified as being really incapable of providing for themselves and are accordingly stigmatized.[32] Moreover, both in an earlier article and in *A Theory of Justice*, Rawls picked up explicitly the (then fairly novel) concept of a "negative income tax" to illustrate how his principles of justice could shape the distributive branch of the institutions of a just society, at a time when that concept was sometimes used in a broad sense that covered the so-called demogrant—that is, an unconditional basic income.[33] Consequently, the Rawlsian case for basic income seems overwhelming. It just needs spelling out.[34]

Yet, John Rawls himself did not agree. He wrote that "those who surf all day off Malibu must find a way to support themselves and would not be entitled to public funds."[35] According to the most straightforward interpretation of Rawls's difference principle, as presented above, people without earnings, whether voluntarily or not, are among the least advantaged and hence entitled to some benefit. How high a benefit? As high as is sustainable, bearing in mind that high levels of both benefits and taxes would presumably induce some workers to leave factories and offices and spend more of their time on the beaches. In order to block off this implication, embarrassingly indulgent—Rawls felt—on Malibu surfers, Rawls proposed to include leisure in the index of social and economic advantages in terms of which his difference principle was formulated. More specifically, he proposed to ascribe to those who choose full-time leisure a virtual income equivalent to the full-time minimum wage.[36] Consequently, full-time Malibu surfers can no longer justly indulge their lifestyle at the expense of the rest of society. If they want to get a real and not just a virtual income, if they want to be fed and housed, they will have to work.

In light of this move, the relationship between basic income and social justice seems settled: a Rawlsian justification of an unconditional basic income is out of the question. But is it really? There is one crucial aspect of Rawls's difference principle which is overlooked both by those who believe that it provides a straightforward justification of an unconditional basic income and by those who believe that it could not possibly provide such a justification. What the difference principle requires is not that the worst-off individuals should be made as well-off as possible in terms of an index of outcomes, as specified by a list of social and economic advantages. What it requires us to maximize is rather *the average value* of this index achieved, over the course of their lives, by the people who occupy the worst social position. In other words, it is not the worst-off individuals' scores, but the worst social positions' average lifetime scores that need to be sustainably maximized.[37]

Is maximizing the average score of people in the worst position not just a rough way of maximizing the score of the worst-off at any given point in time? It would be, if social positions were defined, as Rawls suggests they might be, as income or wealth categories: "Thus all persons with less than half of the median income and wealth may be taken as the least advantaged segment." Such a characterization of the worst-off category "solely in terms of relative income and wealth with no reference to social positions," he writes, "will serve well enough." However, as this passage entails, Rawls thinks of "social positions" as conceptually distinct from income and wealth categories, even though the latter may provide convenient proxies for many practical purposes.[38] A person's social position is therefore best understood as the occupational category, more or less broadly defined, to which she is supposed to belong throughout her life. Examples mentioned by Rawls himself include unskilled workers, farmers, and dairy farmers.[39]

Now, among individuals sharing the same social position in this sense, actual lifetime performance in terms of income, wealth, powers, and prerogatives can vary considerably, as a result of events which combine chance and choice in unequal, generally unspecifiable, proportions. Some keep buying on credit, others work overtime. Some give birth to disabled children, others incur big losses selling houses after costly divorces. Within each position, considerable differences in lifetime levels of income and wealth unavoidably arise as a result of all sorts of unpredictable circumstances. In addition, the average index will vary considerably across social positions, typically as a function of the scarcity of the skills required to occupy them and of the social demand for the services performed within them. Unlike most of the better positions, the worst position is one to which even the "least fortunate" individuals have access.[40] No minimum level of social and economic advantages is guaranteed to these individuals, but only access to a social position with a higher average lifetime level of social and economic advantages than the one offered to the incumbents of the worst social position under any other feasible arrangement.

Paying proper attention to the role played by social positions definitely moves us away from the common yet mistaken *outcome-egalitarian* interpretation of the difference principle, in terms of individual levels of social and economic advantages, and toward an *opportunity-egalitarian* interpretation, in terms of average lifetime levels associated with social positions. What needs to be maximized under this principle is not the outcome (in terms of income, wealth, powers, and prerogatives) actually achieved by the least fortunate, but the average outcome they can hope to achieve by virtue of the social positions they are given access to. What outcome level each individual incumbent of any social position, including the worst one, will achieve over a lifetime will be highly sensitive to individual preferences and choices. Once the difference principle is interpreted in this way, the inclusion of leisure in the index of social and economic advantages has diametrically opposed implications. Under the outcome-egalitarian interpretation, to regard leisure as virtual income, as Rawls proposed, is to strip surfers of their right to a benefit they would otherwise be entitled to, if their leisure were not incorporated in their index. Under the opportunity-egalitarian interpretation, this inclusion pulls in the other direction.

If income and wealth but not leisure feature in the index, a social arrangement with an unconditional basic income will likely do worse by the standards of the difference principle than would one with a work-tested minimum-income scheme that would deny income to full-time surfers. If instead the index is cured of its one-sidedness through the sensible inclusion of leisure time, the optimal option, by the standards of the difference principle, will crucially depend on the relative weights the index places on income and leisure, on the exact characterization of social positions, and on a great many contingent empirical facts. But one thing is certain: once the leisure enjoyed over their lifetimes by the incumbents of a social position no longer counts for nothing, an arrangement that includes an unconditional income and hence makes more room for chosen leisure—career interruption, voluntary part-time work—will have a higher likelihood of doing better, by the standard of the difference principle properly interpreted, than one that is biased against leisure, such as Edmund Phelps's wage subsidy scheme for full-time, low-paid workers (outlined in chapter 2). Ironically, the very move which Rawls thought was needed to prevent his theory from condoning an unconditional basic income actually makes it more sympathetic to it. It does remain impossible to assert categorically that an unconditional basic income can be justified by Rawls's principles, but it has become equallly impossible to categorically deny it.

Indeed, basic income even provides a quite plausible component of what Rawls regards as the only version of capitalism that has the potential of being just. This is what he calls, borrowing an expression from basic-income advocate James Meade, "property-owning democracy"—that is, a regime in which private ownership of the bulk of the means of production is combined with both material and human capital being widely spread.[41] With this in mind, a basic income can be viewed not only as a return on commonly owned capital but also as a capital endowment transferred in small installments to each member of society. And, especially if it is combined with the development of lifelong learning, it can be expected to foster the widespread acquisition of human capital (as argued in chapter 1). Even so, a liberal-egalitarian justification of basic income based on Rawls's difference principle remains far more factually contingent than the one offered in the previous section. And up to the end, Rawls himself remained more attracted to guaranteed employment and wage subsidies than to an unconditional basic income.[42]

Ronald Dworkin Versus the Beachcombers

John Rawls's theory of justice is the most influential but not the only member of the liberal-egalitarian family. The more philosophically inclined among our readers may be interested to find out how another illustrious member of the family, even less indulgent than Rawls of those he calls "scroungers," ends up making room, under some plausible factual conditions, for the justification of an unconditional basic income. Ronald Dworkin's theory of distributive justice as equality of resources is an intellectual tour de force. Its aim is to offer a conception of distributive justice that is better than Rawls's at making people's share of resources both ambition-sensitive (that is, sensitive to preferences for which they can be held responsible) and endowment-insensitive (that is, independent of circumstances for which they cannot be held responsible).[43] For this purpose, he distinguishes impersonal, or external, resources (that is, our material wealth), from personal, or internal, resources (that is, our abilities).

As regards *personal resources*, Dworkin proposes an insurance scheme behind a hypothetical veil of ignorance that can be described as follows. Suppose that we each know the frequency of all talents and handicaps among the members of our society but that a veil of ignorance makes us believe that the probabilities of having any of them are the same for each of us. Suppose further that this veil does not prevent us from knowing our own preferences, including our risk aversion. We should then be able to specify how much we would insure for each possible risk, bearing in mind that the premiums to be paid if lucky will have to cover the indemnities to be received if unlucky, each weighted by the probabilities of the situations that would trigger them. If it could be performed, this exercise would yield a set of person-specific, lump-sum premiums and indemnities, each corresponding to a possible endowment in personal resources of the person concerned. In the real world, each person has such an endowment and, depending on what it happens to be and on the choices she would have made under the veil of ignorance, she will end up with a premium to be paid or an indemnity to be received.[44]

As regards *impersonal resources*, Dworkin initially seemed to propose a distinct device. But in the final formulation of his approach, he proposes to subsume all resources under his insurance scheme. Behind the veil of ignorance that hides their family situation, people are also supposed to be able to insure against being "born to parents who can give or will leave them relatively little."[45]

What emerges is a fascinating construct that involves a frightening amount of intellectual gymnastics and moreover requires information that is unavoidably unavailable (and, even if it were available to some people, could not be expected to be truthfully revealed). Dworkin is aware of these difficulties and therefore falls back on "what level of insurance of different kinds we can safely assume that most reasonable people would have bought" behind the veil of ignorance.[46] The resulting rough approximation, Dworkin conjectures, will be a tax-funded scheme covering a number of specific risks, namely "ordinary handicaps" such as blindness or deafness, but also the lack of sufficient skills to earn some minimum level of income.[47] And the minimum-income scheme to which most reasonable people would sub-scribe, he further conjectures, will guarantee an income level no lower than the community's poverty line. It can take a number of different forms, from unemployment benefit to training-and-jobs programs, more or less dissua-sive for "scroungers," and will need to "stipulate that the beneficiary attempt to mitigate his position by seeking employment."[48] In contrast to what he takes to be Rawls's view, those who opt for "idleness" cannot do so at the expense of the "hard-working middle classes." Rawls's conception of distribu-tive justice, he claims, is inappropriately soft on those who "prefer to comb beaches."[49]

However, as one turns from the demands of justice to policy recommen-dations, this tough stance on beachcombers had to be softened for two prag-matic reasons. First of all, Dworkin conceded from the beginning that, even though the insurance scheme would justify a transfer system targeted exclu-sively at the involuntarily unemployed, "perhaps a more general form of transfer, like a negative income tax, would prove on balance more efficient and fairer, in spite of the difficulties in such schemes. And whatever devices are chosen for bringing the distribution closer to [Dworkin's conception of justice as] equality of resources, some aid undoubtedly goes to those who have avoided rather than sought jobs." This is not to be cheered: "This is to be regretted because it offends one of the two principles [ambition-sensitivity] that together make up equality of resources. But we come closer to that ideal by tolerating that inequity than by denying aid to the far greater number who would work if they could."[50] Second, in later writings, Dworkin proposed adding child poverty to the risks the insurance scheme should give us the possibility of insuring against: "How much insurance would children buy, and on what terms against being born to indigent and unemployed par-ents?"[51] As it is impossible to keep children out of poverty without either depriving them of their parents or keeping their parents out of poverty as well—whether or not they "avoided rather than sought jobs"—this sensible extension of the insurance scheme breeds indulgence for further deviation from what Dworkin's justice would ideally require.

More fundamentally, if one looks closely at the implications of Dworkin's hypothetical insurance scheme, feeding the beachcombers turns out to be more than an ethically regrettable, though pragmatically defensible, devia-tion from justice. It becomes a possible implication of justice itself. For there is no reason that people should care only about achieving a minimum pur-chasing power, irrespective of how little choice they are given about how to earn it. Under Dworkin's veil of ignorance (which hides people's assets but not their desires), the "Crazies" who care exclusively about money will choose to be forced to accept any job if they happen to be poorly skilled, so that they can minimize taxation if they turn out to possess highly lucrative skills. But the "Lazies" who care instead for the quality of their lives will opt for a scheme that gives them a minimum income even if they refuse to perform any of the jobs which family obligations or poor skills happen to give them access to, while making them pay higher taxes if their situation gives them access to high-paid work they do not mind performing.

In this light, it is no longer possible to proclaim, as Dworkin does, that "to reward those who choose not to work with money taken in taxes from those who do work" is "inherently wrong because it is unfair," or "that forced transfers from the ant to the grasshopper are inherently unfair."[52] Although even a modest unconditional basic income is unlikely to be unanimously chosen under the veil of ignorance—the "Crazies" would not opt for it—it seems most plausible that the "Lazies," as characterized above, would choose something like it, not as a free ride on the Crazies' work, but as part of their own actuarially fair hypothetical insurance scheme. Within the framework of the first-best (and unworkable), strictly individualized insurance scheme, the ambition-sensitivity of the scheme does imply that the "Lazies" who sub-scribe to a scheme allowing them to opt out of paid work (in case the only jobs their abilities enable them to do are jobs they do not like) will have to bear the opportunity cost of their choice, in the form of a higher taxation (in case there are lucrative jobs that they will perform with pleasure). But this is consistent with the possibility of transfers, on grounds of justice, to people who choose to remain idle rather than accept jobs they could do but do not like. As to the second-best, more realistic version of the scheme, it is meant to track the choices of "the average person" or of "most reasonable people." Clearly, it should not mimic the Lazies' preferred scheme, but nor should it mimic the Crazies', as too eagerly taken for granted by Dworkin. Departure from the Crazies' preferred scheme is not more or less regrettable than depar-ture from the Lazies'. Consequently, even leaving out pragmatic consider-ations, allowing beachcombers to be frugally fed need not be regarded as a deplorable concession to scroungers, but can conceivably belong, under some contingent yet plausible factual conditions, to the basic structure endorsed by a responsibility-sensitive, egalitarian conception of justice. In Dworkin's case as in Rawls's, however, this remains a highly contingent justification of a modest unconditional income.

Why Liberal-Egalitarians Disagree

The liberal-egalitarian family is not limited to Rawls and Dworkin, and the approaches proposed by its other members lead to still different conclusions on basic income. Thus, Amartya Sen, unlike Rawls and Dworkin, refuses as a matter of principle to ask and answer the question "What is a just society?" He therefore cannot have a view on the question of whether a basic income would be part of a just social arrangement. But he can have a view and wants to have one on whether introducing a basic income would help make a society more just. The metric of justice he offers is one of basic capabilities, such as access to adequate food, housing, clothing, health, and education. If, under given circumstances, introducing a basic income would help extend some of these capabilities in sustainable fashion to a larger part of the population, his conception of justice would support it. But there may be circumstances in which, given the choice, some other policy, such as guaranteed employment would be preferable to an equally affordable basic income.[53]

Like Sen, Brian Barry proposes a conception of justice that is clearly liberal-egalitarian while being pluralistic and to some extent indeterminate. He therefore cannot provide a principled justification of basic income. In his first explicit discussion of the proposal, he was even rather hostile to it, and he remained critical of the possibility of justifying basic income directly from some general principle.[54] But as time went on, he became increasingly adamant that an unconditional basic income constitutes an essential component of a more just society.[55]

Compared to Barry's or Sen's, the advantage of Rawls's and Dworkin's conceptions of distributive justice, from our standpoint, is that, in addition to articulating fundamental ethical intuitions we share, they provide definite sets of principles from which the justification of an unconditional basic income can conceivably be derived, if only under some plausible factual assumptions. Once Rawls's difference principle is interpreted in opportunity-egalitarian fashion and its "productivist" bias corrected through the inclusion of leisure among the social and economic advantages, it can be viewed, in conjunction with the principle of fair equality of opportunity, as an alternative interpretation of our "real freedom for all." And so can Dworkin's equality of resources, once the "pro-Crazy" bias is corrected in what he believes should follow from his hypothetical insurance scheme. Why do their theories nonetheless lead to conclusions about basic income different from ours? Essentially because they are being spelled out against the background of different stylized pictures of our societies and of the inequalities that prevail within them.

For Dworkin, the key idea is that brute luck has provided us with unequal endowments, both personal and impersonal. This is unjust. Not much can be done about inequalities in personal endowments, but the distribution of impersonal endowments can be reshaped to correct the injustice. And his theory spells out how this could be done. The underlying stylized picture of society is plausible enough for people accustomed to the general equilibrium models of neo-classical economics, in which the option sets of economic agents are fully defined by their personal and impersonal endowments and their fates are fully predictable on this basis. In one form or another, this stylized picture is widely accepted, especially among economists interested in distributive justice.[56] But it fits less well with our messy real world, in which countless factors besides what can plausibly be construed as endowments profoundly affect people's life chances, and in particular their access to jobs and other rewarding productive activities. Rather than trying to imagine a way of reshaping the distribution of endowments in a fair way, our own approach to distributive justice proposes lumping together all the factors that affect what we are given and ensuring that the smallest gift is as generous as possible.

Rawls's conception of distributive justice, like ours, avoids this conceptualization in terms of endowment. It does so by relying on a stylized picture that gives a central role to the notion of social position. This picture works best for a society with a number of distinct, stable occupations in which workers tend to stay for their whole careers and beyond (owing to earnings-related retirement pensions), while nonworkers have their own social positions determined by the positions of their spouses in lifelong, stable households. To apply it to today's economy and society, in which people jump up and down between social positions so-defined, stretches the imagination. But it is not impossible. The difference principle simply asks us to focus on the index of social and economic advantages that can be expected by those spending their whole lives in the worst social position, as defined by the index. The situation gets more confusing as soon as part-time work is involved, or interrupted careers, or long-term unemployment, and with all shades of voluntariness present in varying proportions: each may be willing to do some job, but not any job. We then hit head-on the hard question of how to construct the index in terms of which social positions are to be compared, within regimes and across regimes, and in particular the question of how to weight the two components of the index that tend to be inversely correlated: income and leisure.[57] The alternative we propose sidesteps both the need for a nomenclature of social positions and the need to provide an unbiased index that would make them comparable. Instead, it proposes focusing on the gifts we all receive and maximizing the smallest gift.

Maximizing the smallest gift (or more precisely, its value understood as its opportunity cost for others, itself approximated by market prices) is a way of maximizing the power of those who currently have least of it, along two dimensions. It maximizes their power to consume, but also, by broadening the range of occupations they could viably adopt, maximizes their power to choose the sorts of lives they want to live. This approach has limitations of its own—in particular, the fact that it leaves out of the grasp of distributive justice all those gifts we receive that cannot be taxed either directly or indirectly. This includes no doubt some of those that matter most to our lives, such as the love of those we love. Unlike our talents, these cannot be taxed indirectly through taxation of the incomes attached to the positions to which they help give access. But perhaps this is just as well. Perhaps a conception that boosts as much as is sustainable the market power of those with least market power, and thereby (combined with access to education and other services) their ability to resist subjection to bosses, partners, or bureaucrats, will serve us well enough.

This feature makes our version of the liberal-egalitarian approach a close relative of what is sometimes called, following Philip Pettit, a republican approach—that is, a conception of distributive justice that focuses on non-domination or protection against arbitrary interference, not only in the political realm.[58] We are not denying that such an approach could justify an unconditional basic income.[59] But we prefer a theory that better captures a concern for making those who are least free as free as possible to say no *and* yes.

Libertarianism and Common Ownership of the Earth

Could a plausible justification of an unconditional basic income be found outside the liberal-egalitarian (or republican) tradition? In particular, given our argument's emphasis on freedom, could our intuitive case for basic income be accommodated in a libertarian framework? At the core of libertarianism is the view that all adult members of a society have the absolute right to dispose as they wish of their own persons and of the goods they have legitimately acquired. Consequently, taxing the income that a person has earned as a result of voluntary transactions amounts to the unacceptable theft of the fruits of a person's labor. In this light, this approach has little chance of being able to justify the funding of an unconditional basic income. However, all material goods ultimately derive from natural resources which at some point were not owned by anyone. All libertarian theories must therefore stipulate how these natural resources can be legitimately appropriated.

"Right libertarians" invoke the "first come, first served" principle, sometimes combined with a so-called "Lockean proviso" requiring that no person should be worse off than she would have been had there been no private appropriation.[60] For "left libertarians," on the other hand, the value of land and, more generally, of natural resources—including the value that derives from the private appropriation and exploitation of their potential—is owed in equal shares to all members of the human community concerned, arguably the whole of mankind. One could imagine justice so conceived to be achieved by giving everyone a piece of land of equal value. But the bureaucratic complexity and economic inefficiency of trying to do this would be such, under present demographic and technological conditions, that another way of giving concrete expression to this same principle is far more attractive.

This involves taxing land and other natural resources at their full competitive value and sharing the revenues from this tax equally among all members of the community concerned, irrespective of their personal situations and past or present contributions to production.[61] From a "left libertarian" standpoint, funding an unconditional basic income in this way does not amount to extorting from workers and other economic agents part of what they legitimately possess. Nor does it involve any charity or solidarity on the part of the rich for the benefit of the poor. It rather consists in collecting a fee from those who take advantage of natural resources and transferring it to the co-owners of those resources.

For this approach to be operationalized, a number of points need to be clarified. First, the idea is that only the value of "unimproved land," and not what was made with it or built on it, is to be taken into account. This value, meaning the economic rent attached to the plot, is of course mainly determined by its location, or in other words by the "improvements" or lack of them on nearby land. These are what make a plot in Manhattan more expensive than one in Nebraska, rather than, say, the chemical composition of the soil. Thus the question arises: What if I built something on my plot that helped attract investment all around it, and that boosted in turn the value of my plot? Is this increment part of the value of my "unimproved land" and therefore to be shared by all?

Second, the value that must be shared is not just the value of land, but also the value of what lies under that land and indeed what is under the seas. But nonrenewable natural resources unavoidably get depleted. Should we just accept that the stock whose value is to be equally shared will shrink from one generation to the next? Or should each generation increase the stock of capital so as to compensate for its contribution to the depletion of nonrenewable or slowly renewable natural resources? If so, should it adjust the compensation to the expected population growth?

Third, the scarce resources to be shared equally should also include those lying *above* the land—for example, the electromagnetic spectrum, and the atmosphere itself. Can we determine a threshold beyond which the atmosphere is no longer capable of absorbing carbon dioxide without undesirable climate change? And if so, should we fix a tax (or a price of carbon-emission rights) in such a way that emissions are kept below this threshold and distribute its proceeds equally among all human beings?

How high an unconditional basic income could be justified on "left libertarian" grounds depends on the answers to these (very tricky) questions and on (fairly speculative) empirical estimates, to be discussed in chapter 6. Some "left libertarians" have tried to broaden the legitimate tax base, for example, by including those goods left unowned by the deaths of their owners. This would mean abolishing the right of inheritance while maintaining the right of giving *inter vivos,* which can't be prohibited on libertarian grounds any more than market exchanges can.[62] One might be skeptical about how much this would add to the tax yield, as the dramatic difference in treatment of bequest and donation would be bound to trigger an equally dramatic shift from the former to the latter. More fundamentally, this move reflects the libertarians' inability to capture our considered judgments about what a fair distribution requires.[63]

This is even clearer in the eloquent plea for basic income by self-labeled libertarian Matt Zwolinski: "A basic income gives people an option—to exit the labor market, to relocate to a more competitive market, to invest in training, to take an entrepreneurial risk, and so on. And the existence of that option allows them to escape subjection to the will of others. It enables them to say 'no' to proposals that only extreme desperation would ever drive them to accept. It allows them to govern their lives according to their own plans, their own goals, and their own desires. It enables them to be free."[64] This sort of plea we find persuasive enough. But it uses the substantial notion of freedom which we appealed to loosely in the arguments of chapters 1 and 2 and spelled out more rigorously in the present chapter. This approach might be called "real-libertarian" providing it remains clear that it belongs to the liberal-egalitarian family, not to the libertarian one. For libertarianism, understood as a distinct philosophical approach, relies by definition on a system of pre-institutional individual entitlements, which just institutions must respect and protect. Along with other liberal-egalitarian approaches, our own does not operate under such pre-institutional constraints. It may look like a radical extension of a pre-institutional equal right to nature. Instead, it considers that everything is up for distribution without any pre-institutional constraint, but that institutions should be designed in such a way that the distribution of opportunities to which they lead can be regarded as fair and justifiable to all as free and equal persons.

Marxism and the Capitalist Road to Communism

At what might seem to be the polar opposite of the libertarian approach, could Marxist thought offer or at least suggest a distinct yet plausible justification for an unconditional basic income? True, Marx himself was not particularly encouraging. In contrast to the "utopian socialism" of Charles Fourier and others, his own "scientific" approach was not about ethical desirability but about historical necessity. The tone of some of his writings and the presuppositions of his political activism, however, are hardly consistent with this stance. On the contrary, they justify the attempts by some of his followers to work out normative perspectives that could justify the struggle for the replacement of capitalism by socialism, of the private by the collective ownership of the means of production. Two concepts play a crucial role in these attempts— exploitation and alienation—and both are no less relevant to the discussion of an unconditional basic income than to the discussion of socialism.

Exploitation, or the extraction of surplus value, is essentially the appropriation by nonworkers of part of the net product of an economy. Part of the total product in any given period is used to replace the material means of production used up in the production process, from seeds to computers. What is left is the net product, some of which is purchased with the workers' wages. The rest, whether used for investment or consumption, is appropriated by such nonworkers as feudal lords, slave owners, and capitalists. When workers also save and capitalists also work, the picture gets more complicated. But the core of the notion of exploitation can be preserved. There is exploitation if and only if part of the net product is appropriated by virtue of something other than labor.[65] And socialism can then be justified for those who regard exploitation as ethically reprehensible in itself, on the grounds that the collective appropriation of the means of production by the working class entails that workers appropriate the whole of the net product, and hence that exploitation is abolished.

For the justification of a basic-income scheme, this looks at first sight most unpromising. Indeed, an unconditional basic income would seem to be a recipe for the exploitation of workers by those who choose not to work. It is therefore not surprising that some of those fighting against capitalist exploitation should be fiercely hostile to basic income, which they view as extending to all a possibility fortunately confined so far to the capitalist class: living in idleness at the expense of the proletariat. However, concern for the exploitation of working people can also make us look at basic income as a blessing, not a calamity.[66] From this different standpoint, what is problematic in capitalist exploitation is not the parasitism of a small class of capitalists but the fact that a large class of proletarians has no option but to sell them the use of their labor power. What matters, therefore, is the bargaining power conferred by an unconditional basic income to all workers—in particular, to the most vulnerable among them—and the range of attractive alternatives it offers them, from self-employment and cooperatives to taking time off in order to retrain or just to breathe. Not forcing all to work but allowing each not to work is then the best way, not of abolishing capitalist exploitation, but of reducing its extent and shrinking what is most objectionable about it: its obligatory character. It must be conceded, however, that it is not exploitation as such, in the Marxian sense, that is then regarded as unjust. The underlying ethical intuition fits more comfortably in a liberal-egalitarian approach, focusing on a fair distribution of real freedom or opportunities.

An alternative approach, arguably less distant from Marx's own view (as formulated most explicitly in his critique of the Gotha program) does not attribute a direct ethical superiority to socialism over capitalism in connection with the removal of exploitation.[67] It rather regards socialism as instrumentally superior to capitalism in bringing about a state of abundance, itself the condition required for the abolition of *alienation*, understood as the performance of activities that do not have their aim in themselves. The capitalist organization of production—because it lacks central planning, because effective demand chronically fails to match supply, and because the profit motive inhibits the dissemination of innovation—is claimed to hinder the development of productive forces. Socialism, Marx believed, can remove these obstacles and thereby unleash human productivity growth to such an extent that our economy will soon reach a state of abundance. In other words, society will then be in a position to operate in accordance with the principle that defines the communist ideal: "from each according to his capacities, to each according to his needs." The work required to meet everyone's needs will be reduced to such an extent, and will become so pleasant, that everyone will be willing to perform it spontaneously according to their capacities, without any payment being needed to induce them to do so.

There is, however, no reason why one should wait until full abundance to start realizing partially the distributive principle that defines communism. Indeed, if it turns out—in light of historical experience and for deep-seated reasons to which Marx paid insufficient attention—that capitalism does better than socialism at developing the forces of production, this gradual transition to communism could happen in the context of a capitalist economy. The proposal of an unconditional basic income makes a lot of sense in this perspective. While not yet in a state of abundance, our society may plausibly be regarded as *affluent* in the sense that it could cover everyone's fundamental needs unconditionally with a basic income, topped up in some cases to address special needs such as disabilities.[68]

In order to fund this without forced labor, however, producers must have sufficiently strong material incentives to work and train. This means that tax rates on market rewards must remain well under 100 percent. However, as productivity increases, less and less work is required, especially less of the unpleasant work that needs to be compensated with significant net incomes to attract enough takers. Consequently, the proportion of the social product that is distributed according to contribution can gradually decrease and the share that is distributed according to needs can correspondingly increase, with the former gradually reduced to pocket money that tops up the latter. At the limit, the whole of the social product can be distributed according to needs, as alienated labor is no longer necessary to produce enough to cover these needs. Production by human beings is still essential. Robots do not do the whole job. But the work involved in this production is not distinguishable from play: it is so satisfying in itself that enough of it is forthcoming in the absence of any material reward.[69]

It is useful to contrast this "market-communist" justification of an unconditional basic income with the "real-libertarian" justification offered above in terms of maximin real freedom or maximin gift. For this purpose, imagine a capitalist society in which there is no public expenditure apart from an unconditional basic income and no taxation except a linear income tax (as in the figures in chapter 2). Let us further suppose that raising the tax rate produces a negative effect on society's taxable income. As the tax rate increases from o to 100 percent, the sustainable level of the unconditional basic income first rises (this is the "normal range" in which the tax rate increases more than the taxable income shrinks) and then falls (this is the "prohibitive range" in which the taxable income shrinks more than the rate rises). Figure 5.1 illustrates this. Let us further suppose that our economy is affluent in the sense used above—that is, that there is a sustainable level of an unconditional basic income that exceeds what is required to satisfy what the market-communist approach explored here would regard as fundamental needs. At the boundary between the normal and the prohibitive range, the sustainable level of the unconditional basic income reaches a peak (GMax) that corresponds to the tax rate recommended by the real-libertarian approach (1). By contrast, the market-communist approach, concerned as it is to minimize alienation, recommends pushing the tax rate higher (2), thereby depressing the unconditional basic income up to the point at which it just suffices to cover fundamental needs (G*).

Under the market-communist option, both the average taxable income Y and the minimum income G, as secured by the unconditional basic income, are lower than under the real-libertarian option. On the other hand, income inequality, as measured by the ratio of average income to minimum income, is also necessarily lower. So is the ratio of distribution according to contribution to distribution according to needs. And so is the level of net earnings—that is, the gap between per-capita income and basic income. These assertions need to be made with some caution. If the economy is open, the higher tax rate could simply lead many people to perform alienated work and earn high earnings abroad. Even in a closed economy, the high tax rate could induce many people to perform alienated activities in the informal sphere or to earn part of their income in the form of untaxed perks.[70] In this case, a significant part of total income would escape taxation and would keep growing as the tax rate rises. In Figure 5.1, therefore, total income per capita Y' would exceed taxable income per capita Y and fall more slowly than Y in response

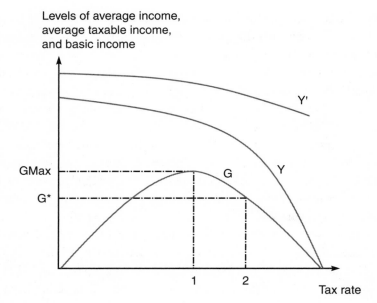

Figure 5.1 Optimal level of basic income from a "real-libertarian" and a "market-communist" perspective

Y: taxable income per capita
Y': total income per capita
Tax rate t: normal range from o to (1), prohibitive range from (1) to 100 percent.
Real-libertarian optimal tax rate (1): corresponds to the maximum sustainable level of basic income GMax
Market-communist optimal tax rate (2): highest tax rate consistent with basic income meeting fundamental needs G*

to higher taxation. Let us leave these complexities aside, however, and assume that the simpler version of our graph (with Y' coinciding with Y) fully captures the impact on both equality and alienation.

How can the market-communist option be justified relative to the real-libertarian one? There are two main possibilities. One is on egalitarian grounds. The market-communist option leads to more equality, as simply measured by the lowest income as a percentage of average income—in Figure 5.1, the ratio of basic income G to per-capita income Y. This egalitarian preference may be rooted in the intrinsic normative importance ascribed to greater equality as such, even at the expense of a lower income for everyone. But it may also be rooted in instrumental considerations—for example, a fear that the inequality needed to secure the economic sustainability of a higher basic income might jeopardize its political stability in a context in which the political system is not insulated from economic inequality; or the expectation that income inequality as such, irrespective of absolute levels, has negative effects on dimensions of real freedom not entirely captured by income levels, such as the health of the worst-off.[71]

The other justification could be called the "de-growth" justification. It rests on the fact that the market-communist option leads to less alienation, as approximated by the average level of pay needed to prompt productive contributions and captured in Figure 5.1 by the difference in absolute terms between per-capita income and basic income. For this justification to stick, one needs to assume that minimizing the volume of alienated activities is what matters, rather than maximizing the real freedom to escape from them, which is greater under the real-libertarian option. This assumption may derive from a perfectionist or illiberal standpoint that maintains it is not work but leisure—not busy-ness and consumption but escaping the rat race and opting for a simple way of living—that is essential to the good life, and alienated activity should therefore be discouraged as much as is compatible with covering everyone's needs. But it may also be inspired by instrumental considerations, concluding that a higher volume of (alienated) production today would come at the expense of its sustainability through time, or that its environmental impact would badly affect real freedom in a way that is not fully captured in income levels.

The intrinsic or perfectionistic versions of both justifications are hard to sustain in liberal societies committed to respecting the diversity of conceptions of the good life. In their instrumental versions, however, the difference from the real-libertarian approach is not fundamental and can be interpreted as an invitation to refine the latter so as to make it less naïve. Moreover, whether or not at the highest sustainable level in relative or absolute terms, a basic income would and should help the survival and development of communist pockets in a capitalist society: not only small, voluntary communities that choose to distribute their production according to needs and not according to contributions (in line with the original model of the Israeli kibbutz), but also large-scale collaborative enterprises that make the collective product of thousands of cooperators spread around the world freely available to whomever may find it useful (as the Wikipedia model does). It can therefore be argued that, in affluent societies, a basic income systematically contributes to making the volume of material production smaller than it could be, to "decommodifying" human labor, and to swelling an "autonomous" sphere irreducible to both the market and the state. However, it does not need to do so as a result of our striving for these effects as aims in themselves. These can also simply be by-products of the pursuit of justice as real freedom for all.

Basic Income and Happiness

At the end of this extensive discussion of possible justifications of an unconditional basic income on the basis of a plausible conception of justice, one might wonder whether it was really necessary to take all this trouble. Can it not be simply argued that a basic income is required to make our society a happier society, or even the happiest possible society?

Such a focus on happiness, if understood as the extent of satisfaction of people's preferences, amounts to adopting some version of the utilitarian conception taken for granted by most twentieth-century economists in their prescriptive pronouncements.[72] To assess the merits of this approach, there is no better starting point than the very last chapter of the founding book of welfare economics. Under the title "A National Minimum Standard of Real Income," A. C. Pigou justifies as follows the introduction of a minimum-income scheme: "economic welfare is best promoted by a minimum standard raised to such a level that the direct good resulting from the transference of the marginal pound transferred to the poor just balances the indirect evil brought about by the consequent reduction [of national income]."[73]

The underlying conjecture is that marginal utility diminishes with the level of income—that is, that the higher a person's income, the less her degree of preference satisfaction is affected by her income rising or falling by one unit. It follows that the maximization of aggregate welfare (or happiness or utility or preference satisfaction) will justify taxing high incomes and transferring the proceeds to those with low (or no) incomes of their own. In other words, a maximally happy society will require some form of minimum income.

It does not follow, however, that this minimum-income scheme should take the form of an unconditional basic income. Returning to ground covered in chapter 1, we can observe that, first, the economies of scale resulting from cohabiting make the standards of living of people living with partners higher than those of people living alone, and this pleads against a strictly individual minimum income with a level independent of the household situation. Second, the general utilitarian argument does not entail universality. Pigou himself mentioned that, with universal transferences, the labor supply reaction "would operate so strongly that the dividend would be seriously injured."[74] The subsequent development of utilitarian optimal tax theory justified sympathy for a means test or at least for prohibitive marginal rates—or rates of clawback—on the lowest income brackets: the disincentives they imply concern only a small and poorly-productive proportion of the people, while the revenues they enable the government to collect for the sake of boosting minimum income are massive.[75]

Third, the general utilitarian argument does not imply that the minimum-income benefits should be obligation-free. True, people who, given the choice, would choose not to work could be expected to increase their level of preference satisfaction thanks to this freedom from obligation. But even leaving aside the possibility that such people might overlook their own long-term interests, it is of course important to take account of the impact on welfare of those who will keep working. First, to provide a given level of minimum income, workers need to be taxed more than they would be if only those willing to work were entitled to transfers. And second, if it is indeed (as we quoted Jon Elster observing) a "widely accepted notion of justice" that it is "unfair for able-bodied people to live off the labor of others," some degree of resentment on the part of workers should also be factored in. Each of these considerations may end up weighing little: the economic cost of enforcing the work test may exceed its benefit, and an obligation-free basic income, if framed as a share in a common inheritance, could be perceived as fair by all. But this cannot be taken for granted. Hence, although there is a strong general utilitarian case for a minimum income provision, it can hardly be interpreted as singling out an individual, universal, and obligation-free basic income as its most promising version.

A second common way of attempting to justify basic income by its contribution to happiness, quite different from the one drawing on welfare economics, appeals to the contribution of basic income to economic growth. The marginal utility of income may diminish as a person's income grows, but as long as it remains positive, the growth of income should be regarded as positive by those who view happiness as the ultimate standard. In the long history of basic income advocacy, from Dennis Milner's 1920 *Higher Production by a Bonus on National Output* to Geoffrey Crocker's 2014 *Economic Necessity of Basic Income,* there has been no lack of pleas based on the putative positive impact of basic income on growth. However, most of the arguments used in such pleas are of the Keynesian variety—often implicitly, sometimes explicitly.[76] Consequently, they fail to single out basic income among many other possible forms of redistribution. True, a basic income would act countercyclically, boosting effective demand in downturns and thereby fostering growth when it is most useful for the sake of absorbing unemployment. However, the same can be said of conditional forms of minimum income or indeed of social transfers generally. It seems hard to argue for basic income's superiority in this respect. Indeed, as mentioned already, because of its freedom from obligation, basic income is attractive to those in affluent societies who advocate a stationary state or even "de-growth," out of concern for intergenerational justice or for other reasons.[77] Nonetheless, as explained in chapter 1, this freedom from obligation when combined with universality can boost the development of human capital and hence productivity. But freedom from obligation is also what facilitates turning higher productivity into more leisure and greater labor quality, rather than into enhanced production and consumption. This should logically make it less attractive than more conditional alternatives for those who want to maximize happiness by maximizing economic growth.

The good news for those who want to defend basic income as conducive to greater happiness is that this does not matter. While there is a strong positive correlation between income and happiness for individuals within a given society, and a weaker one across societies, Richard Easterlin drew attention in 1974 to the fact that the phenomenal growth in real income experienced by affluent societies did not translate into significantly higher preference satisfaction.[78] There are at least three mechanisms at work helping to explain this. First, part of the satisfaction derived from higher income comes from the possession or consumption of so-called *positional goods*—that is, goods that contribute to happiness partly or entirely by virtue of distinguishing their owners from those with no access to them. Second, the acquisition and use of some goods can be *counterproductive* in the sense that, once acquired and used by many, they make each user less happy than if no one had acquired them, typically for reasons of congestion. Third and most generally, preferences are not set once and for all but are *adaptive*. In particular, people's aspiration levels adjust upward as their original preferences get satisfied. Consequently, it is an illusion to believe that growth will make our societies happier, and the fact that basic income is not optimal for growth cannot be an argument against basic income for those aiming to make our societies happier.

In any case, our advice to basic income advocates, in closing this philosophical chapter, is not to pay too much attention to the alleged impact of basic income on happiness, and not only because the belief in such an impact unavoidably rests on highly speculative conjectures. More fundamentally, greater happiness does not make sense as an objective for our societies. One way of substantiating this conviction is to consider what could be interpreted as a generalization of Easterlin's paradox. In his *Division of Labor in Society*, Emile Durkheim points out that, leaving out obligation-induced suicides, there is a significant positive correlation between the rate of suicide and the extent of "civilization" in a sense that covers not only the level of real income but also, for example, the extension of equality of rights between all citizens. He writes that "the true suicide, the sad suicide, is in the endemic state with civilized people. It is even distributed geographically like civilization."[79] The more civilized a society, the larger the proportion of its members who feel so miserable that they put an end to their lives. Assume that this rate of suicide is a good indicator of a society's general level of unhappiness and that Durkheim's paradox is empirically established. Should we therefore give up the effort to make our societies more "civilized," and in particular more just? Durkheim did not think so. Instead, he preferred to "resolutely renounce these utilitarian comparisons" and endorsed Auguste Comte's recommendation to "dismiss as vain and futile the vague metaphysical controversy concerning the increase of man's happiness in the various ages of civilization."[80]

We fully agree. As already suggested by our reference to adaptive preferences in connection with Easterlin's paradox, increasing the aggregate level of happiness as preference satisfaction cannot possibly make sense as a long-term objective, because preferences change. In particular, levels of aspiration are strongly affected by what has been achieved previously. It does not follow that it makes no sense to try to make our societies better societies, and in the first place more just societies. On the contrary, articulating a coherent and plausible conception of justice, as we tried to do in this chapter, is essential. And discussing proposals aimed at making our societies more just, as we have been doing throughout this book, is no less important. Without such proposals, there is no hope—neither for ourselves nor for generations to come. But, for there to be hope, what is being proposed must be not only desirable but also realizable. In the following chapters, we turn to the question of the feasibility, economic and political, of an unconditional basic income.

6

Economically Sustainable? Funding, Experiments, and Transitions

CAN A BASIC INCOME BE SUSTAINABLY FUNDED? A worry often expressed is that, once people are guaranteed a generous obligation-free income, many will work much less or stop working altogether. Of course, it is part of the purpose of a basic income to enable women and men to reduce or interrupt their paid work, or to opt for less remunerative but more gratifying employment, or to settle with their employers for remuneration in terms of work quality rather than pay. Basic-income supporters can welcome all this—unless it dries up the source on which the funding of the basic income depends. This risk arises, many economists critical of basic income point out, not so much because of the freedom from obligation of the minimum income guaranteed to all, but above all, because of the taxation its funding requires. The most straightforward form this taxation can take is the personal income tax, which has tended to become essentially a tax on labor income. And it is the tax profile required by a generous basic income that makes people challenge its sustainability. In this chapter, we want to clarify the core of this challenge, examine how much we can learn from experiments and simulation models about how serious it is, discuss other sources of funding as ways of softening it, and finally assess the merits of three cautious ways of moving forward.

Labor Income

Worries about the sustainability of a basic income have two main sources. The minor one is the risk of inflation. It can be dealt with very briefly. Funding a basic income by redistributing purchasing power within some population, as in most proposals, cannot be expected to generate an overall inflationary pressure, as would funding it by transfers from abroad or by money creation. However, some local inflationary pressure can be expected. To an extent that will vary greatly with the choices made as to the level of the basic income, what it replaces, and how exactly it is funded, there will be some redistribution from relatively high earners to relatively low earners, especially part-time workers, and to the beneficiaries of low social transfers. Hence, if some goods are, at least in the short term, in inelastic supply while being (and remaining after the reform) more than proportionally purchased by net gainers from the introduction of a basic income, some increase in the prices they face, and hence some decrease in the real value of their basic income, can be expected. This holds, in particular, when a basic income is introduced on a large geographical scale. The associated redistributive effect in favor of poorer areas may then boost the price of housing and other local goods, thereby reducing without offsetting the benefit of the redistribution. This possibility needs to be borne in mind but does not endanger the sustainability of the scheme.

This cannot be said about the second main source of concern about the sustainability of a generous basic income: the negative effect it may have, jointly with its funding, on economic incentives. This effect will differ according to the form taken by this funding, and we shall examine a whole range of options later on. But in countries with both a developed income tax system and a developed welfare state, by far the most obvious way of funding a basic income is through the personal income tax. It is the one adopted in most proposals worked out in detail.[1] It is also the only one that lends itself to a formal equivalence with a negative income tax, as discussed in chapter 2. In those countries, it is difficult to imagine funding a significant level of basic income in a foreseeable future without relying at least in large part on this form of taxation. Because of various privileges granted to income from capital, taxing personal income has increasingly become close to equivalent to taxing labor income. And taxing labor income for the sake of funding an unconditional basic income is quite different from subjecting it to social contributions. The latter essentially transform part of a direct wage into an indirect one, in the form of a retirement pension and other social insurance benefits, whereas the former implies a clear reduction in the net return to formal work and to moving to a better-paid job. It is this dwindling of material incentives, added to the comfort of an obligation-free income, that challenges the sustainability of a generous basic income.

The simplest way of formulating this challenge is very misleading. It consists of multiplying the proposed level of basic income by the population concerned, calculating how highly taxable personal income would need to be taxed in order to yield this amount, and adding the corresponding tax rate to the preexisting tax burden. In the context of countries with developed welfare states and tax systems, this does not make sense, because much of the basic income would be "self-financed" in two ways. As mentioned in chapter 1, it would replace all lower social (assistance or insurance) benefits and the lower part of all higher social benefits. And it would also replace the tax exemptions on the lower income brackets of all households and possibly a number of other tax expenditures—for example, on childcare services or private pensions. Depending on the level of the basic income and on the size and structure of existing benefits and tax exemptions, the share of the basic income that is "self-financed" in one of these two ways will vary greatly. For example, the bulk of a basic income pitched at 10 percent of GDP per capita could in many cases be financed in this way, with the net cost then just a small fraction of its gross cost.[2] With higher levels of basic income, the net cost would obviously grow, but it would remain much smaller than the gross cost, and it is the net cost that matters.

More precisely, what matters is the way in which this net cost translates into a new profile of marginal tax rates. The core threat to the sustainability of a basic income that stems from reduced incentives to work resides in a feature that is intrinsic to any shift from a means-tested to a universal minimum-income scheme. It is illustrated under the simplest possible assumptions in Figure 6.1 and can be summed up as follows. Such a shift has a different impact on three categories of taxpayers. Those with a gross income below the minimum income level see their effective marginal rate of taxation (or rate of benefit clawback) dramatically reduced from the 100 percent inherent in a standard means-tested scheme to a far lower one (in our illustration, the linear rate of 25 percent), with a favorable effect on their incentives that can be described as the removal of a poverty trap (see chapter 1). Those with a gross income between the minimum income level and another level located somewhere above the breakeven point of the basic-income scheme see both their net incomes swell and their marginal tax rates increase (in our illustration, from 9 to 25 percent). And those with a still higher income also face an increase in marginal tax rates (the same one in our illustration) but see their net income shrink. The worry is that the welcome improvement of work incentives for people at the very bottom of the earnings ladder comes at the

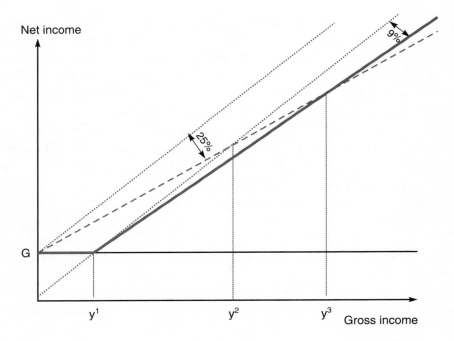

Figure 6.1 Net income with a means-tested minimum-income scheme versus with a basic income

The dotted lines represent the gross income with and without the basic income.
The discontinuous line represents the net income with a basic income.
The continuous line represents the net income with a means-tested minimum income.
y^1 is the breakeven point under the means-tested scheme
y^2 is the breakeven point under the basic-income scheme
y^3 is the point that divides net gainers and net losers from the shift to a basic income

Background assumptions:

· No public expenditure apart from the basic income or means-tested minimum-income scheme.
· 30 percent of the population have a gross income of zero, and 70 percent have a gross income higher than y^1.

Individual basic-income scheme:

· Basic income at 25 percent of average income.
· Linear income tax of 25 percent on all incomes, with the breakeven point at the level of the average income (y^2).

cost of a serious worsening of the incentives for large numbers of more productive workers whose contribution to the economy is far more important. The intermediate category will be particularly induced to work less because of the combined effect of enjoying a higher net income (the "income effect") and of earning less per hour performed (the "substitution effect").

Needless to say, this structural consequence of basic income's universal character captured in our simple illustration takes more complex forms in real life. In particular, it is amplified if the shift is from a household-based, means-tested scheme to an individual basic income at the level of the means-tested scheme for a single person. And it will show up in far higher rates of taxation because of the need to keep funding other public expenditures. In the United States, for example, non-social public expenditure absorbs about 13 percent of GDP, public expenditure on education and health about 12 percent, and other social expenditure about 10 percent (of which 6 percent goes to pensions). In France, the corresponding figures are 17 percent for non-social public expenditure, 12 percent for education and health, and 22 percent for other social expenditure (of which 12 percent goes to pensions).[3] To get a sense of the order of magnitude, suppose that half of the cash part of social expenditures can be dispensed with in the presence of a basic income at 25 percent of GDP. This would yield a tax rate of 55 percent of GDP in the US, and 65 percent in France. Further, part of the GDP does not take the form of personal income and hence cannot be part of the base of a personal income tax. In the euro area, for example, the share of the GDP that takes the form of incomes paid to households is somewhat above two-thirds of GDP.[4] Assuming all public expenditures are to be funded by a linear tax on all these incomes, the rate required would not be 55 or 65 percent but rather 80 or 90, while still ignoring the shrinking of this tax base owing to various exemptions.[5]

These figures must not be interpreted as the part of a society's income that is used for its own purposes by the state, since the introduction of a basic income does not diminish the part of that income that is in the hands of private households. Quite possibly, the opposite is true. But they are relevant as indicators of the marginal taxation implied by a shift to a minimum-income scheme that is at the same time universal, individual, and generous. This challenge cannot be ignored. Part of the response consists in relativizing the importance of material incentives and in stressing the priority of efficient human-capital formation over maximal participation in the labor market (as we did in chapter 1). This is important for the long-term vision.

But more is needed if we are to gain and spread confidence in the sustainability of a generous basic income. To be able to make informed guesses about what would happen if such a basic income were introduced, it must be possible to do better than asking people what they would do if they were given a basic income at a particular level.[6] One can conduct experiments and construct simulation models.

Basic Income Experiments

Sometimes experiments happen without needing to be organized. One example is provided by the Win for Life scheme, a part of Belgium's National Lottery that offers its winners, instead of one big payout, a lifelong monthly payment pitched at 1,000 euros between 1998 and 2007 (about 40 percent of Belgium's GDP per capita at the time) and at 2,000 euros afterwards.[7] Another example is provided by MeinGrundeinkommen, a crowdfunding initiative launched in 2014 by a young Berlin entrepreneur, Michael Bohmeyer, aiming to provide a basic income of 1,000 euros (about 40 percent of Germany's GDP per capita at the time) to volunteers on the condition that they allowed their economic activity to be monitored over the one-year period. The point was to see whether they would work or train less or more, switch to another activity, and so forth.[8]

In both these cases, we are talking about a genuine basic income—in cash, individual, without means test or work test—tried with real people. Yet, little can be inferred from either about what can be expected from the society-wide introduction of a basic income. A first reason for this is that the people who got the basic income were not only a very small sample of the population but also a very biased one consisting of (high-frequency) lottery participants and (highly motivated) basic income fans. A second reason is that there is bound to be a difference in the behavior of the handful of people who received a basic income as the outcome of a lottery or as part of an experiment and how they would have behaved if everyone else in the community had also received it.

These two limitations were overcome in two pilot studies that took place under altogether different circumstances and are often referred to in the basic-income debate. First, in 2008 and 2009, the nearly 1,000 adults below sixty who had been residing in the Namibian village of Otjivero for at least one year received an unconditional monthly basic income of 100 Namibian dollars (about $8, and about 2 percent of Namibia's GDP per capita at the time), while those above sixty kept receiving their state pension of over 500 Namibian dollars. The bulk of the funding came from the German United Evangelical Mission.[9] As all residents in the relevant age group received the payment, there was no individual self-selection bias and the project made it possible to observe a basic-income scheme operating at the level of a whole community.

A more carefully designed experiment was conducted in the Indian state of Madhya Pradesh from June 2011 to November 2012 with funding from UNICEF. Essentially, each adult resident in eight randomly chosen villages was entitled to an unconditional basic income of 200 rupees per month (slightly more than $4, or 6.5 percent of GDP per capita in Madhya Pradesh and 4 percent of GDP per capita in India at the time). This amount was increased to 300 rupees after one year. Children were entitled to half the amount adults received. Twelve similar, randomly chosen villages served as a control group, where no basic income was introduced. Thus, the ascription of effects to the basic-income scheme could be made with greater confidence. Moreover, like in the Namibian case, every resident in the relevant age group was invited to register. Hence, individual sample bias was minimized and the impact of introducing the scheme at the level of a whole community could be observed.[10]

While these two limitations were overcome, they were replaced, as regards their relevance for basic-income proposals in affluent countries, by a more serious one. The modesty, even by Namibian or Indian standards, of the amounts involved and the context in which the basic income was introduced (a place with essentially no social insurance or public assistance for adults below pension age) make the Namibian and Indian pilots hugely different from what introducing a basic income would mean in countries with developed welfare states. Obviously, this huge difference does not prevent the experiments from improving significantly the villagers' lives or from yielding interesting insights into the effects of schemes that alleviate extreme poverty without creating dependency traps. But it undermines any conclusion northern basic-income supporters may be tempted to draw in support of their own proposals.

Moreover, the various experiments mentioned so far suffer from two further defects that limit their relevance as models for real-life schemes. First, with the exception of Win for Life, they are of limited duration. The effect of a basic income is bound to be quite different depending on whether one expects it to last for one year only or for life. Depending on the person and the activity, awareness of the shorter duration may produce more attachment (let's be prudent) or less attachment (let's seize the opportunity) to the person's current activity than would a lifelong scheme. Second, in all four cases, the funding of the scheme is coming from the outside. The effect of the taxation that would be needed if a full-blown basic-income scheme were introduced is in no way taken into account. In the Namibian and Indian cases, for example, much of the new economic activity that could be observed was the predictable outcome of an injection of purchasing power into the local economy.[11] And in the lottery and crowdfunding cases, the net income the beneficiaries could keep earning through their work was not diminished by the additional taxation that would be needed if everyone was to receive 1,000 euros. These two major limitations, intrinsic to any basic-income experiment, prevent us from drawing any firm conclusion about the economic sustainability of a lifelong basic income funded from within the community that enjoys it.[12]

Negative-Income-Tax Experiments

Might more relevant lessons be learned from the older and far more expensive experiments that were conducted in North America in the 1970s? As mentioned in chapter 4, most of these took place in the United States: in New Jersey and Pennsylvania (1968 to 1972), in Iowa and North Carolina (1970 to 1972), in Gary, Indiana (1971 to 1974, focused on black single mothers), and in Seattle and Denver (1970 to 1980, the largest one).[13]

Each experiment consisted of giving randomly selected households from different income categories the benefit of a negative-income-tax scheme (see chapter 2) with different levels of income guarantee and different rates of clawback, and comparing them to control groups with the same characteristics that remained under the preexisting schemes. The amount paid to households with no other income ranged mostly from 50 percent to 150 percent of what was the official poverty line at the time. In the 100 percent version of the New Jersey experiment, for example, the minimum annual income guarantee for a household consisting of two adults was $1,000 per capita (about 21 percent of GDP per capita in 1968). No single adult was included at the start of this experiment, but spouses leaving a household remained entitled to their share of the household's income guarantee. The clawback rate—that is, the percentage of each dollar earned that is offset by a reduction of the benefit received—ranged from 30 percent to 70 percent.[14] The payment of benefits was limited in time, between two years (Iowa and North Carolina) and a maximum of nine years for some recipients in Seattle/Denver. All experiments included households headed by an able-bodied male, which were not eligible for public assistance at the time. Except for the initial New Jersey experiment, they also included single-parent households.

Another negative-income-tax experiment has become particularly popular since it was rediscovered, many decades after it was performed. The so-called Mincome experiment took place in 1975–1978 in the town of Dauphin, in the Canadian province of Manitoba. A household-based negative-income-tax scheme was introduced at 60 percent of the Canadian poverty line with a clawback rate of 50 percent. In 1972, when the experiment was designed, the annual income guarantee for a single adult was fixed at C$1,255 (close to 25 percent of Canadian GDP capita at the time). The amounts were subsequently adjusted to keep track with inflation. Unlike all other North American experiments, this one used a "saturation sample": all households in the town satisfying the income conditions were eligible for the program. A control group was provided by a random sample of low-income families from neighboring rural communities. Because the whole community was involved, some attempt could even be made to distinguish what was due to "individual-level mechanisms" as opposed to "community effects," such as a lower hostility to working-time reduction, and greater opportunities for joint leisure activities in saturated samples than in dispersed samples. The Dauphin experiment, therefore, can claim some specific relevance for estimating the impact of the real introduction of a basic income.[15]

However, this should not be overstated. The relevance of the Dauphin experiment to current basic-income proposals suffers from most of the same limitations as the other negative-tax experiments. First of all, what was being tested in all the North American experiments was not a basic income. True, the benefit was obligation-free. But it was not strictly individual—even though, in the Dauphin case, the amount for a single person was scarcely more than for each member of a couple (C$1,255 versus C$1,172). Above all, it was not universal: in Dauphin, for example, owing to the income condition on participation, only about 20 percent of the residents actually took part in the program, and the benefit was not paid upfront to them. As explained in chapters 1 and 2, even though the schemes could be said to mimic the post-tax-and-transfer profile entailed by some conceivable household-based universal scheme for the bottom part of the income distribution, this should make more than a small difference. Second, what one could hope to estimate with these experiments is at most the difference a household-based negative income tax would make relative to the scheme that would otherwise have applied to the subjects in the experimental group. This differed significantly from one type of household to another, from one place to another, and even sometimes from one time to another in the course of a single experiment.[16] If one wanted to use the outcomes of such experiments to make claims about the introduction of exactly the same scheme in today's situation in a particular country, one would first need to check that the background social protection institutions were sufficiently similar to those that prevailed in seven American states and one Canadian province in the 1970s. This institutional background was very distant from the quasi-absence of public provisions in Namibia or in India today, but was also very different from the comparatively generous conditional minimum-income schemes in place in many European states and even from the present setup in Canada and the United States.

Suppose, however, that both the scheme whose introduction is being considered and the background situation are sufficiently similar to those in some experiment. What we can learn from this experiment about the sustainability of a scheme is still severely limited by the two considerations already mentioned in connection with the basic-income pilot projects and a third one, even more important in our eyes. First, there is the limited duration. In most North American experiments, the duration of payment was limited to three years. This is, of course, anticipated by the subjects, and it is therefore unclear whether they would reduce their labor supply more or less if they expected instead that the scheme would last forever.[17] Moreover, the new scheme may affect social norms, but only over the longer term. Second, enrollment in the experiments cannot be compulsory. As a result, there is likely to be an overrepresentation of households interested in joining the scheme because of their intention to make good use of the options it opens for them.[18] Above all, this excludes from the experiment all those households which would lose as a result of participation because of belonging to an income category that would have to pay for the net cost of the scheme if it were introduced for real. For these two reasons, whatever impact, sharp or weak, on the supply of paid work an experiment might establish, it will always be possible for the opponents of the scheme to claim that this overestimates the sustainability of the scheme because it ignores the impact of the lifelong character of the income guarantee and of the higher tax rates on net contributors. And that claim will be right. Because of these two limitations, even the best-designed experiments with a particular version of a genuine basic income cannot possibly suffice to establish its sustainability if introduced for real.

More important still, for basic-income supporters, is a third limitation. Even the best-designed experiments cannot capture the effects on the labor market which are at the core of the case for basic income versus conditional minimum-income schemes. As explained in chapter 1, the universality of basic income opens the possibility of saying yes to some jobs that are currently not viable and its freedom from obligation opens the possibility of saying no to other jobs, which will therefore need to pay better or improve if they are to have incumbents. Such effects, however, crucial to both the desirability and the sustainability of basic-income schemes, have no chance of showing up in the experiments, partly because of their limited duration but above all because they affect only a few hundreds or thousands of individuals in labor markets of several millions. Often (indeed, always in the case of less developed welfare states), the negative-income-tax or basic-income schemes are pitched at such a level that, relative to existing provisions, they have a significant direct effect in terms of income poverty reduction. The welcome indirect consequences of this reduction can then be usefully documented, as they were in Dauphin and even more in Otjivero and Madhya Pradesh. But the specific impact on the economy of the basic income's being universal and obligation-free cannot show up, because of the small size of the sample relative to the relevant labor market.

As we write this chapter, more experiments are being planned in Finland, the Netherlands, Canada, and elsewhere. Bearing in mind the strong reservations voiced above about their relevance is important to temper unwarranted enthusiasm. It is even more important to prevent a damaging backlash analogous to the one that followed the North American experiments.[19] Not only is there no single thing that could be called "introducing a basic income" but, depending on its level, what it replaces, and how it is funded, the nature of the thing can vary hugely. In addition, none of the measures that have actually been tested so far in affluent countries could be so called. And the effects those measures produced had as much to do with the specific features of the background in which they were introduced as with their own content. Finally, because of the three intrinsic limitations mentioned above— limited duration, exclusion of net contributors, and small size relative to the labor market—while the experimental evidence can still be used to corroborate or refute some "even if" claims, it cannot possibly substantiate grand assertions about the (un)sustainability of a basic income. Owing to the interest they keep triggering in the media even when they are just mere possibilities that may never materialize, all "basic income experiments" are wonderful in so far as they boost awareness of the idea and discussion about its pros and cons. But if their relevance to either the sustainability or the desirability of a basic income is inappropriately framed, their net effect on real-life reform in this direction may turn out to be disastrous.

Econometric Models

If experiments are not very promising in terms of what we can learn from them about the real-life sustainability of basic-income schemes, what else can we turn to? As with any other topic in the social sciences, we must try to infer causal links from correlations. This is fundamentally what is being done in econometric models that claim to predict, often with more assurance than is warranted by their empirical backing, what would happen if a basic income were introduced. This empirical backing typically consists of a large set of observations of marginal net incomes and amounts of work performed by various categories of people differentiated according to gender, number and age of children, partner's income, and so forth. A utility function that increases at a decreasing rate with both income and leisure is imputed either to individuals or to households taken as a single unit as the function their labor-market decisions aim to maximize. Such a utility function can capture both the income effect (the higher the total income, the lower the propensity to work) and the substitution effect (the higher the marginal income, the higher the propensity to work). The parameters of this function are then selected so as to best fit the data. The correlations detectable in these data are turned into conjectural causal relations by being interpreted in light of some sufficiently plausible rational decision-making model.

For the prediction of the effect of introducing a basic income on the labor market, the key causal notion is that of tax elasticity of the labor supply: the percentage decrease of the number of hours some category of people is willing to work that can be expected from a one-percent increase in the marginal tax rate applying to the income earned with this work. How these marginal tax rates (in a broad sense that covers the rates of benefit clawback) would be affected by some basic-income proposal (including its funding by the personal income tax) can be determined on the basis of the specification of the initial situation, the reform being investigated, and the actual distribution in more or less detailed categories of the active population for which the reform is intended. Applying the estimated tax elasticities for the various categories to the changes in income levels and marginal tax rates to which their incomes are subjected yields a prediction of the effect on the labor supply. Typically, for reasons spelled out earlier in this chapter with the help of a stylized comparison, workers whose total net income is increased as a result of receiving a basic income, but whose marginal income shrinks as a result of funding it, will be predicted to reduce their working time quite substantially. Several models of this general sort have now been constructed for a number of countries.[20] The prediction that emerges in all cases is a fall, more or less pronounced, in labor-market participation and average number of hours of work performed.[21]

How should basic-income advocates respond to such findings? Assuming that they are methodologically sound and based on an appropriate and reliable data set, these econometric models have the advantage, relative to experiments, of avoiding the problem of duration and including the responses of net contributors. But they cannot avoid two other important limitations. First, the empirical grounding of whatever prediction is made consists of correlations observed at a particular time and place, in cultural and institutional circumstances that affect labor market behavior. When drawing conclusions from an econometric model about the likely consequences of a prospective reform, it is therefore not enough to check that both the new schemes and the schemes to be replaced are sufficiently similar in the model and in reality. In addition, one must bear in mind that informal gender norms, the availability of childcare and paid leave, pension arrangements, how favorably part-time work is treated by labor-market legislation and by informal social norms, and many other relevant factors can vary significantly from one time and place to another. Great caution must therefore be taken when extrapolating tax elasticities to the reform that is being proposed. It is not because the models are constructed here and now that the data sets they happened to be able to use are relevant for a proposal made for here and now.

Second, these models typically assume that it is the supply of labor that determines the volume of employment. If people do not work or do not work more than they do, it is because this is their best choice, given their income and its expected increase in case they worked more, and not because there are no jobs matching their qualifications. One implication of this assumption is that nothing in the predicted negative effect of basic income on employment is due to the fact that the basic income is obligation-free—that is, not restricted to those working or willing to work. The models make no claim to capture the impact of the presence or absence of a willingness-to-work condition. Instead, they assume that there is no such condition in place or that it is ineffective. What they do claim to capture is the impact of changes in tax profiles that follow from the universal character of the basic income (and hence the lower effective marginal rates on the lowest incomes) and, when it is a feature of the scheme being explored, of its strictly individual character. Another corollary of this exclusive focus on the supply side is that no account is taken of the adjustment of the demand side. As argued in chapter 1, a basic income is meant to make it easier to say yes to some low-paid or uncertainly paid jobs, including self-employment, thereby boosting their creation. It is also meant to make it easier to say no to other low-paid jobs, thereby boosting their wages and increasing workers' eagerness to take them.[22] These economic consequences of the introduction of a basic income are crucial to the case for it. Their being largely or entirely ignored by econometric models—as we saw they are, though for a different reason, by experiments—is a second major reason for not looking at whatever forecasts pop out of the econometricians' black box as if they were infallible prophecies.

Nonetheless, these forecasts cannot just be dismissed. For the reasons mentioned, they cannot give us great confidence in either the sustainability or the unsustainability of a particular income-tax-funded basic-income scheme for a particular country at a particular time. The fact that they will tend to predict a significant reduction in the current labor supply of various categories of women and men should neither surprise nor worry us. If a basic income is to contribute to the realization of a free society and a sane economy, it is essential that this should happen. Whether even a sharp reduction is consistent with sustainability will depend on the longer-term impact on human capital (see chapter 1), which these models cannot capture. However, the reduction in the labor supply can take several forms—in terms of which categories of workers are affected, how much, and in what way—not all equally conducive to the intended effects. With the most problematic underlying assumptions spelled out and explained in honest and lucid fashion, simulation models, cautiously interpreted, can provide valuable information about the ways in which different scenarios are likely to affect the labor supply of different categories. This will not suffice to establish the (un)sustainability of specific basic-income proposals, but could help to fine-tune them.

In light of this overview of what can and cannot be learned from experiments and econometric exercises, what needs to be done by basic-income supporters concerned about the sustainability of their proposals? Two things. One is to explore alternative sources of funding, whether as substitutes or as complements to a personal income tax, among them those which some basic-income advocates regard as the most appropriate, or even sometimes the only appropriate. The other is to explore the merits of various more modest steps in the direction of a generous unconditional basic income.

Capital

Since we are ourselves ecumenical about the way basic income and other public expenditures should be funded (see chapter 5), there will be something unavoidably unprincipled in the quick overview we offer in the following pages. There will also be something intentionally uneven about it, as we want to pay special attention to sources of funding other than income tax that have been proposed by basic-income advocates or are actually used for existing schemes. We shall mention the special reasons that have been advanced for singling out some of them, and mention the main drawbacks, if any, we see with them.

The first option is one to which few basic-income supporters are likely to take exception. We saw that the taxation of personal income has tended to reduce to the taxation of labor income. Indeed, the various experimental and econometric exercises discussed in the previous sections mostly take for granted that taxing income amounts to taxing earnings. Hence there is the obvious suggestion to tax capital more, so that labor can be taxed less. This suggestion can take four concrete forms. The most obvious one consists of reducing the asymmetry in the tax treatment of capital income and labor income, whether by applying a progressive schedule to the total of capital and labor income, by assimilating capital gains—that is, the increase in the value of one's capital—to taxable income, or by scrapping a set of loopholes and unnecessary exemptions. A second way in which one can increase the contribution of capital is by taxing capital directly through a steeply progressive personal-wealth tax. Obviously taxing a stock is not like taxing a flow. For the yield to be sustainable, the rate must remain modest.[23] Third, there is the corporate tax. If firms' profits cannot adequately be taxed at the point at which they swell their individual beneficiaries' income or wealth, they should be taxed before they leave the firms.

Fourth and finally, there is the inheritance tax, or more generally the taxation of all bequests and gifts *inter vivos*. This sort of tax has a special appeal for those who see basic income as a share in a common inheritance. Our own interpretation of this inheritance is very broad and covers what we receive as part of our labor or capital income no less than what we inherit (see chapter 5). But inheritance in the narrow sense is sometimes proposed as an earmarked source of funding for a universal basic endowment (see chapter 2) more than for a basic income (for example, by Bruce Ackerman and Anne Alstott and by Anthony Atkinson).[24] From the standpoint of the person making a donation or a bequest, it may seem an anomaly to have her wealth taxed more when generously giving it away than when selfishly consuming it. But from the standpoint of distributive justice between heirs, it is definitely an anomaly that money received in exchange for nothing should be taxed (if at all) at a far lower rate than is money received in exchange for productive effort.

Each of these four ways of making capital contribute more could help reduce too exclusive a fiscal pressure on labor income. The current asymmetry is mostly justified by the need to encourage risky investment and an entrepreneurial spirit. But, apart from direct political pressure, it is above all explained by the transnational mobility of taxable capital and taxable capital income—including in the form of fictitious transnational transfers of profits by multinationals. Taxation organized on a global or regional scale would suppress or reduce this factor. So can collaboration between national tax authorities in the form of agreements on minimal rates and exchange of fiscal information.[25]

In the history of basic income, there have been more radical proposals that avoid this problem by making capital pay for basic income without its needing to be taxed. If a state owns all means of production, it can simply determine what proportion of the total product it allocates to wages, to investment, and to other expenditures, including, if it so wishes, an unconditional basic income. In a socialist society, in other words, part of the economic surplus can be disbursed as a uniform social dividend without anyone's needing to be taxed. This is possible under centrally planned socialism, but it is also possible under market socialism, where the collective ownership of the means of production is combined with competition among firms and a free labor market. The market socialist models advocated by Oskar Lange, James Yunker, and

John Roemer all include a social dividend.[26] If there is a free labor market—as opposed to a centralized allocation of workers—the relative levels of wages and the social dividend raise incentive issues analogous to those raised by taxation under capitalism, though with more leeway since there is no private capital to be assuaged by sufficient profits.

This option may not be completely ruled out in the few countries in the world in which a significant part of the means of production is still publicly owned.[27] But elsewhere, a wholesale nationalization of the means of production is not exactly in sight. A move in this direction was nonetheless proposed by James Meade as a central component of his "Agathotopian" model.[28] Under his "topsy-turvy nationalization," firms are privately managed but half of their shares are owned by the state. The dividend earned by these state-owned shares can then fund a basic income allocated to each citizen without requiring any taxation. Getting there obviously requires turning a country's public debt, on which interest needs to be paid, into a public endowment that would yield a return to be distributed as an unconditional basic income. One could get there in one step through a huge capital levy, but, Meade notes, "such a step would be out of the question except in a highly revolutionary political atmosphere."[29] The alternative consists of taxing present generations quite heavily in order to create such a surplus that the return on it could pay for the basic income of future generations. But the intergenerational inequality entailed by following this path, even if politically possible, would be difficult to justify.[30]

Nature

Instead of banking on the public ownership or co-ownership of all productive assets, one could bank, more modestly, on the public ownership of one specific type of asset: natural resources. This idea comes in three versions, each of particular relevance to some basic-income schemes. First, the state could own some renewable natural resource, starting with the country's land, and rent it out, and then use the rent to fund a basic income. This was essentially Thomas Paine's proposal for funding a basic endowment for the young and a basic pension for the old. It was also Thomas Spence's and Joseph Charlier's proposal for funding a basic income, but in each case with an extension to all real estate (see chapter 4). Estimating how much of a basic income could be funded out of the rental value of unimproved land raises tricky difficulties, both conceptual and empirical, some of which have already been mentioned in connection with the left-libertarian justification of basic income (chapter 5). One estimate for the US state of Vermont yielded a lower and upper bound of 4 percent and 8 percent of Vermont's GDP in 2008.[31] With contemporary technology, the surface of the earth is not the only scarce permanent resource that is privately appropriated. So is the broadcast spectrum. The same source estimates the associated economic rent at 1.5 percent of GDP, but any such estimate is no doubt very sensitive to local conditions and vulnerable to technical change.[32]

Exactly the same logic can be applied to the atmosphere as soon as one recognizes the limits of its ability to digest our emissions of carbon dioxide without generating major damages. This recognition does not turn the atmosphere into a nonrenewable resource, but into a scarce renewable resource, whose use as a sink for our emissions has an opportunity cost that is arguably best reflected in a price. Given that our atmosphere is a global resource, the most sensible level at which this distribution should in principle operate is clearly the global one, and we shall therefore return to it in chapter 8. But pragmatic approximations may make sense at a national level, and they would be guided by the same logic as the one flowing from the equal ownership of the earth. In the United States, estimates of the level of basic income that could be funded out of the proceeds of a carbon tax vary from 0.7 to 2 percent of GDP per capita.[33] In all these cases, the payment of the rent by the appropriators may look like a tax—the "Georgist" single tax on land, the carbon tax, and so forth—but is in fact rather a fee paid in exchange for the right to use a collectively owned asset.

The second version of the proposal to fund a basic income out of publicly owned natural assets consists of banking on the revenues from the sale of nonrenewable natural resources. This model is illustrated by Iran's universal subsidy scheme funded by an increase in the price of domestically produced oil. In January 2010, the Iranian parliament approved by a narrow majority the so-called "targeted subsidies law." This law brought the comparatively very low domestic price of oil gradually in line with the international price, thereby scrapping an economically perverse implicit subsidy to oil consumption by both Iranian households and firms. About a quarter of the revenues thus generated were meant to subsidize producers directly hit by the price increase. Most of the rest was meant to compensate the seventy million Iranian citizens for the impact of the general price increase on their standard of living by introducing a monthly cash subsidy. This cash payment was initially intended to start at $20 and to gradually rise to $60 per person per month (about 13 percent of GDP per capita). For various reasons, including the sanctions affecting the Iranian economy, the real value of the grant quickly declined and the full universality of the scheme did not last long.[34]

Other schemes that can be viewed as approximating this way of funding a basic income were even more short-lived. In January 2006, the 3.3 million residents of the Canadian province of Alberta received a one-shot tax-free "prosperity bonus" of C$400 (about $350 at the time). The then Premier Ralph Klein had announced that other grants might follow in subsequent years, depending on the province's oil revenues, but none ever did.[35] In February 2011, as the Arab Spring was unfolding, Kuwait's National Assembly decided to pay a one-off cash benefit of 1,000 dinars (about $3,500, or 7 percent of Kuwait's GDP per capita at the time) out of the country's oil revenues to each of its 1.1 million native citizens (not to its 2.4 million foreign residents), officially to commemorate the fiftieth anniversary of independence and the twentieth anniversary of liberation from Iraqi occupation.[36] And between 2010 and 2012, the Mongolian government offered untargeted cash benefits to all its citizens funded by royalties from the country's mining industry.[37] As we are talking here of nonrenewable resources, it is obvious that a basic income funded in this way could not possibly be sustainable.

Hence the third version, which uses the sale of nonrenewable natural resources in order to create a permanent sovereign fund.[38] This model is instantiated by the world's only case of a lasting genuine basic income: the Alaska Permanent Fund (discussed at length in chapter 4). The latter consists of an endowment accumulated thanks to the extraction and sale of Alaska's oil and invested worldwide. Because of its being indexed to the performance of the Permanent Fund in the previous five years, the amount funded in this way has oscillated smoothly but considerably, with an average of about $1,200 per year, or about 2 percent of Alaska's GDP per capita, since the beginning of the century. Many other sovereign funds have been created and developed in a similar way, most notably in Norway, but none of them has made the choice of distributing a regular dividend to all citizens.[39] However, the dividend model has inspired proposals concerning other countries with considerable oil reserves. For example, the idea of setting up a similar system in Iraq was defended in 2003 by several members of the American Congress. And a plan concerning Nigeria was presented and defended in an IMF report coauthored by Columbia University economist Xavier Sala-i-Martin.[40]

With this third version of the idea of an entitlement to an equal share in the value of natural resources, we are back, through a specific path and with the limits it entails, to a publicly owned endowment that yields a basic income as a dividend. In this case, assuming natural resources are publicly owned, it is not only that the basic income requires no taxation once the fund exists, but also that the growth of the fund requires neither taxation nor expropriation. Restriction to the natural resources is a tight constraint, however, and the creation of such a sovereign fund must therefore remain the privilege of a minority of states or sub-states that happen to sit on particularly valuable natural resources and managed to make a successful claim to them.

Money

For those parts of the world that are not so lucky, is there another way of funding a basic income without taxation? One is by exploiting the irrationality of gamblers. Since 1996, the Eastern Band of Cherokee, a Native American tribe in North Carolina, distributes to each of its officially enrolled adult members, regardless of their income, family situation, and place of residence, an equal share in the profits of the casino it runs on its reservation. The number of beneficiaries is not made public, but the tribe has about 7,500 members. And the level of the dividend, about $4,000 on average in the 1990s, is believed to approach $10,000 per year (or close to 25 percent of North Carolina's GDP per capita) in 2015.[41] A slightly less anecdotal illustration is provided by Macau, a casino-dependent semi-autonomous city-region of China with about 600,000 inhabitants that used to be a Portuguese possession. Every year since 2011, the government's "Wealth Partaking Scheme" has been distributing a sum that has fluctuated from 3,000 to 9,000 patacas (from $400 to $1,200, or slightly more than 1 percent of Macau's very high GDP per capita) to each of its permanent residents (and a smaller amount to its non-permanent residents). Each annual scheme is the object of *ad hoc* legislation, without commitment for the following years, which makes it more akin to the Alberta and Kuwait one-off payments than to Alaska's permanent fund.[42] Needless to say, such schemes are not generalizable. They amount to funding the basic incomes of the Cherokee and the Macau residents out of an unintended donation by outsiders, American and Chinese gamblers, respectively.

If there is, next to natural resources, any major way of funding a basic income without taxation, it can only be through money creation. From an early stage, several proponents of a basic income advocated its funding through printing fresh currency. Thus, in the 1930s, Major Douglas's "Social Credit" movement in the United Kingdom and Jacques Duboin's "distributist" movement in France (both discussed in chapter 4) shared the conviction that the best way to prevent the crises of overproduction generated by technical progress was to distribute purchasing power straight to the population instead of relying on the operation of the private banking system.

This idea has usually been dismissed as relying on simplistic economics and as overlooking the deleterious effect of the inflationary pressures its implementation would generate. However, there are two sound rationales for funding either a very modest or a temporary basic income through money creation.[43] The first one, articulated most systematically by Joseph Huber, supposes that central banks can regain, at the expense of private banks, the monopoly of money creation. They can then issue drawing rights to all residents. If these match the annual growth of the real economy, they will not cause inflation. If they exceed it, they will, but a moderate, non-accelerating inflation rate is arguably a good thing to "grease" cyclical fluctuations and structural change. There is some unavoidable uncertainty about the rate of real growth one can expect and some unavoidable fuzziness about the rate of inflation deemed appropriate. Yet, this argument makes room for a sensible monetary funding at a level that would need to fluctuate and could not exceed by much the rate of real growth.[44]

The second rationale requires a far less radical reform of the banking system. It received fresh attention as a result of the 2008 financial crisis and the prolonged stagnation that followed in Europe, despite extremely low, sometimes even negative rates of interest. "Quantitative easing for the people," a direct lump-sum payment to all residents of the Eurozone, has been proposed by mainstream economists as a way of stimulating the economy by boosting consumer demand that could work more quickly and more effectively than the usual technique operating through interest rates and private banks.[45] As a tool for kickstarting the economy, however, this egalitarian "helicopter money" can only be of limited duration. Once the injection of purchasing power—in one go or in a short sequence of payments—has done its job, it should be discontinued.[46]

Instead of relying on the creation of money, one could also think of funding basic income by taxing the circulation of money. The "Tobin tax" on international financial transactions can be viewed as a relatively modest version of such a tax and has also occasionally been proposed as a source of funding for a basic income.[47] As conceived by James Tobin, its main aim was not to generate revenues but to reduce the volatility of financial markets by discouraging speculative transactions. Even very low tax rates would generate a sharp contraction of the tax base. Hence, the yield of a Tobin tax is bound to remain modest. Moreover, for obvious reasons, it can only be introduced at an international level.[48]

However, one could also think of a "super-Tobin tax," a micro-tax on every single electronic money transfer, even from one's own current account to one's savings account. In the debate that preceded the 2016 Swiss referendum on basic income (see chapter 7), a proposal for funding it in this way, at least in the longer term, was seriously discussed.[49] Such a tax has been repeatedly and independently proposed before, including in connection with basic income.[50] It would admittedly require reducing large non-electronic payments to a marginal role—for example, by no longer printing paper money or by giving no legal protection to transactions in paper money, whether domestic or foreign. But it would have the advantage of being pretty painless: just a tiny fee collected automatically from every money transfer in exchange for the privilege of being able to use such a safe, convenient, and sophisticated payment system. This universal transfer tax and no doubt also other new forms of taxation that will become practicable and reliable as a result of further technical innovation must be explored with an open mind, whether to fund a basic income and other public expenditures or to perform the other functions taxation is meant to serve.

Consumption

In the meantime, the taxation of income in the widest possible sense must remain the main source.[51] However, this taxation could operate at the time and place at which the income is spent rather than at the time and place at which it is earned. The main objective difference between an income tax and a consumption tax is obviously that the part of a person's income that is being saved escapes the latter, but not the former. But there is also a subjective difference: an income tax is spontaneously perceived as taking from us part of what we made, whereas a consumption tax is perceived as inflating the price to us of what others made. There are two main ways in which a consumption tax can be implemented.

One is the expenditure tax. It consists of deducting from a person's total income the part that is saved over a given period and taxing the difference.

Tax schemes of this sort have been justified by a concern to foster investment and growth but also, at least if made progressive, by a concern for limiting luxury consumption.[52] This is the sort of tax scheme James Meade proposed for the funding of part of the social dividend in his *Agathotopia*.[53] Implementing it requires a sufficiently sharp division between consumption and saving. What is the status of consumer durables, of the house one lives in, of a flat one occasionally rents out? What about gifts in kind or in cash? Where exactly the line is drawn will depend on the specific reason one has for deviating from income as the tax base. But once the distinction is made, any tax profile can in principle be chosen. Although high earners save a higher proportion of their income, they may still pay a higher proportion of their total income in expenditure tax if the tax profile is sufficiently progressive.

Second, a consumption tax can take the form of a sales tax, of which the European Value Added Tax (VAT) is one form. In all forms of sales tax, the ultimate consumer pays a tax at some given percentage (that can in principle exceed 100 percent, which an income or expenditure tax could not do) over and above the price fixed by the seller. With the ordinary sales tax, sellers transfer the whole of this tax to the government. With the VAT, sellers deduct from the taxes levied through their sales the taxes they paid on purchasing the goods and services they need for their business. Only the value added is taxed. Unlike an income or expenditure tax, a sales tax—whether VAT or not—applies to what is produced abroad as well as at home, while exempting what is exported. Like a linear expenditure tax, a sales tax will tend to tax the incomes of high earners at a lower rate, owing to their saving a higher proportion of their income. As purchases are many and scattered, the regressiveness of the tax profile is far trickier to avoid with a sales tax than with an expenditure tax. One can try to do so by applying different rates to basic goods and to luxury goods. But transnational mobility makes the purchase of many luxury goods—jewels, works of art, fancy holidays—highly responsive to such differences in tax rates.

The idea of a (very modest) basic income not only funded by a sales tax but as a natural correlate of it, irrespective of the latter's main purpose, has come up in the United States from a rather unexpected side. While defending a (proportional) "fair tax" on consumption, Mike Huckabee, in his 2008 campaign to become the Republican presidential candidate, also advocated an unconditional transfer to all residents. His so-called "prebate" was meant to prevent poor people from being further impoverished through taxation. It is fixed at the level of the poverty threshold multiplied by the rate of the consumption tax, and thereby provides an analog to exempting from the personal income tax the income bracket below the poverty threshold. For example, with a poverty threshold at $1,000 per person per month and a consumption tax of 20 percent, a basic income of $200 a month (about 5 percent of GDP per capita at the time) would provide this guarantee.[54]

In the European basic-income discussion, proposals to use VAT as the main source of funding have been playing a prominent role since the 1990s.[55] There are specific reasons for using it if a basic income were ever to be implemented at the level of the European Union or the Eurozone as a whole (see chapter 8). But even at the national level, several influential basic-income advocates have forcefully recommended using the VAT. For example, the political party set up in the late 1990s by Roland Duchâtelet, a Belgian ICT industrialist (see chapter 7), proposed abolishing the wage-based social security contributions and keeping the personal income tax only for high incomes, while raising the rate of VAT from 20 percent to 50 percent in order to fund an unconditional basic income of about 500 euros (23 percent of Belgium's GDP per capita at the time).[56] Similarly, Götz Werner, CEO of a large German drugstore chain and Germany's most flamboyant basic income advocate (see chapter 7), has been proposing since 2005 a VAT-funded basic income of 1,000 euros (about 35 percent of Germany's GDP per capita at the time).[57] Under Werner's influence, VAT was also the main source of funding proposed by the initiators of the 2016 Swiss referendum on basic income (see chapter 7).[58] In most proposals, it is suggested that luxury goods should face higher VAT rates, in order to make the tax profile more progressive.

Whether or not VAT can be made much more progressive in this way, it should not be dismissed too easily as an alternative to the income (or expenditure) tax on the grounds that the latter can be more redistributive. In many OECD countries, where top rates of income tax have tended to fall since the late 1970s, affluent taxpayers enjoy the benefit of deductions, exemptions, tax breaks, discounts, loopholes, the separate taxation of capital income, tax optimization, and sheer evasion, that make its superiority, as regards progressivity, increasingly questionable.[59] By catching in undifferentiated fashion the bulk of consumption out of any sort of income, as opposed to mostly labor income, VAT may under some circumstances prove a no more regressive and a more robust source of funding for a basic income both in a developed and in a less developed context.[60]

Those favoring VAT to fund a basic income sometimes argue that compared to taxing income, taxing consumption will reduce the cost of labor and preserve work incentives. But this is largely due to a short-term illusion. Raising a consumption tax will tend to boost prices and thereby reduce real wages. Why would the relative scarcities and bargaining powers that boost the cost of labor if workers' incomes are taxed more not also operate as a result of a higher taxation of their consumption? Why would the supply of labor be affected by a decline in marginal real wages if caused by lower post-tax wages and not if caused by higher prices? If there is a systematic difference in impact on the cost of labor and work incentives between funding through VAT and funding through income tax, therefore, it can only be to the extent that VAT manages de facto to capture a broader spectrum of incomes at the point of spending than income tax does at the point of earning.[61] There is no fundamental reason for rejecting a VAT or another form of sales tax as a way of funding a basic income, but no fundamental reason for adopting it, either. But VAT can have pragmatic advantages in circumstances in which an income tax is harder to implement or does not work well.

We'll offer a final word on the relevance for basic income of the way in which taxes can be modulated in order to encourage or discourage consumption—and thereby production—in certain directions. One rationale has to do with health, typically when alcohol and tobacco are being taxed more than other commodities either for paternalistic reasons or in order to reduce the burden on collectively funded health care. The other main rationale consists of internalizing environmental externalities and protecting the interests of future generations. For example, the use of fossil fuels can be taxed because of the local pollution they generate—in addition to their contribution to the risk of climate change discussed above. Or the use of private cars, whether or not they use fossil fuels, can be taxed because of the noise they make, the congestion they generate, the dangers they cause, or the public spaces they clutter. Or nonrenewable energy in all its forms can be taxed in order to help conserve it for future generations. These various types of ecotaxes make sense independently of the revenues they yield, but they are sometimes also proposed as appropriate sources for funding a basic income.[62]

There is no fundamental reason that they should be earmarked for this use. But there is often a good reason to link the two. At the time they are introduced, such ecotaxes generate an upward pressure on the prices of the goods immediately concerned and of all other goods and services whose production requires them. If one wishes to compensate for the effect of this rise on the standard of living while preserving the intended incentive, using the proceeds to fund a basic income is an obvious option, as it overcompensates small consumers and undercompensates big ones. The argument is analogous to the one that led to the Iranian policy discussed earlier, but in the Iranian case the compensation was needed because of a rise in the price of a collectively owned asset—domestically extracted oil—whereas here it is needed because of the introduction of a tax that is meant to reduce negative externalities. In both cases, this source of funding is fragile, but for different reasons: the depletion of the country's nonrenewable natural resources in one case, success in changing consumption so as to reduce negative externalities in the other.

What should be retained from this quick gallop through alternative funding sources by people worried about the high rates required by a generous basic income if funded entirely by the income tax? First, that there are plenty of other options, and many of them could help, even a great deal under some specific circumstances—in some cases possibly reducing to little or nothing the upward adjustment of the marginal taxation of labor. But also, second, that none of these alternative sources offers a panacea, or any robust assurance that a generous basic income is economically sustainable, or any reason to believe that, in the short run at any rate, we can dispense with the income tax. It is therefore of great importance to do something else: explore the various ways in which one could cautiously move forward, and discuss their respective merits. This is the mission of the remaining sections of this chapter.

Categorical Basic Income

A first possibility consists of starting with a basic income restricted to some categories of the population. The most obvious restrictions of this sort relate to age. Indeed, there are places in which basic incomes for the young and for the old are already in place.

First, many countries have implemented a universal child-benefit system—that is, a basic income for minors paid to one of their parents, usually their mother, sometimes without any condition apart from permanent residence, sometimes with some condition of school attendance, sometimes also with a differentiation according to the rank of the child or with a top-up for poorer or single-parent families. Many European countries have such a universal child-benefit system. In 2012, the republic of Mongolia became the first developing country to join the club.[63] Universal child-benefit schemes often evolved out of social-insurance schemes funded by employers' social contributions: they were a way for employers to secure an adequate income for all their workers' families without needing to pay to all their workers, including those without families, a wage sufficient for a large family. They possess the advantages of universality explained in our general argument for this feature of an unconditional basic income: higher rate of take-up, absence of stigmatization, and no poverty trap. In addition, compared to means-tested child benefits, they have the advantage of organizing a broader solidarity between those who take on the job of bringing up the next generation and those who do not, and they also avoid creating a household trap for secondary earners in households with children, mostly mothers. With a means-tested child-benefit system, mothers who decide to work not only may face a high marginal tax rate (if the household income is taxed as a whole) but, in addition, they will see their child benefits reduced or even scrapped, causing them to face more dissuasive effective marginal tax rates than any other category. Nonetheless, once funded by general taxation rather than social contributions—a logical step once all children are covered, not just the children of waged workers—universal child benefits have often become the target of short-sighted proposals to means-test them, some of them successful and others defeated or later reversed.[64]

At the other end of the age spectrum, a universal basic pension was already advocated by Thomas Paine (see chapter 4). In the 1930s, at about the same time as Huey Long's "Share our Wealth" movement, Francis Everett Townsend, a Californian doctor, proposed the introduction of a basic pension for all Americans over sixty, funded by a sales tax. His movement gathered ten million members under the banner "Age for Leisure, Youth for Work," but declined after Roosevelt's 1935 Social Security Act, which created a means-tested, old-age assistance program.[65] In 1938, New Zealand was the first country to introduce a noncontributory and non-means-tested pension scheme for the elderly. Called the "New Zealand Superannuation," it became subjected to a means-test in 1985 but was made universal again in 1998. In the 1940s and 1950s, such basic pensions were also introduced in Denmark, Finland, Sweden, and the Netherlands, but only the latter's has been maintained until today (at a high level of about 30 percent of GDP per capita in 2015). In Denmark, the 1 percent top earners are no longer entitled to it. In New Zealand and the Netherlands, the entitlement to the basic pension is dependent upon one's length of residency, but payments are not restricted to people living in the country after 65.[66] Several developing countries also have implemented universal basic pensions. For example, Namibia has had one since 1992 for every permanent resident older than sixty (at about 12 percent of GDP per capita in 2014), and Bolivia introduced an equally unconditional *Renta Dignidad* in 2008 (at about 15 percent of GDP per capita in 2014). Relative to means-tested schemes, the advantages of a universal basic pension are the general advantages of universality mentioned in chapter 1: a higher rate of take-up, the absence of stigmatization, and the reduction of a poverty trap which, in this case, takes more the form of a disincentive to save and accumulate pension rights than that of a disincentive to work. Nonetheless, as in the case of child benefits, some attempts to return to a means-tested system have been successful.[67]

A universal child benefit and a universal basic pension are both most welcome from our point of view. Developing them outside of the social insurance system is a way of providing basic social protection, and the freedom associated with it, beyond the set of people who paid social security contributions to a sufficient extent. Moreover, both the fact that universal child benefits come with no strings attached (other than having children and looking after them) and the fact that the basic pension is independent of past career make it easier for people to reduce their working time when they need to and thereby encourage the sharing of paid employment. In these ways, the effects of universal child benefits and basic pensions converge with those aimed at by an unconditional basic income. Both therefore offer, in many contexts, promising ways of moving forward.

This cannot be said about other ways of introducing a basic income for some subset of the population. For example, one might think of gradually generalizing the entitlement to the basic income beyond the children and the elderly by first extending it to young adults.[68] On a first interpretation, the basic income would be extended cohort by cohort (rather than age group by age group). It would then have the obvious consequence of creating blatant unfairness between cohorts, including in terms of the bargaining power they would enjoy throughout their lives on the labor market. On a second interpretation, the basic income would be granted at any given time, to a particular age group (say, people aged 18 to 21), but not to these same people from the moment they reach the age of 23. This is, in effect, what Bruce Ackerman and Anne Alstott (1999) are proposing with the four $20,000 annual installments of their stakeholder grant.[69] And it also converges with the proposal to generalize to all youngsters the universal student grant currently paid in some countries to those registered as full-time students, thereby avoiding the perverse redistribution in favor of young people from advantaged backgrounds, overrepresented in higher education.[70] Such schemes would not be as structurally unfair as those operating with cohorts. But they could reinforce the obsolete idea that higher education should be concentrated in the early years of adulthood rather than take the form of lifelong learning. And there are, moreover, strong reasons to doubt the wisdom of granting young adults an ephemeral bargaining power that they will lose later in their lives.

Rather than with age categories, some have also proposed to introduce a basic income starting with some occupational categories. A basic income for farmers has been particularly popular among people wanting to get rid of the perversities of the price subsidies that, for a long time, formed the bulk of the European Union's agricultural policy.[71] And between 2005 and 2012, a scheme that could be regarded as a real basic income for artists was in place in the Netherlands.[72] There is an obvious problem with any such categorical scheme. Once significant financial consequences are linked to belonging to such categories, relying on them is bound to unleash bitter disputes about who would qualify as a farmer or as an artist—about how exactly the relevant activity is to be defined, about how full-time the activity needs to be exercised, and so forth—and is more likely to lead to a backlash than to a gradual generalization. Even less attractive would be a restriction to the permanent residents who possess citizenship of the country concerned. Not only would this not cheapen the scheme by very much in most countries, it would also create a labor market in which all workers would see their net wages reduced in order to fund a basic protection which only some would enjoy.

Consequently, as regards the population of working age, no permanent categorical restriction holds much promise. Perhaps the closest to it that could be justified is illustrated by a feature of Brazil's *Bolsa Familia* program (see chapter 3) that seems at first glance to be a defect in its implementation but that makes it more similar to a basic income than other means-tested schemes. Given the impossibility of enforcing an ongoing means test at reasonable cost, once a household is registered in the program because it is deemed to satisfy the income condition, it seems common practice that the administration does not bother to monitor its income for the following six years. Hence, beneficiaries can top up the benefit with additional earnings without limit until the next check. The introduction of a genuine basic income for all Brazilians would require a greater formalization of the economy and a corresponding increase in the Brazilian government's capacity to tax incomes fairly and efficiently. In the meantime, this six-year-at-a-time basic income for the poor can be regarded in a broad sense as a categorical basic income, though one that could not survive long with a more generous level of transfer (the maximum amount of the benefit per person in 2015 was about $13 or 2 percent of Brazil's GDP per capita) or in a context in which a reliable means test is less problematic.[73]

Household Basic Income and Tax Surcharge

So, how might we move cautiously in the direction of a generous basic income for the whole population of working age without triggering fears about the effects of sharply increased marginal rates of income taxation, in the likely event that other forms of funding would only be of marginal help, at least in the short run, or would raise analogous problems? Note that the fears, as spelled out above, do not derive from the freedom from obligation of basic income or its universality in the sense of being paid upfront, but from its being at the same time strictly individual and universal in the sense that incomes from another sources can top it up. These fears therefore affect a generous individual negative income tax just as much as an individual basic income, and can be addressed through three strategies: compromising on individuality, compromising on universality (in the sense indicated), and compromising on generosity.

The first option is best viewed as starting from existing means-tested benefit schemes. As a result of noticing the trap effects of such schemes, several countries reformed them so as to create the possibility of combining benefits and earnings without losing in benefits whatever was gained in earnings. This happened, for instance, in the 2009 reform of the French minimum-income scheme. The former RMI (*revenu minimum d'insertion* or minimum integration income), created in 1988, gave way to the RSA (*revenu de solidarité active* or active solidarity income), which lowered the effective marginal tax rate from 100 percent to 38 percent.[74] The coherence of the tax-and-transfer system requires, however, that, with the same earnings, the ordinary taxpayer and the RSA recipient should not end up with different net incomes. This has been gradually pushing the French minimum-income system in the direction of a simpler and more legible negative income tax applying to all households, as recommended to France's socialist government in two reports it commissioned, one by France Stratégie, France's national planning bureau, the other by the socialist member of the National Assembly Christophe Sirugue.[75]

Similarly, in November 2010, the United Kingdom's conservative government announced the gradual implementation—starting in 2013 and expected to be fully implemented in 2017—of a type of household-based negative income tax called the "universal credit," as recommended by the Centre for Social Justice, a think tank set up by the Conservative minister Ian Duncan-Smith. The objective is to merge several tax credits and cash transfers (including the Jobseeker's Allowance, UK's minimum-income scheme) into a new scheme aimed at giving more financial incentives to low-income people to move into the labor market.[76]

Once the integration with the tax system is completed, what we are getting is a household-based negative-income-tax scheme, restricted to those working or willing to work. However, with financial incentives to work in place, this condition—a willingness to work whose monitoring is often intrusive, costly, and ineffective—could arguably be relaxed. The payment would still not be made upfront to all households, but the profile of post-tax-and-transfer distribution would be the same as with a household-based basic income. Taking the household rather than the individual as the relevant unit makes it possible to take account of economies of scale. A universal income that is lower per capita for the members of a couple than for single people can therefore achieve a given level of poverty reduction at a considerably lower cost than with an individual basic income. And given that existing minimum-income schemes tend to be household-based, it needs milder increases in tax rates in order to replace them without making their beneficiaries worse off. However, taking the household as the relevant unit would obviously come at the expense of losing the simplicity and other important advantages linked to the individual nature of a genuine basic income (see chapter 1).

It is therefore worth turning to a second option: sticking to the strictly individual nature of the basic income or of the refundable tax credit (in the case of a negative income tax) while conceding a very high rate of clawback on this individual benefit—that is, a regressive income tax profile. This is, for example, the option advocated by James Meade in his *Agathotopia:* a "tax surcharge" on the lower bracket of everyone's income.[77] The underlying assumption is that, paradoxically, it is better for the poor to be taxed at a higher rate than the rich—or at least the less poor. More precisely, if one wishes to sustainably maximize the lowest income, the tax profile must be regressive

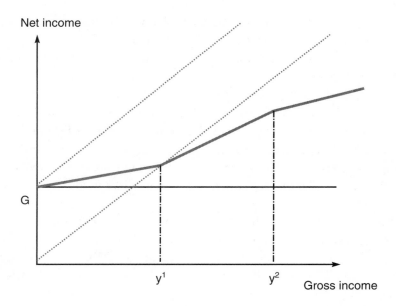

Net income

G

y¹   y²

Gross income

Figure 6.2 Net income with a basic income and a high rate of clawback

In this illustration of the tax surcharge, 75 percent of any additional income is clawed back up to the breakeven level of gross income y^1.

Because this high rate applies to a large portion of the incomes of all taxpayers, it is possible, for a given budget target, to keep the marginal rate far lower for gross incomes between y^1 and y^2.

Beyond y^2, progressivity can hit again.

over the lowest part of the distribution of earnings. The argument is quite simple.[78] If you want to collect a large amount of taxes in a sustainable way, it is best to tax at a high rate income brackets that are densely populated—all taxpayers have part of their income in that bracket—but in which few people have their marginal income. It is not the tax rate applying to this bracket that determines how much most people will gain or lose by working a bit more or a bit less. This reasoning does not exclude making the higher range of the tax profile progressive—that is, taxing some higher brackets at a higher rate than some lower ones. But it motivates a strong presumption in favor of a high effective rate of taxation on the lowest income brackets (see Figure 6.2).

Compared to a linear profile, this regressive profile has the disadvantage of making automatic taxation at source less straightforward. Assuming individual taxation, it also discourages employment sharing within the household: if the lower bracket is more heavily taxed than the next one, concentrating employment in one person makes more economic sense. Above all, it subjects to an explicit confiscatory rate a wide range of low incomes. True, relative to the implicit 100 percent rate implied by strictly income-tested schemes, a marginal tax rate of, say, 75 percent, should be less dissuasive and if the scheme is administered in the form of a basic income paid upfront rather than as a refundable tax credit, the certainty of the floor should further help remove the unemployment trap (see chapters 1 and 2). Still, a permanent and explicit strongly regressive income tax schedule is a serious handicap for this second option.

Partial Basic Income

There is a third option, which has our preference. It preserves the simplicity of an individual basic income and avoids the unattractive regressive tax profile but it settles, for the time being, for what is sometimes called a partial basic income—that is, one that makes no claim to being sufficient to live on if one lives alone. Such a proposal was seriously considered by the Meade Committee on taxation in the United Kingdom in the late 1970s. And it was a central piece in the best scenario for the future of social protection in a report published in 1985 at the request of the Dutch government (see chapter 4). If it is introduced in a context in which a conditional minimum-income scheme is in place, it could for example be pitched at half the income level granted to a couple, with conditional public assistance maintained as a top-up whenever it is required to prevent its recipients from losing out, which would be the case for all one-adult households.[79] A genuine partial basic income would take the form of an individual upfront payment to each adult, but a strictly individual refundable tax credit would already be a step in this direction.[80]

As a measure to be taken right now, such a partial basic income has two main advantages over a "full" one. First, it avoids or at least softens considerably the dilemma illustrated above between, on the one hand, keeping a high rate of clawback on low incomes and thereby a deep poverty trap, and on the other, a sharp increase in the marginal tax rates on a wide range of earnings, with the largely unpredictable effects this would trigger on the labor market.

Second, it avoids creating sudden havoc in the distribution of income: given its strictly individual nature, a "full" basic income and its funding could not avoid making cohabiting adults better off at the expense of worsening the financial situation of households with just one adult. These two advantages are coupled with one disadvantage: if some poor households are not to see their situation significantly worsened, some substantial complement will need to be kept in the form of conditional public assistance.

Needless to say, it is important that the partial basic income should be high enough to make a real difference. Its introduction will not mean a *tabula rasa*. Various conditions would still need to be satisfied and checked for those claiming a benefit on top of their basic income. But there would be far less need for this, partly because the partial basic income would replace all benefits and tax reductions of lesser amounts and partly because of the significant reduction of the depth of the unemployment trap, and possibly even its abolition for households with more than one adult. Most of the people still needing top-ups would be people living alone and therefore on average more in need of attention or guidance by social workers than those living in larger households. It is not only important that the level of the partial basic income be high enough to allow a significant simplification of the benefit system. It is even more important that it be sufficient to produce the emancipatory consequences claimed for it in chapter 1. For there to be a significant increase in the real freedom to say yes or no to particular occupations, it is not necessary that the unconditional income be sufficient to live decently for the whole of one's life, even as a single person in an urban context. A basic income that falls far short of this amount still makes it possible to take a job with lower or less certain earnings, to reduce working time, to acquire further training or education, or to spend more time looking for the right job, all of this further facilitated for many by savings and sharings, loans, and informal solidarity.

In this light, it is important that basic income advocates not waste too much time on the question of what they would regard as a fully adequate level of basic income. Trying to jump in one go to a "full" basic income, however precisely defined, would anyway be irresponsible. There is a difference between, on the one hand, the next step on which we need to get broad agreement in light of its likely consequences and, on the other, the level of basic income that makes most sense as a horizon, a mobilizing utopia, an ultimate goal. Of far greater immediate importance than a quantitative specification of this ultimate goal is the question of what would be suppressed and what kept when a partial basic income gets introduced. Depending on how it is financed and on the other measures included in the reform package, a lower level of basic income can markedly improve the situation of the worst off, while a higher level can worsen it.

Our own conviction is that in many contexts this third option—a partial basic income—offers the most promising way forward, with variations from country to country depending on the structure and size of their tax and transfer system and on political opportunities (see chapter 7). We would echo the advice uttered by the earliest academic advocates of basic income. G. D. H. Cole states: "If it were decided to institute a policy of 'social dividends' payable of right to all citizens as their share in the common heritage, quite apart from the rewards accruing to them from their individual labour, it would no doubt be necessary to begin on a small scale—with payments that would not suddenly upset the whole structure of incomes derived from the various forms of productive service. But the system, once instituted, could be extended progressively."[81]

And James Meade puts it this way: "A social dividend can be started at a very moderate scale financed out of the abolition of existing personal allowances under the income tax, by the reduction of other social benefits, and by some moderate increases of tax rates supplemented at some stage with an element of special levy on the first slice of other income. If the journey is taken at a gentle pace, one can hope ultimately to reach Agathotopian conditions without too much strain on the way."[82]

In many places, even this partial basic income will not be the next feasible step to take. Many other moves can be welcomed as worthwhile progress in the right direction: the introduction of a conditional minimum-income scheme in countries where none exists, the universalization of child benefits and basic pensions, the generalization of refundable tax credits, the development of in-work benefits as a complement to benefits restricted to the involuntarily unemployed, and the introduction of subsidies to voluntary unemployment in the form of benefits for career interruption or working-time reduction. The more of these features are in place, the less of a jump into the unknown the introduction of a basic income will be.

Does this cautious gradual approach suffice to assuage skepticism stemming from the uncertainty that surrounds the consequences of implementing a basic income?[83] In his vigorous critique of the basic-income proposal, Jon Elster notes that "the state of the social sciences is light-years away from allowing us to predict the global net long-term equilibrium effects of major institutional changes, while piecemeal social engineering, through incremental planning or trial-and-error . . . only allows us to estimate local, partial, short-term, or transitional effects."[84]

We agree with this observation, the first part of which was repeatedly paraphrased in our discussion of experiments. However, as Elster recognizes: "A counterargument might run as follows. Very little would be lost by implementing the proposal on a small scale, by a low-level guaranteed income. If it turns out that it has the predicted effect, one could then increase the guaranteed income up to the point, if any, where further increases begin to have adverse effects. . . . In other words, if there is nothing to lose and possibly something to gain, why not give it a chance?"[85]

This is, in effect, what we are proposing. If experiments cannot teach us much about the consequences of a jump to a generous unconditional basic income, let us start with a modest one. This is, after all, what was done in the case of the other two models of social protection. The public-assistance schemes that currently exist in some European countries and even in North American are lavish compared to those first introduced in Flemish cities at the beginning of the sixteenth century, and today's social insurance benefits for the retired ("social security" in the American sense) are sumptuous compared to Bismarck's pioneering old-age pension system. (See chapter 3.) Bismarck did not pick a random sample of workers to check whether they would work less hard or save less than a control group as a result of paying social security contributions and being promised a state pension. Instead, he made industrial workers pay 2 percent of their wages into a fund and entitled them, if they had contributed for at least thirty years, to a pension that could be as low as 19 percent of their wage.[86] Not randomized experiments, but real-life experimentation with initially modest levels for whole municipalities (in the case of public assistance) or whole countries (in the case of social insurance) generated the confidence required to move to more ambitious levels.

Could this be enough to overcome Elster's reticence? It could not. Given the "abundance of actual or potential proposals of equal plausibility," such real-life experiments "are useful, indeed necessary, if the underlying idea is widely held to be valid; they are pointless if the goal is simply to provide inputs to some social analogue of natural selection. Society cannot underwrite the pet ideas of each and every enthusiast who offers a panacea for our problems."[87] The objection to moving forward in the way suggested is therefore not of an economic nature. It is rather rooted in skepticism about the potential political support for the proposal: "The alleged effects are surrounded by massive uncertainty. They 'could' come about, in some suitably abstract sense, but not in a sense that would motivate anyone to political action."[88]

This takes us to the subject of the next chapter.

7

Politically Achievable? Civil Society, Parties, and the Back Door

IS A SUBSTANTIAL BASIC INCOME of, say, 25 percent of GDP per capita affordable? The previous chapter should have made us confident enough that it is, or at least that a partial basic income could responsibly be implemented that would make a real difference while paving the way for subsequent increases in its level. But economic sustainability does not spell political feasibility. True, in many countries, the establishment of a basic income would simply be a further step following on previous achievements—whether those were general means-tested minimum-income schemes, or universal schemes in kind (education and health care), or age-specific schemes (child benefits and retirement pensions)—most of which proved politically robust.[1] Nonetheless, not a single country so far has even tried to provide basic security to its citizens by means of an unconditional basic income.

Unlike economic sustainability, political feasibility must not be treated as a parameter to be taken as a given. It is something that can be shaped by opinion and is indeed our job to help shape.[2] Political feasibility no doubt has something to do with what some call class struggle, and others ascribe to the median voter's self-interest. However, as Thomas Piketty writes, "the history of inequality is shaped by the way economic, social, and political actors view what is just and what is not, as well as by the relative power of those actors and the collective choices that result."[3] The contours of the politically feasible are set by our values no less than by our interests; by our moral attractions and repulsions no less than by the balance of power; by arguments about what is right no less than by calculations of what would best satisfy our greed. If we as authors of this book did not think so, we would not have bothered to write it. This is why political feasibility is intimately linked to ethical justifiability. Indeed, apart from the uncertainty of the effects attributed to the proposal, the reason that Jon Elster believes that basic income "completely lacks the potential for being rooted in a social movement" is precisely that it is ethically objectionable. "Moreover," he writes, "the proposal goes against a widely accepted notion of justice: it is unfair for able-bodied people to live off the labor of others. Most workers would, correctly in my opinion, see the proposal as a recipe for exploitation of the industrious by the lazy."[4]

In chapter 1, and more explicitly in chapter 5, we have countered this claim by arguing for an unconditional basic income as a key component of a free *and* just society. Its impact on the political feasibility of a basic income is nonetheless so great that we shall need to return to it. Before doing so, we want to give a broad overview of the past and present state of public support for basic income and opposition to it; to reflect on the underlying causes; and to explore the resources available in various social and political currents for generating support for the idea.

Public Opinion

One way of assessing the current degree of support for and opposition to basic income consists of consulting the outcomes of opinion polls. Some of these investigate the role played by notions of desert and personal responsibility in attitudes toward welfare schemes; they consistently confirm that guaranteed minimum schemes and unemployment insurance schemes subjected to a willingness-to-work condition enjoy greater popular support than schemes that impose no such condition.[5] However, attitudes towards basic income itself have also been investigated more or less extensively in a number of countries.[6] The results of all surveys must be treated with the usual prudence, owing to the effects of the specific phrasing and framing of the question. This remark applies in particular to surveys about the idea of an unconditional basic income, which is likely to be unfamiliar to the bulk of the respondents and therefore likely to be confused with related ideas. Moreover, respondents are asked to compare a basic income with the status quo as it is or as they perceive it at the time of the survey, which obviously varies greatly from country to country.

A number of surveys were conducted in Europe's Nordic countries, where the welfare state is on the whole more universalistic than elsewhere and where the notion of basic income has some currency. Thus, a poll conducted in Denmark in 1994 found that 40 percent of respondents saw basic income as a "good idea." Similarly, a 2002 Gallup poll conducted in Finland found that 63 percent of Finns thought "a system that would automatically guarantee a certain basic income to all permanent residents" was a "good idea." In the same year, the same question was put to a representative sample of Swedish respondents, and 46 percent of them expressed support for the idea. In Norway, in response to a 2003 survey, two-thirds of a representative sample expressed sympathy for the idea.[7]

More recent surveys in North America and France yielded contrasting outcomes. In a national poll about "government welfare" conducted in August 2011, a representative sample of a thousand likely US voters was asked to respond to this proposition: "The idea would be to provide enough money for everyone to enjoy a modest living regardless of whether or not they choose to work. Do you favor or oppose having the federal government provide every single American with a basic income grant?" Fully 82 percent opposed the idea, and only 11 percent favored it. Broken down by political party lines, 19 percent of likely Democrat voters versus 3 percent of Republicans were in favor. In 2013, a similar survey was conducted with a representative sample of Canadians who were asked, more vaguely, whether they would favor or oppose a "guaranteed annual income policy for Canadians, to replace the current economic assistance programs." Forty-six percent turned out to be at least "somewhat in favor."[8]

The support expressed for basic income was even stronger in a survey conducted in France in 2015, when a representative sample was asked: "Are you in favor of the introduction of a basic income guaranteed to all citizens that would replace most existing benefits?" Sixty percent of the respondents turned out to be in favor (16 percent among them completely) and 40 percent not in favor (19 percent among them not at all). Among Green and far-left voters, nearly 80 percent were in favor; among supporters of the far-right National Front, 51 percent were. If the phrases "whether or not they choose to work" and "which would replace most existing benefits" had been swapped, one can safely conjecture that the gap between American and French public opinion would have looked less wide.[9]

Both phrases were used in the largest opinion poll on basic income to date, a survey conducted in April 2016 by Berlin-based Dalia Research. A representative sample of ten thousand Europeans across twenty-eight countries (and in twenty-one languages) was asked about the proposal of an "income unconditionally paid by the government to every individual regardless of whether they work and irrespective of any other sources of income." The characterization of the proposal also mentioned that the basic income would replace "other social security payments" and would be "high enough to cover all basic needs." Nearly two-thirds (64 percent) of respondents said they would vote yes "if there were a referendum on introducing basic income today." Only 24 percent rejected the idea, while 12 percent said they "would not vote."[10] The results of this survey and of the others mentioned above are not irrelevant to assessing the political prospects of an unconditional basic income in a specific country at a specific point in time. But they are no more than snapshots of the opinions of a public that perhaps understood the idea but had scarcely thought about it.

There is one major exception to this rule: the survey conducted with a representative sample of the Swiss population in the two weeks that followed the June 2016 national referendum about an unconditional basic income. The text submitted to the vote did not specify an amount, but the very high figure of 2,500 Swiss Francs (about the same in dollars) per adult that was mentioned by the initiators is the one that was present throughout the public debate. The overall result of the referendum was 23.1 percent in favor and 76.9 percent against. The post-referendum survey revealed that support was by far the weakest (at just 10 percent) among the oldest group, those over age seventy—which was also the group with the highest rate of voting turnout. But support by the youngest group (up to age thirty) was also slightly below the average (at 22 percent). There was no significant difference by income level, some difference by gender (24 percent of women versus 21.5 percent of men expressed support), and larger differences between city dwellers (32 percent) and rural residents (19 percent), and among professional categories, with the most favorably disposed being the self-employed (36 percent). Asked why they voted as they did, the reason given most often by "yes" voters was their desire to promote the discussion of what they thought was a good idea. The most frequent reason given by "no" voters was their belief that such a basic income could not be financed.[11]

Thanks to the public debate that precedes it, a national referendum creates a great opportunity to conduct a survey with a particularly well-informed public opinion. But this possibility exists only in very few places and cannot arise very often, and it is moreover limited to the particular version of the idea chosen by the initiators of the referendum. In order to assess public receptiveness to basic-income proposals, it is therefore generally more instructive to turn to whatever explicit discussion of the proposal can be found in various components of civil society and the main political families.

Labor Unions

Labor unions—that is, the organizations of the formal sector's waged workers—have been at the forefront of countless progressive fights and played key roles in major achievements. Can they, and will they, also play a major role in the path leading up to a basic income? Looking back at most labor union reactions to the earliest basic-income-like proposals, this does not look likely. When, in 1943, Juliet Rhys-Williams proposed a universal benefit (subjected to willingness to work) for the United Kingdom, it was immediately pointed out that "a scheme which demolished the argument for a family wage was unlikely to be popular with the trade unions." And when the scheme was considered in 1951 by a Royal Commission on Taxation of Profits and Income, the Trade Union Confederation (TUC) published a memorandum criticizing the notion of a basic income paid "irrespective of need," and reasserted its commitment to the social insurance principle, which firmly established workers' rights to social benefits.[12]

A couple of decades later, the American Federation of Labor–Congress of Industrial Organizations (AFL–CIO) had to take a position on President Richard Nixon's 1969 Family Assistance Plan (FAP), which bore some resemblance to a negative-income-tax scheme (see chapter 4). Some of its members regarded it favorably as a possible step towards a more integrated safety net. Yet the AFL–CIO gave priority to a higher minimum wage over the supplementation of low wages by subsidies from the government. "Labor was not stirred by the idea of a guaranteed minimum income," Daniel Patrick Moynihan would later recall. "Still it did not oppose FAP, either in public or in the committee rooms of the Congress, where its power was unmatched."[13] In Canada, the labor unions' reaction came later but was more explicit and even more distrustful.[14]

Things looked very different for a while when a public debate surfaced in Europe in the early 1980s, starting in the Netherlands, this time focused on a genuine basic-income proposal. The Dutch debate was spearheaded from the start by a labor union, the Voedingsbond FNV (Food Union), a component of the country's main labor-union federation. This union was headed from 1984 to 1992 by a woman, Greetje Lubbi, and counted among its members an exceptionally high proportion of women, low-paid workers, and part-time workers. With the Dutch unemployment rate in double digits, the union's leaders advocated a substantial basic income coupled with a sharp reduction in working hours. They also questioned the work ethic and the cultural centrality of waged labor, arguing that a basic income would confer social recognition to "those who do unpaid work, have no income and no social status."[15] However, as they conceded later, "it proved difficult to mobilise members on such an abstract and long-term objective as a basic income," quite remote from "the members' more concrete interests that they were experiencing in daily life."[16] As a result, the Food Union's enthusiasm for basic income ran out of steam. It withered away in the early 1990s and never received the support of the leadership of the federation FNV to which it belonged.[17]

In a very different context, the Congress of South African Trade Unions (COSATU) openly and persistently supported the introduction of a basic income as a measure that would simultaneously advance economic growth, job creation, and the fight against poverty. Informal solidarity in the form of remittances sent by formal-sector workers to their families in the country was a heavy burden for many union members. The implementation of a formal mechanism of solidarity in the form of a basic income would provide a more transparent, more efficient, and less arbitrary redistributive mechanism. Whether for this or other reasons, COSATU officially supported the introduction of a basic income in South Africa. Along with the South African Council of Churches and the South African NGO Coalition (SANGOCO), it founded in 2001 the Basic Income Grant Coalition, pressing for an unconditional basic income of 100 rand per month (about $18 or 8 percent of the country's GDP per capita at the time). In his budget speech of February 2002, Finance Minister Trevor Manuel said the proposal was unaffordable and rejected it as "economic populism." Despite a 2006 endorsement by the minister for social development, Zola Skweyiya, the government of President Thabo Mbeki confirmed its opposition to a basic income and its commitment to a more targeted social-protection system, and COSATU lost interest.[18]

The Dutch food union in the 1980s and COSATU two decades later are not the only cases of official support for basic income by labor unions, but there are not many more. Some unions encouraged reflection on the idea by organizing meetings and publications.[19] Some prominent union leaders advocated the idea in their personal capacities.[20] But the most widespread attitude is one of neglect, sometimes because basic income is viewed as lacking relevance to the immediate future. And in the rare cases in which the idea has been explicitly discussed, it has tended to be energetically rejected.[21]

There is something surprising, prima facie, about this unsympathetic reaction. How could the workers' movement be opposed to a measure that increases workers' bargaining power? An unconditional basic income would not only increase workers' options in and out of employment, and thereby enable them to individually negotiate higher pay or better work conditions; it would also provide a convenient strike fund, and hence a valuable resource for collective action, as workers would keep receiving secure basic incomes while the payment of their wages is interrupted by work stoppage. Strikers would thereby gain ability to face long-lasting resistance from employers.[22] A basic income would also reduce the supply of labor for at least some types of jobs, thereby strengthening the bargaining position of unions as collective actors in the labor market.

Why then do labor unions tend to be unenthusiastic about, indeed often frankly hostile to, a basic income? There are several reasons, unequally present in different contexts and unequally sound.[23] A first one is an occasional confusion between basic income as such and an extreme version of it that entails the abolition of the whole existing transfer system. Such an abolition is strongly resisted by unions for three reasons: it would make some poor households worse off; the social insurance and public assistance systems have specific functions which a basic income could not fulfill; and a large number of welfare-state employees would need to be sacked. As explained earlier, however (in chapters 1 and 6), any sensible basic-income proposal must be viewed as an unconditional floor fully compatible, including in the longer term, with social insurance and public assistance top-ups. Its introduction can and must be calibrated in such a way that, owing to these top-ups, low-income households will not lose out in static terms, while all gain in terms of options open to them. The basic income will not substitute for but rather help social insurance and public assistance better fulfill their specific functions. Consequently, no massive sackings should be feared (or hoped for) in the welfare-state sector. The introduction of a basic income does have the ambition to reduce bureaucratic work thanks to significant simplifications of tax and transfer systems and reduced reliance on conditional benefits. But one can be confident that the gradual implementation of this simpler system will itself be sufficiently complicated that the staff's competence will be needed in the transition period and its trimming will be very gradual.

A second reason for labor unions' lack of enthusiasm is a fear that the introduction of a basic income would trigger a fall in the general wage level, as each household would receive part of its income independent of work. This was, it seems, the main reason behind the American labor movement's reluctance to endorse Nixon's Family Assistance Plan in the 1970s. "Organized labor feared any likely increase in cheap labor stimulated by the removal of work disincentives," as Desmond King writes.[24] It is also evident in the reservations expressed by Michel Jalmain, a national secretary of the CFDT (the French Democratic Confederation of Labor, one of France's main labor unions), that a basic income would amount to subsidizing, at the community's expense, firms that offer precarious and poorly-paid jobs.[25] And it is analogous to what John Maynard Keynes saw as the main reason for the British trade unions' opposition to universal child benefits: "I believe that the trade union movement is actively hostile on the express ground that it fears such allowances would be what I wish them to be, namely, an alternative to higher wages. It would be much better that a man with heavy family burdens to support should receive assistance out of taxation, which is thrown on profits generally, than that an attempt should be made to raise wages paid by his employer to a disproportionate level."[26]

This fear is more serious. But it overlooks two crucial points. First, as explained in chapter 1, the impact of an unconditional basic income on the labor market can be expected to be double-edged. Indeed, it is essential that it should be. Because of its universal nature, a basic income makes some categories of low-paid occupations viable—namely, those that are intrinsically attractive or sufficiently rich in training, while not being viable now because they pay too little or too irregularly. At the same time, because of its being obligation-free, a basic income will make people more reluctant to accept or stick with irksome, training-poor jobs. These will need to pay more to appeal to enough workers. The net effect on the general level of remuneration is therefore necessarily uncertain, while the effect on the average wage of the worst-paid among existing jobs can safely be expected to be positive. Second, a basic income is perfectly compatible with minimum-wage provisions.[27] Such provisions serve various purposes, including the reduction of tax evasion. Much of what justified them before the introduction of a basic income will keep justifying them afterwards. And, as explained in chapter 1, they would not prevent the development of the sort of low-paid employment that the introduction of a basic income aims to encourage. True, one can argue that their level could legitimately be adjusted downward; with a basic income, the same level of disposable income for full-time workers could then be guaranteed with a lower minimum net wage. However, if, as is likely, the basic income is to be funded at least in part by higher taxation of the lower brackets of income (as explained in chapter 6), the pre-tax minimum wage may well need to be maintained to preserve a full-time worker's total net income, basic income included. And then there is no reason for reducing the level of the minimum pre-tax wage, let alone for scrapping it altogether.

A third reason for the unions' resistance, related but distinct, has to do with their role in determining workers' disposable incomes. One aspect of it is just a matter of perception. Obviously, the larger the basic-income component in the total income of a household, the less central the wage component looks. A basic income paid upfront to each member of the household makes the main breadwinner's contribution—and hence the organization to which he or she belongs—look less centrally important to the household in question and to society as a whole. Note that this effect on perception is specific to a genuine basic income and does not affect its negative-income-tax variant: equivalent tax credits show up in higher net wages for breadwinners, especially (but not only) if the negative-income-tax scheme is household-based rather than individual. The net income of the household might be exactly the same—and for the same reason—as under an "equivalent" basic-income scheme, but under a negative income tax there is a bigger proportion that seems to be coming from the remuneration of labor, and hence from what is partly under union control. This is, of course, an illusion—but it is a powerful one and one that union leaders will not find in their interest to expose.

Closely connected to this, but not reducible entirely to perception, is a fourth reason. The wage component of a household's income is negotiated between employer and worker, following a procedure that varies considerably from country to country. Unions derive their bargaining power—which varies greatly, according to the nuisance capacity of the labor-force segment concerned—from the labor they could threaten to withdraw. Social insurance benefits are largely funded out of this wage component and often co-managed by unions. By contrast, a basic income (whether paid upfront or in the guise of a tax credit) is granted by a government to its citizens through a process in which unions are not directly involved—and therefore a process which gives unions less confidence that their members' interests will be properly taken into account. However, this is again to a large extent an illusion, as the tax status of labor income and the (often quite significant) subsidies from general taxation to the funding of social insurance benefits make the incomes that workers owe directly and indirectly to their jobs also highly dependent on democratic decisions.

A fifth reason for labor unions' general lack of enthusiasm for a basic income has to do with their own power. While an unconditional basic income increases the power of workers relative to capitalists, it also increases their power relative to their unions. In case of a prolonged strike, the workers' uninterrupted basic incomes add up to a potential strike fund not only for their union, but for any subset of its members. Collective action may therefore be more difficult for the union leadership to steer. This dispersion of capacity for collective action could sometimes enable a weak subset of workers to defend its legitimate claims. It might also be misused by a subset of relatively privileged workers. In any event, this consequence of the introduction of a basic income is unlikely to be welcomed by union leaders.[28]

Finally, probably the most general and fundamental reason for labor unions' lack of enthusiasm is simply that they believe the introduction of a basic income would not be in the best interest of their core membership, often largely made up of full-time, male workers with stable contracts and decent pay and hence far from representative of the whole working population. In an immediate financial sense, many of these workers are unlikely to gain from a basic income reform, and the best-paid among them are likely to become financially worse off, thanks to the tax adjustments required, especially if the basic income is strictly individual, its level is substantial, and little can be done to get more out of capital income. By contrast, the workers who stand to gain most immediately from a basic income tend not to be unionized. In the United States, for instance, the rate of unionization among full-time workers in 2014 is more than twice that of part-time workers, and the median earnings of non-unionized workers are less than 80 percent of union members' median earnings.[29]

Keynes saw it as "a great misfortune that the self-conscious efforts of the working class to better themselves should be so much concentrated on the effort to raise wages, even to the point of being suspicious, as I fancy the trade unions are, of alternative methods of bettering conditions."[30] Whichever of the factors listed above is most responsible for unions' lack of interest in basic income, there are good grounds to agree with him. But there are also good grounds to believe that labor unions can overcome this misfortune.

Unions can be expected to develop more sympathy for basic income if progress is made along four lines. First, unions must gain enough trust that the redistributive arm of democratic government is able to collect and distribute revenues in a sufficiently fair, efficient, and reliable way. Under present circumstances, this will require, in particular, that governments collaborate far more actively with one another to tax more fairly the part of value added captured by transnationally mobile financial and human capital. Second, unions must come to view themselves as representatives of whole populations of working and potentially working people, including the growing precariat, and not just their shrinking cores of full-time, permanent, male insiders.[31] This they might do by broadening their membership but also by getting their members to identify enough with the situations of others—which may also become their own situation or their children's. Third, it would help if they could stop believing that workers are the creators of the whole of the product, part of which is stolen from them by capitalists, and realize instead that most of today's product is something neither today's workers nor today's capitalists deserve any credit for (as argued in chapter 5). Finally, unions might temper the importance they attach to stable, full-time, lifelong, waged employment and to the net pay that goes with it, and broaden their "laborist" conception of what makes a life worth living.[32]

If you doubt that union leaders will ever be able to overcome the multilayered distrust outlined above, you might be heartened by Andy Stern's recent book, *Raising the Floor*. Stern was until 2010 president of the Service Employees International Union, which with close to two million members is one of the largest labor unions in the United States. He invites his readers "to join in a national conversation to raise the floor and shape the future of jobs, work, and the American Dream, with Universal Basic Income as our guiding star."[33] Having spent time reflecting on the probable impacts of technological change in coming years and decades—as we move "from an industrial economy to one based on digitization"—he came to the conclusion that trying to create satisfying full-time jobs for everyone, as he had been advocating throughout his career, was a lost cause. Rather than give up the American Dream, he saw the need to give it a novel interpretation: "According to the new American Dream, we'll each have the freedom to choose and create the life we want for ourselves and our loved ones, according to our deepest values, without ever having to worry about our basic human needs for food, shelter, and security."[34] To realize this dream, Stern proposes to "institute an unconditional, universal basic income of $1,000 per month for all adults between the ages of eighteen and sixty-four."[35]

Is it at all likely that such a message will be taken seriously by the membership and leadership of today's labor unions? Here are two indications that

it might. In January 2012, German trade unionists set up Gewerkschafterdialog-Grundeinkommen, a "platform for supporting a dialogue on basic income among trade union members," with basic income conceived as a way of strengthening workers' rights. It has been organizing workshops on basic income since then throughout Germany.[36] On July 11, 2016, Unite, the largest British trade union, adopted a motion at its fourth policy conference, in Brighton, in which it noted "the evident inability of our bureaucratically costly social security system, with its dependence on means-testing and frequent arbitrary sanction, to provide an adequate income floor," and expressed its conviction "that a Basic Income, an unconditional, non-withdrawable income paid to everyone, has the potential to offer genuine social security to all while boosting the economy and creating jobs." It sent an invitation to its membership "to actively campaign for a Universal Basic Income."[37]

Employers

What about the employers' side? When something is being advocated on the grounds that it gives greater economic power to those with least economic power, it cannot be expected to be cheered enthusiastically by those who, thanks to their own economic power, can take advantage of other people's dependence. Pointing out, for example, that striking workers will not even need to draw on a strike fund thanks to their basic incomes may be more than enough to make capitalists switch off. It is therefore no surprise that finding an employers' organization that supports an unconditional basic income is even more difficult than finding a labor union that does.

As in the case of labor unions, however, there are some modest exceptions. Since 2010, the German Bund Katholischer Unternehmer, an organization of Catholic entrepreneurs, has been urging the introduction of a negative income tax in Germany, based on a "clear foundation inspired by catholic social thought." In the context of France's 2012 presidential campaign, the Centre des Jeunes Dirigeants d'Entreprise, a French organization of young business leaders, published a white paper advocating a 400 euro basic income (about 12 percent of GDP per capita at the time) to be paid to all residents and funded mainly out of green taxation.[38] Usually, however, employers' organizations ignore the idea. And when they cannot, as was the case during the campaign for the Swiss popular initiative, they firmly oppose it: no organization mobilized as early or as vigorously against the proposal as Economiesuisse, Switzerland's business federation.[39]

Yet some of the most prominent and influential advocates of basic income are successful entrepreneurs. One of them is Roland Duchâtelet, a Belgian businessman active in microchip production and football clubs, who warmed to the idea of basic income in the early 1990s.[40] In 1997, he founded a political party named *Vivant* (Living), with one central proposal: the introduction of an individual and unconditional basic income of 500 euros (about 23 percent of GDP per capita at the time), funded by a steep increase in the Value Added Tax. At Belgium's 1999 federal elections, Vivant won close to 2 percent of the votes thanks to an expensive campaign funded by Duchâtelet. Its success was a bit less in the 2003 elections. In neither case did it attract enough votes to win a seat in the federal parliament. In 2007, Vivant was absorbed by the Flemish liberal party, for which Duchâtelet served one term as a senator. The fizzling-out of his party has not prevented Duchâtelet from remaining a vocal advocate of a "freedom income" that should be coupled, in his view, with a simplification of the tax system and a trimming of an inefficient and meddling welfare bureaucracy.[41]

Another example, even more spectacular, is provided by the German entrepreneur Götz Werner, the founder and CEO of Germany's main drugstore chain, DM, and employer of over 26,000 workers. In 2005, the "Hartz IV" reform of the German welfare state increased the pressure on benefit recipients to seek employment. Werner then started advocating an unconditional basic income first pitched at 1,200 euros (over 50 percent of Germany's GDP per capita at the time), funded by a consumption tax and accompanied by the suppression of all forms of income tax and of many existing transfers. Making a fervent plea for basic income from such an unexpected side, Werner was in high demand as a guest on TV talk shows and in other media. He subsequently published several books in which he refined (and in part toned down) his proposal and spelled out the reasoning behind it. Against the background of an explicit allegiance to Rudolf Steiner's anthroposophical doctrine, Werner views basic income as a key component of an economy that will work better because its workers will work more freely.[42] His approach to basic income as a *Kulturimpuls*, a cultural impulsion, helped inspire the Swiss basic income initiative.

Roland Duchâtelet and Götz Werner are not the only business leaders who advocate basic income publicly.[43] But they are the ones to have done so with the greatest perseverance and impact, and remain outliers in their categories, just like the few major labor leaders who have come out in favor of basic income. If significantly broader support is ever to come from the side of employers, it would most likely be when basic income is clearly part of a deal that couples the firmer basic security it provides with greater labor market flexibility. Support is also most likely to come in the first place from organizations that gather primarily small businesses and the self-employed. As an example, in June 2016, the head of Flanders's UNIZO (the Organization of Self-Employed Entrepreneurs), Karel Van Eetvelt, declared that the basic-income proposal had to be further explored as it could potentially boost entrepreneurship and better protect freelance workers.[44]

From the labor movement and the business world, let us now turn to two components of our societies whose attitude towards basic income can a priori be expected to be more favorable: the precariat and women.

The Precariat

Job seekers, people with short-term or part-time contracts, those enrolled in workfare schemes, the more vulnerable among the self-employed, and more broadly, all those excluded for whatever reason from good jobs that provide material security and positive identification—these are the people commonly gathered under the label "precariat."[45] They include many of the people who stand to gain most, in an immediate sense, from the introduction of a basic income. But this doesn't necessarily mean that the associations that represent them find it obvious to advocate something as general and remote as an unconditional basic income. For example, when the debate on basic income surfaced in Ireland in the 1990s, the Irish National Organization of the Unemployed denounced the proposal. It felt the campaign for a basic income deflected attention from the immediate problems of unemployment and poverty, for which there were more effective remedies—namely, targeted schemes that were cheaper and therefore more realistic.[46]

Nonetheless, a number of associations that have developed outside the traditional labor movement to represent the interests of those now commonly called the precariat have actively militated for basic-income-type proposals. An early example was in the United States in the late 1960s, when the National Welfare Rights Organization (NWRO), a movement of welfare claimants composed mainly of unemployed black women, called upon the federal government to guarantee every American a minimum income in the form of a negative income tax. Aimed at replacing existing public-assistance programs, the NWRO plan was "designed to cover all of the basic needs of a family, whether or not the adults in it were participating in the labor force. . . .

Eligibility was not contingent on personal behavior and did not need to be certified by a caseworker."[47]

On a smaller scale, in the early 1970s, a group of unemployed people in a small town in southern England decided to form a "claimants' union," despite the fact that "the notion of a Union for people out of work sounds contradictory and improbable to people in a dole queue." They started campaigning for an unconditional basic income but faced opposition from the official labor movement. What the latter wanted, in the claimants' view, was just to increase the wages of those who had jobs—thereby making jobs more difficult to get for those without them—and to decrease the taxes on their wages—thereby putting pressure on the transfers to the jobless. Far from wishing to expand the existing welfare state, the claimants wanted to abolish it. They advocated "some form a guaranteed income, a real living income, for people in work and out of it, that would not have to be crawled and grovelled for at the feet of a bureaucratic overlord."[48]

In several other countries, precariat-linked organizations of varying durability, representativeness, and impact made the institution of something like a basic income one of their central claims.[49] Perhaps the most spectacular manifestation of such a movement happened in France. The *Syndicat des Chômeurs* (Union of the Unemployed), founded in 1982, and its successor, the *Mouvement National des Chômeurs et Précaires* (National Movement of the Unemployed and Precarious Workers), founded in 1986, devoted much space to basic income in the pages of their magazine *Partage*. Local associations of self-defined *précaires*, sometimes of libertarian persuasion, subsequently turned this sheer interest into vigorous support.[50] This paved the way to what sociologist Pierre Bourdieu called a "social miracle": a massive mobilization of the French unemployed in the winter of 1997–1998, taking as their main slogan *"un emploi c'est un droit, un revenu c'est un dû!"* ("a job is a right, an income is an entitlement!") at demonstrations and occupations in several French cities.[51] Under the impulse of the precariat-based federation AC! Agir Contre le Chomage (Acting Against Unemployment), founded in 1994, basic income was propelled for the first time into the French public debate, if not quite onto the political agenda.[52]

It is no doubt easier to find an unambiguously positive attitude towards basic income among these associations of precarious workers than among conventional labor unions. At the same time, it must be conceded that these associations themselves tend to be very precarious, often small, and ephemeral. Their members may have more time to devote to militancy than full-time workers do. But they tend to lack the financial and human resources that make for robust social movements: for most of them, it is difficult enough to make ends meet, and many of those with the skills of effective leaders will remain in the precariat only for short periods of time. Moreover, the precariat lacks the sort of intense and regular interaction that the proletariat owes to sharing a workplace. It also lacks an asset analogous to the insiders' labor power, on whose collaboration the operation of the economy depends. And, most seriously perhaps, it faces the challenge of breeding a positive identification with the stigmatized status of the unemployed or precariously employed. One may therefore doubt that precariat associations will ever gain strength even remotely comparable to that of traditional labor organizations, let alone sufficient to secure the introduction of an unconditional basic income.[53]

Women

Women form another and far larger category from which greater support for basic income should be expected than from the mainstream labor movement. Under practically any imaginable basic-income reform, women would benefit far more than men, whether in terms of income or in terms of life options. The reason for this is simple. Since women currently participate to a lesser extent in the labor market and since their average hourly wage is below that of men, a strictly individual basic income is bound to be of greater financial benefit to them, other things remaining equal, whether it is financed through direct or indirect taxation. It will thereby help reduce the pro-male bias in the distribution of earnings and of social insurance benefits.[54] This increase in women's "income of their own" boosts women's freedom in a way celebrated by Virginia Woolf: "Intellectual freedom depends upon material things. Poetry depends upon intellectual freedom. And women have always been poor, not for two hundred years merely, but from the beginning of time. Women have had less intellectual freedom than the sons of Athenian slaves. Women, then, have not had a dog's chance of writing poetry. That is why I have laid so much stress on money and a room of one's own."[55]

The greater freedom afforded to women by firm incomes of their own will enable them not just to write poetry. In one of the negative-income-tax experiments discussed in chapter 6, entitling each member of poor households to a benefit seems to have increased the divorce rate. A follow-up analysis surmised that the "certainty that income will be available during the difficult transition period after a marital dissolution lessens the financial dependence on the marriage of the financially more dependent spouse—the wife, in most cases. Increased independence presumably allows some persons to leave unsatisfactory, perhaps even brutalizing, marriage."[56] And an income of one's own does not only facilitate getting rid of an unsatisfactory partner. It also facilitates giving up an unsatisfactory work life. As Carole Pateman puts it, "a basic income would make available a range of opportunities to women and, if they were willing to live on the income, would allow them to exit from demeaning relationships and jobs."[57] As explained earlier (in chapter 1), a basic income makes it easier to opt for part-time work and take career breaks. It thereby enables in particular poorly-paid women to escape from the double shift and an unbearable life pace. This also showed up in the results of the negative-income-tax experiments through a moderate decrease in the labor supply of secondary earners—mostly married women. As stressed in chapter 6, these results from experiments with what were not quite basic-income initiatives, introduced fifty years ago in specific institutional and cultural contexts, should not be carelessly extrapolated. However, the basic point they illustrate is robust enough. As far as freedom goes, basic income does make a difference, and a bigger difference for those who make more use of the new opportunities they are given. Women are massively overrepresented among these.

For all these reasons, it is not surprising that some feminist associations have put basic income among their central objectives. One early example shows up in a pamphlet with the title *Women and Social Security,* published in 1975 by the Federation of Claimants Unions at the initiative of a union of working-class women living in London. The pamphlet was reprinted in revised forms several times in subsequent years, and each edition of it had a section advocating an unconditional basic-income scheme. Under such a scheme, it said, "each woman would be treated as a separate individual, and never as another person's dependent. This would remove the humiliating investigation of personal relationships which is an integral part of the supplementary benefits scheme"—that is, the means-tested minimum-income scheme then in place in the United Kingdom. "It would," the pamphlet further says, "radically affect the position of women in this society."[58]

While there are clear collective statements of this sort and no lack of defenses of basic income by feminist authors, it certainly cannot be said that there is a broad consensus in the feminist movement in favor of the introduction of a basic income.[59] The most fundamental reason for this is the reticence triggered in some feminist circles by the very fact that women as a group would make greater use than men of the new options created by it. From a feminist standpoint, the problem is not, of course, that the greater freedom offered by the basic income might boost the divorce rate. (This prediction is still used today as an argument against guaranteed income schemes, on the grounds that it is not good for children to grow up in fatherless households.[60]) From a feminist standpoint, the problem is rather the impact on women's participation in labor markets. For a number of mutually-reinforcing reasons— from unashamed discrimination and oppressive gender-specific expectations to the widespread and persistent fact that women tend to be younger than their partners—the female in most couples earns less per hour than the male. If at some point a couple regards it as desirable to reduce its total number of hours of paid work in order to make more time for childcare or other domestic tasks, it is therefore in most cases less costly if the woman stops working or reduces her working time than if the man does. And every time she does it, the gap widens. In combination with other factors and to an extent that is bound to vary greatly from context to context, this fact helps explain the asymmetry between men and women observed not just in the negative-income-tax experiments but also in the actual operation of existing schemes that bear a relevant resemblance to basic income.[61] This asymmetry presents a challenge to the acceptability of a basic income from a feminist standpoint. The suspicion is that some women will use the new options offered by their basic incomes in a shortsighted way, as a result of underestimating the importance for their long-term material security of remaining strongly integrated in the world of work.

Should such questions prevent forever a more resolute support for basic income in the feminist movement? We do not think so, providing two conditions are fulfilled. One is that the overarching objective should not be what Nancy Fraser criticized under the label of "universal breadwinner model."[62] The full-time, lifelong employment that defined the traditional male role is not the sole model of a successful life, and the emancipation of women does not consist of imposing this male model on all of them. It rather consists of giving them more choices, more real freedom to make their lives what they want them to be. As Anne Miller puts it, this must involve reducing rather than reinforcing the existing bias in favor of the "career-oriented" against the "care-oriented."[63] With this bias reduced by the provision of a basic income, it is quite possible, indeed at present most likely, that a higher proportion of women than of men will make use of their widened set of options to reduce their working time. If the feminist concern is to expand women's freedom—rather than to dictate how they use it—there is no reason that this fact should prevent a feminist movement from embracing wholeheartedly the idea of an unconditional basic income. Or at least there is no such reason if a second condition is fulfilled.

This second condition consists of finding a satisfactory way of addressing the following challenge. The unequal extent to which men and women make use of the enhanced possibility of reducing their working time could indirectly reduce the real freedom of women. There are two main mechanisms through which this could happen. One is the lack of role models: not seeing enough women in some positions may induce women to effectively write off life options that are formally as open to them as they are to men. The other mechanism is statistical discrimination: some employers will feel, more than before, that women are less likely than men to work full-time and stick to the job. For this reason, they will allocate jobs and responsibilities more easily to men than to women.

If additional asymmetry is induced by the introduction of a basic income, and it is sufficient to make these effects significant, some side measures could be used to neutralize them. To start with, the form taken by the personal income tax matters a great deal; compared to the joint taxation of the income of the household, a system of strictly individual, progressive taxation would create material incentives for the sharing of employment among household members.[64] Additional, specific measures could be taken to encourage a more even distribution of employment and care work among male and female parents. For example, a top-up parental leave benefit could be allocated in proportion to the number of months taken by the one among the two parents who takes the shortest one. Or the benefit could be higher for paternal than for maternal leaves.[65] Finally, all sorts of measures are needed to facilitate the combination of employment and family responsibilities, from flextime and telework to conveniently located and affordable childcare facilities and appropriate school hours.

The aim to keep in mind throughout is to correct the two effects mentioned above (if they are serious)—not to make sure that women and men make on average the same choices. For there is a crucial distinction between reforms that lead to reduced participation by women in labor markets as a result of reduced freedom and reforms that yield reduced participation thanks to increased freedom. A regression from a universal to a means-tested scheme of child benefits falls into the first category. As explained in chapter 6, it amounts to increasing the rate at which mothers' earnings are taxed, and thereby creates for many of them a household trap. By contrast, if women choose to reduce their paid work as a result of a basic income being introduced, that would be due to their greater freedom, to their greater bargaining power gained as a result, and to their own choices of how to use it. Realizing the importance of this distinction is essential to the defense of basic income from a feminist perspective.[66]

Socialists

To assess the political prospects of basic-income proposals, it is instructive to consider, as we have just done, the attitudes that tend to prevail in some key components of civil society and the reasons behind them. It is no less instructive to explore the positions adopted within the various political families. This is the work of the next few sections. Our exploration will focus disproportionately on the European political landscape, which is at the same time sufficiently differentiated, sufficiently stable, and sufficiently aware of basic-income proposals for some trends to be detectable.[67]

As the mainstream socialist or social-democratic parties tend to be closely linked to the labor movement, one can expect them to display the same general features. There are nonetheless a number of interesting specific episodes worth mentioning. Some of them are scarcely more than anecdotal. For example, Thomas Skidmore (1790–1832), one of the first proponents of an unconditional basic endowment, was leader of the New York Working Men's Party. In chapter 4, other pioneering thinkers appeared. Jacob Kats (1804–1886) belonged, along with Marx and Engels, to the Brussels-based Association Démocratique and founded what could be viewed as the first expression of a Flemish workers' party. As mentioned in chapter 4, it was in his circle that the first known proposal for a nationwide basic income was elaborated. And Edward Bellamy (1850–1898), who advocated a lifelong basic income coupled with a compulsory social service, was actively involved in the early stages of America's short-lived People's Party (1891–1908).

Less anecdotal is the effort made by Dennis Milner, author of *Higher Production by a Bonus on National Output* (1920) and leader of the State Bonus League, to get his unconditional state bonus approved by the British Labour

Party. It was put to a vote at the 1920 party conference but rejected by a two-thirds majority. Not much later, however, George D. H. Cole, an Oxford professor close to the top of the Labour Party (he was the mentor of the future prime minister Harold Wilson), defended it in several of his books, while James Meade, then also in Oxford, recommended in his *Outline of an Economic Policy for a Labour Government* (1935) that greater income inequality should be pursued "first by the development of social services and later by the distribution of a social dividend."[68] The basic-income proposal was marginalized with the adoption and implementation of the Beveridge report by the post-war Labour government.[69]

It briefly resurfaced in 1994, when a Commission on Social Justice was set up at the initiative of John Smith, then leader of the Labour Party, in order to explore the reform of the UK's welfare state half a century after the Beveridge report. According to the Commission, "in a society with a strong work ethic many people would oppose, as giving 'something for nothing,' a scheme deliberately designed to offer unconditional benefits to all." However, "if it turns out to be the case that earnings simply cannot provide a stable income for a growing proportion of people, then the notion of some guaranteed income, outside the labour market, could become increasingly attractive."[70] Another two decades later, in 2016, the Labour Party's pressure group Compass published a report under the title "Universal Basic Income: An Idea Whose Time has Come?" It included a specific partial-basic-income proposal.[71] Commenting on the report, the Labour Party's shadow finance minister John McDonnell declared that basic income "is an idea Labour will be closely looking at over the next few years" and seems to have convinced the Labour Party leader Jeremy Corbyn to look into it. In September 2016, the Labour MPs debated the idea in public for the first time.[72]

The only other major social-democratic party that took the idea of basic income seriously was the Dutch labor party, *Partij van de Arbeid* (PvdA), which participated in many national governments after World War II and headed several of them. As was mentioned in chapter 4, a public debate on basic income was triggered in the early 1980s mainly thanks to the *Voedingsbond* FNV, a union of food sector workers. This could not fail to affect the Dutch Labor Party, then in opposition. At its February 1983 national conference, the proposal was put to a vote and rejected, on the recommendation of the party leadership, by a 60 percent majority. But the minority did not give up, and in 1985, a working group was set up within the party and started publishing, in preparation for the pre-electoral conference of February 1986, four issues of a well-documented magazine entirely devoted to basic income. The latter included detailed discussions of the arguments and expressions of support by prominent party members, such as the economist Jan Tinbergen and former European Commission president Sicco Mansholt. With the party leadership still firmly opposed, the national conference defeated again the basic-income proposal with a majority of about 60 percent.[73] Twenty years later, in June 2016, the idea made a cautious comeback within the party when 61 percent of the PvdA members voted in favor of a motion asking for the inclusion of basic-income experiments within the party platform for the upcoming 2017 general election.[74]

In other countries, social-democratic parties have barely discussed the idea.[75] And those compelled to take explicit stances have sometimes showed themselves to be deeply divided, as was the case with the Swiss socialist party in the run-up to the 2016 referendum.[76] More often, they have simply expressed their hostility.[77] This has not prevented some prominent party members from expressing their sympathy for the idea. For example, in Italy, Achille Occhetto, the general secretary of the *Partito Comunista Italiano* (Italian Communist Party) who turned it in 1991 into an explicitly social-democratic party (the *Partito Democratico della Sinistra*, later *Partito Democratico* or Democratic Party), showed himself very receptive to the basic income idea. In a dialogue with James Meade, he defended the compatibility between a social dividend and the fair remuneration of work. In the context of an increasingly automated economy, he said, "wanting to preserve a rigid link between income and individual labour . . . is sheer proof of retrograde dogmatism."[78] In France, Michel Rocard, who as prime minister introduced in 1988 the means-tested minimum scheme RMI (the *revenu minimum d'insertion,* or minimum integration income, mentioned in chapter 6), later expressed his support for moving towards a basic income via the negative-income-tax scheme proposed by his adviser Roger Godino. Indeed, he was one of the keynote speakers in 2000 in Berlin at the eighth congress of the Basic Income European Network. In Spain, Jordi Sevilla, Minister of Public Administration in José Luis Zapatero's socialist government, proposed in 2001 a tax reform incorporating a basic income. Further afield, in Brazil, Eduardo Matarazzo Suplicy, federal senator for the state of Sao Paulo from 1997 to 2015 and cofounder with Luiz Inacio Lula da Silva of Brazil's *Partido dos Trabalhadores* (Workers' Party), has been campaigning for an unconditional basic income since the mid-1990s; he managed to get both chambers of the parliament to approve and President Lula to sign in January 2004 a law that calls for the gradual implementation of a *renda basica de cidadania* (basic citizenship income) for all Brazilians.[79]

To the left of the social-democratic parties, orthodox communist parties have tended to be even less keen.[80] But some more or less transient alliances of small, far-left parties have seen in basic income part of a radical alternative to today's capitalism. In Finland, for example, the *Vasemmistoliitto* (Left Alliance), born in 1990 of a split from the declining Communist Party and joined by radical ecologists and other small leftist groups, has had a partial basic income on its platform since its inception. This alliance took part in three government coalitions between 1995 and 2014 but never pushed for basic income while sharing governmental power.[81] In Ireland, the small party Democratic Left, born of a split from the Workers' Party in 1992, repeatedly expressed its public support for basic income until it merged with the bigger Labour Party in 1999. In Quebec, the *Union des Forces Progressistes* (Union of Progressive Forces), founded in 2002 by socialists, communists, and ecologists, included a "universal citizen's income" on its electoral platform, until it became *Québec Solidaire* in 2006.[82]

In Spain, the radical left-wing party *Podemos* (We Can) arose in January 2014 out of the *"indignados"* movement that had been unfolding since May 2011 in response to drastic austerity measures. It included a call for basic income in its platform for the May 2014 European election, at which it won 10 percent of the Spanish seats, but withdrew it from its later manifestos. From March 2016 onwards, Yanis Varoufakis, Greece's minister of finance in Syriza's 2015 government and founder of the pan-European political movement Diem, came out very firmly in favor of basic income in successive interviews: "The basic income approach is absolutely essential, but it is not part of the social democratic tradition. . . . Now, either we are going to have a basic income that regulates this new society of ours, or we are going to have very substantial social conflicts."[83]

However, the most significant case of support for basic income by a party to the left of traditional social democracy is provided by the German party *Die Linke* (The Left), a party with strong parliamentary representation, especially from former East German districts. In June 2003, at the initiative of Katja Kipping, at the time its deputy leader, the *Partei des Demokratischen Sozialismus* (Party of Democratic Socialism, or PDS), successor of East Germany's communist party, started promoting an unconditional basic income of 1,000 euros per month as an alternative to the "Hartz reforms" of the German welfare state that were being prepared at the request of the government of Chancellor Gerhard Schröder. In 2007, the PDS became *Die Linke* through a merger with a left-wing segment of the Social Democratic Party under the leadership of the latter's former leader Oskar Lafontaine. Since then, the basic-income proposal has remained very present, though also quite controversial, within the party. It received another boost with the election of Katja Kipping as co-chair of the party in 2012.[84]

In light of this quick overview, the least that can be said is that the basic-income proposal is not central in the doctrine of socialist parties. This should not surprise us. In the first chapter of his classic book *Socialism and the Social Movement in the 19th Century* (1896), Werner Sombart noted:

> It is not too much to say that the glorification of labour is the central point in all Socialist ethics. . . . The world of the future will be a world of work, where the most widely accepted principle shall be: "He who does not work shall not eat." On this all Socialists are agreed. We are not surprised that this is so. When people in the lowest social strata on whom the curse of the most disagreeable work rests (and it is of manual labour, more especially of the lowest kind, that the Socialist thinks in the first instance), when people such as these dream of an ideal state, it will hardly be one in which life is all play and no work. Work there must be, if the necessities of man are to be produced; the Socialist thinkers want only to shorten its duration by more equal distribution.[85]

This interpretation is abundantly corroborated by countless statements by socialist leaders. Thus we have Rosa Luxemburg's forceful assertion in 1918, shortly before being murdered, of "a universal duty to work for all those able to work" *("allgemeine Arbeitspflicht für alle Arbeitsfähigen")*. In her words: "Only somebody who performs some useful work for the public at large, whether by hand or brain, can be entitled to receive from society the means for satisfying his needs. A life of leisure like most of the rich exploiters currently lead will come to an end. A general requirement to work for all who are able to do so, from which small children, the aged and sick are exempted, is a matter of course in a socialist economy."[86]

Decades later and in a very different context, the 1967 Arusha Declaration by Tanzania's first president, socialist Julius Nyerere, similarly states: "A truly socialist state is one in which all people are workers and in which neither capitalism nor feudalism exists. It does not have two classes of people, a lower class of people who work for their living, and an upper class of people who live on the work of others."[87]

Against this "laborist" interpretation of the essence of socialism, it could perhaps be argued that true socialism, in contrast to laborism, must aim to distribute the social surplus among all members of society, rather than only among laborers and directly or indirectly by virtue of their labor. However, if a strong presumption for basic income is to be found in the socialist tradition, it is neither in its social-democratic version nor in its Marxist version (unless stretched in the way suggested in chapter 5). Rather it is in the "utopian socialism" of the likes of Charles Fourier (as discussed in chapter 4), where freedom is given a more central role. For example, when Wilhelm Weitling (1808–1871), one of the first German communists who moved to New York after the failure of Europe's 1848 revolutions, published *Guarantees of Harmony and Freedom*, he emblazoned on its first page a motto: "We want to be free, like the birds in the sky; like them we want to go through life in joyful bands and sweet harmony."[88] In contrast to Sombart's identification of the core of the socialist ideal ("hardly one in which life is all play and no work"), the rehabilitation of the utopian socialist tradition stresses the emancipation from work and its gradual assimilation to play. Such a rehabilitation can be found, for example, at the end of Herbert Marcuse's famous 1967 lecture on "the end of utopia":

> It is no accident that the work of Fourier is becoming topical again among the avant-garde left-wing intelligentsia. As Marx and Engels themselves acknowledged, Fourier was the only one to have made clear this qualitative difference between free and unfree society. And he did not shrink back in fear, as Marx still did, from speaking of a possible society in which work becomes play, a society in which even socially necessary labor can be organized in harmony with the liberated, genuine needs of men.[89]

Liberals

What about liberal parties, in the European or classical sense in which "liberal" is contrasted with "socialist" just as pro-market is with pro-state? It cannot be said that many of them advocate a basic income, but some certainly have done and some still do. In particular, several parties in the European Parliament belonging to the Alliance of Liberals and Democrats for Europe have defended either a straight basic income or something close to it.

In the Netherlands, *Democraten 66* (Democrats 1966, or D66), which was founded in 1966 following a secession of the left of the liberal party *Volkspartij voor Vrijheid en Democratie* (People's Party for Freedom and Democracy), kept a significant parliamentary representation across the next decade and participated in several governments. It came out in favor of basic income on several occasions. In December 1994, the D66 minister for economic affairs, Hans Wijers, embarrassed the labor-liberal coalition government by publicly stating that the Netherlands "were inevitably moving towards a reform resembling basic income."[90] In the aftermath of this incident, D66 published an in-depth report arguing for an unconditional basic income—but dropped it from its party programs in the late 1990s. At its November 2014 congress, however, it adopted a motion in favor of the launch of experiments aimed at assessing the true cost of a basic income. Similarly, Austria's *Liberales Forum* was set up in 1993 by members of the *Freiheitspartei Österreich* (Austrian Freedom Party) who rejected the nationalist anti-immigrant orientation given to the party by Jörg Haider. From 1996 onwards, under the leadership of Heide Schmidt, this small party openly supported the introduction of a negative income tax. In 2014, it was absorbed by *NEOS—Das Neue Österreich* (The New Austria), which still has a negative income tax on its program.

In the United Kingdom, the Liberal Democrats were born in 1988 out of a merger of the heirs of the old liberal party and social-democratic dissidents from the Labour Party. Under the leadership of Paddy Ashdown (from 1989 to 1999), himself a keen advocate of basic income, they prominently featured a "Citizen's Income" in their 1989 and 1994 electoral manifestos, but dropped it later. In Ireland, *Fianna Fáil*, a center-right party founded by Eamon De Valera in 1926 and a major government party through most of Ireland's history, became interested in basic income in the aftermath of its 2011 bad electoral defeat. In July 2015, its spokesman on social protection announced the party's intention to propose replacing social welfare payments by a basic income of at least 230 euros a week for everyone, regardless of means (over 30 percent of Ireland's GDP per capita at the time).[91]

Finland's *Suomen Keskusta* (Finnish Centre), founded in 1906 as the Agrarian League and also a component of the liberal group in the European Parliament, recently gained some prominence in Europe's basic-income discussion. Since the late 1980s, some of its members have been arguing for a basic income, and its youth section in particular has been pushing for it. After the elections of April 2015, the Centre Party became the country's largest party, and its leader, Juha Sipilä, formerly a successful IT businessman, became prime minister. The new government, a coalition with smaller parties, immediately announced its intention to launch a basic-income experiment (as mentioned in chapter 6), the ultimate purpose of which is to "make the system more participatory and strengthen work incentives, reduce bureaucracy, and simplify the now complicated benefit system in a way that ensures the sustainability of public finances."[92]

Beyond Europe, another example is provided by Japan. Guided by Tōru Hashimoto, a popular TV figure turned political leader and elected mayor of Osaka in 2011, the local party *Osaka Ishin no Kai* (Osaka Restoration Party) included in its draft electoral platform for the December 2012 general election an ultra-liberal version of basic income: a cash income of approximately $600 (25 percent of Japan's GDP per capita at the time) replacing the bulk of Japan's social insurance and public assistance programs. However, when in September 2012 Hashimoto launched a national version of his party called *Nihon Ishin no Kai* (Japan's Restoration Party), his support for basic income became more ambiguous. Subsequent versions of the platform refer to a negative income tax, with a renewed emphasis on work requirements.[93]

In addition to these political parties, there are plenty of liberal think tanks that advocate some version of basic income. In France, for example, *Génération Libre* (Free Generation), directed by philosopher Gaspard Koenig, has been playing an important role in drawing attention to the idea in liberal circles and beyond, including by publishing a detailed proposal for France.[94] Meanwhile *Alternative Libérale* (Liberal Alternative), chaired by Louis-Marie Bachelot, advocates a basic income at a subnational level, so that each subnational entity can choose its preferred level and compete with the others.[95] In the United Kingdom, the Adam Smith Institute has released a research report in which it advocates the implementation of an individual negative income tax that "should replace major means-tested benefits."[96]

In all these cases, it is important to look at the details of the proposal—not just at the level of the basic income and how obligation-free it is, but also at what it is meant to replace and how it is supposed to be financed. Depending on these details, we may be close to proposals made by "liberal" democrats in the American sense, such as John Kenneth Galbraith, James Tobin, and others, who managed to get a generous "demogrant" into George McGovern's 1972 electoral platform, or alternatively, close to the negative income tax popularized by Milton Friedman in 1962—or indeed close to the basic income proposed by Charles Murray. In his 2006 book *In Our Hands*, Murray proposes to eliminate all US federal welfare programs (in a broad sense that includes not just Temporary Assistance to Needy Families and food stamps, but also Social Security, Medicare, Medicaid, and the Earned Income Tax Credit) and to distribute the money saved in just two forms: an unconditional basic income of $7,000 per year (about 15 percent of GDP per capita in 2006) for everyone aged 21 or older, and an additional $3,000 ear-marked for a universal health insurance plan.[97] Ten years later, in the week preceding the Swiss referendum, Murray published an update of his pro-posal, with an unambiguous caveat: "A universal basic income will do the good things I claim only if it replaces all other transfer payments and the bureaucracies that oversee them."[98] There is, of course, a huge difference—and not only in terms of political achievability—between Murray's monthly cash payment of $833 (in the updated version) replacing all cash transfers, and a basic income at a similar level fitted under the whole distribution of income, some recalibrated benefits included, as advocated in chapter 1.

Like the business leaders who have come out in favor of basic income, many liberal parties and organizations (in the European sense) are attracted to basic income because of its simple, non-bureaucratic, trap-free, market-friendly operation, which helps make generous transfers more efficient and sustainable. But there are also ultra- or neo-liberals who are mainly attracted to it—and even more to a negative income tax—because they hope it will help phase out more generous systems and indeed because it may lend itself more easily to being phased out in turn. However, it is not difficult for real liberals—people who care for the real freedom of everyone, not just the rich—to find in their tradition plenty to motivate a strong presumption in favor of an unconditional basic income. Our version of the liberal-egalitarian ap-proach to social justice proposes one way of doing so. But John Stuart Mill and even Friedrich Hayek (as discussed in chapter 4) can provide alternative points of departure.

Greens

Ever since its inception in the 1970s, the green movement has consistently displayed unmistakable sympathy for the idea of an unconditional basic in-come.[99] In the late 1970s, the newly-founded British Ecology Party was the first European political formation to explicitly include basic income in its program. Nearly half a century later, what has now become the Green Party of England and Wales still writes in its platform: "Scrap most of the existing benefits apart from disability benefits and Housing benefit. Abolish the income tax personal allowance. Then pay every woman, man and child legally resident in the UK a guaranteed, non-means-tested income, sufficient to cover basic needs—a Basic Income."[100] In 2016, its only representative in the House of Commons, Caroline Lucas, introduced a motion calling the British government to "fund and commission further research into the possibilities offered by the various Basic Income models."[101] In the run-up to the 2014 referendum on Scotland's independence, the Scottish Green Party had also made basic income one of the key components of a hypothetical Scottish welfare system: "A Citizen's Income would sweep away almost all benefits and the state pension and replace them with a simple regular payment to everyone—children, adults and pensioners. This income should be enough to meet the basic needs of everyone."[102]

In the United States, the Green Party has consistently included basic income in its electoral platforms. Thus, the economic program adopted in June 2004 at its Milwaukee convention called unambiguously for the introduction of a "universal basic income." It included a whole paragraph on the topic, still unchanged in the party's 2014 platform: "We call for a universal basic income (sometimes called a guaranteed income, negative income tax, citizen's income, or citizen dividend). This would go to every adult regardless of health, employment, or marital status, in order to minimize government bureaucracy and intrusiveness into people's lives. The amount should be sufficient so that anyone who is unemployed can afford basic food and shelter. State or local governments should supplement that amount from local revenues where the cost of living is high."[103]

In 2007, the Green Party of Canada led by Elizabeth May took a similar position, officially calling for a "guaranteed annual income for all Canadians" at a party convention in Vancouver. In 2011, May became the first Green Party member of the Canadian House of Commons, and since then she has often reiterated her support for a guaranteed annual income.[104] The 2015 electoral platform of the Green Party of Canada includes the following statement: "The Green Party of Canada believes it is time to re-visit a major policy initiative—the use of a negative income tax, or Guaranteed Livable Income for all. . . . The essential plan is to provide a regular payment to every Canadian without regard to a needs test. The level of the payment will be regionally set at a level above poverty, but at a bare subsistence level to encourage additional income generation. No surveillance or follow-up is required."[105]

In the cases of the United States, Canada, and the United Kingdom, the first-past-the-post electoral systems make it hard for green parties to achieve significant political representation and thereby to have direct impact on policy-making.[106] In continental Europe, where proportional representation prevails, most green parties are represented in their respective regional and national parliaments and in the European Parliament, and several of them take part in national and regional government coalitions.[107]

In the Netherlands, the first party with a definitely green flavor was the *Politieke Partij Radikalen* (Political Party of Radicals, or PPR), founded in 1968 by left dissidents of the Catholic Party. In the late 1970s, it joined the food workers' union *Voedingsbond* FNV in pleading vigorously for the introduction of an unconditional basic income. By so doing, it became the first-ever explicitly pro-basic-income party with a parliamentary representation. In 1989, it merged with three other small parties, including the former communist party, to become *GroenLinks* (Green Left), the Netherlands' main green party. Since then, GroenLinks has regularly witnessed clashes between those who regard basic income as a central element of the identity of a green party and those who refuse to deviate from the labor-focused consensus. In 1996, GroenLinks officially endorsed the idea of a modest negative income tax (the *voetinkomen,* or foot income) of 600 gulden per month (12.5 percent of GDP per capita at the time), but it gradually removed references to basic income from its subsequent platforms. In 2012, however, it elected as its leader the economist Bram van Ojik, who published several pro-basic-income pamphlets in his youth on behalf of the PPR.[108] And in February 2015, the national congress of GroenLinks adopted a motion calling for the launch of basic-income experiments in the Netherlands.

In Germany, there has been some interest for a basic income in green circles since the mid-1980s.[109] Thus, the Heinrich Böll Stiftung, the foundation linked to Germany's Green Party *Die Grünen* (The Greens), hosted in 2000 the eighth congress of the Basic Income European Network and in 2004 the founding congress of *Netzwerk Grundeinkommen,* the German basic income network. But when the German debate on basic income really took off around 2005, it was in fierce reaction to the workfare-oriented "Hartz IV" reform of the welfare state realized by a red-green federal coalition. The Green Party, therefore, was deeply divided on this issue. At its congress in Nuremberg in November 2007, it distanced itself from Hartz IV, but the proposal to make an unconditional basic income part of the party program was defeated by a 59 percent majority among the delegates.[110] The idea remains too radical for the party leadership, although that does not prevent its having many supporters among prominent party members.[111]

In other European countries, the picture is not very different, with party memberships often divided on the issue, and very cautious leaderships. In Belgium, both green parties—the French-speaking *Ecolo* and Dutch-speaking *Agalev*—included a basic income in their 1985 programs as a medium-term objective, while never concretizing it into short-term policy proposals.[112] The French Green Party *Les Verts* (The Greens, since 2010 officially named *Europe Ecologie Les Verts*) started debating the issue in the late 1990s. In 1999, it adopted, as a step towards a genuine "citizen's income," the idea of a "guaranteed social income" that would target part-time workers and people involved in "autonomous" activities. In 2013, 70 percent of its affiliates voted in favor of a motion supporting the introduction of a basic income in France.[113] In Ireland, the Green Party was actively involved in the effort that led, in 2002, to the publication by the government of a green paper on the subject, and in monitoring its follow-up, but did nothing about it while in government from 2007 to 2011. In 2013, its leader Eamon Ryan reiterated the Green Party's support for moves towards a basic-income system. In Finland, *Vihreä Liitto* (the Green League) has repeatedly supported basic income since the mid-1990s at the urging of Osmo Soininvaara (who was Finland's Minister for Health and Social Affairs from 2000 to 2002, and party leader from 2001 to 2005). It officially included a monthly basic income of 560 euros for all adults (about 16 percent of GDP per capita) in its electoral platform for the 2015 general election.[114] In Switzerland, the Green Party was the only party with parliamentary representation that called for a "yes" vote in the 2016 referendum (to which we return shortly). According to the post-referendum survey, it was only among its voters that the yeses dominated (56 percent of them said they voted for the idea). But in the parliamentary vote that preceded that referendum, its own deputies were about equally divided.[115]

Added to a frequent lack of internal consensus, the fact that green parties in government have been only junior partners in larger coalitions helps explain why none of them has taken advantage of being in power to press for significant steps in the direction of a basic income. Despite this caveat, it is from green parties that sympathy and support has been coming most generously and most consistently ever since their first appearance on the political scene in the late 1970s.[116] Why is this so? We can name at least three logically independent reasons.

First, it is a core component of green-party doctrine that, owing to environmental constraints, societies must reduce their expectations regarding the growth of material standards of living. This position is less painful to adopt and profess for people who attach comparatively little importance to the possession and consumption of material goods, and comparatively great importance to the enjoyment of pleasurable work and leisure. It is therefore not surprising that people with such preferences should be overrepresented in green parties. As an unconditional basic income would precisely reduce the cost of going for more free time or for a more meaningful but less lucrative job, it is not surprising, either, that members of green parties should tend to favor its introduction. Put differently: a basic income would be good for people who do not find it that terrible to have to consume less, and those are the sort of people green parties attract.

A second reason relates to another core component of green doctrine: the idea that nature and its resources are the common heritage of mankind. Adopting this view is bound to make one receptive to the oldest justification of an unconditional basic income—namely, the common ownership of the earth. Against this background, it is perfectly normal to ask that those who possess the earth, consume its raw materials, or pollute its atmosphere should contribute proportionately to a fund that would pay unconditional dividends to all, generation after generation. How generous such a basic income would be is debatable (as we saw in chapter 6). But once adopted, this perspective makes it much easier to believe that, in contrast to the Left's traditional labor-focused view, a significant part of the national product is not something current producers are entitled to but something that is equally owed to all, no strings attached.

Third, the green movement is against the relentless pursuit of growth but also wants to address the plague of mass unemployment. To the extent that it dissociates income from productive contribution, an unconditional basic income can be viewed as a systemic curb on growth. By turning some employment into voluntary unemployment and thereby sharing the existing jobs among more people, it makes it possible to address involuntary unemployment without productivity increases needing to be constantly translated into a corresponding growth in production. Working-time reductions, whether in the form of shorter working weeks, longer holidays, more paid leaves, or shorter careers, offer an obvious alternative way for pursuing the same goal, and green parties have often proposed these, too, whether or not in combination with a basic income. But a basic income is more appealing at least for the more libertarian, less statist, less laborist components of the green movement.[117]

If basic income can be plausibly viewed as a tool for facilitating "green" lifestyles, as a dividend on common capital, and as a way of reconciling the environmental objective of taming growth with the social objective of reducing unemployment, why is support for it not more vigorous and more unanimous? A first reason is no doubt that if one cares above all for a better environment, one can think of many useful things to do with scarce public resources other than to disseminate them unconditionally, from caring for natural reserves to investing in energy-saving technologies. In particular, for "dark green" people, it would be a shame if the proceeds of energy taxes, carbon taxes, or land taxes were not earmarked for such uses.

A second reason is that if one cares above all for the fate of future generations, one should advocate methods of production that use less natural resources and therefore, nearly unavoidably, more human labor. It does not look like a brilliant idea, from this standpoint, to allocate an income even to those who are not willing to do any work. A simple way of characterizing this tension is by contrasting two ways of addressing the overexploitation of nature. The first is to produce and consume less than what productivity growth would allow and thereby reduce the use of both natural and human resources. The second is to produce and consume the same (or whatever expanded output productivity growth would allow) by compensating a reduction in the use of natural resources by an increase in human labor. Only the first of these two options provides a presumption in favor of a basic income (or a more rigid version of job-sharing). The concern for sustainability alone cannot justify choosing it. What is needed in addition is either a commitment to "post-materialist values"—the intrinsic worth of "voluntary simplicity," a primacy of the spiritual over the material—or a conviction that the point of economic progress is to emancipate people rather than to maximize their consumption potential, albeit across generations. The ultimate reason that green parties are on average far more favorably inclined to a basic income than socialist parties is presumably that awareness of the physical limits to growth has reinforced these two types of value orientation and conversely, as suggested above, that the latter has facilitated the former. As a result, green parties have been more open to challenging the traditional laborist objective of full-time employment for all as a meaningful social objective and, hence also more open to advocating an unconditional basic income.[118]

Christians

In Europe, next to socialists, liberals, and greens, one should not forget the (more or less secularized) Christian-democratic parties which are still a major force in many countries—indeed, they form the core of the European People's Party, the main party federation in the European parliament. Advocacy and debate around basic income is about as scarce within Christian parties as it is within socialist parties, but not quite absent. Consider Dieter Althaus, a member of Angela Merkel's CDU (the Christian Democratic Union of Germany) and prime minister of the East German state of Thuringen (from 2003 to 2009). He proposed in 2006, under the name *solidarisches bürgergeld* (solidary citizen's money), a basic income of 600 euros per month (about 25 percent of Germany's GDP at the time) for every citizen aged 14 or more, funded by a linear income tax of 50 percent and administered in the form of a negative income tax.

Another example is provided by Christine Boutin, France's housing minister (from 2007 to 2009) in President Nicolas Sarkozy's right-of-center government. She is the founder and leader of the *Parti Chrétien-Démocrate* (Christian Democratic Party), as it is called since 2009, having been founded in 2001 as the *Forum des Républicains Sociaux* (Forum of Social Republicans). Asked in 2003 by Prime Minister Jean-Pierre Raffarin to draw up a report on "the fragility of social ties," she surprised France's public opinion by publishing a strong plea in favor of a strictly individual and unconditional "universal dividend," which she has been consistently advocating since then.[119]

More than explicitly Christian political parties, Christian organizations actively involved in public life have been lobbying in favor of a basic income. A striking example is provided by the Justice Commission of the Conference of Religious of Ireland. This organization, led by Father Seán Healy and Sister Brigid Reynolds, has from the beginning of the 1980s vigorously advocated an unconditional basic income. It published many well-documented reports and drew up scenarios for implementing a basic income, taking advantage of a political system that allows faith-based civil society organizations to actively participate in the political decision-making process and influence the political agenda. Thus, in September 2002, the Irish government published a Green Paper on basic income partly inspired by the work of the Justice Commission.[120] In 2009, Healy and Reynolds left the Conference of Religious of Ireland and launched an independent think tank, Social Justice Ireland, "open to anyone—lay or religious, organization or individual—who supports the building of a just society," but both the Christian inspiration and the advocacy of basic income remained prominent.[121] Similarly, in Austria, the *Katholische Sozialakademie* (Catholic Social Academy), an institution of further education linked to the Catholic Church, published in 1985 the first monograph on basic income to appear in German and has played a leading role in the Austrian discussion ever since.[122]

This explicit endorsement of basic income by church-linked organizations is not a catholic monopoly. John Vikström, the Lutheran archbishop of Finland (from 1982 to 1998) went out of his way to make a vibrant plea for basic income in a speech he gave in London in 1998.[123] And it is a Lutheran bishop, Zephania Kameeta, who has spearheaded the campaign for the introduction of a basic income in Namibia. Jointly with two Lutheran missionaries, Claudia and Dirk Haarmann, he inspired a much-publicized pilot experiment in a Namibian village (discussed in chapter 6) that helped stir interest in basic income elsewhere, not least in Lutheran Germany, and he managed to garner the support of the Lutheran world federation.[124] In neighboring South Africa, the South African Council of Churches was one of the most active components in the Basic Income Grant Coalition set up in 2002, and in 2006 the Anglican archbishop and Nobel Peace Prize laureate Desmond Tutu also expressed his firm support.[125] In a more remote past, the plea for a guaranteed minimum income by Baptist minister Martin Luther King, Jr. was no doubt also rooted in his Christian faith.[126]

Support for basic income in the Christian tradition is by no means obvious. True, there is a famous passage in the Gospel of Luke in which Jesus tells the crowd: "Consider the ravens: They do not sow or reap, they have no storeroom or barn; yet God feeds them. And how much more valuable you are than birds! . . . Consider how the wild flowers grow. They do not labor or spin. Yet I tell you, not even Solomon in all his splendor was dressed like one of these. If that is how God clothes the grass of the field, which is here today, and tomorrow is thrown into the fire, how much more will he clothe you—you of little faith!"[127]

But this passage sits uneasily next to two other quotes, hardly less famous and frequently mobilized by critics of basic income.[128] One is much older and brief. God is supposed to have told Adam and Eve when kicking them out of the Garden of Eden: "By the sweat of your brow you will eat your food" (Genesis 3:19). The other, more explicit, is from one of Saint Paul's epistles to the Thessalonians:

> In the name of the Lord Jesus Christ, we command you, brothers, to keep away from every brother who is idle and does not live according to the teaching you received from us. For you yourselves know how you ought to follow our example. We were not idle when we were with you, nor did we eat anyone's food without paying for it. On the contrary, we worked night and day, laboring and toiling so that we would not be a burden to any of you. We did this, not because we do not have the right to such help, but in order to make ourselves a model for you to follow. For even when we were with you, we gave you this rule: "If a man will not work, he shall not eat (Thessalonians 3: 6–10, NIV).

Ever since Vives's plea for a means-tested minimum-income scheme, this passage has been quoted in order to justify the demand that the income guaranteed by public authorities should not be obligation-free but restricted to those willing to work. If it is read carefully, however, the text does not deny the right to subsistence to those who do not work. On the contrary, it denies that one does not have that right, while inviting Christians to follow the visitors' model in not misusing it.[129]

Whether or not one follows this interpretation, it is clear that Christians who want to anchor the advocacy of an unconditional basic income in their religious tradition can appeal to the forceful and repeated assertion of a special concern for the poor. We already quoted in chapter 3, as one of the sources of inspiration for Juan Luis Vives's pioneering plea for public assistance, a famous passage from Saint Ambrose's *De Nabuthae Historia:* "It is the hungry man's bread you withhold, the naked man's cloak that you store away, and the money that you bury in the earth is the price of the poor man's ransom and freedom."[130] This text dating from the fourth century was incorporated around 1150 in the *Decretum Gratiani,* the first code of canon law.[131] It was also quoted approvingly by Thomas Aquinas (1225–1274) in a striking passage of his *Summa Theologiae* that justifies stealing from the uncharitable rich when the poor have no other way of securing their subsistence.[132] However, the experience of centuries of public assistance triggered the worry that this concern for the poor might be implemented in ways that were stigmatizing, degrading, humiliating, and in the end counterproductive. The Christian duty of charity requires that the poor be helped, and from Vives onwards, more and more became persuaded that it was best for the civil authorities to be in charge. But this must be done in a way that respects, indeed restores, the equal dignity of all members of the community as children of God. Hence, imposing conditions that allow officials to invade people's privacy, that force people to accept demeaning jobs, or that require people to demonstrate their own hopelessness is not the way to go. An unconditional basic income makes more sense and is in no way incompatible with promoting as role models, as Saint Paul did, those who "worked night and day, laboring and toiling so that [they] would not be a burden to any of you."

Organizing Without Organization

This quick overview of past, present, and potential support for (and opposition to) basic income does not exactly suggest that the introduction of a generous basic income is imminent anywhere in the world. True, there are a number of organizations, including political parties, advocating basic income, often with great enthusiasm and sometimes with great perseverance. But many are instances of what might be called "cheap support"—support that does not cost much because the supporting organization has little chance of ever being able to put in place what it supports.[133] In the case of green parties, for example, the intensity and clarity of their endorsements seem to be inversely correlated with the probabilities of their governmental participation, itself largely a function of the electoral system. Another quite different illustration is arguably provided by George McGovern. By the time he got the nomination and the prospect of being in power had to be taken more seriously, he dropped his ambitious $1,000 Plan. Later he reflected: "A number of my supporters tell me in retrospect that I never should have changed the $1,000 Plan. They have a point. The Plan was a complicated but basically sound idea. Yet it was also politically disastrous and maddeningly difficult to explain in the midst of a campaign. The misperceptions and misconceptions of it simply could not be laid to rest, no matter how hard we tried. In the end, I offered a different plan to accomplish the same objectives—taking people out of poverty and taking the nation out of the welfare mess."[134]

One may wonder, however, whether political feasibility depends exclusively on existing organizations such as political parties or labor unions. In today's Internet age, perhaps not. The "power of organizing without organizations" has helped basic-income activists to attract media attention via new forms of cooperation outside the realm of traditional politics.[135] If the prospects for the realization of a basic income have made any progress over the last decennia, that is probably more owing to the development of a network of supporters than to the negotiation of electoral programs by political parties, in the best cases sharply divided on the issue. The Basic Income European Network (BIEN), founded in 1986 and expanded worldwide in 2004 as the Basic Income Earth Network, illustrates this potential. Thanks to the internet, running such a network on a continental and even more on a global level has become feasible without the support of some preexisting organization to provide logistic assistance and funding.

BIEN itself has been to a large extent a network of engaged academics sharing and spreading information across borders about relevant events and publications. But some of its affiliate national networks helped trigger and feed nationwide public debates. One interesting case is Germany, where there had been some modest interest in basic-income ideas in the 1980s, in particular among people close to the incipient green movement. However, the fall of the Berlin wall and the subsequent reunification of Germany (in October 1990) created such a daunting challenge for the German welfare state that the discussion about basic income and related ideas practically disappeared for many years.[136] It was spectacularly revived as a reaction to the so-called "Agenda 2010," also known as "Hartz IV," the profound reform of the German welfare state finalized in 2005 by Chancellor Gerhard Schröder's coalition of social democrats and greens. The preparation and implementation of this reform, which greatly toughened the restriction of benefits to those willing to work, triggered not only resistance by organizations clinging to the status quo, but also unprecedented interest in and campaigning for an unconditional basic income. In November 2003, for example, a pro-basic-income poster campaign in German metro stations was launched under the motto *"Freiheit statt Vollbeschäftigung"* ("Freedom Instead of Full Employment"). In July 2004, the *Netzwerk Grundeinkommen* (Basic Income Network) was founded. The debate on basic income soon reached the talk shows and the general press, with the flamboyant drugstore-chain boss Götz Werner and the young *Die Linke* leader Katja Kipping as star actors. Far more books were published on basic income in Germany in just a few years than in the centuries that came before.[137]

Even more remarkable is what happened in Switzerland. In 2008, the German filmmaker Enno Schmidt and the Swiss entrepreneur Daniel Häni, both based in Basel, produced *Grundeinkommen: ein Kulturimpuls*, a "film essay" that paints a simple and attractive picture of basic income, strongly inspired by Götz Werner.[138] The dissemination of this film through the internet in German-speaking Switzerland (representing over 70 percent of the Swiss population) helped prepare the ground for an official popular initiative launched in April 2012 with the following content:

1. The Confederation introduces an unconditional basic income.
2. The basic income must enable the whole population to live a dignified life and to participate in public life.
3. The law will determine the funding and level of the basic income."[139]

The text itself did not stipulate a precise amount, but its presentation on the website of the initiative and subsequent publications by the initiators mentioned a monthly amount of 2,500 Swiss francs per adult (about 39 percent of Switzerland's GDP per capita at the time) and 625 Swiss francs per child.[140] If an initiative gathers over 100,000 validated signatures in eighteen months, Switzerland's federal government is obliged to organize a countrywide referendum within three years, either on the exact text of the initiative or on a counterproposal, to be negotiated with the initiators.

On October 4, 2013, the initiators handed in 126,406 valid signatures to the federal chancellery. On August 27, 2014, after validation of the signatures and examination of the arguments, the Federal Council (Switzerland's national executive) rejected the initiative without making a counterproposal. In its view, "an unconditional basic income would have negative consequences on the economy, the social security system and the cohesion of Swiss society. In particular, the funding of such an income would imply a considerable increase of the fiscal burden." The proposal was subsequently submitted to both chambers of the Swiss Parliament. On May 29, 2015, the Commission of Social Affairs of the National Council (Switzerland's federal house of representatives) recommended by a vote of 19 to 1 (with 5 abstentions) that the proposal for an unconditional basic income be rejected. After a thorough discussion at a plenary session on September 23, 2015, the National Council proceeded to a preliminary plenary vote and endorsed this negative recommendation by a vote of 146 to 14 (with 12 abstentions). On December 18,

2015, the basic income initiative was put up for a final vote in the National Council: 157 voted against, 19 in favor, and 16 abstained. On the same day, the Council of States (the Swiss senate, made up of representatives of the cantons), rejected it by a vote of 40 to 1, with 3 abstentions. In all cases, all the representatives from the center, right, and far-right parties voted against the proposals, while all pro votes and abstentions came from the socialist and green parties, both sharply divided. The degree of support thus ranged from 0 percent in the Federal Council and 2 percent in the Council of States to 10 percent in the final vote of the National Council.[141] A few weeks before the referendum, each Swiss citizen received, as usual, a booklet containing the argument of the initiators of the proposal and the argument of the Federal Council, in this case recommending rejection. On June 5, 2016, the turnout was 46 percent, with 76.9 percent voting against the proposal and 23.1 percent in favor. From its inception in April 2012 to the final vote in June 2016 and beyond, the process triggered a public debate on basic income and a public awareness of the idea unequalled anywhere else in the world and at any time in history.

At about the same time as the Swiss initiative, another popular initiative was launched at the level of the European Union, using a new instrument created by the 2007 Lisbon Treaty and operational since April 2012. To be acceptable, a European Citizens Initiative needs to be initiated by seven EU citizens living in seven different member states and must consist of a proposal that belongs to a domain in which the European Commission has the power to propose legislation. In order to be successful, it must gather at least one million signatures from EU citizens entitled to vote for the European Parliament within the next twelve months, and also reach a threshold number of duly validated signatures in at least seven member states. Successful initiatives are entitled to an official response by the European Commission and to a hearing at the European Parliament. In January 2013, the Commission gave its go-ahead to an initiative with the following weak formulation imposed by the narrow limits of the powers of the European Union in matters of social policy: "Asking the Commission to encourage cooperation between the Member States aiming to explore the Universal Basic Income as a tool to improve their respective social security systems." By January 2014, the required one million signatures was far from reached.[142] Nonetheless, the impact was considerable. In most countries, the initiative created an opportunity to widen the debate to sections of the population previously untouched by it, and in several places it was the first time anything like a debate on basic income had been considered. Moreover, it prompted the creation of several new national networks and a new European network—Unconditional Basic Income Europe—officially created as an international nonprofit organization in February 2015. This is not a reboot of the foundation of BIEN from three decades earlier, but a consequence of the awareness that the European Union itself has now become a locus of power highly relevant to distributive issues and a reflection of the conviction that the time has come to mobilize activists, not only to connect academics.[143]

In many ways, all this is quite impressive, and it is certainly unprecedented. It was at house number 54 in the rue de l'Association (a street in central Brussels meant to honor the constitutional freedom of association) that Joseph Charlier, the first to advocate a basic income on national scale, spent the last years of his life, wondering why so few people paid attention to the "only rational solution to the social problem" he had been advocating since 1848. By coincidence, it was a notary office located in the same street that saw the creation, in February 2015, of the international nonprofit association UBI Europe, gathering activists from all over Europe who advocate some version of Charlier's proposal. Without a doubt, the idea has made some progress since Charlier's time. But is it not still miles away from becoming reality? After all, the European initiative fell far short of the required number of signatures, and even if it had gathered them, nothing at all would have followed in terms of legislation. In Switzerland, a very generous basic-income proposal did gather the required number of signatures and, had it passed, would have become a constitutional right. But it was rejected by a three-to-one majority. Can we turn elsewhere for more hopeful prospects?

Participation Income and the Back Door

Ultimately, for some sort of basic income to be implemented and sustained, sufficiently broad support will need to be secured in public opinion and among political leaders anxious not to alienate a large part of the electorate with a proposal that so blatantly decouples income and productive contribution. The nature of the challenge is vividly presented by economist Robert Frank, who asks us to imagine a group of ten families living off their basic incomes as a rural commune in Colorado:

> Their mornings would be free to drink coffee and engage in extended discussions of politics and the arts. They could hone their musical

skills. They could read novels, write poetry, play nude volleyball. Is it far-fetched to imagine that at least some groups would forsake paid employment in favor of leading lives like these at taxpayer expense? Once such groups formed, wouldn't it be only a matter of time before journalists found them and created an eager audience for reports of their doings? And wouldn't most voters react angrily once footage of the reveling commune members began running on the nightly news? Of course they would, and who could blame them? An Indianapolis dentist with varicose veins rises at 6:00 each morning and drives through heavy traffic on a snow-covered freeway to spend the rest of his day treating patients with bad breath who take offense if they're charged a fee for breaking an appointment without notice. How could such a person not be indignant at the sight of able-bodied people living it up on his tax dollars? In short, it is a pipe dream to imagine that an income grant large enough to lift an urban family from poverty could win or sustain political support for long.[144]

One response consists of trusting the power of the ethical argument articulated in chapter 5, on the assumption—which the argument requires—that the level of basic income in place is sustainable with predictable taxation. The dentist with varicose veins can then rightly be told that he also gets an unconditional basic income and could opt for rural life and nude volleyball. But this can only count as a justification if he is not stuck by surprise with sunk costs in material and human capital investments henceforth heavily taxed, and if the new tax and transfer system is not due to collapse, after all economic agents have adjusted to it.

A second response consists of advocating a partial basic income (as suggested in chapter 6), not just as a first step but as a final destination. This is what Frank himself proposes, in combination with guaranteed employment: "The most direct response to this concern would be to combine a cash grant that is far too small to lift an urban family from poverty with an open offer to pay sub-minimum wages to those willing to perform useful tasks in the public sphere."[145]

A third response, perhaps the most effective one in terms of getting basic income quickly on the political agenda, is the "participation income" first proposed by Anthony Atkinson and later formulated as follows: "One has to ask why, despite finding supporters in all political parties, citizen's income has not yet come close to being introduced. Consideration of this question has led me to the view that, in order to secure political support, it may be necessary for the proponents of citizen's income to compromise: not on the principle that there is no test of means, nor on the principle of independence, but on the unconditional payment."[146]

Like basic income, a participation income is a uniform individual benefit, which can be topped up at will by other incomes. But unlike basic income, it requires a social contribution. In Atkinson's latest formulation, this condition would be fulfilled for those of working age "by full- or part-time waged employment or self-employment, by education, training, or an active job search, by home care for infant children or frail elderly people, or by regular voluntary work in a recognized association. There would be provisions for those unable to participate on the grounds of illness or disability. . . . Reflecting the features of the twenty-first-century labor market, the definition of participation would allow for people holding a portfolio of activities over, say, a thirty-five-hour week, and people may qualify for fractions of this period."[147] In this light, it should be clear that the point of adding the participation condition is not to compress the cost by reducing the number of beneficiaries: "In reality, very few people would be excluded."[148]

On the contrary, one can expect the cost of a participation income scheme to be significantly higher than that of a straight basic-income scheme at the same level because of the controls it requires and the disputes these will generate. When first proposing the participation condition, Atkinson's aim was not to make basic income cheaper. It was rather to secure political acceptability in a post-Thatcher context: "One of the legacies of the Thatcher years has been concern about dependency, and this is not limited to Britain."[149] Hence his conviction that "such a scheme offers the only realistic way in which governments may be persuaded that citizen's income offers a better route forward than the dead end of means-tested assistance."[150] This may be somewhat of an overstatement, but it cannot be denied that Atkinson has a point.[151]

However, as stressed by De Wispelaere and Stirton and recognized by Atkinson himself, the implementation of a participation income creates plenty of administrative challenges.[152] If the condition is taken seriously, the introduction of a participation income would require setting up mechanisms for checking whether an adequate quantity of socially useful activity is being performed. These mechanisms could easily become very cumbersome, given the intrusiveness required in order to check the satisfaction of the thirty-five-hours portfolio condition by activities performed in self-employment, in the domestic sphere, or in voluntary organizations. They would also run a serious risk of corrupting "voluntary" work: associations that rely on volunteering would be given the unpleasant policing role of checking the regular attendance of their "volunteers." In addition, the difficulty of distinguishing what falls within the province of, say, authentic artistic activity—reputed to be socially useful—from what falls within the province of self-indulgence—at best of strictly private interest—illustrates the more general difficulty of establishing a consensual distinction between the socially useful and the rest, once one has decided to discard as the sole criterion the willingness of a private or public employer to pay for the activity.[153]

As a result of these difficulties, one can expect the implementation of a participation income to quickly face an uncomfortable dilemma between costly and intrusive checks on the one hand and arbitrariness on the other. This could create pressure towards reinstating the usual strings—a restriction to those employed or willing to accept employment—at the expense of the scheme's emancipatory impact. But it can also prompt further steps towards an obligation-free basic income. For example, as suggested by James Tobin, a declaration by recipients that they are spending some amount of time on useful activities may be considered sufficient.[154] Or, if there is a specific political concern about young adults, one could confine the participation condition to specific age groups. Study grants given to adult students are obviously conditional on the pursuit of education. A basic income for young adults would amount to universalizing the funding currently reserved for students. It would not be outrageous to make it conditional upon the pursuit of some activity that contributes to their education in a broad sense.[155] Alternatively, some sort of compulsory community service of a few weeks or months could be introduced, that could at the same time, if well conceived, generate some useful by-products, such as strengthening social cohesion by mixing social groups or increasing awareness of the care our environment needs.

After a while, the weakening of the participation condition along one of these paths or indeed its complete removal could be sold, compared to the maintenance of a strict condition, as being in the material interest of all parties: less burdensome for the beneficiaries and the administration in charge of checking that the conditions are fulfilled, and less costly for the taxpayers. Clearly, whether in a stronger or milder version, the participation condition does restrict freedom. But this is no decisive argument against going for it. Purism is the best recipe for getting nowhere.[156] Moreover, whether or not any formal condition of participation is imposed, the introduction of a basic income must in our view be combined, as argued in chapter 1, with a public discourse that values contribution to the community. The firm floor that is provided to all is not there for us to lie on and indulge ourselves, but for us to stand on and do things that make sense to us as well as to others.

In any event, we very much doubt that a generous unconditional basic income will ever be introduced anywhere as a result of a big triumphal revolution. It is more likely to enter through the back door.[157] Certainly it will start with a modest level, and perhaps with some participation condition. Perhaps it will also make its way to reality via a negative income tax, so as to reduce the impact on political feasibility of two powerful yet illusory impressions created by a basic income paid upfront. As described in chapters 1 and 2, these are the impression that the tax burden imposed by the state on the citizens is massively increased, and the impression that tax money is wasted on the rich.[158] On the other hand, once in place, the very universality of a basic-income scheme may contribute to its political resilience.[159] Whether aiming for the front gate or for the back door, the endeavor to institute a basic income needs a vision: not just a dream but an attractive social model, duly scrutinized as regards both its fairness and its sustainability. This model must be articulated and subjected to debate in the public space of our liberal democracies. Serious hope for a fairer society is permitted only if power relations are tamed by the operation of a sufficiently effective deliberative democracy. But more is needed than the vision of a sustainable social model that can be accepted by free and equal persons.

In addition to visionaries, activists are needed—ass-kickers, *indignados,* people who are outraged by the status quo or by new reforms or plans that target the poor more narrowly, watch them more closely, and further reduce the real freedom of those with least of it. There have been and will be plenty of such plans, several of which have become or will become reality.[160] Activists are indispensable to denounce them, to resist them, to push them back. Their fight is likely to be more effective if it is not driven, or not exclusively driven, by self-interest, but also animated by a sense of justice, and if it is not purely defensive but guided by a credible conception of a desirable future, by a coherent set of proposals that are not just the preservation of the status quo or a return to an idealized past, by a realistic utopia. The activists' protests and struggles are being strengthened by the availability of a compelling vision of this sort, but the vision would have no chance of becoming reality if not for them.

It would also have no chance of becoming reality if not for a third category of actors: all the tinkerers, opportunists, piecemeal engineers, and people who have enough of a vision to know in which direction one needs to go. These are people with enough of a feeling for social realities to know what can trigger effective activist energy, but who also have an eye for the cracks in the present system—for the crises that create windows of opportunity, for the conjunctures that are bad enough to feed a widespread desire for change (but not so bad that short-term emergency measures are all that is possible). Good tinkerers are keenly aware of administrative manageability, but also of political palatability; they accurately sense what political actors will dare to do and what they will be proud of having done. They do not recoil at the thought of unholy alliances.[161] They are constantly on the lookout for fruitful compromises, for ways of turning apparent regressions into springboards for further progress, and for steps that can be achieved but not sustained, because they generate new problems that can be solved only through further steps in the desired direction.

The opportunities to be seized are crucially dependent on the specific problems encountered by each country's tax-and-transfer systems, on the vagaries of its political game, and on the tenor of its public discourse. There is therefore no general answer to the question of the best back-door strategy, no answer that can claim validity for all national contexts. For the economic reasons outlined in chapter 6, however, our guess is that it will often involve the cautious introduction of a strictly individual but partial basic income, keeping some parts of existing public assistance system as conditional top-ups. And for political reasons explained in this chapter, our guess is that it may also have to involve, if only for window-dressing purposes, some sort of participation condition.

8

Viable in the Global Era?
Multi-Level Basic Income

So far, we have taken it for granted that the scale at which it makes most sense to introduce a basic income is that of a sovereign state. Ever since Joseph Charlier wrote in the mid-nineteenth century, this is the scale spontaneously adopted by most basic-income advocates. Indeed, some of the expressions commonly used to refer to basic income—state bonus, national dividend, citizen's wage, and citizen's income, for example—suggest an intrinsic connection with a national community. Moreover, we have so far taken for granted that the economic and political feasibility of basic income can be discussed within a purely domestic framework. But so-called "globalization" forces us to look at these issues in a different light. One might even fear that it could inflict a fatal blow to both the desirability and feasibility of a basic income so conceived.

Justice Among Thieves

Let's look at desirability first. We argued in chapter 5 that social justice, understood as a fair distribution of real freedom, requires the introduction of an unconditional basic income. But can one still think about social justice at the level of a particular society taken in isolation? Whether or not our particular conception of social justice is adopted, should one not instead view mankind as a whole as the appropriate community among whose members resources need to be distributed fairly? Political philosophers who are committed, as we are, to a liberal-egalitarian conception of social justice have been discussing this issue intensively since the 1990s. Some, including John Rawls, consider that the demands of egalitarian justice apply only within "peoples"—that is, nation–states—while international justice is character-ized by far weaker principles of fair cooperation and mutual assistance.[1] Others consider that the process of globalization is creating such a degree of world-wide interdependence and intercommunication that making the demands of egalitarian justice stop at national borders becomes increasingly arbitrary. This is also our view. Egalitarian social justice must apply on a global scale.[2]

If this is the case, our conception of justice as real freedom for all requires an unconditional basic income to be introduced and sustainably maximized at the world level. Such a basic income, funded on a global scale, would be required to distribute more fairly the gifts or opportunities that people today enjoy to extremely unequal extents across the globe. As has been repeatedly documented, the most powerful determinant of inter-individual inequality worldwide is the citizenship with which one is born and the as-sociated entitlements.[3] But how are we then to understand the proposals to introduce a basic income in rich countries, to which the bulk of this book has been devoted? Do such proposals not amount, as Hillel Steiner puts it, to "justice among thieves"?[4] The honest answer must be: yes, they do. But it does not follow that discussing such proposals is pointless or that defending them is illegitimate. Why not?

First, just as the injustice of the wider society does not excuse us from pursuing greater justice in our associations and local communities, the injustice of our world does not exempt us from trying to achieve greater justice within our country. Second, what we need in order to achieve justice on a global scale is institutions, not discretionary aid. The relevant question, therefore, is not whether any sum transferred domestically might have made a greater contribu-tion to global justice if paid instead to some poor people in poor countries. It is, rather, whether building the right sort of institutions at the level at which this is now politically feasible, in rich and poor countries alike, can contribute to the building of a just global institutional order. Third, the discussion of national basic-income schemes does not prevent us from beginning to think about the desirability and sustainability of such schemes at a supranational level—as we shall do shortly. For these three reasons, the fact that globalization forces us to adopt a global conception of social justice does not make ethical nonsense of attempts to distribute real freedom more fairly among the residents of a country by introducing a basic income at national level.

So far so good. But does globalization not make economic nonsense of such an attempt? Discussing an unconditional basic income in one country may have made plenty of sense at the time of the brief British debate in the 1920s, at the time of the intense North-American debate in the late 1960s, and perhaps even at the time of the European debates that started in the 1980s. But how could it possibly make any sense in the twenty-first century, in an era in which information, capital, goods, and people are crossing national borders as they have never done before? In this new context, are the prospects for a national basic income not deeply altered? Indeed, have they not dramatically collapsed?[5]

Race to the Bottom

Why is the economic sustainability of an unconditional basic income threatened by globalization? Because of the operation of two mechanisms. One has to do with its attractiveness to potential beneficiaries, the other with its unattractiveness to potential contributors. Neither mechanism constitutes a threat to a welfare state mainly governed by the insurance principle, but both operate fully in the case of an unconditional basic income.

A pure social insurance or contributory system involves no genuine or ex-ante redistribution. The contributions paid out of earnings simply match a set of entitlements to earnings-related retirement pensions, to indemnities for involuntary unemployment, and to other forms of risk compensation. But many aspects of conventional welfare states do involve ex-ante redistribution, typically when child benefits, retirement pensions, sickness pay, or unemployment benefits funded by proportional or progressive contributions are not actuarially equivalent to the contributions paid, but are fixed at the same level for everyone, or not allowed to fall below some floor, or not allowed to rise above some ceiling. Ex-ante or genuine redistribution in this sense— that is, redistribution that does not reduce to the ex-post redistribution inherent in any insurance scheme—is by no means restricted to benefits that are paid to the economically inactive.[6] Ex-ante redistribution also occurs in a form restricted to workers through in-work benefits such as wage subsidies or earned income tax credits for the low-paid. But it is most obviously present when the welfare state includes a general minimum-income guarantee, whether or not it is unconditional in the various senses that are distinctive of a basic income.

If globalization involves the facilitation of international migration, whether worldwide or within a portion of the world such as the European Union, countries with more generous benefit systems—in terms of levels or conditions—will tend to operate as "welfare magnets." For this mechanism to operate, differences in generosity do not need to persuade people to leave their country. It suffices that they help determine the destination of those who are considering migrating.[7] This will put pressure on any scheme that involves significant genuine redistribution, whether it takes the form of cash transfers or in-work benefits, subsidized health care, or subsidized education.[8] The more open the borders of a country with generous and unconditional schemes, the more it will be under pressure to make them less generous and more conditional, in order to stem the selective migration of likely net beneficiaries.

This downward pressure is reinforced by tax competition induced by the desire to keep the net contributors to the redistributive scheme. Even in the absence of any transnational migration of people, the transnational mobility of capital already presents a threat, especially in combination with the transnational mobility of products. If globalization implies that capital can move freely from one country to another and be invested in such a way as to produce goods that can in turn be exported freely from one country to another, profits will be hard to tax by any national government in a globalized economy. However, a high level of taxation of both non-financial capital and high earnings remains possible, as long as the highly-skilled workers that firms need are not too mobile transnationally—and hence not too hard to tax by one or more of the means explored in chapter 6. But as soon as better-paid workers start considering, in sufficiently large numbers, the possibility of moving to countries in which their skills could command higher post-tax returns, high levels of genuine redistribution from both capital and high earners become problematic. Once human capital is thought to be sufficiently mobile, firms will consider settling in places where, for a given cost, they can offer a higher take-home pay. Whether or not these workers and firms actually do move, the fear that they might will lead governments to reduce the rate of taxation on high incomes or to tie benefits more closely to contributions paid, and hence reduce the level or tighten the conditions of genuine redistribution.

Thus, there are twin threats to the economic sustainability of a national basic income arising from globalization—one that stems from the selective immigration of likely net beneficiaries, and one that stems from the selective emigration of net contributors (not only in the form of an actual departure of valuable labor and capital but also, for example, in the form of a fictitious tax-minimizing relocation of the profits of multinational companies or of highly lucrative internet-based activities). Both threats can be addressed by lifting the scale at which the basic income is being introduced. But before exploring this more remote possibility, let us consider what could be done to reduce the vulnerability of basic-income schemes operating at the national level.

Tackling Selective Immigration

The threat of selective immigration is essentially the same as the one faced by the very first conditional-minimum-income schemes introduced at municipal level in the sixteenth century. In the first developed plea for public assistance, as we saw in chapter 3, Juan Luis Vives identified the threat and indicated how, in his view, it should be handled: "Where beggars are able-bodied foreigners, they should be sent back to their cities and villages . . . with provisions for the journey." It is only when they come from "villages and small areas afflicted and ravaged by war"—when they qualify, we would now say, as refugees—that they should be "treated as fellow citizens."[9] Summoned to justify their own scheme, very close to the one recommended by Vives, the magistrates of the city of Ypres went to great lengths to defend a similar position:

> We would be as ready to help anyone, but our resources are scarce enough to mean that we can help perfectly the need of our own poor folks; it is not enough to meet the needs of every man. . . . Those strangers who come to live in our city and to take alms, with a great flock of children, we do not accept. . . . We think there should not be more asked of us than we can give, unless after a period of giving indiscriminately we imprudently bring ourselves to the point where we can no longer help either our own poor or strangers. There is nowhere in the world that can receive and contain all poor people. There is no common chest anywhere that could sustain them all.[10]

When asked to decide whether the scheme complied with Christian doctrine, the censors of the Faculty of Theology of Paris did yield to these pragmatic arguments, but not without expressing their unease: "Whether they are native to the city, or migrants, or from outside it, no one should because of this provision be reduced to the extremes, or nearly the extremes, of destitution."[11]

No such unease is detectable four centuries later in the last paragraph of A. C. Pigou's classic treatise on welfare economics:

> The establishment of an effective minimum standard, if adopted in one country alone, might well lead to a considerable increase in the numbers of the population through the immigration of relatively inefficient poor persons attracted by the prospect of State aid. . . . It is, therefore, to the advantage of a State, which has established a minimum standard above that enjoyed by its neighbours, to forbid the immigration of persons who seem unlikely to attain this minimum without help from the public funds. To this end, idiots, feeble-minded persons, cripples, beggars and vagrants, and persons over or under a certain age may be excluded, unless they are either accompanied by relatives able to support them, or themselves possess an adequate income derived from investments. Unfortunately, however, it is exceedingly difficult to devise machinery which shall be effective in excluding all "undesirable" immigrants without at the same time excluding some that are "desirable."[12]

Passages such as these illustrate the most cruel dilemma faced by people committed to social justice in the more affluent parts of the world: they are torn between sustainable generosity towards their "own poor folks" and generous hospitality to all those "strangers" knocking at the door.[13] This tension is particularly disturbing for basic-income supporters, as the joint appeal of equality and freedom that endears basic income to them should also make them firm supporters of free migration. Surely, the real freedom to choose the way to spend one's life should encompass the freedom to choose where to spend it, and this freedom should not be restricted to those who happen to be born in a privileged part of the planet.

This is an uncomfortable tension, but there are better things to do than mourn a past world of cozy nation–states with sturdy borders, or dream of a future world freed of massive international inequalities and of the irresistible migration pressures they feed. In the meantime, the conflict between these two components of real freedom must be handled. In our conception of global justice, there is no absolute priority for either of them. In particular, there is no fundamental human right of free movement that must be enforced even at the cost of crushing existing redistributive systems. As long as the national level is the highest one at which genuine redistribution can be institutionalized, it needs protection against selective immigration.

The main strategy currently used to protect existing noncontributory schemes is no different from the one recommended by Vives: keep out the potential beneficiaries arriving from elsewhere, unless they come from places ravaged by war. The effectiveness of this strategy is weakened by the un-avoidability of illegal immigration and of subsequent regularizations. And the fences, walls, shipwrecks, and expulsions which its implementation re-quires all illustrate the ugliness of the dilemma involved. The sustainability of (genuine) domestic redistribution imposes firm limits on hospitality. This is true for conditional minimum-income schemes, and is at least as true for an unconditional basic income. Would milder versions of this exclusionary strategy not suffice? There are at least two possibilities.

One consists of imposing a waiting period. Thus, Adam Smith discusses an English rule to the effect that an "undisturbed residence" of forty days is required before poor people can belong to the "own poor" for whom each parish has to provide.[14] In the same vein, the guaranteed-minimum-income scheme for families introduced in the mid-1990s by Governor Cristovam Buarque in the federal district of Brasilia imposed a residence period of ten years before newcomers from other parts of Brazil could claim benefits. A second possibility consists of restricting entitlement to citizens of the country concerned in the strict legal sense of the term. Thus, Japan's 1950 public as-sistance law explicitly states that only Japanese citizens are entitled to the minimum-income scheme. In practice, some foreign residents have been able to access benefits, but only subject to the discretionary power of local agencies.[15] Analogously, China's *Hukou* system entitles migrant families to public health care, public education, and other social services only in the mu-nicipalities from which they originate. This enables Shanghai, for example, to sustain China's highest level of social provision despite the presence of mil-lions of migrants from other provinces on its territory.[16]

Both these versions feature in basic-income proposals. The first one can be illustrated by Brazil's 2004 "citizenship income law" (mentioned in chapter 7), which would restrict the non-Brazilian's entitlement to basic income (once in place) to people who have been living in Brazil for at least five years, and also, in a softer version by a recent US proposal, to make the level of basic in-come depend on the number of years of prior residence.[17] The second version is suggested by the choice of expressions such as "citizen's income" or "citi-zen's wage" to refer to basic income. It is unambiguously illustrated by Joseph

Charlier's "territorial dividend," strictly reserved for those he calls *indigènes* and to descendants of immigrants who can be assimilated only from the third generation.[18] Albeit on a broader scale, it is also illustrated by Jean-Marc Ferry's proposal for a European-Union-wide basic income that would be part of the set of rights defining European citizenship.[19]

Both of these softer versions of the exclusionary strategy face two difficulties that the harder version avoids. One of them is contingent: they may contravene a legal ban on discrimination imposed on a higher level. Where the requirement of a waiting period is concerned, this clash can be illustrated by the first version of the Alaska dividend scheme (laid out in chapter 4), which specified different levels of dividends to which residents are entitled according to their length of residence in the state. The US Supreme Court decided that such differentiation was inconsistent with the Equal Protection Clause of the US Constitution.[20] Where the citizenship requirement is concerned, no member state of the European Union could pass legislation that would grant people different social rights depending on the member state of the European Union of which they are citizens.[21] This is just a contingent difficulty, however. It occurs only when the entity that introduces a noncontributory benefit scheme has to comply with the legal framework of a larger entity in which it is embedded.

There is, however, a second difficulty that is not similarly contingent. The fact that both strategies create two categories of residents, those with full social rights and the others, may be unattractive enough with any income-protection scheme. But it is particularly annoying in the case of a basic income. Unlike benefits that target the economically inactive, a basic income—just as a negative income tax or an earned income tax credit—will benefit workers. While all workers will be taxed, directly or indirectly, at the high rate required to fund the basic-income scheme, those who do not satisfy the condition of minimum residence or citizenship will not receive the basic income (or tax credit) to which all other workers are entitled. If the scheme takes the form of a refundable tax credit, it will have the bizarre consequence that the take-home pay of workers legally performing the same job will differ significantly depending on their length of residence or citizenship status.[22] Moreover, no matter how this basic income is administered, it will involve a major distortion at the lower end of the labor market, with some able to turn down lousy jobs thanks to their unconditional basic income and others forced to accept them because they lack the bargaining power the basic income confers. Once a basic income is in place, the right to work in a country and the right to the basic income must go hand in hand.

Tackling Selective Emigration

The upshot of this exploration of the milder versions of the exclusionary strategy against selective immigration is that they do not provide a credible and attractive alternative to the harder one: shutting the door on many who would like to enter. Regrettably no doubt, if generous national (or, more generally, subglobal) basic incomes are to be made sustainable in the era of globalization, it will therefore not be possible to dispense with some version of the exclusionary strategy.[23] Even this may not be enough to avert a race to the bottom, however. The threat posed by the selective emigration of net contributors also needs to be addressed.[24] How?

One might first think of a strategy strictly symmetric to the one deemed appropriate to limit selective immigration. If it is okay to keep net beneficiaries out, why would it not be okay to keep net contributors in? One strong reason is that the right to emigrate is systematically regarded as a fundamental human right, whereas the right to immigrate is not.[25] There is some hypocrisy in this asymmetry, as people's right to get out is meaningless if there is no country willing to let them in. Nonetheless, the asymmetry makes sense: with no right to emigrate, we are locked up in our country; with no right to immigrate into the country of our choice, not necessarily so. Granting the right to emigrate to people, however, does not entail granting such a right to the wealth they possess, or granting them the right to emigrate without paying back the country's investment in their human capital, and even less granting them the right to evade taxation in their country by localizing elsewhere at least part of their capital or activity. Such restrictions on the right of exit do not annul the right of personal emigration and, if effective, are just as legitimate as the restrictions on the right of entry reluctantly endorsed above.

This is not all that can be done, or perhaps even the main thing that can be done, to stem selective emigration. What creates a threat to the sustainability of a generous noncontributory scheme is not that some net contributors leave, but that they leave because of the higher net return on their human capital they can expect to find abroad. Such a disposition could be countered if one were able to develop some sort of solidaristic patriotism: an attachment to a place, an allegiance or loyalty to the political community it hosts and to the solidarity the latter achieves, that would make high-earners wish to live, work, contribute, and invest locally, rather than shop around for the best post-tax deal. And if solidaristic behavior is not spontaneously forthcoming enough, it can be gently boosted by appropriate transparency and the associated naming and shaming.

Would this not amount to dissuading the highly skilled people of rich countries from moving to poorer countries and improving the latter's lot?[26] In some cases, no doubt. But this patriotism is meant to stem selective mobility across the board: also between rich countries, between poor countries, and from poor to rich countries. In particular, it must inhibit the brain drain from poor countries to rich countries, without preventing people from moving abroad temporarily or even permanently in order to make their country of origin benefit from the skills they learn, the networks they develop, the capital they build up, or the technologies they appropriate while abroad—not just from the remittances they send home. And even if generalized patriotism were to put the brakes more strongly on the migration of the highly skilled from the North to the South than the other way around, it would not follow that this would come at a cost in terms of global justice. For global justice is a matter of distribution not among countries but among individuals. And solidaristic patriotism would do this: it would reduce the threat of selective emigration and thereby strengthen the grip of all countries on the distribution of income among their residents, itself a precondition for the sustainability of genuine redistributive schemes.[27]

How easy or hard it is to handle the threat of selective immigration and emigration will depend on all sorts of local circumstances. In particular, if in the relevant region of the world the languages spoken are different and difficult for non-native speakers to learn—and if, moreover, the associated cultures are distinctive and hard to integrate into—then generous, genuine redistribution will be easier to sustain. Both potential net beneficiaries and current net contributors will balk at the prospect of heavy investments in language learning and cultural adjustment. Moreover, the distinctiveness of national cultures arguably facilitates the development of solidaristic patriotism. For the viability of a national basic income, such a protective shield would, when available, be most welcome. It must be conceded, however, that the very process of globalization tends to erode this protective shield, for two reasons. First, the linguistic obstacles to the immigration of potential net beneficiaries are being eroded by the growth of diasporas that retain their original language and hence provide microenvironments into which newcomers can smoothly integrate. Second, the linguistic obstacles to the emigration of net contributors are being eroded by the spreading of

English as a *lingua franca,* which makes it less burdensome, both domestically and professionally, to settle abroad, especially but not only in the English-speaking part of the world. Nonetheless, as long as they exist, these linguistic differences and the associated cultural differences will keep operating as a brake on transnational migration and thereby reduce the pressure on the sustainability of genuine redistribution. And there are good—though by no means obvious—grounds for wanting at least some of them to persist.[28]

A Global Basic Income?

As mentioned above, the vulnerability that affects a national basic income because of the threat of selective migration can also be addressed by broadening the scale at which redistribution is organized. This is true for the obvious reason that redistribution operating at the level of a larger multinational entity is not vulnerable to migration between the countries it includes. It is also true for a second reason: if some redistribution operates on a broader scale, national redistribution also becomes less vulnerable to selective immigration and emigration. Why? In the absence of redistribution on a broader scale, the arrival of net beneficiaries causes the burden on the country of destination to increase by the whole amount of the net benefit. In the presence of redistribution on a broader scale, by contrast, the stakes are reduced. Before the immigration of net beneficiaries, the country of destination contributed already part of the benefit funded on the broader scale, and after their immigration, other countries will keep contributing to it. Hence, selective immigration is less damaging. And so is selective emigration. In the absence of redistribution on a broader scale, the departure of taxpayers or businesses means the loss of the whole of their contributions for the country they are leaving. If there is redistribution on a broader scale, only part is lost. Consequently, redistribution on a broader scale makes a difference not only because it is itself under less pressure from transborder mobility of both beneficiaries and contributors, but also because it weakens the pressure exercised by transnational mobility on national redistributive schemes. In addition, and more generally, redistribution on a broader scale would soften the cruel dilemma outlined above between country-level solidarity and hospitality towards foreigners, simply because it would diminish the propensity to migrate. With a broad enough scale and a large enough volume of transfers, it could even mean that open borders would no longer be a problem and that the dilemma would vanish.

These considerations support any form of genuine redistribution introduced on a supranational scale. But an unconditional basic income is particularly relevant on this scale, for two reasons. First, if some sort of noncontributory interpersonal transfer system is ever to come into being at a supranational level, it cannot take the form of a complex, subtly-structured welfare state that specifies precisely what qualifies as relevant needs and the conditions under which solidarity will cover them fully, partly, or not at all. It will need to take the crude form of benefits to be accessed under very simple conditions, easy to enforce in a homogeneous way. Second, if an interpersonal supranational transfer system is ever to come into being, it should preferably be designed so as not to create a dependency trap for the countries concerned—that is, an incentive to perpetuate poverty so as to keep transfers flowing. It should therefore provide a floor rather than a net. For these two reasons, a basic income, though not uniquely suitable, would be particularly appropriate.

What could be the broader scales at which one could imagine a basic income being introduced? A worldwide basic income would obviously be best both at protecting itself against selective migration and at protecting all national redistributive schemes. Moreover, it would best fit our conception of social justice as global justice. But is it not so remote a possibility that it is not even worth speculating about? Some people do not think so. The Dutch artist Pieter Kooistra (1922–1998) set up a foundation named *UNO Inkomen Voor Alle Mensen* (A United Nations Income for All People) in order to propagate his proposal for a small unconditional income for each human being, to be funded by issuing an ad hoc currency that could not be hoarded.[29] Many others have come to similar proposals, usually inspired by the generous desire to substantially alleviate world poverty with a simple tool at a moderate expense for the rich of the planet, or by the need to make good use of the (supposedly) large revenues generated by global taxes that have a rationale of their own.[30]

Perhaps the least fanciful family of proposals along these lines is rooted at the core of the climate-change debate. A consensus has gradually formed around the claim that the atmosphere of the earth has only a limited capacity to digest carbon emissions without triggering climatic phenomena likely to be very damaging for large parts of mankind. As the causes of these phenomena are essentially of a global nature, global collective action is required and will be forthcoming with the appropriate speed and zeal only if all parties involved can regard the form taken by this action as a fair deal. But what counts as a fair deal? The most satisfactory interpretation is neither in terms of *cooperative* justice (how should the cost of producing a public good be shared among those who benefit from it?) nor in terms of *reparative* justice (how should the cost of compensating for a public harm be shared among those who caused it?) but in terms of *distributive* justice: how is the value of scarce resources to be distributed among those entitled to them? More specifically, the carbon-absorbing capacity of the atmosphere is a renewable but scarce natural resource to which all human beings, present and future, have an equal claim.

The best way of realizing worldwide "climate justice" so conceived consists of three steps. First, determine, albeit approximately, the threshold which global carbon emissions cannot exceed without creating serious damage. Second, sell to the highest bidders the emission rights that match this threshold for a given period. The uniform equilibrium price that is determined through an auction of this type will percolate into the prices of all goods worldwide in proportion to their direct and indirect carbon content, and accordingly affect consumption and production patterns, including traveling and housing habits. Third, distribute the (huge) revenues from such an auction equally to all those with an equal right to make use of the "digestion power" of the atmosphere—that is, to all human beings.[31] As pointed out in chapter 6, this would amount to something closely analogous, on a global scale, to the funding of a basic income by a tax on land.

If this is what a fair deal requires, a worldwide basic income is still not around the corner, but it is no longer a mere pipe dream. Some implementation challenges no doubt need to be addressed. Distributing the proceeds to governments in proportion to the sizes of their populations may look like a promising step forward, but it can be expected to trigger a backlash if some governments misreport the relevant data or siphon a big chunk of the proceeds before they reach the population. More promising is a transnational scheme that involves a guarantee of reaching individuals, not just governments. To make it more manageable, one might consider restricting it initially to individuals aged over sixty or sixty-five. In countries with a developed guaranteed pension system, the scheme can then take the form of a modest "global" component in the benefit paid by the government to each elderly citizen. In countries with no such system, new administrative machinery will have to be designed but, as the exemplary case of the South African noncontributory

Table 8.1. Percentage shares of world population and carbon emissions, 2012 (United States, European Union, China, Africa)

	US	EU	CN	AF
Share of world population	4.4	7.0	19.1	15.5
Share of world population 65+	7.7	16.2	20.3	6.8
Share of world carbon emissions	16.3	11.7	25.1	3.7

- The share of the population (total or elderly) determines the size of the gross financial benefit from the scheme.
- The share of emissions determines the size of the gross financial contribution to the scheme.
- The difference between the former and the latter determines the size of the net benefit (if positive) or of the net contribution (if negative).

Data Sources: Authors' calculations based on Total Carbon Dioxide Emissions from the Consumption of Energy: US Energy Information Administration (http://www.eia.gov/cfapps/ipdbproject /IEDIndex3.cfm) and (for population figures) United Nations, *World Population Prospects: The 2015 Revision.*

pension suggests, the fact that transfers are concentrated on a subset of the population—and can therefore be higher per capita than if spread more thinly among people of all ages—means that delivery, security, and monitoring costs can be kept at a fraction of the benefit paid out.

Restricting the worldwide basic income, at least initially, to the elderly will have additional advantages. By contributing to security in old age, it will arguably foster the transition to lower birthrates in those countries in which that transition has not yet happened, as the insurance motive for having children will be structurally weakened. Further, by making the aggregate benefit dependent on the number of people who reach an advanced age, this strategy should strengthen government incentives to improve public health, education, and other determinants of longevity. Furthermore, by being initially strongly biased in favor of richer countries in which life expectancy is higher, it will increase the probability of the scheme's being accepted while paving the way for a smooth increase in transfers from richer to poorer countries as the ratios of old to young gradually converge.

As a quick and rough calculation with easily accessible data suffices to show, however, one needs to be careful about the choice of cutoff age. (See Table 8.1.) If the proceeds of a carbon tax are shared in proportion to *total* population, the US, China, and the EU will be big net contributors, and Africa a big beneficiary. If instead the proceeds are shared in proportion to the population over sixty-five, Africa's net benefit will shrink dramatically, while the net contribution of China will be reduced slightly, that of the US reduced greatly, and that of the EU turned into a net benefit. For the time being, at any rate, sixty-five would not be a defensible cutoff age.

In any case, this specific proposal is made only by way of illustration. There is nothing ethically special about carbon emissions as regards global justice. What the latter demands is a fair and sustainable distribution of real freedom among all members of mankind. Even if the revenues from emission rights were distributed fairly, we would still be a long way from it. But the very unequal way in which this scarce common resource is currently being used and the urgency of finding a solution that is not only bearable for future generations but also fair within the present one should provide an opportunity to move forward.

The European Union as a Transfer Union

Even justified by climate justice, even restricted to the elderly, a global basic income may still be too wild a dream to deserve in-depth study. But what about a regional basic income, one introduced at the level of a multinational entity encompassing a subset of the world's nations? One might think of NAFTA, Mercosur, or ASEAN.[32] But both because of the unprecedented process of supranational institution-building that has given it its present shape and because of the nature of the problems it faces as a result, there is one supranational entity for which the idea of a basic income is arguably less extravagant than for any other: the European Union. Both the opportunities for a basic income at that level and the difficulties it raises are of sufficiently broad relevance to deserve close examination. Admittedly, no extent of redistribution at the European level would avoid the tension with a global conception of social justice. The gang would be enlarged, but justice would still be pursued among thieves. Yet, the learning process involved in developing supranational redistributive institutions at the European level and in fashioning the political institutions needed to sustain them is far from irrelevant to the pursuit of global justice. In addition to this broader usefulness it may claim, there are four good reasons for developing redistribution across the borders of Europe's member states—four good reasons, that is, for turning the European Union into a *transfer union*.

The first reason has to do with the very survival of the so-called European social model. A transfer union is needed to address the challenge of selective immigration and emigration in a region of the world in which it is particularly intense, owing to the fourfold freedom of movement—of capital, goods, services, and people—enshrined in the European Treaties. Under the pressure of this intra-European mobility, European member states are increasingly forced to lift their competitiveness above all other concerns and are therefore less and less able to organize at the national level the genuine redistribution required by social justice. Genuine redistribution at the level of the European Union would not escape the pressure stemming from globalization, but it would not be subjected to the far greater pressure weighing on its member states immersed in the European single market. Moreover, as explained above, having some of the genuine redistribution performed by a larger entity makes it easier for its components to keep redistributing generously at their own level and thereby to save from extinction the so-called European social model.

Second, a transfer union is needed to secure the viability of "Schengen"— that is, of the right of free movement for European citizens within the European Union. Cross-border redistribution would reduce not only selective migration, but migration generally in a context in which it can plausibly be regarded as excessive. A naïve economic analysis might consider voluntary migration to be necessarily a contributor to economic efficiency, since it systematically moves factors of production to locations where they are more productive. Such an analysis neglects the negative externalities created both in the communities of origin, thereby deprived of some of their more enterprising members, and in the communities of destination, which have to cope with the educational and cultural integration of migrant families. But whether or not the current level of migration is deemed optimal from the standpoint of economic efficiency, it puts strong political pressure on the freedom of movement, as witnessed not only by the Brexit vote but also by converging opinion surveys in other countries. The freedom-unfriendly response now advocated by many consists of restoring or rethickening the internal borders of the European Union. But there is also a freedom-friendly response, which consists of enabling, say, Romanian or Bulgarian families to remain more easily close to their roots thanks to an EU-wide transfer system. Even in the far more homogeneous context of large nation–states, where internal migration tends to be less problematic, part of the argument for nationwide redistribution has been its function as demographic stabilizer.[33] If the Schengen agreement and the intra-European freedom of movement are to survive politically, turning the European Union into a transfer union is indispensable.

Third, a transfer union is needed to secure the viability of the euro. After much thinking and not too much hesitation, a number of European countries decided in 1992 to go for a common currency.[34] There were warnings, but the European Union did not heed them. It went ahead in 2002, and less than a decade later, the Eurozone was caught in an acute crisis because the less competitive member states had lost the power to devalue their separate currencies. Why did such a crisis erupt in the euro area, while the fifty United States, each similarly disabled, seem to have been coping happily with their single currency for many decades, despite divergences in competitiveness that can be no less dramatic than between European countries? As pointed out, especially by American economists both before the euro was born and after it got into trouble, the fundamental reason is that, in Paul Krugman's compact formulation, "unlike US states, European countries weren't part of a single nation with a unified budget and a labor market tied together by a common language."[35] More explicitly, the United States can rely on two powerful stabilizers, which are far weaker in the European Union.

The first one is interstate migration. The proportion of Americans who move from one state to another is about eight times the proportion of Europeans who move from one member state to another.[36] This is to a significant extent a reflection of the fact that Europe's linguistic and cultural diversity makes moving from one European member state to another on average far less promising in economic terms and far costlier in personal terms than moving from one state to another in the United States. Moving from Attica to Bavaria cannot be expected to be as smooth as moving from South Dakota to California.[37] As we can safely expect this linguistic differentiation to endure, we cannot expect the migration gap with the United States to vanish— at least not until Europe's welfare states are dismantled to such an extent that workers will be massively driven to expatriation, notwithstanding all linguistic and cultural obstacles. Indeed, as argued above, the far greater negative externalities associated with migration in a context of linguistic diversity make it desirable to stabilize the population at the expense of further reducing the potential of migration as an economic stabilizer.

This leaves us with the second powerful stabilizer in the United States: a redistributive tax-and-transfer system that may be far more modest than in many member states of the European Union but that operates overwhelmingly across all fifty states—that is, at the scale of the whole currency area. In the United States, whenever the economic situation of one state worsens relative to others, there is some automatic compensation in the form of in-creased transfers and reduced taxes paid by households and firms located in that state. Early estimates used by American economists to explain why the dollar was sustainable whereas the euro would not be, suggested that about 40 percent of each drop in the GDP in one state was offset by an increase in net transfers from (or decrease in net contributions to) other states. The anal-ogous level of compensation by the EU-wide tax-and-transfer system was and is less than 1 percent.[38] The fact that the American welfare state operates essentially at the federal level means that the impact of growing unemploy-ment on both the revenue and the expenditure sides of a state's budget is far less than if it were operating at the state level, and it is therefore at far less risk of triggering a vicious spiral of increasing budget deficits, swelling public debts, worsening ratings, higher interest rates, and deepening deficits. More-over, higher net transfers mean an injection of effective demand that helps sustain the local economy.

The picture is altogether different in the Eurozone. When hit for what-ever reason (from decreases in foreign demand for some of its main traded products to competitiveness-boosting reforms in other member states) by economic shocks or steady declines, a member-state of the Eurozone is not helped by the transfer system operating within its borders. On the contrary, the more developed its welfare state, the heavier the impact on its public budget of the unemployment generated by its lower competitiveness. And whether it takes the form of higher taxes or less generous benefits or both, the effort to keep the deficit under control will depress domestic effective de-mand, without any noteworthy compensation from an increase in net trans-fers from the rest of the Union. Given that the first stabilizing mechanism—interstate migration—is unpromising, the future of the euro cannot be safe without developing the second one: systematic EU-wide transfers. This gives us a third reason for wanting these.

And there is yet a further reason. The Brexit vote and more generally the upsurge of right-wing and left-wing populism throughout Europe should have made us realize that the European Union cannot hope to regain its le-gitimacy in the eyes of the bulk of its citizens if it keeps being perceived as reducing their social protection in the name of competitiveness—in other words, if it keeps pampering the "movers" while seemingly forgetting the "stay at homes." A European Union that claims to care for all its citizens must show it. In order to facilitate German unification and generate broad allegiance to his emerging *Reich*, Otto von Bismarck created the first national old-age pension system (as related in chapter 3). "The pensions," he said in 1889, "will teach also the ordinary man to regard the Reich as a beneficent institution."[39] Appropriately designed, an EU-wide transfer system could perform an analogous function. It would share in a tangible way, among all European citizens, some of the material benefits which European integration no doubt generates—whether by securing lasting peace, by stimulating productivity, or by realizing all sorts of economies of scale—but which are distributed very unequally.

These are four strong reasons for having a transfer union. Skepticism, however, is not lacking.[40] What form could and should this transfer union take? Could it be a pure insurance scheme between member states, without ex ante redistribution, designed to buffer asymmetric shocks? Such a scheme would help stabilize the euro, but would serve less well the other three functions listed above, and it would have the (arguably) unacceptable implication that richer countries could turn out to be net beneficiaries. What about a transposition, at the level of the Union, of the *Finanzausgleich* (financial equalization) that operates between the budgets of Germany's *Länder?* This would plant the seed of permanent conflict, with contributor member states wanting to interfere with the way "their" monies were spent by the governments of beneficiary member states. The most promising tool is different. In existing federal states, the four functions listed above have never been best served by comparatively small transfers between or to the budgets of the federated entities; rather, they have been best served by huge systems of interpersonal transfers that cross the borders of these entities and are funded at the federal level. Does this mean that we need a federal welfare state at the European level analogous to the American one? The EU member states' elaborate welfare states are very different from each other in both design and funding. They are the path-dependent outcomes of tough struggles, lengthy debates, and laborious compromises. Merging them all into a single EU-wide uniform system may be just about thinkable, but whether it is desirable is more than dubious and it is definitely not doable in anything like the foreseeable future. Let us therefore forget the idea of an EU-wide mega–welfare state and explore more modest forms of cross-border interpersonal redistribution that leave the structure of all national welfare states essentially intact.

One proposal along these lines was made by Philippe Schmitter and Michael Bauer. They called for the gradual introduction of an EU-wide *Eurostipendium* targeting the poorest European citizens. They proposed paying 80 euros per month (about 4 percent of EU GDP per capita at the time) to each European citizen with an income below one-third of the average income in the European Union (then consisting of fifteen member states).[41] This proposal suffers from three major defects. First, it would instantiate (admittedly, to an extent limited by the low level of the transfer) an extreme form of the poverty trap created, as we saw in chapter 1, by means-tested schemes; citizens who earned just below one-third of the average European income would receive a benefit of 80 euros, while those who earned slightly more would receive nothing and thereby end up worse-off than some of those earning less. Second, it would create perverse incentives that could be characterized as an inequality trap at the country level. Consider two countries with an identical GDP per capita. The country in which incomes were more unequally distributed would have a higher proportion of its population below the chosen threshold. In whatever way the scheme is funded, the country with a more unequal distribution would benefit more from the proposed scheme (or contribute less to it) than the one with the more equal distribution. Third, the implementation of such a scheme would need to enforce a homogeneous definition of the income to be taken into account for the sake of assessing whether some household fell below the threshold. What can be included in this income (homegrown food, home ownership, the earnings of one's cohabiting partner, and so forth) or excluded from it (work-related expenses, alimonies, financial burden of dependent children, and so forth)? How intrusive can or must income tests be? These are highly sensitive issues which are unlikely to be resolved with workable uniform solutions at supranational level.

The Eurodividend

Given these difficulties, a proposal that is apparently more radical is actually more realistic.[42] It consists in introducing a genuine unconditional basic income throughout the European Union (or at least the Eurozone) at a level that can vary according to the average cost of living in each of the member states. Something resembling such an EU-wide basic income was proposed as early as 1975, as an efficient alternative to European regional and agricultural policy, in a report to the European Parliament's Economic and Monetary Affairs Committee by Brandon Rhys-Williams, a rather eccentric conservative member of the European Parliament.[43] At a more abstract level, it has been defended by philosopher Jean-Marc Ferry as a central component of

European citizenship.[44] More recently, it surfaced in the limited form of an occasional universal payment by the European Central Bank to all Europeans as a way of kickstarting the European economy (as discussed in chapter 6). Our own proposal consists in a eurodividend of 200 euros on average per month and per person (representing about 7.5 percent of the GDP per capita of the European Union in 2015), with a higher amount in countries with high costs of living, and a lower one in countries with low costs of living. This scheme avoids in one swoop all three defects of Schmitter and Bauer's euro-stipendium proposal. There is no risk of poor households suffering decreases in their net incomes as their earnings increase, since incomes are simply added to the eurodividend. Nor is there a risk that countries would be punished for adopting policies that reduce inequality and poverty (with a given average income), since the level of transnational transfer is not determined by the number of people who fall below the chosen threshold. Moreover, since there is no income condition, there is no need for a homogeneous definition and monitoring of personal income in order to determine the level of benefit.

How is this eurodividend to be funded? We discussed at some length (in chapter 6) the main options for funding a basic income at national level. But the most appropriate options at one level are not necessarily the most promising at another level. Take personal-income taxation, the most straightforward choice at national level. It would require a uniform definition of taxable income across member states, and therefore raise a problem analogous to the one mentioned above in connection with the Schmitter-Bauer means-tested scheme. Reaching an agreement on a uniform personal-income tax base is bound to be so contentious and laborious that it would be most unwise to bank on it. Social-security contributions, in several member states the main source of funding of the welfare state, are no more promising. They should wisely be reserved for the funding of national social-insurance schemes. On the other hand, there may be specific opportunities at the EU level—for example, Rhys-Williams has pointed to probable savings in what is by far the biggest item in the EU budget, the common agricultural policy. However, part of this expenditure arguably serves valuable non-redistributive purposes, and even if the bulk of the corresponding revenues could be reallocated to the funding of a eurodividend for all European citizens, the level of the latter could not exceed 10 euros per month (about 0.5 percent of the EU's GDP per capita in 2015).[45]

It is therefore indispensable to turn to forms of taxation that would be specifically appropriate at the European level. One of them is money creation by the European Central Bank. But, as explained in chapter 6, this could not fund a stable level of benefit but only a fluctuating top-up. Another tempting option is the financial transaction tax, also known as the Tobin tax. On the basis of 2012 estimates for the European Union, a yield-maximizing, EU-wide Tobin tax could, under fairly optimistic assumptions, fund a basic income of no more than 10 euros per person and per month. Moreover, revenues from such a tax can be expected to fluctuate widely with speculative movements, and such revenues can easily be overestimated, as the tax elasticity of the tax base may increase once speculators find loopholes or shift to more lucrative endeavors.[46]

What about a carbon tax (as described in chapter 6) or, rather, a fee to be paid for the right to use some of the carbon quotas allocated to the EU? The sale of the permits currently covered by the Emission Trading System is estimated to yield 21 billion euros annually by 2020, or the equivalent of a monthly eurodividend of about 3.5 euros. However, most carbon emissions are not subjected to the trading system. If all were, the yield would be higher. Under reasonable assumptions, it could fund a eurodividend of up to 17 euros per month. Consequently, even under very favorable assumptions—100 percent of the permits auctioned, 100 percent of the proceeds allocated to the eurodividend—the level of the dividend that could be funded in this way remains very modest, subject to fluctuations that affect the market-clearing price of the permits, and exposed, moreover, to the long-term downward impact of the fee on the volume of the demand for emission permits.[47]

A further possibility worth considering is a tax on the use of fossil energy (also described in chapter 6). The base of such a tax is meant to incorporate the negative effects of carbon emissions, but also of local externalities and resource depletion.[48] It is, of course, a necessary feature of a basic income funded in this way that it should redistribute from countries with high levels of fossil-energy consumption to countries with low levels. This is not problematic if differences in energy consumption are essentially determined by differences in wealth—which is generally the case across regions of the world, but less so across member states of the European Union. It is also not problematic if differences are essentially determined by the extent to which the various countries adopt effective energy-saving strategies, as this is how appropriate incentives are supposed to work. However, a country's level of energy consumption is also affected by some of its natural features—in particular, how cold its climate happens to be. As it is difficult to argue that the populations of Northern countries should pay the price of their choices to remain in the cold places where their ancestors happened to settle, it is unlikely that such a tax could ever be regarded as fair if implemented at the EU level.

The taxation of capital would not face this difficulty and, because of its transnational mobility, supranational taxation is especially appropriate. One form it could take is an EU-wide progressive wealth tax. Thomas Piketty estimates that such a tax, at sustainable rates, could yield up to 2 percent of the European Union's GDP, or the equivalent of a monthly basic income of about 40 euros.[49] The fact that so few member states have such a tax so far might be an argument in its favor, as there would be less disparate arrangements to harmonize. But it might also be an indication that instituting an EU-wide wealth tax would be even more difficult than instituting an EU-wide income tax; in both cases, the big challenge would be agreeing on a common operational definition of the tax base.

An EU-wide corporate tax might therefore provide a more promising alternative. The rates at which profits are being taxed at source vary widely across member states of the European Union, from 0 percent in Estonia to about 30 percent or more in Belgium, France, Italy, and Germany. Repeatedly, proposals to stop the tax competition which this variation feeds and reflects have called for harmonizing corporate tax rates across member states, or at least imposing a minimum rate, and also, more ambitiously, organizing corporate taxation at the EU or Eurozone level. For the moment, there is no common definition of the corporate tax base, but the part of the GDP that accrues to financial and non-financial corporations can be regarded as its ceiling. This corresponds to about 16 percent of GDP in both the EU and the Eurozone in 2014. With an EU-wide rate of 30 percent, this could fund a basic income of about 100 euros per month (or nearly 5 percent of GDP per capita in 2015). This is a very maximalist estimate, however, not only because of the broad definition of the tax base and the selection of a high tax rate but also because it disregards any effect of the increased tax rate on the tax base. Besides, the fact that an agreement could not even be reached on a minimum for national rates makes this avenue, too, a rather remote prospect.[50]

In our view, the most promising avenue is provided by the most Europeanized of all existing taxes: the Value Added Tax (VAT). This indirect tax is paid, ultimately by the final consumer, in proportion to the value added to the product at every stage in its production. The VAT is sometimes proposed for the funding of a national basic income (as seen in chapter 6), but it has specific advantages for the funding of an EU-wide basic income. Unlike the definition of personal income, wealth, or corporate profits, the definition of value added for tax purposes is already homogenized at EU level. It needed to be, because VAT is used to fund part of the EU budget, and because the determination of VAT rates by each member state is constrained by EU legislation. Using the present conventions, one can estimate that each percent of VAT applied to the harmonized tax base of all member states (including those benefitting currently from reduced rates) would yield annual revenues on the order of 60 billion, or about 10 euros per month per capita. Because the European Union's GDP is slightly more than twice this harmonized value added tax base, a VAT of 1 percent corresponds to somewhat less than 0.5 percent of GDP. To get a basic income averaging 200 euros per person and per month (in 2016), the EU-wide VAT rate would need to be around 19 percent.[51]

One could conceivably differentiate or restrict the transfer along the age dimension. The amount could be lower for children, for example, or higher for the elderly. Also, rather than jumping straight to a basic income for all, one could phase it in in steps, starting with a specific age group (as discussed in chapter 6). For example, to help member states cope with the aging of their populations, one could start by allocating all revenues to the 12 percent of Europeans older than 70: a 6 percent VAT would give them unconditional basic pensions of about 500 euros per month.[52] More plausibly, perhaps, given Europe's low birthrate and the European Union's professed concern with child poverty, one could start by targeting the 10 percent of Europeans younger than 10: just a 1 percent VAT, for example, would be sufficient to fund a monthly child benefit of 100 euros.[53] As the age structure varies significantly from one member state to another, the choice between these various formulas for initiating the eurodividend is far from distributively neutral across countries.

We are not offering our VAT-funded eurodividend of 200 euros as a fully-thought-through, duly fine-tuned proposal, but as a baseline for serious thinking about the best way of organizing something unprecedented: a transnational interpersonal transfer scheme. Among the objections that it may give rise to, let us consider just three. First of all, does it make sense to add 19 percent to rates of VAT that are already above 20 percent in some member states? This is not what we are proposing. Neither the new tax nor the new benefit will simply be piled on top of existing taxes and benefits. On the benefit side, the dividend will form the bottom layer of all existing benefits, with the rest subsisting, if their current level is higher, in the form of conditional top-ups. At the same time, the eurodividend is not meant to swell automatically all net earnings. It can be viewed as equivalent to a uniform tax credit that would replace standard tax exemptions on the lower income brackets of every income tax payer. Hence, national budgets would benefit from no longer having to cover the bottom 200 euros of all benefits, and from the suppression of corresponding tax expenditures. Member states could accordingly adjust downward the national tax burden. The most straightforward option is to lower the national component of VAT. But the specific tax and benefit structure of each member state might make other options more attractive.[54]

A second objection is that, for at least some of the four functions mentioned to justify the eurodividend, other instruments might be more effective. Take, for example, the economic stabilization required to secure the viability of the euro. To see how a VAT-funded eurodividend contributes to it, consider the situation of a member state that is suddenly hit by a lasting increase in its rate of unemployment. Under the present setup, the whole of the decrease in tax revenues and the full cost of the unemployed person's replacement income will need to be borne by the budget of the country concerned. In the absence of high mobility and without the possibility of devaluation, the impact on the public deficit and debt can trap the country in a scary spiral. A VAT-funded eurodividend does not cancel this impact, but it attenuates it in two ways. The fall in its revenues is reduced because part of the reduction in the yield of the country's VAT is spread all over the European Union. And the increase in expenditure is reduced because the bottom layer of the incomes of households hit by unemployment takes the form of a eurodividend funded at the EU level, with only the country-level top-ups needing to come out of national revenues. Thus, the fact that the volume of EU-funded benefits paid out in a country hit by a shock would remain unchanged does not prevent the scheme from having a stabilizing effect. It is nonetheless true that this effect would be stronger if the volume of benefits paid out of the common purse were responsive to the economic conjuncture, as would be the case with an EU-funded unemployment insurance scheme.[55] This sort of scheme raises some difficulties which a eurodividend avoids. In particular, it requires a sufficiently uniform definition of what counts as involuntary unemployment and therefore a top-down intrusion into a sensitive area of national social policy. Moreover, to the extent that it operates as an insurance system—that is, without ex ante redistribution—it cannot rule out the embarrassing possibility that poorer countries will end up subsidizing richer ones. Above all, a eurodividend also serves three other functions which an unemployment insurance scheme would not serve as well. And it fits into a broader project for a free society and a sane economy, in which basic incomes at more than one level have an important role to play.

A third objection questions the political feasibility of anything resembling such a eurodividend. According to the existing European treaties, social policy is the preserve of member states. Of course, these treaties could be changed, and the growing awareness of the four reasons listed above for moving to a transfer union is exerting pressure in this direction. But it is hard to imagine a eurodividend emerging smoothly from an intergovernmental negotiation in which national representatives are being judged by their capacity to bring home a net gain for their compatriots. Like the development of national welfare states, the political plausibility of an EU-wide redistributive scheme depends on the emergence of a *demos* that encompasses the whole population concerned. Such a demos can only be said to exist if there are EU-wide political parties pushing for policies that can be regarded as fair throughout the Union and claiming to serve Europe's general interest. And it can only be robust if it is backed by a pan-European civil society with a capacity for lively cross-border discussion and effective mobilization.[56]

If only because of the language barriers, a common demos is much harder to achieve at the European level than at the national one. Yet, in various ways, an EU-wide demos is slowly emerging. Since 2012, over twenty European "citizen's initiatives"—including one on basic income itself (as described in chapter 7)—have been launched, with three of them managing to attract more than one million signatures across the European Union. And in 2014, for the first time, there were declared candidates for the presidency of the European Commission who had to formulate and defend a program before all European citizens during the election campaign for the European Parliament. At the same time, English is spreading fast as Europe's lingua franca, and the civil society active in Brussels is growing by the day. Yet, there is still a long way to go. Less long than for a worldwide basic income, but long enough to keep seeing, in Europe too, the national level as the most relevant level for the immediate introduction of a basic income. Any EU-level cross-border transfer scheme, once in place, would make it easier to sustain national schemes, but we should not wait for the former to be in place before moving ahead with the latter.

Basic Income for Diverse Populations

We have considered above how globalization challenges the economic sustainability of a national basic income and how this challenge might be addressed both by measures taken at the national level and by introducing a basic income on a large scale. But globalization not only affects the economic sustainability of national basic incomes. It also affects their political feasibility. In particular, ongoing immigration tends to make populations more heterogeneous in racial, religious, and linguistic terms, and this ethnic heterogeneity tends to weaken the political sustainability of a generous redistributive system through two distinct mechanisms.

First, the degree of heterogeneity affects the extent to which net contributors to the transfer system identify with (those whom they perceive as) its net beneficiaries—that is, the extent to which they regard them as "their own people" to whom they owe solidarity. This challenge is not new. We saw earlier that, in the defense of their public assistance scheme, the magistrates of the City of Ypres stated quite bluntly that they did not feel they had to take care of strangers: "We prefer our own citizens, whose persons and manners we know, to strangers with whom we have no acquaintance. We are duty bound to look after them, because they are members with us of one political body."[57]

The "strangers" are now among us. When genuinely redistributive schemes are perceived to disproportionately benefit them, the resentment of those who fund them tends to block their expansion and even to jeopardize their viability.[58] Second, institutionalized solidarity can also be expected to be weaker in a heterogeneous society because ethnic differences generate obstacles to smooth communication and mutual trust within the category that can expect to gain most from generous redistributive schemes. Such obstacles make it more difficult for net beneficiaries to coordinate, organize, and fight together.[59]

As a result of the conjunction of these two mechanisms, one can expect institutionalized redistribution to be less generous, other things equal, in more heterogeneous societies than in more homogeneous ones.[60] If globalization means a constant flow of migrants, then invoking a race to the bottom driven by tax and social competition would not even be necessary to predict gloomy prospects for a generous unconditional basic income in a globalized context. The economic constraint will not be binding if the political constraint tightened by growing ethnic diversity stops redistribution before its economic sustainability is at risk.

In this context, would the introduction of an obligation-free basic income not make things even worse, by allowing immigrants to remain disconnected from the formal labor market and thereby prevented from integrating into their host society? In some contexts, it would instead tend to reduce that problem, since a basic income, being universal, removes or reduces the unemployment trap created by means-tested schemes and thereby facilitates economic integration (as explained in chapter 1). Yet, owing to linguistic hurdles, to residential and educational segregation, or to the size of immigrant communities with shared origins, this may not be sufficient to break the vicious cycle of self-perpetuating, underprivileged ghettos. If this is the case, some participation condition may make sense, including compulsory language courses for those not competent enough in the official language of the host country or even compulsory civil service of limited duration. The imposition of such a condition might make sense, and not only because, if well designed, it could strengthen social cohesion and thereby the political sustainability of redistribution. It would also recognize that the provision of opportunities that give substance to the real freedom of immigrants requires more instruments—in particular, linguistic competence—than just the payment of a cash grant.

In contrast with the challenge of economic sustainability, it is obvious that the challenge of political feasibility arising from cultural heterogeneity cannot be addressed by lifting the basic-income scheme to the level of a larger entity, unavoidably even more diverse. Lowering it to a more decentralized, subnational scale may sometimes help.[61] But compared to social protection models that rely on the notion of solidarity, the basic income model is particularly suited to culturally diverse political entities of any size. Solidarity requires a specific, culturally sensitive definition of what counts as being unlucky (involuntarily unemployed, unemployable, involuntarily pregnant, depressed, addicted, and so forth) and therefore entitled to help of a certain type up to a certain point from other people who can similarly expect help if their turns come to be unlucky. By contrast, basic income, conceived as the fair distribution of an inheritance, requires only that people sharing a territory should all regard themselves and each other as free and equal members of one political community. Achieving this in a diverse population should be less difficult than preserving the sort of solidarity that traditional welfare states presuppose. But it will still require daily efforts and smart initiatives in all domains, from electoral systems to urban planning to the school curriculum, and a framing of the identity of the political community that recognizes and values its internal diversity. All of this is crucial to the political viability of an unconditional basic income, but also to many other aspects of the quality of our common life, including the flourishing of an ethos of mutual service.

The upshot of the discussion in this chapter should be clear enough: in order to move forward under current circumstances, one can and must tread several paths simultaneously. Every opportunity must be seized to move, however modestly at first, towards something that starts resembling a world-wide basic income—most promisingly, in the context of striving for a fair deal on global warming. Every opportunity must also be seized to move towards something that starts resembling a supranational, though still geographically limited, basic income—most promisingly, at the level of the European Union—as an anticipation of what should one day be achieved on a higher, global scale and as a contribution to the sustainability of what can be achieved right now on a lower, national scale. Finally, one can trust that sufficient leeway has been kept at the national level, and there is still ample room to reform existing welfare states in such a way that they can incorporate at their very core at least a modest unconditional basic income. These three levels are not rival but complementary. The stronger the global or regional floor, the less pressure on genuine intranational redistribution, and hence the more sustainable a national basic income.

Epilogue

WE ARGUED IN THIS BOOK FOR THE introduction of a regular cash income, paid on an individual basis, without means test or work test, as a central ingredient of the institutional framework of a free, fair, and sustainable society. We indicated why a basic income is to be preferred to related proposals like a basic endowment, a negative income tax, or a compulsory reduction in the maximum length of the working week. We sketched the history of the other two models of social protection—public assistance and social insurance—and traced, against this background, the slow emergence of the basic income idea long before its sudden recent popularity.

We considered the ethical objection that challenges the right to an income for those who choose not to work; spelled out the liberal-egalitarian conception of justice that provides a principled answer to this objection; explained why other conceptions of justice lead to different positions; and explored how rival philosophical approaches could arrive at the same position with alternative justifications. We examined the question of whether a substantial basic income is affordable and economically sustainable, and indicated why we believe a partial basic income funded by an income tax and supplemented by public assistance and social insurance top-ups is the best way forward in the context of a developed welfare state. We surveyed the attitudes toward basic income to be found in organized civil society and in political families; indicated what pushed some in the direction of basic income and some away from it; and made suggestions about how to overcome indifference and hostility. Finally, we recognized that globalization, while contributing to the need for a basic income, does not make its implementation any easier—and we explored various strategies for dealing with this unprecedented challenge.

Is what we have been arguing for utopian? It certainly is, first in the sense that it doesn't exist and never has existed anywhere at a significant level, giving people good cause to suspect it is impossible. It is also utopian in the sense that it is a vision of a better world. Looking across the histories of our societies' institutional frameworks, it is clear that many of the elements we take for granted today were utopian in this twofold sense not that long ago. These elements include the abolition of slavery, the taxation of personal income, universal suffrage, free universal education, and the existence of the European Union. There is a feature that the basic income utopia possesses more than any other: that its implementation would facilitate many other utopian changes. It would support the realization of many ideas, both individual and collective, both local and global, that increasingly find themselves crushed under the pressure of market-imposed competitiveness.

Anyone doubting the power of utopian thinking would be well advised to listen to one of the main intellectual fathers of the "neoliberalism" that has been declared triumphant these days by its friends and even more by its foes. In 1949, long before anyone guessed such triumph was in the offing, Friedrich Hayek wrote: "The main lesson which the true liberal must learn from the success of the socialists is that it was their courage to be Utopian which gained them the support of the intellectuals and thereby an influence on public opinion which is daily making possible what only recently seemed utterly remote." The lesson Hayek learned from the socialists, we must now learn from him: "We must make the building of a free society once more an intellectual adventure, a deed of courage. What we lack is a liberal Utopia."[1] Correct, Mr. Hayek. But the free-society utopia we need today differs profoundly from yours. It must be a utopia of real freedom for all that frees us from the dictatorship of the market and thereby helps save our planet.

Creating this utopia of a truly free society, needless to say, cannot be reduced to instituting an unconditional basic income. No less important are universal basic health care and education, lifelong learning, universal access to quality information on the internet, a healthy environment, and smart town planning. All these are vital to enhancing what we can do on our own, but even more important—because what we can individually do will still remain very little— to expanding what each of us can do in collaboration with others, both nearby and far away, including through meaningful democratic participation. But the sturdy floor provided to individuals by an unconditional basic income is key.

And how shall we reach this utopia? Probably through a series of moves that admit change through the back door more often than through the front gate. Machiavellian thinking will need to play a significant role, in two distinct senses. We will need to think, as Machiavelli did in his *Discorsi*, about how the design of political institutions affects the political feasibility of our proposals. And we will need to think, as "Machiavellians" are reputed to do, about how best to exploit political opportunities. Rather than hope for one spectacular event of earth-shattering scale, we should bank on thousands of occasions cleverly used for short-term relief accruing to long-term progress. There will be disappointments and regressions, as there were in the fights for universal suffrage and against slavery. Utopian visions do not turn real in a day, but they guide us and strengthen us through the effort. And one day we shall wonder why it took us so long to fit beneath our feet a solid floor on which we can all stand. What used to be regarded as the fantasy of a handful of lunatics will then have become an irreversible and self-evident achievement.

Notes

1. The Instrument of Freedom

1. Brynjolfsson and McAfee (2014) and Frey and Osborne (2014) provided influential forecasts. Often presented in eloquent and dramatic fashion, the anticipation of this "second machine age" has been playing a major role in motivating the need to take the idea of basic income seriously. See, for example, Santens 2014, Huff 2015, Srnicek and Williams 2015, Mason 2015 (284–286), Reich 2015 (chapters 22–23), Stern 2016 (chapter 3), Bregman 2016 (chapter 4), Walker 2016 (chapter 5), Thornhill and Atkins 2016, Wenger 2016, Reed and Lansley 2016, Reeves 2016, Murray 2016, and so forth.

2. Growing inequality or polarization can happen within each country in the world, rich or poor, without happening worldwide—for example, as a result of a steady increase of average income in two large and comparatively poor countries, China and India. See Milanovic 2016 for an overview.

3. On these many factors and their interaction, see the vast literature from Wood 1994 to Milanovic 2016. On the less-often noticed impact of shifting social norms on the tracking of (putative) productivity by wages, see Frank and Cook's (1995: chapter 3) insightful analysis.

4. Jan Pen (1971: 48–59) proposed to represent the distribution of earnings as a parade of people of increasing heights whose heights are proportional to their gross earnings. Suppose the parade lasts for an hour, that you are an average earner and hence of average height, and that you are watching a parade of US residents aged 18–59 either working or actively looking for work, first in 1980 and next in 2014. In both cases, you have to stretch your neck in the last couple of minutes to watch the giants walk by, but far more in 2014 than in 1980. In 1980, you have to wait about four minutes after the half hour before seeing people of your height walk by. In 2014, it takes five more minutes before you can look at marchers eye-to-eye. In other words, the median marcher—the half-hour person—has shrunk relative to the average marcher. What about those whose gross income does not reach the poverty line (here simply assumed to be $1,000 a month in 2014 and the same percentage of average income in 1980)? These are the marchers so small that their heads barely reach your knees. Their crowd fills the first nine minutes in 1980. It fills another three in 2014. We thank André Decoster,

Kevin Spiritus, and Toon Vanheukelom for these estimates, based on the following sources: IPUMS-CPS (Current Population Survey), INCWAGE (Wage and salary income), IN-CBUS (Non-farm business income), and INCFARM (Farm income). Incomes from government programs, capital income, and transfers between households are excluded. The poverty line is taken to be $1,000 per month in the 2014 survey, or $8,580 per year in 1999 prices. This corresponds to 26.7 percent of average income. The same percentage is applied to the 1980 data.

5. The United Kingdom illustrates an extreme form of this trend with the rise of zero-hour contracts—that is, contracts that require the full-time availability of the employee but do not guarantee in advance any specific number of hours. The rise of low-paid self-employment is another major manifestation of this trend. In the UK, self-employment accounted for 40 percent of the jobs created between 2010 and 2014. By the end of that period, one in seven workers were self-employed, with average earnings 20 percent lower than in 2006 (see Roberts 2014 and Cohen 2014). Guy Standing (2011, 2014a) documents the rise of this "precariat" as a core element in his plea for the urgency of introducing an unconditional basic income.

6. The job loss caused by automation has been a recurrent theme in twentieth-century pleas for a guaranteed income (see chapter 4), from Douglas (1924) Duboin (1932, 1945), and Theobald (1963) to Cook (1979: 4), Voedingsbond (1981: 1–4), Roberts (1982), Gerhardt and Weber (1983: 72–5), Meyer (1986), Brittan (1988), and so forth.

7. An analogous remark could be made about the impact of education. Misled by the strong correlation between education level and the probability of employment, one might be tempted to see education as the key to full employment. But with a massively higher average level of education, the risk of unemployment has obviously not been correspondingly reduced.

8. vanden Heuvel and Cohen 2014.

9. Suplicy's Confucian formula could also describe labor leader Andy Stern's (2016: 185) conviction: "My support for UBI is born from a belief that we must attack poverty at its core—a lack of income—rather than treating its symptoms." But indignation about the current way of securing a minimum income is what drove him to an unconditional basic income: "I've also seen how much the welfare system humiliates poor people and punishes the unemployed—the terrible indignity of standing in the unemployment line for hours, then having to prove that you've been out looking for a job at least five times that month, even though there aren't any jobs" (Stern 2016: 187). The freedom-unfriendly character of existing schemes is no doubt also part of what made Milton Friedman want to find an alternative (see chapter 2). He quotes a description of "those poor suckers on welfare" by a young man writing on welfare programs in Harlem: "They're the people whose freedom is really being interfered with by government officials. They can't move from one place to another without the permission of their welfare worker. They can't buy dishes for their kitchen without getting a purchase order. Their whole lives are controlled by the welfare workers" (Friedman 1973a: 27).

10. In BIEN's original statutes (1988), basic income was defined as "an income unconditionally granted to all on an individual basis, without means test or work requirement." It

was slightly amended at BIEN's Seoul congress (2016): "a periodic cash payment unconditionally delivered to all on an individual basis, without means test or work requirement." On BIEN, see chapter 4 and www.basic income.org.

11. "Basic income" was used, for example, by the US Commission on Income Maintenance Programs, which recommended a "basic income support program" in its final report in 1969 (Heineman 1969: 57), and in the booklets given to families taking part in the negative-income-tax experiments in New Jersey (Kershaw and Fair 1976: 211–225). See chapters 4 and 6.

12. For example, the proposal made by the initiators of the 2016 Swiss referendum (see chapter 7) gives minors a basic income pitched at one-quarter of the basic income for adults, and in Philippe Defeyt's (2016) detailed basic-income proposal for Belgium, a child gets half of what an adult gets. However, in the existing Alaska Dividend scheme (chapter 4) and in some proposals involving more generous amounts (e.g., Miller 1983), the amount of the basic income is the same, irrespective of age. Universal child-benefit schemes, already in place in some countries, can be viewed as important steps towards a genuine basic income (see chapter 6).

13. Even in the case of relatively small amounts, the question of how thinly the payments should be spread can be the subject of hot debates. Thus, in 2005, the Alaskan House of Representatives discussed a bill aiming to allow Alaskans to opt for a quarterly payment of their dividend, instead of the annual one. The bill was rejected because some regarded it as expressing an unjustified act of paternalism: "those who misspend their dividends should be allowed to 'wallow in their irresponsibility,'" one representative said (*Anchorage Daily News*, March 30, 2005).

14. Stern 2016: 215.

15. These illustrative amounts are calculated using Word Bank estimates for GDP per capita in 2015: http://data.worldbank.org/indicator/NY.GDP.PCAP.CD and http://data .worldbank.org/indicator/NY.GDP.PCAP.PP.CD. Both here and in the presentation of specific schemes and proposals, we use Gross Domestic Product (GDP) per capita rather than the Gross National Product (GNP) per capita (which includes net receipts from the rest of the world) or the national income per capita (which excludes the consumption of fixed capital by government and households), mainly because of the easy availability of relevant data. In most cases, this choice is unimportant. In some, however, especially when the entities considered are small, the sum of the incomes earned by the residents of a territory (GNP) can diverge significantly, upward or downward, from the incomes generated within that territory (GDP). Luxembourg's GNP, for example, is only two-thirds of its GDP. As globalization tightens its grip, such divergences are likely to become more frequent and deeper (see Milanovic 2016: 237).

16. For example, Senator George McGovern's demogrant proposal of $1,000 per year (see chapter 4) corresponded to 16 percent of GDP per capita at the time, Charles Murray's (2016) proposal of $10,000 per year (see chapter 7) to 18 percent, and labor leader Andy Stern's (2016: 201) proposal of $12,000 per year (see chapter 7) to 21.5 percent, while the Alaska

dividend (see chapter 4) never reached 4 percent of Alaska's GDP per capita and the amount mentioned for adults by the initiators of the 2016 Swiss referendum (see chapter 7) was close to 40 percent of Switzerland's GDP per capita.

17. According to the criteria and figures of the US Census Bureau (2015), the weighted average of the money income before taxes that defines the poverty line is $12,331 per annum for an "unrelated adult" under 65 years, and $15,871 per annum for a household consisting of two adults with the head of the household under 65 years and no dependent children. The US Census Bureau defines poverty in absolute terms, using 48 different thresholds depending on family composition, in order to assess the number of Americans who cannot afford basic food expenditure. These official thresholds do not vary geographically. See the discussion of the appropriate level of a basic income in the US context by Walker (2016: 3–7), who defends a basic income of $10,000 per year.

18. The European Union defines "being at risk of poverty" by reference to a threshold corresponding to 60 percent of each country's median equivalized post-tax-and-transfer income. "Equivalized" means that the income of each member of the household is calculated by dividing the total household income by its size with a weight of 1 given to the first adult, 0.5 to each other member aged 14 or more, and 0.3 to each member aged less than 14. Thus, according to the Luxembourg Income Study database, the median equivalized income in the United States was $31.955 in 2013. Sixty percent of this on a monthly basis comes close to $1,600—that is, significantly above 25 percent of GDP per capita.

19. Sociologist Richard Sennett (2003: 140–1), for example, takes for granted, in his discussion of basic income, that it would replace all other benefits.

20. See, for example, the "food stamps" program introduced in the United States in 1964 (and renamed Supplemental Nutrition Assistance Program or SNAP in 2008). The main program meant to implement Brazilian President Lula's Zero Hunger campaign in 2003 also took this form but was soon merged into the comprehensive cash program *Bolsa Familia*.

21. See, for example, Gupta 2014 for arguments relating in particular to India; Matthews 2014 on the basis of a controlled experiment in Mexico; Cunha 2014; Salemi-Isfahani 2014:9 in connection with Iran's cash transfer program; and Hanlon et al. 2010 for a forceful plea on the basis of a broad overview.

22. Even food vouchers can have a depressing effect on the local economy if the latter is largely informal, and hence at a disadvantage in being recognized as entitled to accept earmarked vouchers.

23. As Rutger Bregman (2016: 58) puts it: "The great thing about money is that people can use it to buy things they need, instead of things that self-appointed experts think they need." By contrast, Paul and Percival Goodman (1947/1960: 200) argued for in-kind provision. They believed each citizen should be entitled free of charge to "food, uniform clothing, group accommodation outside metropolitan areas, medical service, transportation" and offered a freedom-based argument for it: "If freedom is the aim, everything beyond the minimum must be rigorously excluded, even if it should be extremely cheap to provide; for it is more important to limit political intervention than to raise the standard of living."

24. Sometimes, temporary situations may last forever. Thus the Red Crescent has been providing for many years a basic income in kind to the (now over 150,000) Sahrawi refugees who have been living in Algeria since 1975. Rations of food, clothing, and other necessaries funded by the European Commission's Development Department and the UN's World Food program are distributed unconditionally to all dwellers of the refugee camps (van Male 2003).

25. For extensive discussions of cash versus kind, see Myrdal 1945, Thurow 1974, 1977, Rothstein 1998, Currie and Gahvari 2008.

26. A scheme can be individual in either sense without being individual in the other. For example, Belgium's minimum-income scheme is less generous to each member of a couple than to a person living alone, but makes an equal payment to each of them separately. Conversely, Iran's 2010 "targeted subsidies law" entitled each Iranian citizen to an equal amount, but required the payment to be made to the (generally male) head of the household (Tabatabai 2011).

27. This presumption may rest on research showing that the purchasing behavior of mothers shows more concern for the welfare of their children than that of fathers (see e.g., Ringen 1997; Woolley 2004) and/or on the fact that, on average, the female members of couples are more vulnerable, both physically and financially, and therefore need more protection. And it may also make sense, in some contexts, to make the entitlement to this basic income contingent on the parents' ensuring that the children undergo health checks or attend school. However, this condition must be enforced with appropriate mildness: its effect must be to induce all households to make their children benefit from these important services, not to deprive of their entitlements some of the most vulnerable among them.

28. Note that not all proposals made under the "basic income" label satisfy this condition. For example, Joachim Mitschke's (1985, 2004) *Bürgergeld* is paid at a lower level to each member of a couple than to a single, and so are Murphy and Reed's (2013: 31) "basic income payments."

29. In most countries, it takes mainly and sometimes exclusively the form of a reduced rate for cohabiting adults, for example 75 percent of what a single adult gets in France's *Revenu de Solidarité Active*, 77 percent in Swizerland's *Sozialhilfe*, 72 percent in the Dutch *Bijstand*, 67 percent in Belgium's *Revenu d'intégration* (all data for 2015). In some countries (for example, France, Switzerland, the United Kingdom), it also takes the form of a separate housing allowance the level of which increases with the size of a household, but less than proportionally to the number of its members.

30. Thus, in April 2015, the Belgian federal government decided to monitor gas and water bills in order to detect fraud by social claimants pretending to live alone ("Te lage energiefactuur verraadt fraude," *De Morgen*, 9 April 2015).

31. This general point echoes the more specific critique that led in the US to the demise of the AFDC (Aid to Families with Dependent Children, replaced in 1996 by Temporary Assistance to Needy Families): for single mothers, having an able-bodied man around the house causes them to forfeit their payments (see e.g. Goodin 1982: 162). As James Tobin (1966: 34) put it: "Too often a father can provide for his children only by leaving both them and their mother."

32. We are here leaving aside a fourth reason sometimes invoked in favor of universality: its level of generosity being more politically resilient (see chapter 7).

33. For example, France Stratégie (2014b: 85) reports that the rate of take-up of France's means-tested minimum-income scheme ("Revenu de Solidarité Active") is about 50 percent and sees 80 percent as an ambitious target. For further illustrations, see Skocpol 1991, Atkinson 1993a, Korpi and Palme 1998, Bradshaw 2012, Warin 2012, Brady and Bostic 2015, Edin and Shaefer 2015. In his particularly forceful plea against means-testing, Brian Barry (2005: 210–11) stresses that many of those supposed to claim the benefits "will be among the least educated members of the population—including the shameful proportion who are illiterate. Many of them will be trying to juggle two jobs and children, so they are hardly in a position to find out about benefits and fill out complex forms." Anthony Atkinson (2015: 211–12) further notes that both the complication aspect and the stigmatization aspect have been growing in importance owing to application procedures that are increasingly demanding in terms of computer literacy on the one hand and to adverse publicity in the media on the other.

34. Note that the negative impact of stigmatization on take-up is not universally deplored. Thus, according to Peter T. Bauer (1981: 20), redistribution towards the less productive "impairs the prospects of a society. This outcome is especially likely when the less productive receive support without stigma and, indeed, as of right." Stigmatization has also sometimes been recommended as a "self-targeting" filtering device: if one makes access to the benefit conditional on a humiliating test, only the truly needy will come forward (see Lang and Weiss 1990). Needless to say, such a recommendation rests on ethical premises different from ours.

35. See Piketty 1999: 28. Bill Jordan (1991: 6) writes that, with means-tested schemes, "the unemployment trap operates strongly because of the insecurity as well as the inadequacy of the earning, and because of the delays and inefficiency associated with reclaiming." See Delvaux and Cappi 1990 and Jordan et al. 1992 for some empirical evidence.

36. Asserting that means-tested schemes create a trap does not amount to asserting that people never take jobs that do not pay more than the benefits they lose by taking them. It sometimes makes sense to take such jobs because the benefits are expected to decrease after some time, or because of the prospects offered by the jobs. But it does not follow that there is no freedom-restricting trap, that there is nothing preventing the unemployed from taking a job. First, it is difficult to qualify as "voluntary" the unemployment of those who, given the expenses or risks associated with the jobs to which they have access, cannot reasonably afford to work. Second, the very fact that poorly-paid jobs do not increase the income of those who take them often means that they are too unpromising, in terms of expected productivity, for employers to bother offering them, even when no minimum-wage legislation would prevent them from doing so.

37. It follows that the introduction of a universal basic income does not imply that minimum-wage legislation provisions need to be scrapped. We return to this point in connection with the attitude of labor unions towards basic-income proposals (chapter 7).

38. Being obligation-free in this sense does not make the introduction of a basic income incompatible with a moral duty to contribute. We return to this important point later in this chapter, and in chapters 5 and 7.

39. For an overview of European countries, see Saraceno 2010.

40. Jordan 1973: 17.

41. From the beginning of the European discussion on basic income, this possible fall in wages has sometimes been praised by supporters of basic income because of its positive impact on employment. Cook (1979: 6–7), for example, notes the slowing down of labor-saving technical change, and Ashby (1984: 17) notes employers "no longer be[ing] required to pay the subsistence component of income." But it has also been frequently invoked as a strong reason for rejecting basic income, denounced as "a subsidy to employers who refuse to pay adequate wages" (Workers Party 1985: 17, 34).

42. This intended effect on the remuneration of lousy jobs was already prominent in Joseph Charlier's (1848: 37) early plea for an unconditional basic income (see chapter 4).

43. The impact of a basic income on wages, Atkinson (1984: 29) writes, "is sometimes couched in terms of employers being able to reduce wages, but the assumptions made about the working of the labour market are critical to the conclusions drawn. If, for example, labour supply is reduced, then there may be upward pressure on wages—although total earned income may still fall." We return to this question in chapters 6 and 7.

44. Hayek (1945: 522) was right to stress "that practically every individual has some advantage over all others because he possesses unique information of which beneficial use might be made, but of which use can be made only if the decisions depending on it are left to him or are made with his active cooperation." What a basic income does is empower those with least power in such a way that they too can make the best use of the valuable local knowledge that only they possess.

45. The idea that a guaranteed income (obligation-free though not universal in his proposal) would go hand in hand with an improvement of the quality of work was well expressed long ago by Charles Fourier (1836: 49): "Next, as the masses, once an abundant minimum is guaranteed to them, would want to work only a little or not at all, one would need to discover and organize a regime of attractive industry which would guarantee that people would keep working despite their well-being." This is a recurrent theme in the plea for an unconditional income guarantee. See, for example, Galbraith (1973: 1) in the very different context of twentieth-century North America: "Nor can it be held against the concept of an alternative income that some economic tasks will no longer be performed. Numerous ill-paid services of the more derogatory sort . . . are now performed by people who have no alternative source of income or, at a minimum, are persuaded by the convenient social virtue that reputability requires them to take useless and demeaning jobs. Given an alternative source of income, some so employed would not work. The services they render would disappear. This should be viewed not as a loss but as a modest advance in the general state of civilization."

46. Atkinson and Stiglitz 1980: 22.

47. Kameeta 2009: vii.

48. For example, the real hourly wage of middle-aged men in the United States nearly doubled in real terms from about $8 in 1975 to about $16 in 2013 (see http://blogs.ft.com /ftdata/2014/07/04/wages-over-the-long-run). Suppose the marginal tax rate on this category of workers was 25 percent in 1975. Their marginal net wage was therefore $6. This marginal net wage (and hence, supposedly, the material incentive to work) could be preserved in 2013 while raising the marginal tax rate to 62.5 percent!

49. Cole 1949: 147.

50. Townsend 1968: 108. More provocatively, David Graeber (2014a) makes the same point as follows: "I always talk about prisons, where people are fed, clothed, they've got shelter; they could just sit around all day. But actually, they use work as a way of rewarding them. You know, if you don't behave yourself, we won't let you work in the prison laundry. I mean people want to work. Nobody just wants to sit around, it's boring." In his fascinating "essay in utopian politico-economic theory," Joseph Carens (1981) goes further: even the idea of a 100 percent tax on labor income is not intrinsically inconsistent with economic efficiency. It is just a matter of non-material incentives taking over.

51. The specific relevance of basic income for the development of these types of enterprises plays a significant role in the economic case for it. See, for example Brittan 1973, 2001 and Nooteboom 1986 on self-employment; Casassas 2016, Wright 2015: 436 and Stern 2016: 190 on workers' cooperatives; Meade 1989, 1995 on capital-labor partnerships (profit-sharing enterprises); and Obinger 2014 on "alternative entrepreneurship."

52. See, for example, Bovenberg and van der Ploeg 1995, Krause-Junk 1996.

53. Evelyn Forget's (2011) analysis of the results of the guaranteed-income experiment held in the 1970s in the city of Dauphin, Canada, is often cited in support of this claim. However, as always when attempting to draw conclusions from experiments (see chapter 6), it is important to identify carefully both the scheme that was being tested (which was not a basic income) and the situation it replaced (which was, for some households, the absence of any kind of income support).

54. This combination of security and flexibility has been at the core of the economic case for basic income since the beginning of the European debate: see Standing 1986, 1999, Van Parijs 1990.

55. If people are no longer forced to sell their labor power in order to survive, they are no longer commodities. This is the reason that Gøsta Esping-Andersen (1990: 47), who coined the expression, viewed a "social wage . . . paid to citizens regardless of cause"—that is, a basic income—as a "highly advanced case" of de-commodification. One way of formulating the fundamental reason that basic income is such a good proposal is precisely that it contributes to de-commodification in this sense while contributing to commodification in the sense of enabling people currently excluded from employment to get out of the employment trap.

56. Simon Birnbaum (2012: chapter 6) offers an in-depth discussion of the relationship between the sustainability of a basic income and the work ethic. He argues in favor of the compatibility and complementarity between a sustainable basic income and a moral obliga-

tion of contribution to society (not necessarily in the form of paid employment), rather than merely a moral appreciation of it as a laudable virtue.

57. Keynes 1930a/1972: 325, 328–9. And two pages further: "We shall once more value ends above means and prefer the good to the useful. We shall honour those who can teach us how to pluck the hour and the day virtuously and well, the delightful people who are capable of taking direct enjoyment in things, the lilies of the field who toil not, neither do they spin. But beware! The time for all this is not yet. For at least another hundred years we must pretend to ourselves and to every one that fair is foul and foul is fair; for foul is useful and fair is not. Avarice and usury and precaution must be our gods for a little longer still. For only they can lead us out of the tunnel of economic necessity into daylight" (Keynes 1930a/1972: 331). Owing to limits to growth that Keynes did not anticipate—perhaps also to a post-World War II growth rate he underestimated—the time for a serious rethink is coming sooner than he predicted.

58. Thus we paraphrase a neat diagnosis by one of the earliest European advocates of basic income, the Dutch professor of social medicine Jan Pieter Kuiper (1976). As documented by Juliet Schor (1993), some Americans are overworked because they earn too much (say, one hour less a week would mean giving up a new swimming pool) and others because they earn too little (say, one hour less a week would mean junk food for the kids).

59. A basic income is often defended as an alternative to full employment, though not always by distinguishing clearly between these two interpretations. See, for example, Robert Theobald 1967, Claus Offe 1992, 1996a, Fritz Scharpf 1993, James Meade 1995, Jean-Marc Ferry 1995, André Gorz 1997, Yoland Bresson 1999. On the relationship between basic income, wage subsidies, and working time reduction, see chapter 2. Resistance to technological change and the banning of volunteering are two other (worse) ways of pursuing full employment (whether in the bad or the good sense) for which basic income provides an alternative.

60. Less consumption in the rich countries does not entail less production in rich countries, as global justice arguably requires permanent cross-border transfers (see chapter 8).

2. Basic Income and Its Cousins

1. We do not discuss here more comprehensive "realist utopias" such as John Rawls's (1971: section 42, 2001: section 41) "property-owning democracy," an institutional framework that we believe is consistent with an unconditional basic income (see chapter 5). Nor do we discuss socialism, defined by the collective ownership of the means of production, also in principle compatible with basic income—indeed, according to some (Roland 1986, Wright 1986), a precondition for its sustainability. (See chapter 6 of Van Parijs 1995 for an in-depth discussion of the relationship between basic income and socialism.)

2. Thomas Paine proposed an endowment at age 21 combined with a pension from age 50, funded by a land tax (see chapter 4). Thomas Skidmore (1790–1832) proposed in his book *The Rights of Man to Property* (1829: 218–9) that the value of all properties belonging to the people

who die in the course of a particular year should be distributed equally among all those who reach adulthood during that same year. The idea of an endowment given to young adults resurfaced later from time to time. The French philosopher François Huet (1814–1869) suggested distinguishing in people's assets between what they owe to their own effort and what they inherited. People should be entitled to dispose of the former part as they wish, whereas the latter part should be taxed at 100 percent upon their death and used to finance a basic endowment in two installments, one-third at age 14 and the rest at age 25 (Huet, 1853: 262, 271–4). For a well-documented overview of early basic endowment proposals, see Cunliffe and Erreygers 2004, and for in-depth discussions of basic endowment versus basic income, see Dowding et al. eds. 2003, Wright ed. 2006, and the discussion between White 2015 and Wright 2015.

3. Stuart White (2015: 427–428) argues for some degree of "convertibility" of a basic income into a "basic capital" through its partial mortgageability, so as to combine the advantages of a basic endowment and a basic income. Karl Widerquist (2012) also defends a combination of a basic endowment and a basic income. At birth, every US citizen would be entitled to a "citizens' capital account" consisting of a basic endowment of $50,000. Part of the returns can be withdrawn to be used as a (partial) basic income, while the rest is reinvested. As the account grows, the possibility of withdrawing larger returns grows accordingly.

4. For example, the much publicized "baby bond" inspired by Julian Le Grand (2003) and introduced by the Blair government in the United Kingdom in 2005 under the label of "Child Trust Fund" consisted of 250 pounds for every newborn child, with an additional 250 pounds for the children of the poorest third of households. It was abolished in 2011. More seriously, Spain introduced in July 2007 a universal birth bonus *(prestación por nacimiento)* of 2,500 euros per child, irrespective of the family situation, in order to counteract population decline. It was abolished in 2010 in the aftermath of the 2008 economic crisis. But even in this case, the amount involved pales in relationship to the amounts currently distributed in many countries in the form of universal child benefits. In Belgium, for example, these average over $25,000 per child over the period of entitlement (for an overview of child benefits in developed countries, see www.oecd.org/els/family/database.htm).

5. Ackerman and Alstott (2006: 45) also suggest a different and far stingier interpretation: "Stakeholders who have done well with their $80,000 must pay back their stake, with interest, upon their death." If the grant is supposed to be returned to society with the interest it could have generated over this period if invested safely, the best thing to do for any dutiful beneficiary is precisely this: invest it safely. Under this interpretation, the stakeholder's grant is not really an endowment at all, but rather a loan, and its equivalent in terms of a monthly basic income is not $300 or $400 but zero. In a milder, and perhaps more sensible, construal of the clawback clause, what needs to be returned to society is not the capital plus interest, but only the capital. In this case, the "equivalent" basic income simply corresponds to the "social dividend" yielded by a person's personal share of society's capital. Under the assumptions made above, this would come to $150.

6. In Ackerman and Alstott's view, part of the funding of the basic endowment should come from a reduction of public expenditure (higher education, mortgage relief, and so forth), which is less naturally coupled with a basic income. On the other hand, a basic income would be naturally combined with (and largely funded by) a restructuring of tax-and-transfer systems (see chapter 6).

7. A basic endowment might seem more egalitarian than a basic income since those dying at, say, 25 will have received exactly the same amount as those dying at 85. But this is a misleading appearance. First, given that the end of life is generally unforeseen, this scarcely makes a difference to the "injustice" stemming from the inequality in the length of people's lives: the person dying at 25 may have turned her endowment into an annuity most of which will be left unconsumed or, worse still, devoted it entirely to an investment which has not yet started to bear fruit. Moreover, given the persistent difference between women's and men's life expectancies, an equal basic endowment turned into actuarially equivalent annuities would give women lower basic incomes than men.

8. Ackerman and Alstott 2006: 45.

9. Ackerman and Alstott are aware of this drawback of a pure endowment, and their specific proposal is therefore a compromise between a basic endowment and a basic income. First, those who fail to complete high school are obliged to turn their stakes into annuities: basic income as a consolation prize for the school dropouts. Second, a basic pension for the elderly prevents the young from blowing the part of their stake that is needed to secure them a minimum standard of living if and when they reach old age. However, even with the stakes reduced to the 21–65 stretch and with the set of potential stake-blowers shrunk to the 80 percent of each cohort who complete high school, the room for a highly inegalitarian distribution of the freedom given by the endowment remains considerable.

10. Anthony Atkinson, for example, supports the idea of a capital endowment in combination with ongoing payments (2015: 169–172).

11. Cournot 1838/1980: chapter VI.

12. Lerner 1944 and Stigler 1946.

13. Friedman 1962: chapter XII. Friedman (1947: 416) concluded his long review of Lerner's *Economics of Control* (Lerner 1944) by noting that "the proposals in the book have considerable suggestive value and may stimulate others to useful and important work in developing them," without mentioning the negative income tax specifically. When reminded of Stigler's (1946: 365) brief discussion of the negative income tax ("There is great attractiveness in the proposal that we extend the personal income tax to the lowest income brackets with negative rates in these brackets. Such a scheme could achieve equality of treatment with what appears to be a (large) minimum of administrative machinery. If the negative rates are appropriately graduated, we may still retain some measure of incentive for a family to increase its income"), Friedman (2000) responded: "Since we were very close to one another, I suspect we did talk about it but I do not recall doing so. It is clear from his statement as well as from my own later on that the idea was very much in the air and was not a completely novel one."

14. See Friedman 1973a/1975: 30: "Early in his campaign, Senator McGovern came out with a proposal to give a grant of $1,000 to every person in the country. That was really a form of negative income tax." And more explicitly: "A basic or citizen's income is not an alternative to a negative income tax. It is simply another way to introduce a negative income tax if it is accompanied with a positive income tax with no exemption. A basic income of a thousand units with a 20 percent rate on earned income is equivalent to a negative income tax with an exemption of five thousand units and a 20 percent rate below and above five thousand units" (Friedman 2000).

15. Milton Friedman (1962: 192 and, more explicitly, 1968: 111–12) uses a different but equivalent characterization of the negative income tax. He starts from the *breakeven point*— that is, the income level that triggers no transfer either way. The difference between the income of a household and this breakeven point is *positive taxable income* if the household's income exceeds the breakeven point and it is *negative taxable income* if it falls short of the breakeven point. In the illustration above, the breakeven point is $4,000. Hence, a household with no income has a negative taxable income of $4,000, one with an income of $2,000 has a negative taxable income of $2,000, and one with an income of $8,000 has a positive taxable income of $4,000. If the tax rate is 25 percent over both the negative and the positive range, it follows that the first two households receive negative taxes of $1,000 and $500, respectively, while the third household pays a positive tax of $1,000. This characterization is strictly equivalent to the one used in the text as a uniform refundable tax credit. The latter has the advantage of making the close connection with basic income more intuitive.

16. Petersen 1997: 58.

17. A standard means-tested scheme (as represented in Figure 2.1) can therefore be viewed as a limiting case of a negative income tax. It corresponds to the case in which the breakeven point (the income level from which positive transfers stop) coincides with the minimum income (as in Figure 2.1), whereas the breakeven point is twice the minimum income level with a negative income tax rate of 50 percent (as in Figure 2.3), and four times that level with a rate of 25 percent (as in the numerical example above). Put differently, in standard means-tested schemes, the negative tax rate (that is, the rate at which the benefit is increased as a function of the gap between the breakeven point and the income of a household) is 100 percent and the overall tax schedule is as regressive as it could be (the negative tax rate of 100 percent is much higher than the positive tax rate).

18. This is fully recognized by Friedman (1973b/1975: 201): "The poor need regular assistance. They cannot wait until the end of the year. Of course. The negative income tax, like the positive income tax, would be put on an advance basis. Employed persons entitled to the negative income tax would have supplements added to their paychecks, just as most of us now have positive taxes withheld. Persons without wages would file advance estimates and receive estimated amounts due to them weekly or monthly. Once a year, all would file a return that would adjust for under- or over-payments."

19. Milton Friedman (1973b/1975: 201) himself stresses the perversity of this uncertainty trap inherent in existing conditional welfare arrangements, but overlooks the fact that it is

shared, relative to a basic income paid upfront to all, by his negative-income-tax scheme: "A welfare recipient now hesitates to take a job even if it pays more than he gets on welfare because, if he loses the job, it may take him (or her) many months to get back on relief. There is no such disincentive under a negative income tax." See also Friedman 1973a: 28: "If someone on welfare finds a job and gets off welfare, and then the job disappears—as so many marginal jobs do—it's going to take him some time to get through all the red tape to get back onto the program. This discourages job seeking."

20. In his discussion of Roger Godino's (1999) proposal of a form of negative income tax, Thomas Piketty (1999: 28) mentions two general disadvantages of a negative income tax compared with a universal basic income. One is greater stigmatization of the recipients. The other, which he finds more important, is the uncertainty trap it creates, in the same way as France's existing means-tested minimum-income scheme. He therefore has the same objection to both: "As working for a few months might make me lose the benefit of the minimum-income scheme for several terms at the end of this period of activity, then why take such a risk?" In the final chapter of his introductory book on economic inequality, he rehearses this last argument as one of the "subtle advantages" of basic income over removals of the poverty trap with existing fiscal instruments and also mentions the "left libertarian" argument that "a universal transfer allows for a less inquisitorial social policy" (Piketty 2015a: 113). However, a remark in a more recent publication suggests that he has not quite made up his mind: "Needless to say, I am also in favor of a basic income for all adults with insufficient market income. However I am not convinced by the idea that all adults should receive this cash transfer. In developed countries with a generous social state, most full-time workers pay more taxes than whatever level of basic income they could possibly be allocated. In my view, it makes more sense to reduce their tax burden, rather than to give them access to a cash transfer, which would then have to be financed by higher taxes. But obviously this is a legitimate matter for debate and disagreement" (Piketty 2015b: 154).

21. Foucault 1979/2008: 206.

22. Tobin et al. (1967: 21–23) examined two methods of payment: "automatic payments of full basic allowances to all families, except those who waive payment in order to avoid withholding of the offsetting tax on other earnings" and "payment of *net* benefits upon execution of a declaration of estimated income," while those making no such declaration would receive the credit in the form of reductions of their tax bills. Both methods Tobin and his co-authors found workable, but their preference was for automatic payments: "The declaration method imposes the burden of initiative on those who need payments; the automatic payment method places the burden on those who do not want them. It may be argued that the latter are more likely to have the needed financial literacy and paperwork sophistication."

23. To illustrate, consider a population of 10 million with a GDP per capita of $4,000 per month. A basic income of $1,000 requires an income tax of $.25 \times 4,000 \times 10 \text{ Mn} = 10,000 \text{ Mn}$, irrespective of the distribution of income. By contrast, the volume of taxation required by an "equivalent" negative income tax depends on the distribution of gross income. For example, if there are five million people earning $2,000 gross and five million earning $6,000, the

former are not taxed at all; they receive instead a transfer of $1,000-(.25\times2000)=500$. The latter each have a tax liability of $(.25\times6000)-1000=500$. Multiplied by five million, this amounts to 2.500 Mn or 6.25 percent of total income $(4,000\times10\text{ Mn})$, four times less than the "equivalent" basic-income scheme. An illusory difference, economists will no doubt say. But one that matters a great deal, political scientists may respond, especially if the press is unable or unwilling to understand and explain the difference between apparent and real cost.

24. Here is James Tobin's (2001) account: "The general public was suspicious that the pure NIT would discourage work and didn't want to spend money with that effect. The NIT experiments were thought to have shown that a household's supply of labor would be diminished by demogrants. This effect was confined to secondary workers and it was neither surprising nor very large. But it had an immense effect adverse to the NIT. The EITC was the result." See also Howard 1997: chapter 3, Ventry 2000, and Steensland 2008: 178–179 on this episode in the history of US social policy, and Nichols and Rothstein 2015 on the development and impact of EITC.

25. To give an idea of the sums involved, for the fiscal year 2016, a single person with one qualifying child gets a maximum credit of about $280 per month. The credit is completely phased out when the household income reaches $3,275 per month ("Earned Income Tax Credits Parameters, 1975–2016," Tax Policy Center, Washington DC, January 2016). We abstract here from various complications regarding the categories of income taken into account. See Nichols and Rothstein 2015 for details.

26. Nichols and Rothstein 2015: 52.

27. On these various defects of EITC, see, for example, Nichols and Rothstein 2015: 29, Bhargava and Manoli 2015: 348–9, Shipler 2004: 15, Holt 2015, and Stern 2016: 158. France's *Prime Pour l'Emploi* faced similar challenges. An advance payment procedure was also tried, but cancelled in 2010.

28. Sykes et al. 2015: 260.

29. Stern 2016: 158.

30. In Ireland, where a means-tested minimum income is in place, the think tank *Social Justice Ireland* (2010: 25–28) has been arguing explicitly for a refundable tax credit restricted to individuals "significantly attached to the labor force" as a path towards a genuine basic income. The possibility of such a transition is explored in greater detail in Van Parijs et al. 2000.

31. Phelps 1994, 1997, 2001.

32. See esp. Phelps 1997: 108, 112, 119, 148 for his objections to various other types of employment subsidies. Next to these, Phelps (1997: 150–3) also discusses subsidies to education and training, and rejects them for several reasons: the full effects would materialize only after a generation; raising the earnings of the low-paid by some given amount in this manner is likely to be far more expensive than through direct wage subsidies; and it would be hard to motivate learning in the absence of a realistic prospect of improved wages.

33. Phelps 1997: 133.

34. Phelps 1997: 111–112, 189.

35. Phelps 1997: 163.

36. Phelps 1997: 138–142, 166.

37. Phelps 1997: 15, 173.

38. Elsewhere, Phelps (1997: 165) hints briefly at a distinct normative foundation: "Unlike those who would dispense welfare willy-nilly to anyone whose income falls below a certain level, I believe that the only genuine entitlement is a reward of self-support and integration for those willing to fulfill a social contract with their fellow citizens by working and earning." The cost of the scheme is worth paying, Phelps (1997: 136) claims, because of the "pride and self-respect" workers would gain "from the sense of having met their end of the social contract—of having acted justly." See chapter 5 for a discussion of the reciprocity-based challenge to an obligation-free basic income.

39. See Harvey 2006, 2011, 2012, 2014, Representative George Miller's 2013 bill "Local Jobs for America Act" (2013), and Gregg and Layard's (2009) job-guarantee proposal for the United Kingdom. See also Handler 2004, Standing 2012, Lewis 2012, and Noguchi 2012 for critical discussions and Tanghe 1989, 2014 for a historical survey of the guaranteed work idea. India's National Rural Employment Guarantee is arguably the most massive real-life approximation of a guaranteed employment scheme. We are not denying that, relative to the absence of income support, it can constitute major progress.

40. Jordan 1994.

41. See, for example, Kaus 1992. Similarly, at the time of England's New Poor Laws (see chapter 3), it was recognized that forcing the unemployed into workhouses was far more expensive than providing them with a minimum of subsistence: "the marginal cost of workhouse relief was nearly double the cost of outdoor relief" (Boyer 1990: 203).

42. Stern 2016: 164–5.

43. Elster 1988.

44. As proposed, for example by Frank 2014, Painter and Thoung 2015: 21–22, or Atkinson 2015: 137–47.

45. Adret 1977, Coote, Franklin, and Simms 2010.

46. Marx 1867/1962: chapter 8.

47. How does this square with the claim sometimes made that France's reduction of the official working week from thirty-nine to thirty-five hours in 1998–2000 caused a significant increase in employment (see, for example, Gubian et al. 2004)? First, the measure was not compulsory across the board but induced by selective tax incentives that made it possible to soften the downward impact on net weekly wages and the upward impact on hourly labor cost, thereby alleviating our first dilemma. This amounts to mixing the working-time-reduction strategy with public subsidies to wages, and it is therefore very hard, if not impossible, to determine whether the impact on unemployment is due to the former or to the latter. Second, while the immediate positive effect on employment seems established, the longer-term impact is controversial (see Gianella 2006). Reorganizing the production process so as to take a higher hourly labor cost into account takes time. Once it has happened, the short-term effect may well vanish.

48. In order to solve the first dilemma, it has repeatedly been proposed that a substantial working-time reduction should be coupled with a basic income (starting with van Ojik 1983: 29 and Krätke 1985: 5–6). This would work, but the other two dilemmas would remain. Moreover, if basic income works on its own as a job-sharing device, why do we need compulsory working-time reduction? One reason given (Mückenberger and al. 1987: 18–20) is that the latter would prevent a dualization between well-paid full-time workers and poorly paid part-timers. But the increase in the marginal tax rates for high earners and the facilitation of training should inhibit this process. And both are implied by a basic income. (See chapters 1 and 6.)

49. See Brittan 1983 for a neat formulation of this point.

3. Prehistory: Public Assistance and Social Insurance

1. This is the only passage that could justify ascribing to Thomas More the proposal of something like a guaranteed minimum income. Whether it does justify it depends on the interpretation to be given to "aliquis proventus vitae" (some income for life) in the following sentence of the Latin text: *"cum potius multo fuerit providendum, uti aliquis esset proventus vitae, ne cuiquam tam dira sit furandi primum, dehinc pereundi necessitas"* (More 1516/1978: 44), which can be translated literally as: "while it would have been much better to ensure that there would be some income for life and that for no one there would be such a terrible necessity first to steal and next to perish."

2. More 1516/1978: 49.

3. Erasmus's letter to More (1518) is quoted in the foreword to Vives (1533/1943: v). Juan Luis Vives's letter to Francis Craneveldt (1525) is quoted by Tobriner (1999: 17).

4. The story is related by Thomas Aquinas in his *Summa Theologica*, with the quote here as it was translated by the Fathers of English Dominican Province, 1912.

5. Vives 1526/2010: 95.

6. Vives 1526/2010: 67, 98. This "criminological" argument for a minimum income will regularly reappear in subsequent pleas for a guaranteed minimum income. According to Charles Fourier (1803/2004: 100), for example, "it is easy to prove that all social crimes committed out of ambition proceed from the poverty of the people." But what the argument is most often used to justify is the joint fight against poverty and idleness. This was certainly the case for Vives but also, nearly three centuries later, for workhouse supporter Jeremy Bentham: "When a man has no other option than to rob or starve, the choice can hardly be regarded as an uncertain one" (quoted in Quinn 1994: 87). Andrew Schotter (1985:68–80) starts from the same argument ("if a person with no market options is hungry, he may be forced to obtain food in non-market ways") to justify not a guaranteed income but rather employment subsidies à la Phelps (see chapter 2), up to the point where the cost to the taxpayer exceeds the benefit from reduced crime.

7. Vives 1526/2010: 72.

8. Vives 1526/2010: 73 and 75–6.

9. Vives 1526/2010: 73.

10. Vives 1526/2010: 89, 81, 76, 78.

11. Vives 1526/2010: 83–4, 87, 99.

12. Since 1522 in Nuremberg, since 1523 in Strasbourg, since 1524 in Leisnig, since 1525 in Zurich, Mons, and Ypres. (See Fantazzi 2008: 96, and Spicker 2010: ix–x.)

13. Quoted by Spicker (2010: ix).

14. Vives made sure he did not sound like a revolutionary. He maintained a role for religious institutions and said he would write on another occasion to bishops and abbots (Vives 1526/2010: 74). He also made room for the possibility that one should "introduce at the beginning the simplest measures, and only later, little by little and unnoticed, the difficult ones" (Vives 1526/2010: 90). In his *De Communione rerum ad Germanos inferiores*, published in 1535, he attacked fiercely the far more radically egalitarian reforms advocated by the Anabaptists (see Fernandez-Santamaria 1998: 177–95).

15. It is at the initiative of the magistrates of Ypres that a Flemish translation of Vives's book was published in Antwerp two years later (see the foreword to Vives 1533/1943). The Ypres document is now available in modern English (Spicker 2010: 101–140).

16. In their judgment, the Paris theologians insisted that rich people should retain the right and the duty to help the poor, that the municipality should not, for the purposes of the scheme, sequester the goods of the Church ("This would not be the act of virtuous and faithful Catholics but of impious heretics, Waldensians, Wycliffites or Lutherans") and that "no decree should forbid public begging by religious mendicants, who are approved by the Church" (full text in Spicker 2010: 141–143).

17. City of Ypres, 1531/2010: 135.

18. Lille in 1527, Ghent in 1535, Brussels and Breda in 1539, Louvain in 1541, and Bruges in 1564 (see Fantazzi 2008: 96–97). In parallel, the French King François I created in 1544 a Poor Board in charge of organizing poor relief (Régnard 1889).

19. Fantazzi 2008: 109–10. A partial English translation had to wait until the end of the twentieth century (Tobriner 1999) and full translations until the twenty-first (Fantazzi and Matheeusen 2002 and Spicker 2010).

20. In Spain, Vives's ideas led in 1545 to a fierce controversy between theologians Domingo de Soto and Juan de Robles. De Soto's *In causa pauperum deliberatio* forcefully objected to the repression of begging and hence to the obligation to work. De Robles was also opposed to the full secularization of poor relief but had more sympathy for the pragmatic considerations guiding Vives's proposal and supported the regulation of begging (Fernandez-Santamaria 1998: 166–76, Arrizabalaga 1999: 156, Fantazzi 2008: 107–8). In the Low Countries, the Augustinian monk Lorenzo de Villavicencio published a book attacking Vives's ideas in 1564. He requested that a book published two years earlier by Vives's follower Gilles Wyts should be consigned to the flames in a public square, but failed to convince the theologians of the University of Louvain (Fantazzi 2008: 108–9).

21. On the influence of Vives and the Ypres scheme in England, see Tobriner 1999: 23, Fantazzi 2008: 110, and Spicker 2010: xv–xix.

22. Workhouses were also set up in other European cities, especially in Germany (see Harrington 1999 and Foucault 1961/2006: part I, chapter 2). And they did not remain for long a European peculiarity. In Japan, the first workhouses were established in the late seventeenth century (Garon 1997: 30).

23. See Boyer 1990: 94–9, Knott 1986: 13, and Dyer 2012. In an address to the parliament in 1699, King William III expressed his worry that "the increase of the poor is become a burthen to the kingdom" and declared that the able-bodied should be "compelled to labour" (Nicholls 1854: 371).

24. For details, see Tobriner 1999: 25–28.

25. Beyond the immediate reactions, the Speenhamland system was the subject of a huge scholarly literature, including a famous chapter in Karl Polanyi's (1944/1957) *Great Transformation*. See Boyer 1990 and Block and Somers 2003 for useful critical overviews.

26. Burke 1795: 251, 261, 270, 280.

27. Quoted by Boyer (1990: 53).

28. Malthus 1798/1976: 54–55.

29. Malthus 1826: 339.

30. This formulation is from the sixth and definitive edition of Malthus's essay (Book IV, Chapter VIII, section 7). On Malthus's critique of the Poor Laws, see Boyer 1990: 56–59.

31. Even in Japan, also in the 1830s, the prominent moralist and economist Ninomiya Sontoku (1787–1856) expressed a very similar opposition to any form of cash assistance to the poor: "Grants in money, or release from taxes, will in no way help them in their distress. Indeed, one secret of their salvation lies in withdrawing all monetary help from them. Such help only induces avarice and indolence, and is a fruitful source of dissensions among the people" (quoted in Garon 1997: 31).

32. Ricardo 1817/1957: 105–6.

33. Hegel 1820/1991: section 245.

34. Tocqueville 1833/1967: 8.

35. Tocqueville 1835/1997: 37.

36. Tocqueville added, however: "But individual charity seems quite weak when faced with the progressive development of the industrial classes and all the evils which civilization joins to the inestimable goods it produces." If it is too weak, is there anything one can do? "At this point my horizon widens on all sides. My subject grows. I see a path opening up, which I cannot follow at this moment." Tocqueville's gloomy analysis ended with this open question, which he intended answering in another memoir. But he never did. See Himmelfarb 1997: 11–13 on the unfinished second Memoir.

37. Bentham 1796/2001: 39.

38. Bentham 1796/2001: 44–5.

39. On Bentham and the Poor Laws, see Himmelfarb 1970 and Kelly 1990: 114–136.

40. Quoted by Boyer (1990: 61).

41. For example, Friedrich Engels (1845/2009: 292) states in his *Condition of the Working Class in England:* "So frankly, so boldly has the conception never yet been formulated, that

the non-possessing class exists solely for the purpose of being exploited, and of starving when the property-holders can no longer make use of it. Hence it is that this New Poor Law has contributed so greatly to accelerate the labour movement." The most famous critique of the New Poor Law and the workhouses is arguably to be found in Charles Dickens's *Oliver Twist* (1838).

42. This is by no means a unanimous view in the French Enlightenment. For example, the first edition of the *Encyclopédie* (1757, vol. 7, 73) contains an entry "Fondation" by Turgot which could have been written by the fiercest critics of the English Poor Laws: "To maintain free of charge a large number of men amounts to bribing idleness and all the disorders it generates; it is making the condition of the idler preferable to that of the working man. . . . Suppose that a state is so well managed that it has no poor, the establishment of free aid for a number of men would create poor people at once, that is would make it in the self interest of as many people to become poor by giving up their occupations."

43. Montesquieu 1748, chapter XXIII, 134.

44. Rousseau 1754/1971: 234.

45. Rousseau 1762/2011, Book I, section IX; Book II, section XI; Book III, section 15.

46. Rousseau 1789/1996: 64.

47. Forrest 1981: 13–19. For a detailed history and description of the French *dépôts de mendicité*, see Peny 2011. The *dépôts de mendicité* are also discussed by Michel Foucault (1961/2006: 404–405) in his *History of Madness*.

48. *Gazette Nationale*, July 16, 1790, quoted by Regnard (1889: 266–267). On Larochefoucault-Liancourt and the *comité de mendicité* (later *comité des secours publics*), see Forrest 1981: 20–30.

49. Maximilien de Robespierre, "Discours sur les troubles frumentaires d'Eure-et-Loir," December 2, 1792, quoted by Soboul (1962: 326–7).

50. Outline of a new declaration of human rights read at the Jacobin Club on April 21, 1793, quoted by Godechot (1970: 72).

51. Constitution of June 24, 1793, Article 21 (Godechot 1970: 82). Godechot (1970: 69–77) provides a vivid description of the context in which the 1793 constitution was prepared and adopted.

52. This striking passage, Kant's only discussion of the distribution of income, continues as follows: "The wealthy have acquired an obligation to the commonwealth, since they owe their existence to an act of submitting to its protection and care, which they need in order to live; on this obligation the state now bases its right to contribute what is theirs to maintaining their fellow citizens. This can be done either by imposing a tax on the property or commerce of citizens, or by establishing funds and using the interests from them, not for the needs of the state (for it is rich), but for the needs of the people. It will do this by way of coercion (since we are speaking here only of the right of the state against the people), by public taxation, not merely by voluntary contributions" (Kant 1797/1996, Part II, Section 1, 100–101). For a careful discussion of Kant's views on the State's duty to support the poor, see Zylberman forthcoming.

53. Fichte (1800/2012) adds, however: "there ought to be no idlers in it either," and further: "Everyone must work and has, if he works, enough to live on."

54. Condorcet 1795/1988: 273–4.

55. A less general but nonetheless unambiguous formulation of the same idea is one century older. Daniel Defoe's *Essay upon Projects* (1697/1999) includes a proposal for a "pension office" that starts as follows: "That all sorts of people who are labouring people and of honest repute, of what calling or condition soever, men or women (beggars and soldiers excepted), who, being sound of their limbs and under fifty years of age, shall come to the said office and enter their names, trades, and places of abode into a register to be kept for that purpose, and shall pay down at the time of the said entering the sum of sixpence, and from thence one shilling per quarter, shall every one have an assurance under the seal of the said office for these following conditions." The conditions covered were injuries ("drunkenness and quarrels excepted"), illness, infirmity, and death. Consistently with this defense of social insurance, in his later essay on *Giving Alms no Charity* (1704), Defoe strongly criticized both the poorhouses that disturbed the operation of the labor market and private people practicing charity ("they encourage vagrants and by a mistaken zeal do more harm than good"), but did not reiterate his earlier proposal as an alternative.

56. In unpublished writings from about the same period, Jeremy Bentham also suggested a social insurance system that could be made compulsory, at least for the better paid workers—that is, those "whose earnings shall appear to admit of a surplus sufficient to insure them against the fall in question [from a situation of greater comfort to a situation of less comfort], by the purchase of a superannuation annuity, sufficient for their maintenance according to the Home-Provision System, during the remainder of their days." (*Writings on the Poor Laws* I, 193–7).

57. According to the Belgian socialist leader César De Paepe (1841–1890), for example, a "general insurance against all accidents, against all risks and perils" must be "the object of a large public service, organized in a unified way and on a large scale" (De Paepe 1889: 304–5).

58. See Perrin 1983: 36–42 and de Swaan 1988: 187–192. As emphasized by De Deken and Rueschemeyer (1992: 102–3), the scheme was restricted to industrial workers, best organized and therefore most threatening, and excluded workers in agriculture and the cottage industry, who often faced far worse conditions. On Leopold Krug's (1810) early proposal of a flat-rate pension funded by flat-rate social contributions, see Schmähl 1992.

59. These quotes are from Jaurès's contribution to a heated parliamentary debate about public assistance for the elderly on July 12, 1905 (*Journal officiel du 13 juillet 1905, Débats parlementaires, Chambre des députés, 8e législature, Compte-rendu—143e séance, séance du 12 juillet 1905,* 2890–92). Léon Mirman, another left-wing *député,* argued against social insurance on the grounds that it was creating a split between waged and non-waged workers. See Hatzfeld 1989: 65–79.

60. Castel 1995: 288–290.

61. See Baldwin 1990 for an insightful account of this process.

62. For a succinct presentation, see, for example, King 1995: 181–82.

63. In Canada, a federal assistance plan, first called Canada Assistance Plan and later Canada Social Transfer, was launched in the 1960s to provide provinces with financial support in the field of public assistance. Federal rules included prohibition of minimum residency requirements for public assistance, but provinces were nonetheless left largely free to develop their own policies. As a consequence, there is now great diversity across the country even if all provinces provide their residents with some sort of income support.

64. See Flora 1986 and Frazer and Marlier 2009 for overviews of the situation in Europe; regarding Japan, see Vanderborght and Sekine 2014: 21–22.

65. On South Africa's noncontributory pension scheme, see Case and Deaton 1998, Letlhokwa 2013, and Surrender 2015.

66. Lo Vuolo 2013.

4. History: From Utopian Dream to Worldwide Movement

1. The connection with the many basic-income proposals made independently over the next two centuries was only made in the 1980s. See Van Parijs 1992: 11–12.

2. In his influential *Rights of Man*, published a few years earlier in response to Burke's *Reflections on the Revolution in France*, Paine already proposed what he saw as a humane alternative to the Poor Laws, "those instruments of torture" (Paine 1791/1974: 431). But this plan remained more remote from a universal basic income than the one contained in *Agrarian Justice*. The components that come closest to it are (1) a means-tested benefit for every child under fourteen "enjoining the parents of such children to send them to school," (2) a means-tested pension from age fifty, expected to be claimed "not as a matter of grace and favour, but of right" by about one-third of the elderly so defined, and (3) a universal right to a small baby bonus expected to be taken up on behalf of one-fourth of the newborn by "every woman who should make the demand, and none will make it whose circumstances do not require it" (Paine 1791/1974, chapter V, 425–9).

3. Paine 1796/1974: 612–13.

4. Paine 1796/1974: 618.

5. Note that the scheme sketched in Condorcet's (1795/1988: 274) seminal formulation of the idea of social insurance includes both an old-age pension ("securing to those who reach old age a relief that is the product of what they saved") and an endowment for the young ("giving to those children who become old enough to work by themselves and found a new family the advantage of a capital required by the development of their activity") but the justification and hence the funding are fundamentally different: both of Condorcet's schemes are meant to be funded by savings made earlier by the beneficiaries themselves and by those prevented by an early death from reaching the age at which they could benefit.

6. Ambrose 1927: 47.

7. Vives 1526: 46.

8. Locke 1689, First Treatise, chapter 4, section 42.

9. Locke 1989, Second Treatise, chapter 5, sections 32 and 34.

10. Paine 1796/1974: 617, 611, 612–613.

11. Spence 1797/2004: 81.

12. None of his earlier writings seems to include this proposal, though. Some of them do mention the collection of rents, but *The Real Rights of Man* (Spence 1775/1982) mentions only targeted poor relief as one of the possible uses of the revenues ("Then you may behold the rent which the people have paid into the parish treasuries, employed by each parish . . . in maintaining and relieving its own poor, and people out of work"), while *A Supplement to the History of Robinson Crusoe* (Spence 1782/1982) leaves their use completely open. ("A small rent or rate, shall, according to the determination of the parishioners, be paid by every person, suitable to the valuation of the houses and land he possesses, to the parish treasury to be put to such uses as the majority please.") On Thomas Spence and subsequent early advocates of basic income, see Cunliffe and Erreygers 2004 and Bonnett and Armstrong 2014. On the contrast between Paine and Spence, see King and Marangos 2006.

13. Spence 1797/2004: 87.

14. Spence 1797/2004: 88.

15. Paine 1796/1974: 620.

16. The quotes above are from Anonymous 1848/1963: 963–4, authors' own translation. The document was discovered and put into context by Erreygers and Cunliffe (2006). The most plausible conjecture attributes the authorship to Napoleon De Keyser, a rather mysterious radical farmer, who published a few years later, also in Flemish, a book which contained a number of detailed proposals, including a cash endowment for young adults and a quarterly equal distribution of the revenues from renting the land (De Keyser 1854/2004). On De Keyser, see Cunliffe and Erreygers 2004: xix. On Marx's circle in 1848, see Matoba 2006.

17. Charlier 1848: especially 51, 57, 75, 94, 102.

18. Charlier 1848: 39.

19. Charlier 1848: 105, 51.

20. Charlier, 1848, 1871, 1894a, 1894b.

21. Charlier 1848: 43, Charlier 1894a: 56, Charlier 1871: 47, Charlier 1848: 37, and Charlier 1848: 37.

22. Letter to Hector Denis, June 25, 1894. From the Archive of the Institut Emile Vandervelde, Brussels, discovered by Guido Erreygers.

23. John Cunliffe and Guido Erreygers rescued Charlier from this total oblivion. See Cunliffe and Erreygers 2001 for a presentation of Charlier's contribution, and Cunliffe and Erreygers eds. 2004 for an English translation of some excerpts from his work.

24. Mill 1848/1904 Book V, Chapter XI, section 13.

25. Mill 1848/1904: 967; first edition, 536, 538.

26. Mill 1848/1904: 968–969, first edition 537–538. Note, however, that the beneficiaries of this legal guarantee of subsistence would be deprived of the right to vote, by virtue of what Mill presented in his *Considerations on Representative Government* as the main legitimate exception to the principle of universal suffrage: "I regard it as required by first principles that the receipt of parish relief should be a peremptory disqualification for the franchise. He who

can not by his labor suffice for his own support, has no claim to the privilege of helping himself to the money of others. . . . As a condition of the franchise, a term should be fixed, say five years previous to the registry, during which the applicant's name has not been on the parish books as a recipient of relief" (Mill 1861: Chapter VIII, 332–3). It is not obvious, however, that these considerations are still meant to apply if the "legal guarantee of subsistence" were to be secured through Mill's Fourierist scheme to be discussed below.

27. Mill 1849: xxix.

28. Mill 1849: Book II, chapter I, section 4. Mill kept this sympathy for Fourier's version of socialism up to the end of his life. See Mill 1879/1987: 132: "The principal of these [forms of socialism that recognize the difficulties of Communism] is Fourierism, a system which, if only as a specimen of intellectual ingenuity, is highly worthy of the attention of any student either of society or of the human mind."

29. Engels 1880/2008: 33.

30. Fourier 1836/1967: 49.

31. In earlier writings, Fourier (1822/1966: 276) advocated, along with many of his French predecessors, not only a means test but also a work test: "The preservative remedy would be to secure to the people work in case of health, and assistance, a social minimum, in case of infirmity." See Cunliffe and Erreygers 2001: 464–465. Similar targeted schemes were proposed on similar grounds by Fourier's English contemporaries William Cobbett (1827), Samuel Read (1829), and George Poulett Scrope (1833). See Horne 1988 for an overview.

32. Here is the passage in full: "Consequently, laziness has vanished: one will be able to forward the minimum to the poor members with the certainty that they will have gained more than their cost by the end of the year. Thus, the establishment of the proposed regime will eradicate misery and begging, the plagues of societies based on anarchic competition and fragmentation. It would be impossible today to forward the minimum to the people: they would fall straight away into idleness, given that work is repugnant. This is why England's Poor Laws led to nothing but the growth of the hideous sore of pauperism. Forwarding the minimum is the basis of freedom and the guarantee of the emancipation of the proletarian. No freedom without minimum. No minimum without industrial attraction. This is what the emancipation of the masses is all about" (Considerant 1845: 49).

33. A similar passage in Mill's posthumous essay *On Socialism* is equally unambiguous: "a certain minimum having first been set apart for the subsistence of every member of the community, whether capable or not of labor, the society divides the remainder of the produce among the different groups, in such shares as it finds attract to each the amount of labor required" (Mill 1879/1987: 133). In a passage of his *History of Socialist Thought*, G. D. H. Cole (1953: 310) confirms this interpretation: Mill "praised the Fourieristes, or rather that form of Fourierism which assigned in the first place a basic income to all and then distributed the balance of the product in shares to capital, talent or responsibility, and work actually done."

34. Mill 1870/1969: chapter VII.

35. In his *Progress and Poverty* (1879/1953), Henry George argued that land being our common property, society should tax land values entirely, while exempting from taxation all

productive activities. But he did not earmark the revenues of his tax for the funding of a basic income. What remains after deduction of the legitimate expenses of government could be divided, "if we wanted to, among the whole community, share and share alike. Or we could give every boy a small capital for a start when he came of age, every girl a dower, every widow an annuity, every aged person a pension, out of this common estate" (George 1881: 64). The increasing land values represent "a manifest provision for social needs—a fund belonging to society as a whole, with which we may take care of the widow and the orphan and those who fall by the wayside, with which we may provide for public education, meet public expenses, and do all the things that an advancing civilization makes more and more necessary for society to do on behalf of its members" (George 1887/2009: 276). Today, however, many self-declared "Georgists" support more firmly the implementation of a basic income or social dividend funded by a land tax (Smith 2006), and some contemporary "left libertarian" political philosophers who support an unconditional basic income view themselves as heirs of Henry George. (See chapter 5.)

36. Russell 1918/1966: 80–81.

37. Russell 1918/1966: 118–119.

38. Russell 1918/1966: 127.

39. Russell 1932/1976: 14.

40. Russell 1918/1966: 127. This is a mild version of what can be found in the earlier anarchist tradition. In his *Conquest of Bread*, Peter Kropotkin (1892/1985: 153–154) leaned towards maintaining a formal work condition. Worker associations could require, for example, "that, from twenty to forty five or fifty years of age, you consecrate four or five hours a day to some work recognized as necessary to existence." However, he did not exclude, as an alternative, the use of (tough) moral sanctions: "If you are absolutely incapable of producing anything useful, or if you refuse to do it, then live like an isolated man or like an invalid. If we are rich enough to give you the necessities of life we shall be delighted to give them to you. You are a man, and you have a right to live. But as you wish to live under special conditions, and leave the ranks, it is more than probable that you will suffer for it in your daily relations with other citizens. You will be looked upon as a ghost of bourgeois society, unless friends of yours, discovering you to be a talent, kindly free you from all moral obligations by doing all the necessary work for you."

41. Milner 1918: 129–130.

42. Pickard 1919.

43. On the Milners, Bertram Pickard, Major Douglas, James Meade, G. D. H. Cole, and other aspects of this first public debate on basic income, see Walter Van Trier's (1995) dissertation.

44. Douglas 1920, 1924.

45. Less well known than Major Douglas, Charles Marshall Hattersley (1922/2004) produced his own version of social credit theory and helped spread it in Canada, where a federal Social Credit Party developed from the mid-1930s onwards. A Social Credit Party governed the province of Alberta from 1935 to 1971 but dropped the social credit doctrine after 1944

and has not managed to win a provincial seat since the early 1980s (see Bell 1993, Hesketh 1997). Social credit parties were also active in other provinces, such as British Columbia, Ontario, and Quebec. In Australia, where Douglas himself made public appearances in 1934, a small "Douglas credit movement" developed in the early 1930s, where it tried but failed to associate with the Labor Party (Berzins 1969). In New Zealand, the social credit movement also spread in the 1930s—as an "avalanche" and a "plague," according to its critics at the time (Miller 1987: 20)—and gave rise to a Social Credit Political League in 1953, which even today continues to exist as a small political party under the name Democrats for Social Credit. On basic income and theories of social credit, see Heydorn 2014.

46. "We may come to a 'state bonus', or to 'Dividends for All'—to use two names which have been adopted by advocates of giving every citizen, quite apart from his work, a certain minimum claim to a share in the annual social product" (Cole 1929: 199).

47. Cole 1929, 1935, 1953. The concept of "social dividend" appears in the 1935 book and "basic income" appears in the 1953 book.

48. Cole 1935: 235.

49. Cole 1935: 236. Note that thirty pages further on, Cole introduces a willingness-to-work condition: "But under the new system the social dividend would be payable to able-bodied persons only on condition that they were ready to work, and there would have to be means whereby a man's receipt of the social dividend could be questioned on grounds of proved unwillingness to perform his part of the common service.[. . .] But in order to be entitled to receive the social dividend, an able-bodied citizen would have to be prepared to work up to a standard sufficient to justify his claim to share in the common heritage of society" (Cole 1935: 263–4). Why is such a condition needed, one may wonder, if it is not to provide economic incentives? Presumably because of the reciprocity concern we discuss in chapter 5. No such condition features, it seems, in any of Cole's later formulations of the social dividend proposal.

50. Meade 1935/1988, 1937, 1938, 1948, 1971.

51. Meade 1989, 1993, 1995. Around the same time and place that the notion of a "social dividend" appeared in the writings of Cole and Meade, it also surfaced in a famous discussion on market socialism by two professors at the London School of Economics, Oskar Lange (1904–1965) and Abba Lerner (1903–1982): in reply to a remark by Lerner (1936), Lange (1937: 143–4) made clear that the expression "social dividend," which he used to refer to the return on capital—collectively owned under market socialism—had to be understood as a contribution-independent payment to all citizens.

52. See Rhys-Williams 1943: 145–146. While universal, her scheme was certainly not obligation-free: "Each adult citizen would sign a contract with the state, promising to work to the best of their ability—full-time for men, part-time for single women and young widows without dependent children—in return for subsistence. Those who chose not to sign or fulfill the social contract would not be eligible for benefits" (Sloman 2016).

53. As explained in the final report (Meade ed. 1978: 278–279, 294), the Committee discussed a full social dividend proposal at 40 percent of average earnings with an additional

15 percent for other expenditures. It noted: "The full social dividend is effective, simple to understand and administer, but the basic rate of tax is likely to be so high as to affect incentives over a wide range and to give rise to political difficulties." And it concluded: "The position taken by the Committee is that the full social dividend with a high basic rate of tax is unlikely to attract sufficient political support for it to be worth considering further." It considered next the "modified social dividend" with a surcharge on the lower income bracket, as discussed in chapter 6. It rejected it on the ground that "the high rate of tax of the first band is considered to have potentially serious disincentive effects and to introduce major administrative difficulties." It therefore considered in more detail "the two-tier social dividend"— that is, a partial basic income at 20 percent of average earnings to all families irrespective of need and employment, combined with a conditional benefit at 30 percent to the involuntarily unemployed, the retired, and the incapacitated. However, it recommended in the end the less novel "New Beveridge scheme" (unconditional family allowances plus social insurance for the involuntarily unemployed, the retired, and the incapacitated plus means-tested benefits when the other provisions prove insufficient).

54. Quoted by Wachtel 1955: vii–viii, 101–2, 105–6.

55. Duboin 1932, 1998. Similar ideas are to be found among members of the French "personalist" movement (Charbonneau and Ellul 1935/1999) and in the "federalist" movement led by Alexandre Marc (1972, 1988).

56. Goodman and Goodman 1947/1960: 198.

57. Long 1934, 1935.

58. On Huey Long and his Share Our Wealth movement, see Brinkley 1981 and Amenta et al. 1994.

59. Theobald 1961, 1963, 1967. The Canadian media theorist Marshall McLuhan was among the authors gathered by Theobald for his collective volume on the "guaranteed income" (Theobald ed. 1967). In his chapter, McLuhan (1967: 205) argues that automation creates room for "the kind of 'leisure' that has always been known to the individual artist and creative person: the leisure of fulfillment resulting from the fullest use of one's powers." In this context, he writes, "the guaranteed income that results from automation could therefore be understood to include that quite unquantifiable factor of joy and satisfaction that results from a free and full disclosure of one's powers in any task organized to permit such [creative] activity."

60. Theobald 1967: 23.

61. Theobald 1966: 103.

62. Theobald 1963: 156. See, for example, Hazlitt 1968: 109 and Friedman 1968: 112. The poverty trap created by such a design did not seem to bother Theobald (1966: 101): "while a work-incentive feature is probably necessary to ensure passage of legislation, the size of the premium should be kept to a minimum."

63. Theobald 1966: 115.

64. Ad Hoc Committee 1964. On the report and its impact, see Steensland 2008: 42–44.

65. On Friedman's theory of economic freedom and its link with a negative income tax, see Preiss 2015.

66. Friedman 1962: 191–192.

67. Friedman 1968: 115–16.

68. Friedman 1973a/1975: 30 and Friedman 1973b/1975: 199.

69. Friedman 1968: 117–8. In *Capitalism and Freedom*, Friedman (1962:190–1) was slightly more categorical. He presented private charity as "in many ways the most desirable" recourse against poverty, but justified governmental action to alleviate poverty on the basis of the argument that in impersonal communities we will only contribute to the poverty relief we want if we are assured that everyone else does.

70. Friedman 1972/1975: 207.

71. Friedman 1973a/1975: 27.

72. Hayek 1944/1986: 89–90.

73. Hayek 1979: 55.

74. Hayek 1979: 141–2.

75. Karl Popper (1948/1963: 361), Hayek's close friend, converged on the policy conclusion, though without the same principled justification and with even less institutional precision: "Do not aim at establishing happiness by political means. Rather aim at elimination of concrete miseries. Or, in more practical terms: fight for the elimination of poverty by direct means—for example by making sure that everybody has a minimum income."

76. Tobin developed his proposal independently of Friedman's: "At some point [in the 1960s] I became aware of Friedman's proposal, but I thought it was confined to a negative income tax rate equal to the lowest income tax bracket tax rate, and that didn't seem to me to offer substantial help" (Tobin 2001). But he is likely to have been inspired by other proposals such as the "negative rates taxation" proposed by Robert J. Lampman (1965), according to Tobin (*New York Times*, March 8, 1997) "the intellectual architect of the war on poverty."

77. Tobin 1965, 1968.

78. "The essential characteristic of demogrants is that the payment is made to all families in the potential eligible group, regardless of income" (Tobin et al. 1967: 161 fn 4). The term "demogrant" was commonly used in the 1960s to refer to "a payment made to all persons above or below a certain age, with no other eligibility conditions except perhaps residence in the country" (Burns 1965: 132). It was first used to refer to proposals for universal child benefits and later for universal retirement pensions. In the 1970s, it started being applied to George McGovern's proposal and to similar proposals.

79. Galbraith 1958: 329–30.

80. Galbraith 1966: 21.

81. Galbraith 1969: 264.

82. Galbraith 1969: 243. The 1958 version of this chapter consisted mostly in the discussion of the proposal of a "cyclically graduated compensation," an unemployment benefit that rises when unemployment rises and falls when it falls (Galbraith 1958: 298–305). There is no trace of this proposal in the 1969 edition.

83. Galbraith 1999a/2001: 312. Galbraith (1999b) returned to this subject in an interview published the same year in the *Los Angeles Times:* "I have long been persuaded that a rich

country such as the United States must give everybody the assurance of a basic income. This can be afforded and would be a major source of social tranquility. It will be said that this will cause some people to avoid work, but we must always keep in mind that leisure is a peculiar thing. Leisure is very good for the rich, quite good for Harvard professors—and very bad for the poor. The wealthier you are, the more you are thought to be entitled to leisure. For anyone on welfare, leisure is a bad thing. I am prepared to take a tolerant attitude on this matter."

84. "Economists Urge Assured Income" was the headline in the *New York Times* on May 27, 1968. Milton Friedman did not support this petition. Here is Tobin's account: "This petition was formulated and circulated by a young MIT assistant professor who had been a student of mine at Yale. . . . I thought it was successful. But Friedman wouldn't join. That was a disappointment to the hope that this proposal might have wide non-political and non-ideological support. This also confirmed my previous suspicion that Friedman's support of NIT was half-hearted" (Tobin 2001). And Friedman's explanation: "At this date, more than three decades later, I do not have any specific recollection of what my reason was for refusing to sign the particular document. However, in general, I have always been reluctant to sign round-robin documents. I have preferred to speak for myself on my own and sign my own name. It may well also be that I found I had some difference of opinion with the particular words in the document in question" (Friedman 2000).

85. See Steensland 2008: 58. See also the personal account by the NWRO leader Wade Rathke (2001: 39).

86. King 1967: 162–164.

87. Johnson 1968.

88. See Heineman 1969, chapter 5: 57, 59.

89. Steensland 2008: 139.

90. Nixon 1969.

91. See Moynihan 1973, Lenkowsky 1986, Steensland 2008, and Caputo 2012 for extensive accounts.

92. McGovern's (1972) proposal was published in the *New York Review of Books* in May 1972, with a foreword by economist Wassily Leontief.

93. On this episode, see especially Steensland 2008: 174–176.

94. Galbraith (1972: 27) wrote: "Mr. Nixon cannot effectively attack the principle of a guaranteed minimum income; he—greatly to his credit—has proposed one himself. He will attack McGovern for urging that the minimum be brought to a reasonable level, to a level where it protects not only the family that is without employment but those whose weakness in the labor market makes them the natural object of exploitation. The McGovern plan, it should be noted, provides what is lacking in all present welfare arrangements—namely, a voluntary incentive to take a job. The man who is now on welfare and takes a job at wages around the welfare level of payment gives up all his welfare income. He has, in effect, a 100 percent tax on his additional income. It is only human to wonder why one should bother to work. The new design ensures that the man who works will always have more money than the man who does not."

95. McGovern 1977: 226.

96. McGovern 1977: 227. See also Galbraith 1975: 151: "When Professor Milton Friedman proposed a guaranteed income for the poor, it was considered (quite correctly) as an act of creative imagination. When a Republican Administration proposed it to Congress, it was a mark of conservative statesmanship. When George McGovern, running for President, advanced a close variant on slightly more generous terms, it was condemned by conservatives as the dream of a fiscal maniac."

97. See Burtless 1990 for an informative account.

98. We shall return to this alleged increase in chapter 7, in connection with the feminist discussion of basic income.

99. Quoted by Steensland 2008: 215.

100. Thus, in 1971, Canada's federal Senate published the Croll report, which recommended the introduction of a negative income tax with a maximum benefit pitched at 70 percent of the poverty threshold. In Quebec, the Castonguay-Nepveu report, also published in 1971, included a proposal for a "general social benefits regime" that was similar to Nixon's Family Assistance Plan. However, Canada's most widely discussed proposal for a guaranteed income is to be found in the much later "Macdonald Report" by the Royal Commission on the Economic Union and Developments Prospects (1986). Its "Universal Income Security Program" (UISP) included a negative income tax and even a modest "demogrant," but faced fierce criticisms from across the political spectrum and was never implemented. On the history of the Canadian debate, see Mulvale and Vanderborght 2012.

101. In Australia, the Henderson Commission, established in 1972 by the conservative McMahon government, published in April 1975 a detailed plan for a "series of guaranteed minimum income payments to all citizens, set at a level sufficient to make it very difficult to fall into poverty." (Australian Government Commission of Inquiry into Poverty 1975: 73). However, this plan was never adopted by the legislature (see Tomlinson 2012).

102. For details about the origins, development, and potential dissemination of Alaska's Permanent Fund, see Hammond 1994, Goldsmith 2005, and Widerquist and Howard eds. 2012a and 2012b. The levels of the dividend since 1982 can be found on the website of the Alaska Permanent Fund: https://pfd.alaska.gov/Division-Info/Summary-of-Applications-and-Payments.

103. Hammond 1994: 251.

104. Hammond 1994: 253.

105. Hammond 1994: 254.

106. Stoffaës 1974.

107. Stoleru 1974a.

108. Greffe 1978: 279, 286.

109. Foucault 1979/2008: 205.

110. Foucault 1979/2008: 207.

111. Jordan 1973. See also his subsequent books on the subject (Jordan 1976, 1987, 1996).

112. Kuiper 1975, 1976, 1977.

113. Meyer, Petersen, and Sorensen 1978.

114. See Dekkers and Nooteboom 1988 for a defense of the WRR proposal, and Groot and van der Veen 2000: 201–206 for an overview of the discussion it triggered. Basic income resurfaced repeatedly in the next three decades in the Netherlands (see chapter 7), but never to the extent it did in 1985.

115. Lubbers 1985: 23.

116. Balkenende 1985: 482.

117. Lubbers 1985: 29.

118. The *Basic Income Research Group* was renamed in 1998 the *Citizen's Income Trust*. Its initial core consisted of sociologist Bill Jordan, economist Anne Miller, and Hermione Parker (1928–2007), parliamentary assistant to conservative MP Brandon Rhys-Williams, himself the son of Juliet Rhys-Williams and author of the first proposal of a basic income at European level (see chapter 8). On the history of the basic-income debate in the United Kingdom, see Torry 2012. In the Netherlands, a network was created in 1987 under the name *Stichting Werkplaats Basisinkomen* (changed into *Vereniging Basisinkomen* in 1991). Other countries had to wait until the following decade or later, when the creation of national networks was stimulated by the development of the international network (BIEN) and later by the 2013 European Citizen's Initiative (see chapter 7).

119. The Collectif Charles Fourier, coordinated by sociologist Paul-Marie Boulanger, economist Philippe Defeyt, and philosopher Philippe Van Parijs, published a special issue of *La Revue Nouvelle* (Collectif Charles Fourier 1985), the first French-language volume devoted to basic income since the long-forgotten Joseph Charlier. With a scenario about the impact of basic income on the future of work, it won a prize from the King Baudouin Foundation in November 1984, and used this prize to organize the conference at which BIEN was founded. Participants in the Louvain-la-Neuve conference included Claus Offe from Germany, Edwin Morley-Fletcher from Italy, Peter Ashby, Bill Jordan, Anne Miller, Hermione Parker, and Guy Standing from Britain; Yoland Bresson and Marie-Louise Duboin from France; Georg Vobruba from Austria; Gunnar Adler-Karlsson, Jan-Otto Anderson, and Niels Meyer from the Nordic countries; Alexander de Roo, Nic Douben, Greetje Lubbi, and Robert van der Veen from the Netherlands; and Koen Raes, Gérard Roland, and Walter Van Trier from Belgium.

120. In 2016, over twenty-five national and regional networks had been accepted as affiliates of BIEN. See the list of national networks on www.basic income.org. The biennial congresses of the Basic Income European Network were held at the University of Louvain (Louvain-la-Neuve, Belgium, September 1986), the University of Antwerp (Belgium, September 1988), the European University Institute (Florence, Italy, September 1990), the University of Paris-Val-de-Marne (France, September 1992), Goldsmith College (London, United Kingdom, September 1994), The United Nations Center (Vienna, Austria, September 1996), the University of Amsterdam (Netherlands, September 1998), the Wissenschaftszentrum Berlin (Berlin, October 2000), the International Labour Office (Geneva, Switzerland, September 2002), and the Forum Universal de las Culturas (Barcelona, Spain, September 2004).

Those of the Basic Income Earth Network were held at the University of Cape Town (South Africa, November 2006), University College Dublin (Ireland, June 2008), the University of Sao Paulo (Brazil, July 2010), the Wolf-Ferrari Haus (Ottobrunn, Germany, September 2012), McGill University (Montreal, Canada, June 2014), and Sogang University (Seoul, South Korea, July 2016).

5. Ethically Justifiable? Free Riding Versus Fair Shares

1. Elster 1986: 719.

2. This aspect is stressed by sociologist Alain Caillé (1987, 1994, 1996) and the MAUSS *(Mouvement Anti-Utilitariste dans les Sciences Sociales)* in their plea for the substitution of an obligation-free income for work-tested benefits that kill spontaneous reciprocity.

3. The quotes are taken from its Articles 1, 3, and 5, respectively.

4. Some mild version of this position is sometimes expressed even by two authors whose writings generally seem supportive of an unconditional basic income (see chapter 4). Thus, for Bertrand Russell (1932/1976: 22–23), "four hours' work a day should entitle a man to the necessities and elementary comforts of life, and the rest of his time should be his to use as he might see fit"; and for G. D. H. Cole (1935: 264), "in order to be entitled to receive the social dividend, an able-bodied citizen would have to be prepared to work up to a standard sufficient to justify his claim to share in the common heritage of society."

5. See Gorz 1980, 1983, 1985, 1988, and 1992 for his defense of a basic income coupled with a social service, and Gorz 1997 for his defense of an unconditional basic income. On Gorz's conversion to an obligation-free basic income, see Van Parijs 2009.

6. Gorz 1984: 16.

7. For further discussion of the relationship between basic income and reciprocity, see White 1996, 1997, 2003a, 2003b, Van Parijs 1997, Widerquist 1999, van Donselaar 2009, 2015. Reciprocity, in the sense entailed by the indictment of free riding, is crucially distinct from the much broader "criterion of reciprocity" which John Rawls (1999: 14) says must be satisfied by any acceptable set of principles of justice. This criterion requires that the terms of cooperation should be reasonable for all to accept as free and equal persons, rather than just accepted under pressure or because of manipulation. The conception of justice as real freedom for all, presented in the next section, is meant to satisfy this broader criterion while contradicting the conception of justice as reciprocity adopted, for the sake of the argument, in the present section.

8. Nor is it a problem for Vives (1526/2010: 81), who congratulates the Roman Emperor Justinian for promulgating a law that "allows no-one to live in idleness." The constitutions of some countries contain similar declarations, but this does not exactly suffice to prevent double standards. Article 27 of Japan's Constitution, for example, asserts that "all people shall have the right and the obligation to work" (Yamamori and Vanderborght 2014: 4–5). More elusively, article 1 of the Italian Constitution makes Italy "a democratic republic founded on labor."

9. Russell 1932/1976: 17.

10. Galbraith 1999b.

11. More quotations from Galbraith along these lines can be found in chapter 4. In addition, an obligation for the poor to work is only acceptable if there is a genuine possibility for them to get access to work. A universal income, or the related schemes discussed in chapter 2, should help. But only the government as employer of last resort could provide a genuine right to work, and this faces in our view the decisive objections discussed in chapter 2.

12. Jan Pieter Kuiper (1977: 511), a professor at the Calvinist university of Amsterdam (see chapter 4), presented his plea for an unconditional basic income as a plea for "the same freedom of choice in the contribution to production as in the contribution to reproduction." In his reflection on the reactions to his basic-income proposal (Kuiper 1982: 279), he noted: "Striking is the emotional character of much criticism. . . . The vehemence of the resistance evokes that with which the decoupling of sexuality and reproduction was disputed."

13. A different analogy between occupational and sexual morality is not affected by this trend. One classic interpretation of the incest taboo (Lévi-Strauss 1967: chapter IV) is that it forces individuals to quit the small circle of the close of kin and thereby to strengthen social cohesion. The obligation to find employment could be said to perform an analogous function.

14. It is sometimes claimed that dropping the obligation to work would signal to unemployed people that society does not need their work. This is correct. But can the unemployed really be fooled into believing that the contribution of each of them is indispensable? It is important to organize our societies so as to enable all their members, as far as possible, to have access to useful activities they like doing and do well, and we have argued for basic income precisely as a way of helping achieve this objective (see chapter 1). But from the facilitation of useful contributions there is no reason to leap to the imposition of allegedly indispensable contributions.

15. The analogy has its limits. Non-producers benefit from the activity of today's producers and at the latter's expense, since the surplus the latter can appropriate shrinks as a result of the former's existence. By contrast, while non-reproducers analogously benefit (through the sustainability of their pensions, the survival of their civilization, the cheerfulness of their parks) from the activity (procreation and education) of reproducers, this happens less necessarily at the latter's expense. This is an asymmetry, sometimes captured by the contrast between parasitism and sheer free riding (Gauthier 1986, van Donselaar 2009). The various points made in the present section are relevant to this accusation of parasitism (worse than just free riding), but the fundamental answer will be given below: the alleged parasites are not harming their alleged victims but simply taking their fair share of an inheritance, a share systematically smaller than the one appropriated by their "victims."

16. See Krebs 2000 for a philosophical defense of a proposal first publicized in the 1970s by the International Wages for Housework campaign (Dalla Costa and James 1975).

17. Michel Bauwens and Rogier De Langhe (2015) propose a variant of this argument: "Even though it is unconditional, a basic income is not "money for nothing," but rather a

lump sum compensation for participation in the commons." Therefore, "the plea for a basic income is not a plea for an alternative social security, but rather a plea for an alternative funding of civil society." It reflects "a renewed confidence in ourselves and the new means we have for organizing ourselves."

18. Appealing to a conception of distributive justice in order to justify a basic income is quite different from claiming that the right to a basic income is a human right. The latter claim rests on a confusion between an unconditional right to an income and a right to an unconditional income. Suppose one can say—on the basis of some ethical theory of human rights or of public international law—that there is something like a human right to an income sufficient, say, to cover basic human needs, or to be lifted out of poverty, or to live in dignity. It does not follow that this sufficient income should be guaranteed to each household through uniform individual cash payments to its members without means test or work requirement. The rhetoric of human rights should not be dismissed, as it is often politically effective, but it is no substitute for a serious philosophical justification.

19. This conception and its implications for the justification of a basic income are spelled out in Van Parijs 1995 and subjected to critical scrutiny in Krebs ed. 2000, Reeve and Williams eds. 2003, van Donselaar 2009, Birnbaum 2012.

20. Such a choice behind a veil of ignorance, in the spirit of Daniels 1985 or Dworkin 2000: ch. 8, provides a better way of handling inequalities related to handicaps than the criterion of undominated diversity operating as a prior constraint on the maximization of the unconditional cash basic income, as presented and defended in Van Parijs 1995: chapter 3. However, it generates similar policy implications, including, in conditions under which an unconditional income could not lift all out of poverty, targeted transfers that are not strictly individual or universal or obligation-free. (See the discussion of the opulence condition in Van Parijs 1995: 86–87.)

21. Bellamy 1888/1983: 82–83.

22. Cole 1944: 144.

23. Simon 2001: 35–36.

24. "In the US, even a flat tax of 70 percent would support all governmental programs (about half the total tax) and allow payment, with the remainder, of a patrimony of about $8,000 per annum per inhabitant, or $25,000 for a family of three" (Simon 2001: 36). In a letter to the Basic Income European Network, Simon (1998: 8) supplemented his general argument with the following remark: "Of course, I am not so naive as to believe that my 70 percent tax is politically viable in the US at present, but looking toward the future, it is none too soon to find answers to the arguments of those who think they have a solid moral right to retain all the wealth they 'earn.'"

25. In addition to Bellamy, Cole, and Simon, the idea of basic income as the distribution of a common inheritance in this broad sense has also been stressed by Marie-Louise Duboin (1988), Gar Alperovitz (1994), and Ronald Dore (2001). In all cases, the choice of the scale at which what "we" have collectively received should be distributed is obviously crucial. We leave it aside here but shall turn to it squarely in our last chapter.

26. The view defended here can be understood as a radical extension of the call for an equal distribution of what is left by the deceased, or of the part of what they leave that they inherited themselves, as defended, for example, by François Huet (1853: 263–75), Eugenio Rignano (1919) or Robert Nozick (1989: 30–33), and simultaneously as a radical extension of the idea, to be found in Paine, Spence, or Charlier, that we are all owed an equal share of the rent on land. (See chapter 4.)

27. This view stands in sharp contrast to the ethical stance commonly induced by Karl Marx's "revelation of the mystery of capitalist production," which distinguishes him fundamentally, according to Engels (1880/2008: chapter 3), from utopian socialism. What Marx showed, he writes, is "that the appropriation of unpaid labor is the basis of the capitalist mode of production and of the exploitation of the worker that occurs under it; that even if the capitalist buys the labor power of his laborer at its full value as a commodity on the market, he yet extracts more value from it than he paid for." According to our own view, the crucial reality to be uncovered behind the market-governed remuneration of factors of production is not that the capitalists appropriate the value created by the workers, but that both capitalists and workers appropriate—very unequally between these two categories and within each of them—the value inherited from the past.

28. Van Parijs (1991, 1995: chapter 4) uses so-called efficiency-wage theories of involuntary unemployment, as developed by Akerlof (1982), Shapiro and Stiglitz (1984), and others, as a starting point for explaining the gift-distributing nature of our economy. If employers pay workers more than what they could get away with—that is, the workers' reservation wage, workers are filled with such gratitude (Akerlof) or fear (Shapiro and Stiglitz) that their productivity is boosted. It directly follows that the wage level that maximizes profits (and hence can be expected to prevail at equilibrium) will systematically exceed the wage level that clears the market—that is, a wage low enough for the supply not to exceed the demand. In other words, contrary to what is predicted by standard "Walrasian" models (with productivity unresponsive to the pay level), involuntary unemployment can be expected to persist at equilibrium. Even in the most perfectly competitive circumstances—full information, costless entry and exit, no wage legislation or collective bargaining, and so forth—it thus appears that people endowed with exactly the same personal and impersonal assets will receive very unequal gifts, in the form of employment rents systematically generated by the labor market.

29. For further discussion of the dependency of this stylized picture of the world on the pervasiveness of the market, see especially Sturn and Dujmovits 2000 and Van Parijs 2001: sections 3–4.

30. "Liberal" in this broad philosophical sense should therefore be sharply distinguished both from "liberal" in the American political sense (libertarians are philosophical liberals) and from "liberal" in the European political sense (socialists can be philosophical liberals).

31. Rawls 1971: sections 11–16, Rawls 2001: sections 14–18.

32. This connection with Rawls's "social bases of self-respect" is even sometimes explicitly made by researchers investigating the effects of basic-income-type reforms. Thus, in his detailed study of Mincome, a Canadian negative-income experiment conducted in the city of

Dauphin, Canada, in the 1970s (see chapter 6), Calnitsky (2016) documents powerful effects in terms of social stigma. Thus, one Mincome recipient said: "I like Mincome in that one is left alone, never harassed or made to feel like you had to crawl to receive an almighty dollar." Calnitsky (2016: 64) comments: "The seeds of Rawls's 'social bases of self-respect' were planted."

33. Rawls 1967: 41; Rawls 1971: 275.

34. See Van Parijs 1988, Prats 1996, and Blais 1999.

35. Rawls 1988: 455 fn7. This reference to Malibu surfers goes back to a long breakfast conversation on the occasion of the conference organized in Paris in November 1987 to mark the publication of the French edition of *A Theory of Justice*. Rawls then objected to this "Rawlsian" justification of an unconditional basic income, as sketched in Van Parijs's (1988) contribution to the conference. In his own considered judgment, Rawls said, Malibu surfers could not legitimately expect to have their way of life subsidized by the public purse. He restated this view in the footnote quoted above, which he added to the written version of the lecture he gave in Paris. A revised version of the lecture appeared subsequently as a chapter of *Political Liberalism*. Rawls (1993: 182 fn9) there supplemented as follows the corresponding footnote: "Plainly, this brief remark is not intended as endorsing any particular social policy at all. To do that would require a careful study of the circumstances."

36. See Rawls 1988: 257; 1993: 181–2; 2001: 179. An earlier, less precise version of the same idea can be found in Rawls's (1974: 253) response to Richard Musgrave (1974), who accused him of an illiberal bias in favor of the meditative activities of a monk at the expense of the lucrative activities of a consultant.

37. The importance of this distinction and its relevance for the justification of an unconditional income were overlooked in Van Parijs 1988 and are explained in Van Parijs 2002: section II.

38. Rawls 1971: 98.

39. Rawls 1971: 96. Note that Rawls occasionally calls social positions "starting places" (1971: 96) or "so-called starting places" (1971: 100). To be able to make sense of Rawls's principle of fair equality of opportunity as defining fair access to unequally attractive social positions, however, a social position cannot be defined as a social class in which one grows up, but rather as an occupational category one joins.

40. Rawls 1971: 102. See also Rawls 1988: 258–9: "The least advantaged are defined very roughly, as the overlap between those who are least favoured by each of the three main kinds of contingencies. Thus this group includes persons whose family and class origins are more disadvantaged than others, whose natural endowments have permitted them to fare less well, and whose fortune and luck have been relatively less favourable."

41. White (2015) argues that a basic endowment (see chapter 2) is a more appropriate way to achieve a "property-owning democracy" than a basic income. If a basic income was in place, citizens should therefore be allowed to convert (part of) their basic income into a lump-sum "basic capital."

42. "Society as employer of last resort through general or local government, or other social and economic policies," Rawls (1999: 50) wrote in his last book, is one of the requirements

for achieving "stability for the right reasons." An earlier draft included at this point a footnote, scrapped in the published version, that mentioned "Ned Phelps's idea of rewarding work." Guaranteed employment and Phelps's wage subsidies, discussed in chapter 2, clearly enjoyed the later Rawls's prima facie preference over an unconditional basic income or negative income tax.

43. On this dual criterion, see especially Dworkin 1981: 311, 2000: 322–324, and 2006: 98, 103–104. The distinction between preferences (or ambition or choice) and circumstances (or endowment or luck) is far from unproblematic and has been the subject of a huge philosophical debate.

44. Dworkin 1981: 276–277, 292–295. Endowment-insensitivity is achieved by asking each to assume that probabilities of good and bad brute luck are the same for all. Ambition-sensitivity requires that people should bear the consequences of the choices they make—or rather of the choices that can plausibly be attributed to them under those hypothetical circumstances.

45. Dworkin 1981. Dworkin's initial formulation—using the parable of shipwrecked people taking part in an auction with each an equal number of clamshells—seemed to justify a 100 percent taxation of inheritance and the equal distribution of the proceeds. But he cautiously left aside "the troublesome issue of bequest" (Dworkin 1981: 334–335). He later suggested: "we can imagine guardians contracting for insurance against their charges' having the bad luck to be born to parents who can give or will leave them relatively little" (Dworkin 2000: 347–348). In his final formulation, he offers "a different (and now I think better) description of gift and inheritance tax as insurance premium. On this different account, such taxes fall not on the donor, as my discussion assumed, but on the recipient of the gift or bequest" (Dworkin 2004: 353). This amounts to expanding the hypothetical insurance scheme in such a way that it covers both personal and impersonal resources.

46. Dworkin 2000: 345, 2006: 115–116.

47. Dworkin 1981: 277–279.

48. Dworkin 2000: 335–8. See also Dworkin 1981: 325–326, 2002: 114. In the earlier formulation, the guaranteed income scheme was more optimistically expected to be no lower than the unemployment benefits and minimum wages in the United Kingdom and the United States (Dworkin 1981: 320). In order to accommodate some mildly paternalistic considerations and to tackle free riding, part of this scheme could be provided in kind, especially in the form of a basic health care package (2002: 114–5). The funding will use a progressive income tax rather than differentiated lump-sum taxes on endowments, because of the practical difficulty of identifying and assessing the value of a person's talents (Dworkin 1981: 325–326, 2002: 126–129).

49. See Dworkin 2000: 330–331, 2006: 104. As should be clear from the above, this critique is not exactly fair to Rawls for two reasons. First, it shows no awareness of Rawls's inclusion of leisure into the index of advantage, precisely motivated by criticisms of this sort. Second, it adopts the common misconstruction of the difference principle as applying to individual scores rather than to lifetime expectations associated with social positions.

50. Dworkin 1983: 208.

51. Steensland 2008: 139.

52. Dworkin 2000: 329.

53. Sen 2009.

54. Barry 1992, 1996a, 1996b.

55. Barry 1994, 1997, 2000, 2005: 209–14.

56. A similar stylized picture underlies, for example, Hal Varian's (1975/1979) income fairness as equality of earning power, Bruce Ackerman's (1980) undominated diversity if interpreted as a principle of distributive justice (Van Parijs 1995: chapter 3), Thomas Piketty's (1994) maximal equal liberty, Richard Arneson's (1989, 1991) equal opportunity for welfare, and the "principle of redress" considered and rejected by Rawls (1971: section 17).

57. As we have argued, the solution proposed by Rawls himself is biased against leisure. On the other hand, a welfarist resolution—lumping income and leisure together into some interpersonally comparable utility—is unacceptable to him. Moreover, as Rawls (1974: 253) recognized from an early stage, the very notion of leisure "calls for clarification." (Does changing diapers count as leisure? Helping children with their homework? Reading bedtime stories to them? Taking them on bike rides? Where is the boundary?)

58. Pettit 1999.

59. See Raventos 1999, 2007, Casassas 2007, Casassas and Birnbaum 2008, Birnbaum 2012. See also Karl Widerquist's (2011, 2013) related approach in terms of "effective control self-ownership"—that is, "the effective power to accept or refuse active cooperation with other willing people," and Jenkins's (2014) justification of basic income from a standpoint inspired by Iris Marion Young's critique of the income focus of distributive justice.

60. See, for example, Murray Rothbard (1982: 48–50) for the "first come, first served" view, and Robert Nozick (1974: 178–9) for the Lockean proviso view. Nozick refers in this context to Charles Fourier's justification for a compensatory minimum income guarantee (see chapter 4), but he argues that the indirect benefits of the private appropriation of land are such that there would be scarcely anything to compensate.

61. As explained in chapter 4, this sort of argument for an unconditional basic endowment or basic income as a way of translating everyone's right to an equal share of the value of the earth can be traced to Thomas Paine (1796/1974), Thomas Spence (1797/2004), and Joseph Charlier (1848). It has been revived by contemporary left libertarians such as Hillel Steiner (1992, 1994) and Michael Otsuka (2003). See Vallentyne and Steiner eds. 2000a and 2000b for an anthology.

62. See Steiner 1992: 83–86 and Steiner 1994: Epilogue. See also Otsuka 2003: 35–9 for further discussion. As mentioned in chapter 4, Joseph Charlier (1848) proposed a gradual assimilation of inherited buildings to land: only half of the ownership of a new building could be bequeathed to private heirs, who themselves could only bequeath half of the remainder to their own heirs, and the remaining quarter could only be transferred one more time before the whole building would join land as collectively owned property.

63. A more radical move, reminiscent of Kant's argument (chapter 3), sticks to an historical entitlement framework but can no longer be called libertarian. James Kearl (1977: 79) argues

that the collective definition of private rights over property "can realistically be thought of as a productive factor and thus as generating a rightful claim to a share of the output." Hence: "The state can, in fact, use its coercive apparatus to force some individuals to help others, since within the limits we have defined, it has been a contributor to the fruits of their labor" (Kearl 1977: 81). Michael Davis (1987: 593) similarly argues that "taxation (within certain limits) is simply returning to the government what it has produced (or rather, returning the equivalent in money). To refuse to pay taxes is not to keep what belongs to you but to withhold what belongs to another. Not taxation but 'tax rebellion' is theft." Yanis Varoufakis's (2016) argument for a universal basic dividend funded out of a "Commons Capital Depository" shares essentially the same ethical foundation. To the extent that it remains based on some producer entitlement (or creators, keepers) idea—and hence particularly relevant as an ad hoc response to libertarians—this sort of argument is compatible with yet crucially different from the liberal-egalitarian gift-equalization argument. The gift contained in our earnings owes a lot to the institutional framework currently provided by the government, but also to natural conditions and a long history of innovation and capital accumulation, and indeed to random events in our personal lives.

64. Zwolinski 2013, 2011, 2014. In his plea for basic income, Zwolinski (2013) appeals to the authority of Friedrich Hayek's—far from orthodox-libertarian—argument for a guaranteed income as an essential part of a "free society" (see chapter 4). On libertarianism and basic income, see also Griffith 2015.

65. Marx borrowed the ethically laden expression "exploitation" from "utopian socialist" Saint-Simon (Ansart 1984: 34). In *Capital*, Marx (1867/1962: ch. 7 section 1), uses the concept of "rate of exploitation" *(Exploitationsgrad)* as equivalent to the rate of surplus value *(Mehrwertrate),* but he also (Marx 1867/1962: ch. 24 section 1) makes a less neutral use of the Saint-Simonian expression "exploitation of man by man" *(Ausbeutung des Menschen durch den Menschen).*

66. See Howard 2005: 127–134 on this contrast, and Howard 2015b: sections 3–4 for a comprehensive discussion of the relationship between Marxism and basic income.

67. Marx 1875/1962.

68. It has been objected (for example, by Raes 1985 and 1988/2013) that this suggestion rests on a profound misunderstanding of the Marxist approach: it focuses on the mode of distribution, whereas Marx insisted on changing the mode of production—that is, the property relations governing the means of production. The latter is true. But changing the mode of production in this sense is not an end in itself but just a means of boosting the development of the productive forces in order to create the economic precondition for a communist society in which everyone's material needs are satisfied without work needing to be remunerated. We are here leaving open the question of whether some feasible form of socialism could be better at securing the sustainability of such a society with a high unconditional basic income. The point is that in the hierarchy of means and ends the latter is more fundamental than the former. Moreover, as we have stressed repeatedly, introducing an unconditional basic income is far more than a change in the distribution of income. It is rather a

change in the distribution of economic power, and thereby in the mode of production, interpreted as referring to the nature, quality, and distribution of work.

69. This "capitalist road to communism" is presented and discussed in Van Parijs 1985 and in van der Veen and Van Parijs 1986a, 1986b, and 2006.

70. Some forms of non-pecuniary remuneration (for example a cozier work environment) may count as reductions in the alienation of labor, while others (for example, company cars or generous business lunches) should simply count as material rewards that evade taxation and hence be added to total per-capita income Y'.

71. See, for example, Glyn and Miliband eds. 1994, Wilkinson and Pickett 2009, Stiglitz 2012.

72. Some basic-income advocates do so very explicitly. For example, Mark Walker (2016: 142) claims that a basic income "will increase aggregate utility" and should be defended on the basis of a version of utilitarianism "that says the right course of action for individuals and societies is the one that maximizes aggregate happiness" (2016: 119).

73. Pigou 1920/1932: 761.

74. Pigou 1920/1932: 730.

75. Mirrlees 1971.

76. Most explicitly, see William Jackson 1999 and the argument behind a sporadic basic income as "quantitative easing for the people" (to be discussed in chapter 6).

77. See, for example, Johnson 1973, Arnsperger 2011, Arnsperger and Johnson 2011, or Mylondo 2010, 2012.

78. Easterlin 1974, 2010.

79. Durkheim 1893/2007: 247.

80. Durkheim 1893/2007: 250–251.

6. Economically Sustainable? Funding, Experiments, and Transitions

1. See, among others, Parker 1989 and Torry 2016 for the United Kingdom, Reynolds and Healy 1995 for Ireland, Gilain and Van Parijs 1996 and Defeyt 2016 for Belgium, de Basquiat and Koenig 2014 and Hyafil and Laurentjoye 2016 for France, Arcarons et al. 2014 for Spain, Bouchet 2015 for Luxembourg, Teixeira 2015 for Portugal, and Boadway et al. 2016 for Canada. In most cases, the funding of the basic income is part of the general income tax scheme. In some, however, such as Helmut Pelzer's (1996) Ulm model for Germany, an earmarked proportional tax is levied on an income base broader than the one on which personal income tax is levied.

2. According to a detailed micro-simulation exercise conducted with Belgian data for 1992 (Gilain and Van Parijs 1996), 40 percent of the cost of a monthly basic income of the equivalent of 200 euros (or 13 percent of Belgium's GDP per capita at the time) could be covered by the scrapping of lower benefits and the reduction of higher ones by the amount of the basic income. With an average tax-exempted income tax bracket on the order of 400 euros per month (including the exemption for adult children in the household) and with

about half the adult population assumed to fully benefit from this exemption, taxing this tax bracket at 25 percent would pay for roughly another quarter of the total cost; taxing it at 50 percent would pay for one half. Taking this (50 percent) and the self-financing by benefits (40 percent) into account, there would then remain 10 percent of the gross cost (or 1.25 percent of GDP) to be financed by additional taxation.

3. Piketty and Saez 2012: Figure 1.

4. 2014 figures, source: http://ec.europa.eu/eurostat/web/sector-accounts/data/annual-data.

5. Some bold attempts have been made to estimate the tax elasticity of the income tax base as a whole. Most of them lead to elasticities between 0.1 and 0.4. Using what they regard as a reasonable intermediate estimate of 0.25, Piketty and Saez (2012: section 3.2) reckon that, if only linear taxation is considered, a flat rate of 80 percent—and an even higher average rate in case of non-linear taxation—would sustainably maximize the tax yield, and hence the level of the basic income, with a given level of other public expenditures. Of course, the cautionary remarks about econometric exercises made above apply here too, especially as regards the extrapolation to varying times and places. As noted by Piketty and Saez (2012: 4.1.3), the sustainable tax yield is sensitive to the extent of trans-national mobility. As the world market becomes more integrated, one can expect a rise in the tax elasticity of migration—that is, in the sensitivity of transnational moves to international differences in tax rates, and therefore also a rise in the tax elasticity of the tax base and a fall in the highest sustainable tax yield. We return in chapter 8 to the challenge this generates.

6. When, as part of the largest survey on basic income so far (see chapter 7), a representative sample of 10,000 Europeans was asked in April 2016 how they would react if given an income "high enough to cover all basic needs" "regardless of whether they work and irrespective of any other sources of income," only 7 percent replied that they would "work less" (https://daliaresearch.com/).

7. Marx and Peters (2004, 2006) conducted interviews with beneficiaries of the initial amount and tried to compare their labor-market behavior with a control sample composed of unlucky regular lottery ticket buyers.

8. See www.mein-grundeinkommen.de and a presentation of the initiative in www.zeit .de/wirtschaft/2014-09/bedingungsloses-grundeinkommen-crowdfunding-bohmeyer. By June 2016, forty annual basic incomes had been funded in this way. In 2016, a similar crowd-funded initiative was launched in San Francisco. See http://mybasicincome.org/.

9. In later years, the payment was reduced and became more sporadic, as a function of donations. There was no control group systematically observed in parallel. See Haarmann and Haarmann 2007, 2012 for a presentation and an assessment by the initiators of the pilot project; Osterkamp 2013a, 2013b for a critical account; and http://allafrica.com/stories /201407170971 for an update.

10. See Davala et al. 2015: 31–48 for a detailed presentation of the experimental set-up.

11. In the Namibian and Indian cases, as the villages concerned are very poor, most of the funding would need to come from elsewhere in the country anyway. Consequently, the effects of the local experiment would not be very different in these villages in case of real introduc-

tion. Moreover, given the modest level, even in relative terms, the (sustainable) affordability is not in doubt especially in the Indian case, because the scrapping of perverse subsidies could cover much of the cost (Standing 2014b, Davala et al. 2015: 206–8, Bardhan 2016).

12. In 2016, the US charity *GiveDirectly* announced its intention to launch a basic-income experiment in Kenya. It is considering monthly payments of around $30 per month (about 25 percent of GDP per capita in Kenya in 2015) to 6,000 residents of several treatment villages for a period of over ten years. See Faye and Niehaus 2016 and https://givedirectly.org /basic-income. The longer duration, if confirmed, increases the relevance of this experiment, without removing the other limitations, especially as regards any extrapolation to basic-income proposals in more developed countries.

13. Informative presentations of the experimental designs and of the main results can be found in Whiteford 1981, Burtless 1986, Greenberg and Shroder 2004, Widerquist 2005, Levine et al. 2005. All experiments were funded by public agencies, in association with universities. The greatest share of the budgets went to cover research and administrative costs, rather than to transfer payments as such. For instance, the research and administration cost of the New Jersey and Pennsylvania experiment amounted to about 70 percent of the total cost (Kershaw and Fair 1976: 18).

14. On the New Jersey experiments, see in particular Skidmore 1975, Pechman and Timpane 1975, Kershaw and Fair 1976, Rossi and Lyall 1976.

15. See Forget 2011, Calnitsky and Latner 2015, Calnitsky 2016. Using a "difference-in-difference" model, Calnitsky and Latner (2015) estimate that about 70 percent of the 11.3 percent reduction in labor-market participation is due to individual-level mechanisms, while 30 percent can be attributed to community effects. Another experiment was performed simultaneously with a dispersed sample of low-income households in Winnipeg, the provincial capital. Both experiments were jointly funded by the federal and the provincial government. Owing to dwindling interest, they were interrupted before the end of the period for which they were planned. The results of the Winnipeg experiment were not analyzed until the nineties (Hum and Simpson 1991, 1993, 2001), those of the Dauphin experiment even later (Forget 2011).

16. The importance of the baseline relative to which the effects are being estimated was highlighted by a change that occurred in the course of the New Jersey–Pennsylvania experiment. The initial design was such that most of the families in the sample were not eligible for welfare payments such as AFDC—namely, families headed by able-bodied males aged between eighteen and fifty-eight. However, new regulations introduced in New Jersey in 1969, three months after the start of the experiment, made many of these eligible for AFDC transfers. What was henceforth being tested in the case of these families, by comparing the experimental sample with the control group, was no longer NIT versus virtually nothing, but NIT versus AFDC (assuming the new regulations were successfully implemented). See Rossi and Lyall 1976: 75–83 and Whiteford 1981: 55.

17. The main exception was the Seattle-Denver experiment, in which some families received transfer payments for up to nine years. Moffit and Kehrer (1981: 110–12) conjecture

that the income effect would be stronger with a permanent scheme (a higher income prompts less working-time reduction if you know that it is only temporary), while the substitution effect would be weaker (a higher effective marginal tax rate prompts more working-time reduction if you know that it is only temporary), which leaves the sign of the net effect of a longer duration undetermined, and even more its size.

18. In the case of the New Jersey–Pennsylvania experiment, Kershaw and Fair (1976: 41–44) provide an overview of the main reasons given by eligible people for refusing enrollment. Among them, the "work ethic" plays a significant role: "He's a proud young man who finally insisted that he did not believe in taking money for nothing."

19. In 2015, Finland's right-of-center government (see chapter 7) announced its intention to launch a randomized basic-income experiment. A working group was set up and published a report in March 2016, exploring a number of options as regards both the nature of the scheme and the design of the experiment (Kangas and Pulkka 2016). The preferred option was for a modest individual basic income of around 550 euros paid to a random sample of 3,000 to 6,000 Finnish residents aged between 25 and 58 with low incomes or an unstable work history, possibly combined with a saturated sample in one municipality. The experiment is currently scheduled to start in January 2017 and last for two years. See Kalliomaa-Puha et al. 2016 and the working group's website: http://www.kela.fi/web/en/experimental-study-on-a-universal-basic-income. In the Netherlands, four cities (Utrecht, Tilburg, Wageningen, and Groningen) got permission to set up, starting in 2017, modest experiments in the direction of a basic income by allowing a randomly selected set of current beneficiaries of public assistance to receive their benefits either without means test (that is, combinable with earnings within a wider range than before) or without work test (that is, without the current "participation" condition) or both (Loek Groot, personal communication, January 2016). In Canada, in 2016, the Finance Committee of Canada's House of Commons recommended that the federal government "implement a pilot project consistent with the concept of a guaranteed income" (Canada, 2016: 71), while senator Art Eggleton introduced a motion encouraging the government "to evaluate the cost and impact of implementing a national basic income program based on a negative income tax" (Canadian Senate, First Session, 42nd Parliament, Volume 150, Issue 18, 25th February 2016). At the provincial level, the 2016 budget of the liberal government of the province of Ontario (Canada) included a plan for a basic-income pilot project (Ontario 2016: 132). Also in 2016, Prime Minister Philippe Couillard of Quebec asked his minister of employment François Blais, a long-standing basic-income advocate (see Blais 2002), to explore the feasibility of a basic-income experiment in the province.

20. See, for example, Scutella 2004 for Australia; Colombo et al. 2008, Horstschräer et al. 2010 and Jessen et al. 2015 for Germany; Clavet et al. 2013 for Quebec; Colombino and Narazani 2013 and Colombino 2015 for Italy; de Jager et al. 1994 and Jongen et al. 2014, 2015 for the Netherlands; Müller 2004 for Switzerland; Colombino et al. 2010 for Denmark, Italy, Portugal, and the UK.

21. For example, in one of the most elaborate of these models, the Dutch Central Planning Office (Jongen et al. 2014, 2015) simulates the impact of a basic income of 687 euros (about 25 percent of Dutch GDP in 2014), which corresponds to what is received by each member of a couple without other income from the existing means-tested minimum-income scheme, and about 70 percent of what is received by a single person. Such a level of basic income (joined with other public expenditures that need to be funded by the personal income tax) is shown to require a flat tax of 56.5 percent, higher than the current highest marginal rate (52 percent). In terms of full-time equivalents, the model predicts a fall of employment by 5.3 percent overall, and of up to 17.7 percent among cohabiting women with at least one minor child. It uses data from a period of low unemployment (2006–2009) and assumes that the volume of employment is determined exclusively by the supply side of the market. It explicitly ignores any effect on prices and wages.

22. For example, the Dutch study quoted before (Jongen et al. 2014, 2015) predicts a particularly high fall in employment among cohabiting women with at least one minor child. As it reflects an expansion of the options open to them, this fall is a welcome primary manifestation of the associated increase in their bargaining power. An intended and predictable secondary manifestation, as undetectable in these econometric models as in short-term experiments with small samples, is an increase in the remuneration of the jobs concerned, which will in turn reduce the fall to be expected in the labor supply.

23. Thomas Piketty (2014: 518, 531–32) reckons that a modest yet steeply progressive worldwide tax (1 percent between 1 and 5 million euros and 2 percent above 5 million), if realizable, could yield revenues up to 3 or 4 percent of the world GDP.

24. Ackerman and Alstott 1999, Atkinson 2015.

25. On tax competition and the difficulty of addressing it, see Genschel and Schwartz 2011 and Genschel and Seekopf 2016.

26. Lange 1937, Yunker 1977, Roemer 1992, 1996. Yunker (1977: 113–121) estimated for the US in 1972 that the "social dividend" (that is, "the direct distribution equally among all the citizen body of property income accruing to the state-owned enterprises under socialism" would amount to $417 per year and per adult, or about 7 percent of GDP per capita at the time).

27. According to some (for example, Van Trier 1992), the transition from socialism to capitalism in East-European countries was a missed opportunity to get there without too much difficulty.

28. Meade 1989: 34–8; 1995: 54–62.

29. Meade 1995: 62.

30. Atkinson (1993d) estimates that a basic income at 15 percent of national income per capita could be funded sustainably in this way (to be supplemented, as proposed by Meade, by part of the yield of an expenditure tax). Getting there is not economically impossible, he argues—from the late 1940s to the late 1970s, the UK rose from a public debt of over 100 percent of GDP to a net worth of the public sector of 100 percent—but the unfairness to the transition generations is a decisive obstacle.

31. Flomenhoft 2013: 101–2, 105. Referring explicitly to Thomas Paine's guess about the total value of unimproved land—one-tenth of national wealth or one-half of national income—Thomas Piketty (2014: 196–8) estimates that the value of unimproved urban and rural land should amount (with a substantial margin of uncertainty) to between 50 and 100 percent of GDP. This makes the Vermont estimates for the associated level of rent look rather high.

32. Flomenhoft 2013: 99–100, 105. With the exception of air (more precisely, the capacity of our atmosphere to absorb carbon dioxide—to which we return), the rent associated with other renewable natural resources such as water or wind totals less than 1 percent of Vermont's GDP. In a similar spirit, Peter Barnes (2014) proposes charging rent for community-owned assets, both natural (atmosphere, electromagnetic spectrum) and institutional (monetary infrastructure, intellectual property protection) and distributing the proceeds as an annual dividend of $5,000 per person (nearly 10 percent of US GDP per capita at the time).

33. Boyce and Riddle (2010) estimate that with a unit price of $25 (in 2020), it would be possible to fund a dividend of about $33 per month (0.7 percent of US GDP per capita in 2015), while Nystrom and Luckow (2014) propose a carbon fee that could fund a monthly basic income of $100 per adult (about 2 percent of GDP per capita) and $50 per child. See also Howard 2012, 2015a, Hansen 2014. A very modest version of such a scheme already exists in California, in the form of a "California Climate Credit" (a lump sum reduction of the electricity bill) granted to every residential electricity customer and funded by the sale to power plants and industries of carbon pollution permits. The credit varies from one provider to another and is on the order of $60 annually for most of them in 2015 (http://www.cpuc.ca.gov/PUC/energy/capandtrade/climatecredit.htm, consulted on August 20, 2015). In the same vein but more ambitiously, in July 2014, congressman Chris Van Hollen (Democrat from Maryland) proposed the creation of a "Healthy Climate Dividend" paid electronically each quarter to every American and funded out of 100 percent of the proceeds of the auction of all US carbon emission permits (https://vanhollen.house.gov/media-center/press-releases/van-hollen-introduces-the-healthy-climate-and-family-security-act-of).

34. Started in October 2010, the first phase of the scheme granted a small, equal basic income to every citizen, with two major qualifications: (1) the payment for all members of each household was made to its official head—that is, mostly to men; (2) non-Iranian residents—mostly Iraqi and Afghan refugees—were not entitled to the grant. See Tabatabai 2011, 2012 for a detailed account, and Salehi-Isfahani 2014 on the key importance of cash transfers in this reform. In January 2012, however, the government announced its intention to increase the amount of the grant to most households, while inviting the 14 percent wealthiest households to waive their entitlement on a voluntary basis. In October 2013, the parliament decided to remove the top 30 percent of Iran's households from the cash subsidies system, and in April 2014 the government decided to stop payment of the subsidies to all middle- and higher-income households. (See www.brookings.edu/blog/markaz/2013/11/01/iran-press-report-the-quest-to-cut-cash-subsidies/ and www.al-monitor.com/pulse/originals/2014/04/iran-subsidy-reform-efforts-corruption.html#.) In September 2015, the amount per

person and per month was 455,000 Iranian rials, or $13.4 (about 3 percent of Iran's GDP per capita; information provided by Mehdad Yousefian).

35. See "Alberta Could Hand Out More Prosperity Cheques: Klein," CBC News, 19 April 2006. http://www.cbc.ca/news/canada/alberta-could-hand-out-more-prosperity-cheques -klein-1.603707.

36. "Oil Wealth Likely to Keep Gulf Calm," *Al Jazeera*, January 18, 2011, http://www .aljazeera.com/news/middleeast/2011/01/20111884114254827.html. See also International Monetary Fund 2011.

37. See Gelders 2015. After the 2012 elections, the Mongolian government stopped these payments and reinstated the Child Money Program, a quasi-universal child-benefit scheme that had existed prior to 2008, and made it universal.

38. Even in the case of permanent resources (such as land or the broadcast spectrum), it may be wise to create a permanent fund. The resource itself may never get depleted, but its value is likely to fluctuate through time. A fund invested in a sufficiently diversified portfolio would help protect the sustainability of the payment.

39. Cummine (2011: 16–17) suspects that "managerial elitism" may explain this lack of enthusiasm: "Exaggerating the downside of dividends serves as a useful justificatory tool for current SWF [Sovereign Wealth Fund] arrangements where significant national savings stay under the direct and relatively autonomous control of financial managers." Contrary to what is sometimes asserted, there is no basic income paid out of an oil fund in the gulf states, only generous conditional benefits reserved for their citizens.

40. See Clemons 2003 for the Iraqi plan (about which there was even a survey, with 59 percent of the American citizens in the sample expressing themselves in favor and 23 percent against), and Sala-i-Martin and Subramanian 2003 for the Nigerian plan. More recently, a somewhat similar proposal was made by Reed and Lansley (2016) for the United Kingdom: a "social wealth fund" should be created with dividends from "natural resources, minerals, urban land and the electromagnetic spectrum, and/or parts of the financial system" and an unconditional basic income should be funded with part of the proceeds.

41. See Akee et al. 2010, 2013, Sutter 2015. Tribal members can be mixed race. In order to be entitled to enroll for membership, a minimum blood quantum of 1/16 is required (Akee 2013: 2).

42. The trilingual official site of the Wealth Partaking Scheme is www.planocp.gov.mo.

43. In addition to proposals for funding a basic income through the distribution of a legal tender by a national or supranational central bank, there have been proposals to fund a basic income with alternative currencies, especially virtual cryptocurrencies. For example, the Worldwide Globals Organization (www.i-globals.org) wants to "demonstrate how the vast majority of people around the world can collectively create an unconditional universal basic income for themselves" by setting up the following scheme: "Every person on earth over the age of 18 can become a member of the WGO for just 25$ or 25¢ for a 4-year membership. In return, members receive 20, 40 or 100 Globals (the equivalent of 200, 400 or 1,000 US Dollars) every month depending upon their citizenships and nationalities" (July 8, 2015). As far as we can see, even the most honest, sophisticated, and ambitious scheme relying on an

alternative currency faces at least one decisive obstacle: the community using it can only be created on a voluntary basis, and its beneficiaries, therefore, cannot distribute a basic income, however modest, to all members of any (territorially defined) society.

44. Joseph Huber (1998) mentions an amount of 500 euros per month for Germany (24 percent of Germany's GDP at the time), to be quickly phased out, however, as the recipient's income increases. In his view, "tax-levied government money and central-bank-issued drawing rights could be combined to any proportion required," but using the latter as well as the former would, he argues, put the economic and political viability of basic income on a firmer footing. See also Huber 1999, Huber and Robertson 2000.

45. Thus, Oxford economist John Mullbauer (2014) recommended that the European Central Bank should pay 500 euros to every Eurozone resident. A similar proposal was made in August 2016 by 35 economists as a way to stimulate the British economy after the Brexit vote (www.theguardian.com/business/2016/aug/03/cash-handouts-are-best-way-to-boost-growth-say-economists). There are modest precedents elsewhere. For example, in January 2009, Taiwan's government handed out shopping vouchers worth $107 to the country's nearly 23 million residents in order to stimulate the island's economy (http://news.bbc.co.uk/2/hi/asia-pacific/7836458.stm).

46. Moreover, the administrative hassle of organizing a payment to all residents would be excessive for just some occasional payments. As argued by Sas and Spiritus (2015), a basic income funded in this way is therefore best viewed as a provisional top-up on a basic income funded from a different source. Arguably, the amount could then also be adjusted (slightly!) downwards in periods of overheating.

47. For example by Bresson (1999), who advocated a worldwide basic income funded by a 1 percent tax on financial transactions. The *Association pour la taxation des transactions financières et pour l'action citoyenne* (ATTAC), founded in Paris 1998 with the introduction of a Tobin Tax as its main aim, soon started discussing and advocating other ideas. Its German branch, in particular, became actively involved in the discussion and advocacy of basic income. See, for instance, Rätz et al. 2005.

48. Tobin 1978. In chapter 8, we discuss this option as a source of funding for a eurodividend and mention an estimate of 10 euros per month as the maximum level of basic income that could be funded by a Tobin tax introduced at EU level.

49. The most prominent advocate of this micro-tax, in the Swiss context, was socialist politician Oswald Sigg, former vice-chancellor and former spokesman of the Swiss government. He developed his proposal in collaboration with Marc Chesney and Anton Gunzinger, professors at the Zurich Polytechnic School, under the label *Automatische Mikrosteuer auf dem Gesamtzahlungsverkehr* (automatic micro-tax on the total circulation of payments). See www.watson.ch/Schweiz/Interview/568982879-Bedingungsloses-Grundeinkommen-l%C3%A4sst-sich-nicht-finanzieren--Oswald-Sigg-hat-da-eine-neue-Idee.

50. A basic income funded in this way is a component of the "social capitalism" advocated by Yona Friedman (2000): a strictly individual and unconditional basic income for each citizen at 20 percent of GDP per capita, funded by a tax on all electronic payments (including

deposits) of 1.5 percent (paper money is abolished, and no coin is worth more than 10 euros) and coupled with a privatization of all public services (education, health, and so forth) except the judiciary and the police. Less radically, Edgar L. Feige (2000) proposed an "automated payment transaction tax" of 0.6 percent applying to all electronic payments as a replacement for the income tax (not for social security contributions). A very similar "total-economic-activity tax" was proposed for South Africa by Margaret Legum (2004). And Brazil used it for some time in order to fund part of its federal social programs. For a discussion of the history, advantages, and disadvantages of such a universal transfer tax, see Rosseels 2009.

51. We are not considering here social insurance contributions in the strict sense as a possible source of funding for basic income. Their function as insurance premiums paid by workers is to fund the coverage of risks they are exposed to by paying for earnings-related unemployment benefits, old-age pensions, sickness pay, and so forth. To the extent that existing social contributions or payroll taxes go beyond this insurance function, they can be assimilated to the taxation of labor income.

52. See, respectively, Kaldor 1955 and Skidelsky and Skidelsky 2012: 17.

53. Meade 1989.

54. Walker (2016: 24–29) also argues that a VAT is "a straightforward means" to finance a basic income in the United States. He estimates that a VAT of 14 percent on all goods and services could fund a basic income of $10,000 per year.

55. They may also start playing a greater role in the United States. See Stern 2016: 213: "I would strongly consider levying a value added tax (VAT) of five to ten percent on the consumption of goods and services, with all the revenue going to the funding of UBI."

56. See Duchâtelet 1994 for the first formulation of his plan. In its most developed presentation, Duchâtelet (2004: 115–129) proposed funding in this way a "freedom income" of 400 euros per month for young adults aged between 18 and 25, a basic income of 540 euros per month for all adults aged between 25 and 65 (about 18 percent of Belgium's GDP per capita in 2004), a uniform child benefit of 135 euros per month for all children under 18, and a basic pension of 800 euros per month for those over 65.

57. See Werner 2006, 2007, Werner and Presse eds. 2007. Before Duchâtelet and Werner, Bart Nooteboom (1984: 5), then head of the study center of the Dutch association of small businesses, had also advocated a VAT-funded basic income.

58. It is the only source mentioned in the 2008 film that launched the campaign for the Swiss initiative on basic income (Daniel Häni and Enno Schmid, *Grundeinkommen—ein kulturimpuls*, Tvgrundeinkommen 2008, www.youtube.com/watch?v=ExRs75isitw) and the preferred source in Christian Müller and Daniel Staub 2016: 67–68. In the more detailed proposal from BIEN Suisse (Kundig 2010), a "Social Value Added Tax" is combined with the personal income tax.

59. Moreover, consumption taxes in general are less regressive from a lifecycle perspective than they look from a snapshot perspective, as at least some of the rich consume more than their current income at late stages in their lives. Thus, Fullerton and Rogers (1993: 228–232) argued that a broad-based VAT is likely to be proportional to lifetime income.

60. In the context of a less developed country, see Pieter le Roux's (2006) plea for a VAT-funded basic income in South Africa.

61. There are further differences sometimes used in favor of VAT, such as the fact that imports are subjected to it while exports are not, which is good for the country concerned (though not so good for its trade partners). Another is that, in contrast with the income tax case, employers and employees will have no incentive to collude through the substitution of untaxed compensation in kind for taxable income. But this is again largely an illusion: a nice meal will be VAT-deductible if offered to an employee as a business lunch, but not if paid for by the employee with his monthly pay. Moreover, in both cases, there is of course not only this incentive towards more (untaxed) "consumption within the firm," or, in other words, in-kind advantages, but also towards more (untaxed) "production outside the firm"—that is, unpaid activities within the household or community (see chapter 1).

62. For early proposals of this sort, see Robertson 1989, 1994, Genet and Van Parijs 1992, Davidson 1995.

63. See Bradshaw 2012, Van Mechelen and Bradshaw 2013, Ferrarini et al. 2013 and Ortiz 2015 for comprehensive comparative overviews of child-benefit schemes. On the Mongolian scheme, Gelders (2015) mentions in this connection the tension between international organizations on the issue of universality versus means-testing. Financial institutions (IMF, World Bank) tend to recommend targeting so as to achieve poverty reduction at the lowest fiscal cost, whereas UNICEF recommends universality because of the higher rate of take-up among the poor.

64. In Canada, for example, a (taxable) Universal Childcare Benefit was introduced at the federal level in 2006. At the initiative of minister Jean-Yves Duclos, however, Justin Trudeau's liberal government, in 2015, made the system more generous for children in poor households and degressive with household income. In Japan, a universal child benefit *(Kodomo Teate)* was introduced in 2010, but it was heavily criticized since its inception and in 2012 the government had to introduce an income threshold beyond which families were no longer entitled to the benefit (Abe 2014).

65. Longman 1987: 229–234.

66. See St John and Willmore 2001 on the New Zealand scheme, St John 2016 for a detailed discussion of its resemblance to basic income, and Abrahamson and Wehner 2003: section 1 on the Danish People's pension. Since 1986, Japan has also had a universal basic-pension scheme aimed at covering all residents, but a significant proportion of the unemployed and self-employed do not register in the system (Vanderborght and Sekine 2014: 18).

67. Thus, Finland and Sweden transformed their universal pensions into noncontributory top-ups on insufficient earnings-related pensions in 2001 and 2003, respectively. See Goedemé (2013: 111–12) for an overview of noncontributory pension schemes in Europe.

68. Bidadanure (2014: 162–164) discusses two variants of a basic income targeted at people under 35 years old, a cohort-specific and an age-specific "Youth Basic Income," but argues that, all things considered, a basic income for all, irrespective of age, is a superior alternative.

69. Ackerman and Alstott 1999.

70. Non-means-tested student grants exist in Denmark, Finland, and Sweden, and Belgium's universal child benefits for children up to age 25 in full-time education can be assimilated to them (see European Commission 2014b).

71. See, for example, Schmitt 1980, Gerhardt and Weber 1983: 88–9, and Lavagne and Naud 1992.

72. In 1999, the Netherlands adopted a "law on income support for artists" *(Wet inkomensvoorziening kunstenaars)*, providing an income-tested minimum income for people whose activity was acknowledged to be "artistic" by a certified body. In 2005, this law was turned into a "law on work and income for artists" *(Wet werk en inkomen kunstenaars)*, which provided that artists could benefit from a transfer pitched at 70 percent of the means-tested guaranteed minimum income, and supplement this guarantee with their own earnings (up to a total of 125 percent of the minimum income), for a maximum of 4 years. In 2008, 3,700 artists received a transfer payment (see Ijdens et al. 2010 for further details). This law was abolished in 2012, on the grounds that artists did not deserve a specific treatment, and were expected to be actively searching for ("real") work.

73. See Francisco Nobrega's (2015) plea for an officialization of this limited de facto "universality" of the Bolsa Família scheme: "After entering the monthly grant system the newcomer would have a generous time interval before the grant expires. This longer interval will remove the "poverty trap" long enough for progress out of the grant system. In case a lack of income remains, the person / family will apply, near the end of the allotted time, to stay in the system." And see chapter 7 on Senator Suplicy's 2004 basic-income law.

74. Similarly, beneficiaries of Australia's income-tested minimum income (the *Newstart Allowance*) can earn up to A\$48 per fortnight before their allowance is reduced. Additional earnings are taxed at rates lower than 100 percent. The UK's jobseekers' allowance offers a similar pattern.

75. France Stratégie 2014a, 2014b, 2014c, Christophe Sirugue 2016. France Strategie, the former Commissariat Général du Plan, now directed by Jean Pisani-Ferry, recommended a merger of the various existing schemes (both of a means-tested minimum income and an earned income tax credit type) into a single scheme of "activity and solidarity allowances designed as a negative income tax." See especially France Stratégie 2014a: 157; 2014b: 85; 2014c: 34–36. Christophe Sirugue's (2016) preferred option integrates ten different schemes into a single one with the same sort of profile. In both cases, at least a mild willingness-to-work test keeps being imposed. A similar proposal had been made earlier by Roger Godino (1999) under the label *allocation compensatrice de revenu* ("compensatory income transfer") and mentioned in several official reports intended to feed reflection on the future of employment, including one by Pisani-Ferry (2000).

76. See United Kingdom 2015 and Jordan 2011. Similarly, in Germany, where negative income tax proposals have been made from the right and the left since the 1970s (Engels, Mitschke and Starkloff 1973, Mitschke 1985, Scharpf 1993, 1994), the structure in place since the 2005 "Hartz IV" reform (see chapter 7) is also one that facilitates the combination of benefits and low earnings, with a strengthened willingness-to-work test. About half of the

recipients of the means-tested minimum-income scheme [*Arbeitslosengeld II*] are "working poor."

77. Meade (1989: 37) argues that it is impossible to achieve an adequate social dividend with a proportional tax "simply because the marginal rates of tax on increased earnings and profits combined with the assurance of the substantial unconditional income represented by the social dividend introduced an unacceptably large general disincentive for enterprising work and investment." He therefore proposes a 60 percent rate on the lower bracket and 45 percent above instead of 50 percent everywhere. Such a regressive tax profile is also proposed by Dilnot, Kay, and Morris (1984: 74–79) for their two-tier system, by Joachim Mitschke (1985) for his *Bürgergeld,* and by Roger Godino (1999, 2002) for his *allocation compensatrice de revenu.* As these examples illustrate, this second option can be combined with the first one (household-based rather than individual) in order to keep the increase of marginal tax rates within narrower limits.

78. This "Rawlsian" or maximin argument (see chapter 5) for a regressive tax profile in the lower range (analogous to the utilitarian argument mentioned in chapter 5) can be found in Atkinson and Stiglitz 1980: 420–1, Piketty 1997, Piketty and Saez 2012: chapter 4.1. Such a regressive profile can be far better for the worst-off than one, such as Friedman's (see chapter 4), that involves a linear tax profile, and even than one involving a sharply progressive profile. It all depends on the level of minimum income they aim *and* manage to fund in a sustainable way.

79. Suppose for example that the initial situation in the country concerned is one with a means-tested minimum scheme at the level of $1,000 per month for a single adult, and $700 per month for each member of a couple. The unconditional but partial basic income could then be fixed at $700 per month for each adult. A single adult with no other income would be entitled to a conditional top-up of $300. The same outcome can be achieved with a lower individual partial basic income of $400 combined with a fixed amount per household of $600 (see Gerhardt and Weber 1983: 79). In some proposals, the top-up also takes the form of a housing supplement of variable size (e.g., Parker 1982).

80. Such a step was made in the Netherlands in 2001, when a tax reform created an individual refundable tax credit—2,100 euros per year, or about 7 percent of Dutch GDP per capita at the time—to which not only every taxpayer was entitled but also the non-working partners of every taxpayer, thus leaving very few adults in the country without either a benefit or an individual tax credit. The reform was made at the initiative of the liberal finance minister Gerrit Zalm, who had declared, in 1993, in his capacity as head of the Dutch Planning Bureau, that such a reform would be the next step towards a partial basic income (See Groot and van der Veen 2000). In 2009, however, the government decided that the scheme would be gradually phased out, and that it would stop altogether in 2024 (see: http://financieel.infonu.nl/belasting/105964-algemene-heffingskorting-2014-omhoog.html). In the same vein, congressman Bob Filner (Democrat, San Diego) submitted a bill to the US Congress in May 2006 proposing to transform the standard income tax deduction into an indi-

vidual refundable tax credit of $2,000 per adult (about 4 percent of GDP per capita at the time) and half of that per child (see Sheahen 2012: 148).

81. Cole 1944: 147. A decade earlier, Cole (1935: 235) seemed to be more impatient: "The aim should be, as speedily as possible, to make the dividends large enough to cover the whole of the minimum needs of every citizen. Being paid as a civic right, it will be of equal amount for all, or rather for all adults, with appropriate allowances for children. It should be from the beginning at least large enough to cover the bare physical necessities of every family in the community." But the "payments that would not suddenly upset the whole structure of incomes" he had in mind in 1944 may have been considered by him "large enough to cover the bare physical necessities of every family."

82. Meade 1989: 45.

83. As noted long ago by John Stuart Mill (1979: chapter 4) and Oskar Lange (1937: 134–135), an analogous gradual transition to socialism understood as state ownership of the means of production is harder to imagine.

84. Elster 1986: 709.

85. Elster 1986: 720.

86. Deppe and Foerster 2014: 8.

87. Elster 1986: 720.

88. Elster 1986: 719.

7. Politically Achievable? Civil Society, Parties, and the Back Door

1. G. D. H. Cole (1944: 147–8), for example, saw universal free health care and education as natural stepping stones to a universal basic income: "If the state assumes the responsibility of seeing to it that all its citizens are to be given the chance of free health service and free education up to a secondary stage . . . what is there utopian in suggesting that a share in the product of industry ought to accrue to every citizen as a money payment which he can spend freely, as well as in the form of certain freely provided services? It is a step further, I agree, but it is a step further on a road on which we have already agreed to travel a good deal of the way."

2. It is our job, at least, as participants in a public debate. For a committee expected by a government to make recommendations for immediate implementation, the legitimate constraints are arguably different. In its report on the reform of British taxation, for example, the committee led by James Meade (Meade ed. 1978: 279) can be forgiven for writing: "The position taken by the Committee is that the full social dividend with a high basic rate of tax is unlikely to attract sufficient political support for it to be worth considering further." And France Stratégie (2014c: 23–24) can similarly be excused for writing in its report on the future of France's social policy: "This proposal [of a universal and unconditional basic income] knocks against the fact . . . that the social acceptability of a basic income without any link with employment is not established."

3. Piketty 2014: 20.

4. Elster 1986: 709, 719.

5. See for instance Miller 1992, Swift et al. 1999, Reeskens and van Oorschot 2013, Taylor-Gooby 2013.

6. Relevant surveys were conducted in Denmark (Goul Andersen 1996), Sweden and Finland (Anderson and Kangas 2005), Norway (Bay and Pedersen 2006), the United States (Rasmussen Report 2011), Brazil (Waltenberg 2013), Japan (Itaba 2014, Takamatsu and Tachibanaki 2014), and France (IFOP 2015).

7. See, respectively, Goul Andersen 1996 (Denmark), Andersson and Kangas 2005 (Finland and Sweden), Bay and Pedersen 2006 (Norway).

8. See, respectively, Rasmussen Reports, Government Welfare and Income Grants, survey conducted August 29–30, 2011 (http://www.rasmussenreports.com) and Trudeau Foundation 2013: 3.

9. See IFOP 2015. Relevant surveys were also conducted in other countries, but the formulation of the question has often been too vague to allow the assumption that respondents were expressing an opinion about an unconditional basic income. In Japan, for example, a survey asked a large sample in Osaka and Tokyo whether they would support "the idea that the government covers the minimum necessary cost of living" (Itaba 2014: 175). One-third supported it, one-third rejected it, and one-third had no opinion. But there are, of course, other ways of covering the minimum necessary cost of living than through a basic income. In Catalonia, by contrast, the question was more precise. In July 2015, 1,800 residents were asked what they thought of a basic income of 650 euros financed by a transfer from the 20 percent richest to the rest of the population. Fully 72 percent answered they were in favor (GESOP 2015: 4).

10. The results of this survey were presented by Dalia Research at the conference on "The Future of Work" held in Zurich on May 4, 2016. See https://daliaresearch.com/.

11. See Tables 1.2, 3.1, 3.2, and 3.4 in Colombo et al. 2016, which contains many more interesting data. We thank the authors for having given us access to their report before publication.

12. Sloman 2016: 209, 213.

13. Moynihan 1973: 276–7. On the US labor movement, see also Desmond King (1995: 208): "Organized labor has been glad to support selective noncontributory programs allocated on a means-tested basis for nonunion members but has been disinclined to mobilize its political strength to build universal public welfare programs."

14. The Canadian Labor Congress denounced the "neoliberal inspiration" of the "Guaranteed Annual Income" proposed in 1986 by the Macdonald Royal Commission on the Economic Union and Development Prospects. (See Haddow 1993, 1994.)

15. Lubbi 1991: 15.

16. van Berkel et al. 1993: 22–24.

17. See Voedingsbond 1981 for an early statement of the position of the Voedingsbond on basic income and see van Berkel et al. 1993 for an in-depth analysis of its exceptional role.

The Voedingsbond FNV hosted the headquarters of the Dutch Basic Income Network from 1987 to 1997.

18. On the South African debate on basic income, see Peter 2002, Standing and Samson eds. 2003, COSATU 2010, Seekings and Matisonn 2013.

19. In Italy, the Research Centre of the main trade-union confederation (CGIL—*Confederazione Generale Italiana del Lavoro*) organized a series of conferences and publications on basic income from 1987 to 1992 but never managed to get the idea adopted by the organization (Sacconi 1992). In Colombia, the *Escuela Nacional Sindical,* a union-linked educational institution based in Medellin, devoted an entire issue of its journal *Cultura y Trabajo* (2002) to basic income and made it the theme of its twenty-fifth anniversary celebrations (Giraldo Ramirez, 2003). In Spain, the Basque Trade Union *Esker Sindikalaren Konbergentzia* devoted two full issues of its magazine *Gaiak* to the subject in 2002 and 2005.

20. In Ireland, Rosheen Callender, one of the leaders of the ITGWU (Irish Transport and General Worker's Union, which merged with the Federated Workers' Union of Ireland in 1990 to form SIPTU, Ireland's largest trade union), publicly supported the idea in the 1980s (Callender 1985, 1986). In Canada, Michel Chartrand—one of the historical figures of Quebec's trade union movement—became, in his personal capacity, one of the most mediatized supporters of the proposal (Bertrand et Chartrand 1999, Wernerus 2004, Vanderborght 2006). More recently, in the Netherlands, Reinier Castelein (2016), the leader of the small trade union *Unie* (Union), argued that, in response to automation, a basic income would help to achieve a better distribution of time, work, and income (Castelein 2016), while Doekle Terpstra, former leader of the large *Christelijk Nationaal Vakverbond* (CNV—"Christian Trade Union Federation")—advocated basic income as an important part of a "new social contract" made necessary by the failure of current activation policies (*De Volkskrant,* May 31, 2016). Most impressive is the extensive plea by US labor leader Andy Stern (2016), to which we turn shortly.

21. One articulate and eloquent example of the hostile attitude of labor unions toward basic income can be found in the speech given in Switzerland's Council of States (the Swiss senate) by one of its (socialist) members, Paul Rechscheiner, chairman of the *Schweizerische Gewerkschaftsbund* (SGB—"Swiss Federation of Trade Unions"), Switzerland's largest labor-union federation, as part of the parliamentary debate on the popular initiative on basic income. Full employment must remain the objective, he insists, and social insurance is there to protect workers against risks, often above the strict minimum: "A basic income is too much when there is no need, and not enough when there is one." Another illustration is provided by the *Confédération des Syndicats Chrétiens* (CSC—"Confederation of Christian Trade Unions"), Belgium's largest trade-union federation. In 1985, shortly after the first appearance of basic income in Belgium's public debate, it published a document in which the idea was described as a "silly and worrying utopia . . . against which trade unionism would one day have to fight" (CSC 1985). In January 2002, a preparatory report for its national congress included a section unambiguously entitled "No Basic Income" (CSC 2002: 42, Vanderborght 2006). A more recent contribution by one of its leaders expresses a timid opening to

"those who believe in basic income as a useful utopia, as a horizon towards which one can walk cautiously, with one's feet in reality" (Van Keirsbilck 2015: 24).

22. This feature did not escape labor leader Andy Stern (2016: 188): "UBI is a game-changer for labor. As basic income advocate Timothy Roscoe Carter points out: 'In any negotiation, a person who can walk away from a deal can always exploit a person who cannot. Capitalists can always walk away from labor, because they can just live off the capital they would otherwise invest. It will never be fair until labor can just walk away. A basic income is the ultimate permanent strike fund.'"

23. For further discussion of this question, see also Vanderborght 2006.

24. King 1995.

25. Jalmain 1999.

26. Keynes 1930b/1981: 14.

27. This is contrary to what is frequently asserted by critics of basic income from the left. See, for example, Clerc 2003 and Alaluf 2014: 36–37.

28. In some countries, there is an additional, more contingent factor that may help to explain the hostility of the union leadership. In Scandinavian countries and in Belgium, the countries with the world's highest rates of unionization, the unions' income partly consists of remuneration for the services they provide to unemployed workers. Unions are allocated some proportion of the unemployment benefits they are in charge of distributing and/or of the unemployment funds they are entitled to manage (Van Rie et al. 2011). If unemployment benefits shrink into mere top-ups on each family's basic incomes, and if moreover the rate of involuntary unemployment shrinks thanks to the job-sharing and untrapping effects expected from the reform, this source of income is unavoidably threatened. One may no doubt prefer less perverse ways of providing labor unions with a legitimate payment for the useful role they play. In the meantime, this may help explain the fierceness of some reactions.

29. Specifically, 12.3 percent versus 5.8 percent and $776 versus $980 per week in 2015 (Bureau of Labor Statistics 2016). Our point about the relevance of unionized workers being comparatively privileged holds whatever the direction of the causal link that explains the correlation between unionization and pay level.

30. Keynes 1930b/1981: 13.

31. As Andy Stern (2016: 147) puts it: "The people running unions, unfortunately, have not been creative enough, to date, in responding to the challenges of a changing economy, as evidenced in their slow response to Uber, Airbnb, and other disruptive ventures, and in the difficulties unions have faced while trying to organize freelancers."

32. In David Graeber's (2014b) forceful formulation: "I'm thinking of a labor movement, but one very different than the kind we've already seen. A labor movement that manages to finally ditch all traces of the ideology that says that work is a value in itself, but rather redefines labor as caring for other people."

33. Stern 2016: 222.

34. Stern 2016: 200.

35. Stern 2016: 201. To get things moving in the United States, Stern (2016: 219) even proposes to "put a constitutional amendment for UBI" and to get "an independent candidate to run for president in 2020 or 2024 for the Basic Income Party. . . . To have a major candidate for president articulating the need for a basic income would catapult our issue and stimulate a national debate."

36. See http://www.gewerkschafterdialog-grundeinkommen.de/category/home

37. This was motion 54, submitted by West Midlands / Community, Youth Work, and Not for Profit. The full text features in the *Preliminary Agenda* of Unite's fourth policy conference, July 11–15, 2016: 36–37 (http://www.unitenow.co.uk/index.php/documents/documents /policy-conference-2016/362-unite-policy-conference-2016-preliminary-agenda/file). In September 2016, UK's Trade Union Congress passed a resolution submitted by Unite with the following wording: "Congress believes that the TUC should acknowledge Universal Basic Income and argue for a progressive system that would be easier for people to navigate, paid individually and that is complementary to comprehensive public services and childcare provision" (https://www.tuc.org.uk/sites/default/files/Congress_2016_GPC_Report_Digital. pdf).

38. See, respectively, Sommer 2016: 82 and Centre des Jeunes Dirigeants d'Entreprise 2011.

39. Economiesuisse 2012.

40. Duchâtelet 1994.

41. On the history of *Vivant*, see Vanderborght 2002.

42. Werner and Hardorp 2005, Werner 2006, 2007, Werner and Presse 2007, Werner and Goehler 2010.

43. Other major businessmen who came out in favor of a basic income include Pierre Bergé (1991: chapter 14), CEO of the French fashion design company Yves Saint Laurent; Charles Sirois (1999: 147–9), CEO of the Canadian telecommunication company Telesystem and cofounder (in 2011) of the center-right political party *Coalition Avenir Québec* (CAQ— "Coalition for Quebec's Future"); and Josef Zotter, CEO of the Austrian chocolate firm Zotter (http://derstandard.at/2000019681222/Schelling-Arbeitslosengeld-in-Oesterreich-ist -zu-hoch). In a neighboring category, see also the plea by Peter De Keyzer (2013: chapter 10), the chief economist of Belgium's largest bank, BNP Paribas Belgium.

44. *De Morgen*, June 9, 2016. In the Netherlands, one of the most consistent advocates of basic income from an early stage is Bart Nooteboom, for many years director of the think tank linked to the Dutch association of medium-size and small firms. See Nooteboom 1986 and Dekkers and Nooteboom 1988.

45. The term "precariat" originates in the Italian anarchist tradition. It has been widely used in French sociology, for example, by Robert Castel (2009). It has been popularized in English by Guy Standing (2011, 2014a).

46. Allen 1997, Bond 1977.

47. Kornbluh 2007: 143. The original plan is formulated in National Welfare Rights Organization (1969/2003). The NWRO's plan never reached the political agenda, but the

organization took part in the discussions of Nixon's Family Assistance Plan, insisting that transfer payments were to be made truly universal rather than targeted at families with children. On the NWRO, see also Piven and Cloward 1993: 320–30.

48. Bill Jordan's 1973 essay offers a well-documented and insightful case study of the aspirations, potential, and difficulties of this local precariat initiative. On its advocacy for basic income, see especially Jordan 1973: 27, 70, 72–3, and also Jordan 1986.

49. In the late 1970s, Australia's Unemployed Workers Movement (1979) asserted in its statutes that one of its goals "is to campaign for the establishment of a Guaranteed-minimum-income scheme in Australia that will provide everyone with an adequate human standard of living." In Canada, the National Anti-Poverty Organization (NAPO), founded in 1971 by over two hundred anti-poverty groups and now renamed Canada Without Poverty, has been advocating a countrywide "guaranteed adequate income" since the early 1980s and launched a national campaign in its favor in 2007. In 1984, during the hearings of the Macdonald Commission, the *Fédération Québécoise Anti-Pauvreté* (Quebec's Anti-Poverty Federation) also explicitly defended a basic income (Tremblay 1984). In the Netherlands, the *Landelijk Beraad Uitkeringsgerechtigden* (National Council of Welfare Claimants) started advocating the introduction of a substantial basic income from 1986 onwards and was one of the founding associations of the Dutch basic income network in 1987 (Landelijk Beraad Uitkeringsgerechtigden 1986, Hogenboom and Janssen 1986).

50. Geffroy 2002.

51. Bourdieu 1998.

52. Guilloteau and Revel 1999, Fumagalli and Lazzaratto eds. 1999. Impressed by the extent and duration of the troubles, Lionel Jospin, France's socialist prime minister at the time, asked the social welfare department to draw up a report on the "problems raised by the movements of the unemployed" (Join-Lambert 1998). One section has a very revealing title: "Towards the Merger of All Minima and, Beyond That, Towards a Basic Income?" While the document answers the question in an ambiguous way, it inaugurates a series of official studies on the reform of social minima, with explicit discussions of basic income and the negative income tax.

53. The possession of a (good) job can be viewed as creating a class division analogous to the possession of (significant) capital, but for the reasons just sketched, the weaker party in this new class conflict is less well armed than the weaker party in the older one. See Van Parijs 1987b.

54. In the United States, for example, the mean gross earnings of women are 66.5 percent of men's ($36,900 versus $55,443, figures for 2013 are at https://www.census.gov/hhes/www /cpstables/032014/perinc/pinc10R_000.htm) and 57 percent of women are in the labor force, compared to 69.2 of men (figures for 2014, Bureau of Labor Statistics 2015: 9–10). Taking these percentages into account, the mean annual earnings (when including those with zero earnings) were about $21,000 for women and $39,000 for men. To get a better sense of the difference, consider a basic income of $1,000 per month funded entirely by a flat tax of 40 percent on earnings. On average, women would gain $120 per month (+17 percent) while

men would lose $120 (-9 percent) starting from a situation with no redistribution. In order to assess the extent of the additional redistribution from men to women generated by a specific basic income reform in a particular national context, one would need to take a close look at what it replaces and at how much redistribution from men to women (if any) is achieved by what it replaces.

55. Woolf 1929/1977: 103.

56. Hannan and Tuma 1990: 1271–2. The putative impact on the divorce rate in the Seattle–Denver experiments was one of the most disputed in the scientific literature on the negative-income-tax experiments. From a first analysis, Hannan et al. (1977: 1186) concluded that "income maintenance raises the rate of marital dissolution." In the final report, Hannan et al. (1983: 259) went further, stating that the schemes tested in these experiments "dramatically increased the rate at which marriages dissolved among white and black couples, and decreased the rate at which Chicano women entered marriages." Their estimates, however, became the object of an intense controversy. In their reanalysis, Cain and Wissoker (1990a: 1237) claimed instead that "the NIT had no effect on the rate of marital breakups among the participants." See Hannan and Tuma's (1990) reply and Cain and Wissoker's (1990b) rejoinder.

57. Pateman 2011: 7.

58. See Federation of Claimants Unions 1985a: 35 and 1985b: 44 and the discussion in Yamamori 2014. In February 2016, on the occasion of its Women's Conference, the public service union UNISON, one of UK's largest unions and one in which women are overrepresented, called for an exploration of "the potential of a Universal Basic Income as a more woman-friendly direction for future welfare policy" (UNISON 2016: 12). The message is less precise but, being voiced by women in a labor union rather than a claimants union, it has a higher chance of being heard.

59. See, among others, Miller 1988, Saraceno 1989, Withorn 1993/2013, Morini 1999, McKay 2001, 2005, 2007, Alstott 2001, Pateman 2006, 2011, Elgarte 2008, Zelleke 2008, Yamashita 2014, Furukubo 2014, Shulevitz 2016.

60. See, for example, Salam 2014.

61. For example, Belgium introduced in the 1980s a gender-neutral career interruption scheme with a small lump-sum benefit for anyone taking it in both the private and the public sector. As far as the private-sector scheme is concerned (renamed "time credit" in 2002), women made up 62 percent of the beneficiaries in 2010, and 95 percent of those with at least one child less than 8 years old (Van Hove et al. 2010: Table 61). Note, however, that 58 percent of the women who took advantage of the scheme did so by reducing their working time from five to four days a week (58 percent in 2010) and that less than 8 percent did so by (temporarily) giving up their job altogether (Van Hove 2010: Table 62).

62. Fraser 1997.

63. Miller 1988.

64. This constitutes an advantage, from a feminist standpoint, for a partial basic income over a full basic income with a surcharge on the lower brackets (see chapter 6). With a partial

basic income, the individual taxation of a couple can be progressive from the lower bracket. With a surcharge, by contrast, it is by definition regressive in that range, and therefore encourages the concentration of employment in one person.

65. The "virility premium" proposed by Vielle and Van Parijs (2001) consists of doubling the lump-sum parental-leave benefit (in place in Belgium at the time) for fathers only, and funding this measure by a small percentage increase in the personal income tax of men only. Both on the benefit side and on the tax side, some countries might regard this as conflicting with the constitutional principle of equality. Note, however, that, given the pay gap, earnings-related parental-leave benefits amount to something quite similar.

66. For further discussion of feminist concerns about basic income, see Orloff 1990/2013, Parker 1993, Fitzpatrick 1999b/2013, Eydoux and Silvera 2000, Robeyns 2001a, 2001b, Van Parijs 2001, 2015b, Baker 2008, Bergmann 2008, Gheaus 2008, O'Reilly 2008, Danaher 2014, Blaschke et al. eds. 2016.

67. The most significant appearances of basic income ideas in American politics date back to the late 1960s and early 1970s and are covered in chapter 4.

68. See Cole 1929, 1935, 1944 and Meade 1935. On Milner's pioneering effort, see also chapter 4.

69. James Meade was also one of the leading economists at the time of Clement Attlee's labor government (1945–1951), which implemented the Beveridge plan, and he later chaired a commission on the reform of taxation that ended up recommending a "new Beveridge plan" rather than its chief contender, a partial basic income (see chapter 6). Later in his life, he was less politically active but remained strongly committed to basic income up to the end (Meade 1989, 1991, 1993, 1995).

70. Commission for Social Justice 1994: 262–3.

71. Reed and Lansley 2016.

72. *Guardian*, June 6, 2016. The Compass report proposed a weekly individual basic income of 71 pounds for adults aged over 25 (about 13 percent of GDP per capita) combined with conditional top-ups (Reed and Lansley 2016: 17). Something similar may be happening with New Zealand's Labour Party. The idea of a local or regional basic-income experiment features among the "ten big ideas" put forward by its Future of Work Commission (2016: 9). And its leader (since 2014) Andrew Little, former head of New Zealand's largest trade union (the Engineering, Printing, and Manufacturing Union, or EPMU), has expressed his interest in a basic income on several occasions (Rankin 2016: 34).

73. On the Dutch debate, see Van Parijs 1988, Groot and van der Veen 2000.

74. Even though the motion explicitly used the expression "basic income," it actually referred to a negative income tax. In its reaction, the party leadership promised to take the motion into account in its election platform, while insisting that the party's ultimate goal remains to achieve full employment (see http://www.pvda.nl/berichten/2016/06/Moties+politieke+ledenraad+4+juni+2016).

75. France may turn out to be an exception. But it is too early to tell. Several prominent members of the *Parti Socialiste* (PS), including former Prime Minister Manuel Valls and, less

ambiguously, deputies Delphine Batho, Eduardo Rihan-Cypel, and Benoit Hamon asserted publicly their support for the idea. Basic income even found its way into the preparatory document for the socialist party's program for the 2017 presidential election, but still in a very cautious way. The sympathetic section devoted to it notes that the "universal existence income" raises many questions regarding its financing, its acceptability, and impact on wages and other social policies, and ends with a commitment to set up a working group on the subject (Parti Socialiste 2016: 39–40). In North America, the closest there is to an established social democratic party, Canada's New Democratic Party (NDP), discussed basic income and a negative income tax in the late 1960s. But it never went further than a subcommittee adopting a vague motion in favor of the implementation of a negative income tax at its 1969 party convention (Mulvale and Vanderborght 2012: 185).

76. At a two-thirds majority, the Swiss *Sozialdemokratische Partei der Schweiz* (SP— "Social-Democratic Party of Switzerland," or "Parti Socialiste Suisse" in French) officially recommended a "no" vote (http://www.nzz.ch/schweiz/eidgenoessische-abstimmungen -parolenspiegel-fuer-den-5-juni-ld.16727) and the socialist member of the federal executive spoke vigorously against the proposal. But in the final parliamentary vote, fifteen socialist deputies voted in favor, thirteen against, and thirteen abstained (see https://www.parlament .ch/de/ratsbetrieb/amtliches-bulletin/amtliches-bulletin-die-verhandlungen?SubjectId =36389), and according to the post-referendum survey (Colombo et al. 2016: Table 3.1), 39 percent of the socialist voters voted yes, far above the overall yes score (23.1 percent).

77. This is particularly clear in Nordic countries, regarded as the paradigms of social-democratic regimes. See Christensen 2000: 311–14 on Denmark and Anderson and Kangas 2005 on Sweden. In Belgium, after Paul Magnette, number two of the French-speaking *Parti Socialiste* (PS—"Socialist Party") and Minister-President of the Walloon Region, had declared in an interview that basic income was what history was taking us to *("dans le sens de l'histoire"),* the party chairman, former federal prime minister Elio di Rupo, was quick to warn that "basic income is a Trojan horse for dismantling Belgium's welfare state" (see *La Libre Belgique,* June 7, 2016 and *Le Soir,* July 1, 2016, respectively).

78. *L'Espresso,* October 15, 1989.

79. Article 1 of the law gives "all Brazilians resident in the country as well as all foreigners who have been residents for at least five years, regardless of their social and economic condition, the right to receive annually a monetary benefit." However, it also says that the full scope of the measure "will have to be achieved in stages, at the discretion of the Executive Branch, giving priority to the most needy sections of the population." For the time being, this amounts to means-tested cash transfers of the *Bolsa Familia* sort. (See chapter 3). For further discussion of the significance of this law, see Suplicy 2006, 2011 and Lavinas 2013.

80. The French *Parti Communiste* (PCF—Communist Party), for example, is more receptive to the ideas of its member Bernard Friot (2012), who argues in favor of the introduction of a "lifelong wage" *(salaire à vie)* paid to all workers and all the involuntarily unemployed, at a level that would vary according to each worker's democratic ascription to one of four levels of qualification. See Réseau Salariat 2014.

81. Koistinen and Perkiö 2014.

82. *Québec Solidaire* has included a means-tested but obligation-free and individual "guaranteed minimum income" in its 2012 and 2014 electoral platform for provincial elections. According to its 2014 platform (Québec Solidaire 2014: 10) it would provide individuals with no other income with an annual transfer of C$12,600 (about 28 percent of Québec's GDP per capita).

83. *Economist,* March 31, 2016. See also, more explicitly, Varoufakis 2016.

84. See Kipping 2016a on her fifteen years of fighting for basic income, and Kipping 2016b for her keynote speech at the sixteenth congress of the Basic Income Earth Network in Seoul.

85. Sombart 1896/1905: 25.

86. Luxemburg 1918.

87. Nyerere 1968: 15.

88. Weitling 1845.

89. Marcuse 1967.

90. See *NRC Handelsblad,* December 17, 1994. Minister Wijers was backed up by the (right-liberal) minister of finance Gerrit Zalm (VVD), but opposed by ministers from the Labor party (PvdA). Prime Minister Wim Kok (PvdA) avoided the clash by asserting the need for "a careful study of what it is possible to do, in the long term, with this idea." He never took the initiative to put it back on the agenda.

91. *Sunday Times,* July 5, 2015. In Belgium, both the Flemish liberal party *Open VLD* ("Open Flemish Liberals and Democrats," which absorbed Roland Duchâtelet's basic-income-focused party Vivant in 2007) and the French-speaking liberal party MR ("Reformist Movement") count among their members fervent advocates of basic income (for example, the young deputies Nele Lijnen in one case and Georges-Louis Bouchez in the other) and they both took the initiative to organize public debates on basic income in 2015 and 2016.

92. See Koistinen and Perkiö 2014 on the history of the Finnish discussion, and Kalliomaa-Puha et al. 2016 on Finland's basic-income experiment.

93. Kobayashi 2014. To this list of (classical) liberal politicians, one could add Hugh Segal, federal senator for the Conservative Party (2005–2014) and one of Canada's most vocal proponents of basic income. In February 2008, he introduced a motion in the federal Senate calling for "a fulsome study on the feasibility of a Guaranteed Annual Income" (Mulvale and Vanderborght 2012: 185). "Such a guaranteed annual income," Segal (2012: 10) writes, "would be a serious pillar of that opportunity [fair access to the economic mainstream], as important to us as universal education, safe communities and health insurance."

94. de Basquiat and Koenig 2014.

95. Bachelot 2011.

96. Story 2015, Andrews 2015.

97. Murray 2006.

98. Murray 2016.

99. Even before there was much of a sign that green concerns would lead to the formation of political parties, the connection between basic income and these concerns was stressed by some of basic income's early advocates. For example, Lionel Stoleru (1974a: 308) wrote in France: "By asking ourselves how to achieve such moderation [the moderation of growth in rich countries required by the solution of some of the contradictions of capitalism], we realized that this problem was fundamentally the same as the problem of putting into place a basic guarantee for every citizen"; and Steven Cook (1979: 6) wrote in the United Kingdom: "We need to encourage such responsible exploration of voluntary low-consumption life styles if we are to be able to adapt successfully to likely changes in world society, as the shortage of energy and other resources increasingly makes itself felt and as experience of 'affluence' leads to greater emphasis on personal fulfillment rather than material consumption."

100. Green Party 2015a: 54. In its detailed proposal, the Green Party (2015b) proposed to implement a basic income of 80 pounds per week for adults (around $450 per month, or 12 percent of UK's GDP per capita at the time).

101. Early day motion 974, January 19, 2016. This motion was supported by 35 members of the Scottish Assembly, mainly from the Scottish National Party (23) and the Labour Party (8).

102. Scottish Green Party 2014.

103. See http://www.gp.org/platform/2004/economics.html#241660) for the 2004 program and http://www.gp.org/what-we-believe/our-platform/17-platform/41-iv-economic-justice -and-sustainability for the 2014 version.

104. See, for instance, May's interview with the online platform *Leaders and Legacies,* January 12, 2015: "We Can't Eliminate Child Poverty if the Parents are Poor: Elizabeth May."

105. http://www.greenparty.ca/en/policy/vision-green/people/poverty. See also the plan for a "Guaranteed Livable Income" released by the Green Party in July 2015 (http:// northumberlandview.ca/index.php?module=news&type=user&func=display&sid=35595). Further examples include the Green Party of New Zealand (2014: 2), which declared it wanted to "investigate the implementation of a Universal Basic Income for every New Zealander" as part of its income-support policy, and Japan's small green party *Midori no Tō,* founded in 2012 in the aftermath of the Fukushima Daiichi nuclear disaster, which also included basic income in its electoral platform (Vanderborght and Sekine 2014: 29).

106. A first-past-the-post system can be favorable to a pro-basic-income party if it is regionally based. This is unlikely to be the case but actually happened in Canada. At the 1972 federal election, for example, Raoul Caouette's Social Credit Party, being concentrated in Alberta, fared respectably with a platform that included an expensive system of universal guaranteed income payments (Leman 1980: 146).

107. This has been the case at the national level in Finland (1995–2002 and 2007–2015), France (1997–2002 and 2012–2014), Germany (1998–2005), Belgium (1999–2003), Ireland (2007–2011), and the Czech Republic (2007–2009).

108. See van Ojik 1982, 1983, 1985, 1989, and van Ojik and Teulings 1990. Next to Groenlinks, a much smaller green party called *De Groenen* (The Greens), founded in 1983, has

consistently advocated a basic income but never achieved any parliamentary representation, and stopped taking part in national elections in 1998.

109. See Offe 1985 and the collections edited by eco-libertarian Thomas Schmid (1984) and by Green Party parliamentary assistant Michael Opielka (Opielka and Vobruba 1986, Opielka and Ostner 1987).

110. See www.stern.de/politik/deutschland/parteitag-gruene-gegen-grundeinkommen -fuer-alle-603477.

111. Among them are Andrea Fischer, who resigned as health minister (1998–2001) in the first Schröder government; Wolfgang Strengmann-Kuhn, member of Germany's federal parliament and the party's spokesperson on social policy; and Gerald Häfner, the member of the European Parliament who hosted the launch of the European Citizens' initiative on basic income in 2012.

112. On *Ecolo's* 1985 program, see Lechat 2014. On *Agalev's* 1985 program, see https:// nl.wikipedia.org/wiki/Economisch_programma_van_Mechelen.

113. The author of this proposal, Senator Jean Desessard, submitted a similar motion to the French Senate in February 2016, calling for the French government to "take the necessary steps towards the implementation of an unconditional basic income." All ten Green senators voted in favor of the motion, along with one senator from the right-of-center party Les Républicains. Two hundred senators voted against it (French Senate, scrutin 227, May 19, 2016).

114. Osmo Soininvaara, personal communication August 4, 2015. This proposal includes a 41 percent flat tax on annual incomes below 50,000 euros and 49 percent above. It was micro-simulated with a model provided by the Finnish Parliament.

115. See http://www.gruene.ch/gruene/de/kampagnen/abstimmungen/grundeinkommen -.html for the recommendation; Colombo et al. 2016: table 3.1 for the survey; and https://www.parlament.ch/de/ratsbetrieb/amtliches-bulletin/amtliches-bulletin-die -verhandlungen?SubjectId=36389 for the parliamentary vote. At the final vote in the National Council, four Green deputies voted in favor, five against, and three abstained.

116. In addition to national developments, the idea of basic income has been actively promoted by several Green members of the European Parliament from several member states, such as Alexander de Roo (Netherlands), Sepp Kusstatscher (Italy), Pascal Canfin (France), Jean Lambert (United Kingdom), and Carl Schlyter (Sweden). In 2013, Green MEPs were overrepresented among those who signed the European Citizens' Initiative in favor of basic income.

117. See our arguments above about basic income's relationship with a sane economy (chapter 1) and growth (chapter 5). For further discussion of the relationship between basic income and the doctrine of the Green movement, see Fitzpatrick 1999a/2013, Van Parijs 1987a/2013, 2009.

118. In a few countries, part of the more libertarian component of the Left has been attracted more recently to pirate parties, the first of which was founded in Sweden in 2006. Their activism mainly focuses on the fight against intellectual property, but it has been broad-

ened to include civil liberties, transparent government, and also often an unconditional basic income. Basic income featured prominently, for example, in the manifesto of Germany's *Piratenpartei Deutschland* for the 2013 general election. In 2015, the three members of parliament from Iceland's *Píratar* submitted a motion asking the government to establish a working group to explore its feasibility in the country (http://www.althingi.is/altext/145/s/0454 .html). And, along with the Green Party, Switzerland's *Piratenpartei* is the only Swiss party that called for a "yes" vote in the 2016 referendum on basic income.

119. Boutin 2003.

120. Ireland 2002.

121. See Healy and Reynold's many publications, from Reynolds and Healy eds. 1995 to Healy and Reynolds 2000 and Healy et al. 2013. In 2008, the Justice Commission of CORI hosted the Twelfth Congress of the Basic Income Earth Network.

122. Büchele and Wohlgennant 1985. In 1996, the *Katholische Sozialakademie* hosted the Sixth Congress of the Basic Income Earth Network and it has housed the Austrian basic income network (*Netzwerk Grundeinkommen und sozialer Zusammenhalt*) since its creation in October 2002.

123. In a speech at the Finnish Institute in London in 1998, John Vikström argued that with a basic income "even working a little would be possible and would make sense. The system would not push people into idleness and divide citizens into winners and losers as cruelly as is the case now. I look at the question from the point of view of human dignity. A basic income paid to everyone would be less humiliating than the present benefit system can sometimes become." (*Basic Income* 29, newsletter of the Basic Income European Network, Spring 1998).

124. At a meeting in Lund, Sweden, in March 2007, the Council of the Lutheran World Federation "expressed its support for initiatives by member churches to address poverty in their own contexts, and recognized especially the work of the Evangelical Lutheran Church in the Republic of Namibia in the coalition to promote the establishment of a Basic Income Grant in Namibia." See Haarmann and Haarmann 2005, 2007, 2012.

125. In his message to the 2006 Cape Town congress of the Basic Income Earth Network, Desmond Tutu declared: "Friends, I don't need to remind you of the importance and benefits of campaigns such as the basic income movement that are designed to enhance the dignity, well-being, and inclusion of all people and to move us closer to our vision of social equity." (This message is made available by the *Desmond Tutu Peace Foundation* at https://www.youtube.com/watch?v=oISeAG7nmg8.)

126. "There is nothing except shortsightedness to prevent us from guaranteeing an annual minimum—and livable—income for every American family. . . . There is nothing to keep us from remolding a recalcitrant status quo with bruised hands until we have fashioned it into a brotherhood" (King 1967: 189). See also, from the same period, the book-length discussion of basic income by Methodist minister Philip Wogaman (1968: 79): "Guaranteed income as a secure economic floor will make it possible for men to become what God intended them to become by free response. The fact that many will doubtless abuse this freedom is a risk which God has taken in creating man in the first place."

127. Luke 12: 24–28 (New International Version). The other relevant passage in the Gospel is Mark 2: 23–26, where Jesus defends the right of his disciples to pick grain from fields to feed themselves on the Sabbath. Charles Fourier (1829: 431) mobilized this passage to justify the right to a minimum income: "Jesus, through these words, enshrines the right to take what one needs where one finds it, and this right entails the duty to secure a minimum to the people; as long as this duty is not recognized, there is no social pact."

128. In 2000, a Brussels labor court explicitly quoted the sentence from Genesis when rejecting the claim of a welfare recipient who was invoking the right to an unconditional basic income and arguing against the legal obligation for public assistance recipients to be actively seeking employment (Dumont 2012: 413).

129. The Greek original uses the word εξουσία (2 Thessalonians: 3, 9), usually translated as right, power, or authority. In whatever way it is best translated, it is obvious that it could not have in Saint Paul's Greek the same connotations as any of these modern terms. The closer its meaning is to that of the modern term "right," the more compatible this passage turns out to be with the right to an obligation-free income (in the sense specified in chapter 1), albeit combined with a work ethos.

130. Here is the whole passage taken from the English translation of the *De Nabuthae Historia* (Ambrose 1927): "Is it iniquitous of God that he does not distribute the means of life to us equally? So that you have riches and abundance while others are needy and in want? Is it to confer a crown on you for the proof of your kindness and on the others for their virtue of patience? You have received wealth of God, and you deem yourself to act in no way unjustly if you use it for your own ends, if you alone obtain the sustenance of the lives of many? What is more grasping, more greedy, than one who turns the food of many, not to his own use, but his own delicacy and abundance? It is no less a crime to take from him that has than to refuse to succor the needy when you can and are well off. It is the hungry man's bread you withhold, the naked man's cloak that you store away, and the money that you bury in the earth is the price of the poor man's ransom and freedom" (Dist. xlvii, can. Sicut ii).

131. Gratianus 1140/1990.

132. "Hence whatever certain people have in superabundance is due, by natural law, to the purpose of succoring the poor. . . . [If] the need be so manifest and urgent, that it is evident that the present need must be remedied by whatever means be at hand (for instance when a person is in some imminent danger, and there is no other possible remedy), then it is lawful for a man to succor his own need by means of another's property, by taking it either openly or secretly: nor is this properly speaking theft or robbery." (*Summa Theologiae*, Part II.2, Question 66, Art. 7: Is it lawful to thieve in case of necessity?)

133. De Wispelaere (2016: 2–3) characterizes "cheap political support" as the "expressed support without either the commitment or the capacity to engage in the necessary political action to build a sustainable coalition."

134. McGovern 1974: 137.

135. Shirky 2008.

136. Claus Offe (1992, 1996a, 1996b) and Fritz Scharpf (1993, 1994, 1995, 2000) are prominent exceptions.

137. These include: bestsellers by businessman Götz Werner (2007, 2010), collections or monographs by people close to the left party (Blaschke, Otto, and Schepers 2010, 2012), the Greens (Jacobi and Strengmann-Kuhn 2012), the Attac movement (Rätz et al. 2005, Rätz and Krampertz 2011), the Christian-Democratic party (Althaus and Binkert eds. 2010), and the Catholic church (Schulte-Basta 2010). See also Füllsack 2006, Hosang 2008, Franzmann 2010 for broad collections and www.grundeinkommen.de/die-idee/literatur for an extensive bibliography.

138. The 2008 film and other videos can be downloaded from http://grundeinkommen .tv/grundeinkommen-ein-kulturimpuls.

139. Another popular initiative proposing an unconditional basic income funded by a tax on nonrenewable energy was launched in May 2010 but failed to gather the required number of signatures. The initiators of the 2012 initiative first thought of specifying that the basic income would be funded by the value added tax but dropped the idea in order not to reduce support for the proposal. See http://de.wikipedia.org/wiki/Initiative_Grundeinkommen.

140. Häni and Kovce 2015: 168 and Müller and Staub 2016: 56–65.

141. For the press release by the Federal Council, see www.news.admin.ch/dokumentation /00002/00015/index.html?lang=fr&msg-id=5420. For the results of all parliamentary votes on this popular initiative, see https://www.parlament.ch/de/ratsbetrieb/amtliches-bulletin /amtliches-bulletin-die-verhandlungen?SubjectId=36389). Many thanks to Nenad Stojanovic for helping us with some of the subtleties of Swiss politics.

142. Over 285,000 signatures were collected, with the threshold reached in six of them (Bulgaria, Slovenia, Croatia, Belgium, Estonia, and the Netherlands). Had the proportion of signatures been the same among European citizens for the European Citizens' Initiative on basic income as among Swiss citizens for their popular initiative on the same subject, the European initiative, rather than garnering fewer than 300,000 signatures, would have garnered more than ten million. This huge gap is not hard to explain. First, there is the difference between, on the one hand, an age-old institution to which the Swiss population is accustomed at every level of government, and on the other, an institutional innovation, particularly unfamiliar in those EU member states in which direct democracy is completely unknown. Second, the EU initiative had to cope with a shorter time to collect signatures (twelve months instead of eighteen in Switzerland) and some teething problems with the registration system. Third, because it had to remain within the limits of the Commission's legislative powers, the phrasing of the proposal had to remain much weaker—and hence less exciting—in the EU case than in the Swiss case. Fourth, what would be triggered in case of success was far less than in the Swiss case: not a binding impact on the EU's fundamental law, but just a letter from the Commission and some Committee time at the Parliament. Finally, while the linguistic hurdle to effective campaigning is not insignificant in Switzerland, it is daunting at the level of the Union, with its twenty-four official languages.

143. For more on the goals of Unconditional Basic Income Europe, see its website: http://basic income-europe.org.

144. Frank 2014.

145. Frank 2014.

146. Atkinson 1993b; 1996a: 68.

147. Atkinson's 2015: 219.

148. Atkinson 2015: 221.

149. Atkinson 1996b: 67; 1996c: 94.

150. Atkinson 1998: 149.

151. In his most recent formulation, Atkinson adds a second rationale: the participation condition "conveys a positive message about 'reciprocity.'" This message is not only "more likely to garner political support." It is also "intrinsically justified" (Atkinson 2015: 221). Our chapter 5 addresses the issue of intrinsic justification.

152. De Wispelaere and Stirton 2007, Atkinson 2015: 220–221. In later writings, De Wispelaere and Stirton (2011, 2012) correctly stress that one should not exaggerate the comparative simplicity of a pure basic income if it does not replace all existing transfers. They further point out that a basic-income scheme needs to have a reliable way of registering all those entitled, of making the payment to them, and of correcting mistakes. This is all true, but the challenge of checking the satisfaction of the participation condition is of a different order of magnitude.

153. Labor leader Andy Stern (2016: 196–7) briefly considered such a "participatory income" that requires people to volunteer or work at activities that are "truly beneficial to society." But he then found himself remembering why he thought "that UBI should be simple and pure and not tied to any requirements at all. By turning UBI into a platform for a more committed and engaged citizenry, aren't we making it too layered and complicated to succeed? Aren't we opening it up to endless debates on what we, as Americans, should value and do, instead of leaving those issues up to the more efficient, free-choice mechanism of people simply spending their money?" (Stern 2016: 197).

154. See the following account of a conversation with James Tobin in New Haven in April 1998: "But however economically and socially sound, there is something politically tricky about these large unconditional handouts to everyone. . . . The need for a general guaranteed income system remains as strong as ever. But one could design it in a way that would accommodate to some extent the puritan concerns. This would certainly be good for its general cultural acceptance, and hence its political feasibility. It may also be good in itself—Tobin confesses to some ambivalence on this—providing the "contribution" condition is understood in a sufficiently broad sense. Rather than excluding any nonworking able-bodied adult from the right to the grant, he favors subjecting that right to the beneficiary declaring that (s)he is spending a minimum amount of time performing a socially useful activity (looking after one's children and volunteering for a church would count just as much as paid work). More than this amendment may be needed to assuage the fear for welfare loafers and to get again a new ambitious project on the track. But this is a task for another generation" (Van Parijs 1998: 7).

155. Some variant of this is proposed by Painter and Young (2015: 20) for the United Kingdom. While advocating an unconditional basic income for all adults, they suggest that those aged 18–25 should sign a publicized "contribution contract" with their local community. In sharp contrast with the idea of a basic income restricted to young adults (briefly considered in chapter 6), this type of mild paternalism should help assuage the fear hinted at in chapter 1 that many young adults, if given a modest unconditional income, will opt to enjoy life in a shortsighted mode, sharing accommodation and topping up their basic income with casual, often informal work—only to discover later on that, in order to raise a family, they should have made the effort to improve their earning power.

156. Andy Stern (2016: 202–3) seems to agree: "As I've learned in twenty-five years of trying to make big changes in Washington, most politicians' second choice if their own favorite proposal is not supported is to do nothing—a recipe for political gridlock. There is only one antidote to gridlock—a willingness to compromise." But he also warns: "Step-by-step approaches end up raising more concerns and resistance than they either soothe or squelch." He therefore advises: "once we have a broad consensus on the basic principles and framework for universal basic income, and certainly on the disbursement number and category of people covered, I could envision an incremental or phased-in approach if it really appeared to be the best way to move forward."

157. Vanderborght 2004a, 2004b. Basic-income proposals that try instead to enter through the front gate are likely to encounter strong resistance on the grounds that they clash with the fundamental principles that underlie the tax-and-transfer institutions in place. Thus, after considering Juliet Rhys-Williams's (1943) proposal for integrating social benefits and tax allowances into a basic-income scheme, the chairman of the British Board of Inland Revenue dismissed it on the grounds that it mixed systems embodying different principles: "income tax was based on the concept of taxable capacity . . . whereas social security was designed to prevent citizens from suffering material want as a result of unemployment, sickness, or old age." (Sloman 2016: 209). Similarly, France Stratégie (2014c: 24) rejected the unconditional-basic-income proposal because it would undermine rather than reinforce "both the effectiveness and the legitimacy of our model and its foundations (protection and mutualization of risks)."

158. This political obstacle to universality was noted by A. C. Pigou (1920/1932: section IV.X.8) in connection with the possibility of instituting a universal basic income as a generalization of what was then advocated by supporters of universal pensions and a universal "endowment of motherhood": "In any event, among practical politicians the device of universalizing grants to large categories of persons, irrespective of their individual needs, is greatly disliked. There is no real question of pressing it far enough to do away with the need for differential transferences based directly on the poverty of recipients."

159. As argued, for example, by Korpi and Palme 1998 and as might be illustrated by Alaska's dividend scheme (see chapter 4). See Van Lancker and Van Mechelen 2015 for a discussion of the view that universality makes generous levels more resilient.

160. See, for example, Schroeder et al. 2015 on the trends in six European welfare states from 1998 to 2014.

161. As often noted (for example, by Werdemann 2014 and De Wispelaere 2016), basic income has supporters in different parties, not all with the same version of basic income as their top choice. This diversity may not prevent a cross-party coalition from going part of the way, but it cannot but inspire some caution among coalition partners.

8. Viable in the Global Era? Multi-Level Basic Income

1. Rawls 1999.

2. This is not the place to justify this position. It is spelled out and defended in Van Parijs 1995 (chapter 6; 2007; 2011: section 1.9) and in Rawls and Van Parijs 2003.

3. See, for example, Shachar 2009, Milanovic 2016.

4. Steiner 2003.

5. According to the survey conducted after the Swiss referendum on basic income, 36 percent of those who voted yes and 65 percent of those who voted no agreed that the introduction of a basic income should be decided on an international level and that doing it alone would damage Switzerland (Colombo et al. 2016: Table 3.5).

6. This distinction between sheer ex-post or insurance-based redistribution and ex-ante or genuine redistribution is orthogonal to the distinction made in chapter 1 between transfer schemes that involve ex-ante or upfront payments (that is, payments that are made irrespective of the beneficiaries' incomes), and schemes that operate through ex-post or means-tested payments (that is, payments made selectively in light of prior information about the beneficiaries' incomes). A means-tested minimum-income scheme is ex-ante in the first sense and ex-post in the latter, while a private pension scheme is ex-ante in the second sense but not in the first one.

7. For discussions of the "welfare magnet" thesis, see Peterson and Rom 1990, Peterson 1995 and Borjas 1999 for the United States, and Razin and Wahba 2015 for Europe.

8. As regards this pressure, the key distinction is not work-tested versus obligation-free, or in-work versus out-of-work, but contributory versus noncontributory. To illustrate: Atkinson (2015: 143–4) notes that internal mobility within the European Union threatens the viability of subsidized employment and therefore recommends restricting the latter to the long-term unemployed who are registered in the United Kingdom and have paid social security contributions. Similarly, in his discussion of various scenarios for the implementation of a basic income in Europe, James Meade (1991) stresses the importance of harmonization, not in order to avoid a concentration of idlers in countries with a basic income but to avoid a concentration in those countries of poorly productive activities.

9. Vives 1526/2010: 73.

10. City of Ypres 1531/2010: 129.

11. Spicker 2010: 141.

12. Pigou 1920/1932: 766–7.

13. See Howard 2006 for a discussion of this dilemma. In their apology for their choice of one horn of the dilemma, the magistrates of Ypres considered that reason settled the matter:

"If we cannot keep both strangers and citizens, because we do not have enough resources, then reason tells us that we should leave the lesser advantage [avoiding "the few evils that would come of putting out a few"] to keep the greater one [avoiding the "ruin and decay of this good law"]" (City of Ypres 1531/2010: 136). Note that the dilemma arises even in the absence of redistributive schemes, as unlimited immigration would mean competition for jobs, housing, and other amenities between a constant flow of fresh immigrants and at least some of the least advantaged sections of the local population. And it arises, with a redistributive scheme in place, even if all immigrants wish to work, and do work. The dilemma is sharpened with a redistributive scheme because its very survival is threatened by the inflow of net beneficiaries, as the magistrates of Ypres were anxious to point out.

14. Smith 1776/1977: ch.10.

15. In 2014, the Supreme Court of Japan confirmed that "foreigners do not possess the right to receive assistance based on the law, and are only limited to being subjects for public assistance in a practical sense, on the basis of administrative decisions" ("Supreme Court Rules Permanent Residents Ineligible for Public Assistance," *Asahi Shimbun*, July 19, 2014). One implication is that foreigners cannot appeal against the rejection of their application for benefits.

16. On the *Hukou* system and its impact on social exclusion, see for instance Nyland et al. 2014.

17. Jesse Spafford (2013) proposes that the amount of the basic income to which an immigrant is entitled would increase with the number of years of residence in the country (rising, for example, by $2,000 per year, up to the full amount of $18,000). This is analogous to the scheme initially envisaged in Alaska but struck down by the US Supreme Court.

18. Charlier 1848: 75.

19. Ferry 1995, 2010. Note that the Alaska dividend scheme is not restricted to American citizens. Thus, in 2015, nearly 10 percent of all applicants to the dividend reported being born in a "foreign country" (Permanent Fund Dividend Division 2015: 40).

20. For details on the *Zobel v. Williams* case (June 14, 1982), see http://law2.umkc.edu/faculty/projects/ftrials/conlaw/zobel.html. For the definitive version of the eligibility conditions, see https://pfd.alaska.gov/Eligibility/EligibilityRequirements.

21. Strictly speaking, the Dano Ruling of the Court of Justice of the European Union of November 11, 2014 (Case C-333/13, *Elisabeta Dano, Florin Dano v. Jobcenter Leipzig*) does allow some indirect discrimination on grounds of national citizenship. According to this ruling, each member state must "have the possibility of refusing to grant social benefits to economically inactive Union citizens who exercise their right to freedom of movement solely in order to obtain another Member State's social assistance although they do not have sufficient resources to claim a right of residence" (Court of Justice of the European Union, press release 146/14). If the condition "solely in order to" is presumed not to be met whenever economically inactive Union citizens are exercising their right to freedom of movement by returning to the member state of which they are citizens, this ruling can be interpreted as allowing member states to grant more social rights to some of their own citizens than to similarly situated citizens of other member states.

22. Bizarre but not unthinkable. As a compromise between open and closed borders, Milanovic (2016: 231) suggests the creation of a less valuable "intermediate level of citizenship" that "might involve higher taxation." See also Iida 2014 for a discussion of the option of reserving the basic income for citizens in Japan.

23. Why has the Alaska scheme proved sustainable, despite free movement within the United States and quasi-immediate entitlement to the dividend? This has little to do with the borders of the United States as a whole being far from open, and a lot more to do with the fact that the dividend has been pitched, on average, at about 2 percent of Alaska's GDP per capita (see chapter 6).

24. Selective emigration was less of a concern for the early municipal public-assistance schemes than selective immigration. Yet it is presumably such a concern that induced John Locke (1697) to recommend "that in all cities and towns corporate the poor's tax be not levied by distinct parishes, but by one equal tax throughout the whole corporation."

25. Including, for example, in John Rawls's (1999: 74) theory of international justice.

26. See Steiner 2003 for a critique of this "solidaristic patriotism" and, for a response, Van Parijs 2003b: 209–212.

27. The emigration of beneficiaries, not only of net contributors, also poses a problem for basic-income schemes. If the bottom part of the pension of every retiree in a country is formed by an unconditional basic income, what happens if some people choose to retire abroad? Do they lose the right to this part of their pension, since they no longer reside in the country? Do they retain the whole of it, no matter what? Do they keep part of it in proportion to the number of years they spent in the country? Some complications of this sort are unavoidable with a basic income and significant migration, as they are with existing noncontributory basic pension schemes (see chapter 6). The Alaska dividend scheme also had to make provisions for emigrants: residents who leave Alaska might remain eligible, but at all times during their absence, they must demonstrate their intention "to remain an Alaska resident indefinitely." Strict guidelines define the conditions under which recipients remain entitled to the dividend despite being absent from Alaska. See https://pfd.alaska.gov/Eligibility/AbsenceGuidelines.

28. See Van Parijs 2011 (chapters 5 and 6) on why the preservation of this linguistic differentiation, though not desirable in itself, is nonetheless required by social justice as parity of esteem.

29. Kooistra 1983, 1994.

30. See, for example, Canadian economist Myron Frankman's (1998, 2004) plea for a "planet-wide citizen's income" funded by a planet-wide progressive income tax, Belgian journalist Dirk Barrez's (1999) campaign for "10 francs a day worldwide," French economist Yoland Bresson's (1999) proposal of a Tobin-tax funded global basic income, and perhaps German philosopher Thomas Pogge's (1994, 2001) proposal of a "global resources dividend" to be funded out of a tax on the use or sale of the natural resources of the earth. While noncommittal about the most appropriate way of implementing this dividend, Pogge (2005: 4) notes that "something like a Global Basic Income may well be part of the best plan."

31. For a hint in this direction, see Glaeser 2011: 221. And for a developed argument, see Busilacchi 2009.

32. See Howard 2007 and Howard and Glover 2014 for a stimulating discussion of a NAFTA-level basic income.

33. This was one of the arguments used by James Tobin et al. (1967: 14) in favor of a federal negative income tax in the United States: "Although migration from agriculture and low income rural areas should be encouraged, it might well be desirable on both economic and social grounds to reverse the present tide of migration into a limited number of large northern urban areas. One of the purposes of establishing a national NIT program is to guarantee a decent minimum standard of life to Americans wherever they reside." The expected reduction in demographic pressure on Brazil's big cities was also one of the arguments that persuaded President Fernando Henrique Cardoso in October 1996 to launch a federal income support program throughout Brazil.

34. This was a bold move of which some illustrious friends of basic income quoted elsewhere in this book would have approved. John Stuart Mill (1848: Book III, Chapter XX, 372), for example, predicted that "the progress of political improvement" would lead all countries to share the same currency. "So much of barbarism, however, still remains in the transactions of the most civilized nations, that almost all independent countries choose to assert their nationality by having, to their own inconvenience and that of their neighbours, a peculiar currency of their own." As to James Meade (see relevant discussions in chapters 4, 6, and 7), while agreeing in principle, he urged caution. In the first-ever academic article discussing the possibility of a European monetary union, he stressed that a common currency requires "what would amount to a single European government" with extensive powers, including the power "to carry out an effective special-area policy for depressed regions in Europe." A monetary union, he wrote, "is ultimately desirable; let us hope that it will prove ultimately practicable; but it is not a starter at the moment, and it would be a great shame to sacrifice the present real political possibilities of building a commercial free-trade area to this ideal of simultaneous monetary and budgetary integration" (Meade 1957: 388).

35. Krugman 2011. Amartya Sen's (2012) diagnosis is essentially the same: "A unified currency in a politically united federal country (such as in the United States of America) survives through means (such as substantial population movements and significant transfers) that are not available to a politically disunited Europe. Sooner or later the difficult question of the long-run viability of the euro would have to be addressed." Martin Feldstein (1992, 1997, 2012) had repeatedly warned against the euro project on similar grounds long before it was launched.

36. According to the OECD (2012), this proportion was, in 2010, 2.4 percent for the United States and 0.29 percent for the European Union. For a discussion of these estimates, see European Commission 2014a: 282–283. Note that this simple quantitative comparison is biased as a result of the difference in the number and average size of the components (50 states versus 28 member states). But the deep gap remains when this bias is corrected, especially

if one disregards the temporary upsurge of migration from the eastern member states after the 2004 enlargement. And it is only partly explained by the fact that the proportion of Americans who change residence every year—whether or not in the same state—is about three times the proportion of Europeans who do so. See also Jauer et al. 2014.

37. This linguistic dimension (put simplistically: "No common currency without common language!"), present in Krugman's quote above, is also emphasized by other predictors of the failure of the euro. Thus, Martin Feldstein (1997: 36) warned that "although the legal barriers to labor mobility within the European Union have been eliminated, language and custom impede both temporary and long-term movement within Europe. As long as Europeans speak ten different languages, cross-border movement in response to job availability will be far less than movement among American regions." And Milton Friedman (1998): "The characteristics that make Australia and the United States favorable for a common currency are that the populations all speak the same language or some approximation to it."

38. On the basis of such an estimate, Sala-i-Martin and Sachs (1991: 20) concluded, "the creation of a unified currency without a federal insurance scheme, could very well lead the project to an eventual failure."

39. Cited by Ritter (1904/1983: 29). See also De Deken and Rueschemeyer's (1992: 102) political analysis of the birth of Germany's social insurance system: "The government fully expected that the creation of this social insurance system would cause the favoured groups of workers to feel greater loyalty towards the state."

40. For example, Martin Feldstein (2012: 111): "the euro has thus caused tensions and conflicts within Europe that would not otherwise have existed. Further steps toward a permanent fiscal union would only exacerbate these tensions." And Luuk van Middelaar (2013: 262): "For a variety of reasons, the concept of European benefit payments is not taken seriously either by politicians or by voters. It would have a huge impact on national economies and would disrupt relations between member states and their citizens. With pressure on uniform, nationwide support systems increasing in many countries, a European welfare state is barely conceivable."

41. Schmitter and Bauer 2001.

42. As argued in detail in Van Parijs and Vanderborght 2001.

43. Brandon Rhys-Williams was the son of Juliet Rhys-Williams, who advocated a universal benefit during World War II (see chapter 4). One key component of the "European social contract" he proposed consisted of harmonizing the basic welfare systems of what was then the European Economic Community. A first step could be made with a unified community-wide child-benefit system which individual countries would be free to top up. A further step forward would be a basic income in the form of "a full-scale tax-credit system incorporating a structure of positive personal allowances as a feature of the community tax system." This EU-wide basic-income scheme would "provide an opportunity to carry through a regional policy at personal level, since it would . . . carry purchasing power outwards from the centres of wealth to the districts and even into the houses where incomes are below the average." Moreover, "it would help to raise the incomes of farmers with low earn-

ings without interfering with the prices of their products," and thus provide a partial alternative to the Common Agricultural Policy (a large program aimed at supporting European farmers, with an annual budget that amounts to about 40 percent of the total budget of the European Union). This "European Social Contract," Brandon Rhys-Williams thought, would "combine the benefits of security and unity afforded to the citizens of communist societies with the personal freedom and self-respect which are the best characteristics of the property-owning democracies." All quotes from Parker 1990.

44. Ferry 1995, 2000, 2014.

45. The European Union's annual expenditure on agriculture amounts to about sixty billion euros in 2015 (see http://europa.eu/european-union/topics/budget_en) or 118 euros per capita. Independently of Rhys-Williams, Lavagne and Naud (1992) also proposed using this source of funding for an EU-wide basic income.

46. A 2012 study by the European Commission estimates its yield, if applied to the whole of the EU, at about 57 billion euros annually. The estimate is based on a tax rate of 0.1 percent for securities and of 0.01 percent of the notional value for derivatives agreements, payable by each side of a transaction. See the "Financial Transaction Tax" document released by the European Commission in May 2012 (http://ec.europa.eu/taxation_customs/taxation/other_taxes/financial_sector/index_en.htm).

47. The 3.5 euro estimate is based on European Commission 2012: 24, table 7. The much higher estimate of 17 euros is a speculative guess (for which we are indebted to our colleague Vincent Van Steenberghe), as the equilibrium price that would emerge depends on the ceiling chosen (which may go down) and the rate of economic growth (which keeps fluctuating). With 4 to 5 Bn tons of CO_2-equivalent and a price of 20 euros per ton, this could yield up to 100 Bn euros and hence fund a eurodividend of up to 17 euros per month, on the assumption that all permits are allocated through the auction (instead of a percentage rising gradually from 20 percent in 2013 to 70 percent in 2070, as currently decided at EU level). Estimates for Germany taken separately yield higher dividend levels of about 20 euros per month (Schachtschneider 2012) because they take as their point of departure Germany's current quota, largely determined on the basis of the historically given level of emissions, and assume that their value is to be shared exclusively among the German population. This also explains why the estimates for the US are even higher (see chapter 6).

48. Genet and Van Parijs (1992) estimated that the tax burden on energy use in the (then) twelve-member European Union could have funded an EU-wide basic income of about 20 euros per person per month, and that a tax that would internalize all negative environmental externalities (as assessed by a Delft-based research center) could have funded a monthly basic income of up to 100 euros (about 7 percent of GDP per capita of at the time).

49. Piketty 2014: 528–9, 572. Piketty's (Table S 5.1) proposal is an annual tax of 1 percent on fortunes between one and five million euros, and of 2 percent on fortunes above five million. It would affect 2.5 percent of population.

50. The estimate for the tax base is derived from http://ec.europa.eu/eurostat/web/sector-accounts/data/annual-data. This is also the tax base used in the Bruegel think tank's proposal

for a Eurozone-wide unemployment benefit funded by a Eurozone-wide corporate tax (see Pisani-Ferry et al. 2013: 9, fn 10).

51. For our purposes, a rough estimate suffices. More refined estimates would need to take into account some complexities related to the 50 percent capping clause mentioned below, and related to the possible impact of the new tax profile on the tax base (bearing in mind the adjustments in domestic tax systems to be discussed shortly), not to mention the implications of the Brexit. The VAT part of the funding of the EU's current budget can be sketchily presented as follows. Starting from the VAT revenues in each member state and the pattern of tax rates on different categories of goods and services, one calculates for each member state a harmonized VAT base by dividing the VAT revenues by a weighted sum of the VAT rates. Abstracting from lower rates that apply temporarily to some countries, 0.3 percent of this tax base is collected by the EU in every member state, subject to the tax base not exceeding 50 percent of GDP (a ceiling imposed to prevent poorer countries from contributing at a higher rate than richer ones because of a higher propensity to consume). See European Union 2008: 234 for further details about the structure and European Union 2011 for further details about the amounts.

52. The population data used for these estimates are drawn from http://epp.eurostat.ec .europa.eu/portal/page/portal/population/data/database. See Goedemé and Van Lancker 2009 for a discussion of an EU-wide universal basic pension.

53. Starting with EU-level child benefits has been proposed by Atkinson 1996d, 2015: 222–223 and Levy et al. 2006.

54. Working out the redistributive impact of a specific combination of eurodividend, EU-wide VAT increase, and readjustment of national tax-and-transfer schemes would need to be done using the European tax and benefit simulation model EUROMOD, along the lines of what Bargain et al. (2012) did for a full and partial replacement of the member states' income-tax and cash-benefit systems by a European one. However, simulating the impact of changes in VAT rates on the real incomes of various types of households is more complex than simulating the impact of changes in income tax rates.

55. For example, of the type proposed by Dullien (2014a, 2014b).

56. These political preconditions are further spelled out and discussed in Van Parijs 2015a.

57. City of Ypres 1531/2010: 127–8.

58. In a survey conducted in Norway, support for basic income declined dramatically when respondents were told that non-Norwegian residents would be eligible for the scheme (see Bay and Pedersen 2006).

59. For this sort of reason, Marx and Engels were hostile to the immigration of Irishmen into the industrial towns of the North of England (see Brown 1992).

60. See, for example, Quadagno 1995, Alesina et al. 2003, Desmet et al. 2005, and the essays collected in Van Parijs ed. 2003a and in Banting and Kymlicka eds. 2006, 2016. The latter essays document but also qualify the two mechanisms mentioned below, and explore the ways in which they are and can be counteracted, whether deliberately or not.

61. For unrelated reasons, the only two entities which have had a genuine (though low) basic income for some years—Alaska (see chapter 4) and Macau (see chapter 6)—are subnational. More relevant are the cases of Catalonia and Scotland. The socialist-led Catalan government that came to power in 2003 commissioned a feasibility study for a Catalan basic income, and in March 2004, two left-nationalist parties in the ruling coalition, *Iniciativa per Catalunya-verdo* and *Esquerra republicana de Catalunya*, submitted a basic income bill to the Catalan Parliament (see Arcarons et al. 2005, Casassas et al. 2012). At its March 2016 conference, the Scottish National Party adopted a motion to the effect that "a basic or universal income can potentially provide a foundation to eradicate poverty, make work pay and ensure all our citizens can live in dignity" and that it "should be considered as a possibility when designing the welfare state of an independent Scotland" (see http://www.independent.co.uk/news/uk/politics/universal-basic-income-snp-scotland-independent-conference-vote-a6931846.html). Albeit at the expense of its economic sustainability, the political feasibility of a basic income may be greater at a subnational level, not only because of its greater homogeneity, but also because of its potential attractiveness to (sub-)nationalist movements for strengthening the subnational identity.

Epilogue

1. Hayek 1949: 194.

Bibliography

Reference Note

The literature on basic income has become so massive that the following list of references can make no claim to offering anything like an exhaustive bibliography on the subject. Introductory books available in English include Fitzpatrick (1999c), Blais (2002), Raventos (2007), Sheahen (2012), and Torry (2013, 2015). Widerquist et al. (2013) provides a comprehensive anthology of contemporary research. Cunliffe and Erreygers eds. (2004) provides a collection of contributions by forerunners of the idea. *Basic Income Studies* (http://www.degruyter .com/view/j/bis) is a multidisciplinary journal devoted entirely to basic income. Useful websites (in English) include:

> Basic Income Earth Network (BIEN): http://www.basicincome.org
> Unconditional Basic Income Europe (UBI-E): http://basicincome-europe.org
> United States Basic Income Guarantee Network (USBIG): http://www.usbig.net
> Citizen's Income Trust (UK): http://citizensincome.org/

References

Abe, Aya K. 2014. "Is There a Future for a Universal Cash Benefit in Japan? The Case of Kodomo Teate (Child Benefit)." In Yannick Vanderborght and Toru Yamamori, eds., *Basic Income in Japan: Prospects of a Radical Idea in a Transforming Welfare State*, 49–67. New York: Palgrave Macmillan.

Abrahamson, Peter, and Cecilie Wehner. 2003. "Pension Reforms in Denmark." November, Department of Sociology, University of Copenhagen. http://www.lse.ac.uk/european Institute/research/hellenicObservatory/pdf/pensions_conference/AbrahamsonWehner -Pensions.pdf.

Ackerman, Bruce. 1980. *Social Justice in the Liberal State*. New Haven: Yale University Press.

Ackerman, Bruce, and Anne Alstott. 1999. *The Stakeholder Society*. New Haven: Yale University Press.

———. 2006. "Why Stakeholding?" In Erik Olin Wright, ed., *Redesigning Distribution*, 43–65. New York: Verso.

Ad Hoc Committee on the Triple Revolution. 1964. "The Triple Revolution." *International Socialist Review* 24(3): 85–89. https://www.marxists.org/history/etol/newspape/isr/vol25/no03/adhoc.html.

Adler-Karlsson, Gunnar. 1979. "The Unimportance of Full Employment." *IFDA Dossier* 2: 216–226.

———. 1981. "Probleme des Wirtschaftswachstums und der Wirtschaftsgesinnung. Utopie eines besseren Lebens." *Mitteilungsdienst der Verbraucher-Zentrale NRW* 23: 40–63.

Adret. 1977. *Travailler deux heures par jour*. Paris: Le Seuil.

Akee, Randall, William E. Copeland, Gordon Keeler, Adrian Angold, and E. Jane Costello. 2010. "Parents' Incomes and Children's Outcomes: A Quasi-Experiment Using Transfer Payments from Casino Profits." *American Economic Journal: Applied Economics* 2(1): 86–115.

Akee, Randall, Emilia Simeonova, William E. Copeland, Adrian Angold, and E. Jane Costello. 2013. "Young Adult Obesity and Household Income: Effects of Unconditional Cash Transfers." *American Economic Journal: Applied Economics* 5(2): 1–28.

Akerlof, George A. 1982. "Labor Contracts as Partial Gift Exchange." In George A. Akerlof, ed., *An Economic Theorist's Book of Tales*, 145–174. Cambridge: Cambridge University Press, 1984.

Akerlof, George A., and Janet L. Yellen. 1986. "Introduction." In George A. Akerlof and Janet L. Yellen, eds., *Efficiency Wage Models of the Labor Market*, 1–22. Cambridge: Cambridge University Press.

Alaluf, Mateo. 2014. *L'allocation universelle. Nouveau label de précarité*. Mons: Couleur Livres.

Albeda, Wim. 1984. *De Crisis van de Werkloosheid en de Verzorgingsstaat. Analyse en Perspectief*. Kampen NL: Kok.

Alesina, Alberto, Arnaud Devleeschauwer, William Easterly, Sergio Kurlat, and Romain Wacziarg. 2003. "Fractionalization." *Journal of Economic Growth* 8: 155–194.

Allen, Mike. 1997. "What Does Basic Income Offer the Long-Term Unemployed?" Dublin: Irish National Organisation of the Unemployed.

Alperovitz, Gar. 1994. "Distributing Our Technological Inheritance." *Technology Review* 97: 31–36.

Alstott, Anne. 2001. "Good for Women." In Philippe Van Parijs et al., *What's Wrong with a Free Lunch?* 75–79. Boston: Beacon Press.

Althaus, Dieter, and Hermann Binkert, eds. 2010. *Solidarisches Bürgergeld: Freiheit nachhaltig und ganzheitlich sichern*. Norderstedt: Books on Demand GmbH.

Ambrose. 1927. *S. Ambrosii De Nabuthae: A commentary*, trans. Martin McGuire. Washington DC: Catholic University of America.

Amenta, Edwin, Kathleen Dunleavy, and Mary Bernstein. 1994. "Stolen Thunder? Huey Long's 'Share Our Wealth,' Political Mediation, and the Second New Deal." *American Sociological Review* 59(5): 678–702.

Anderson, Jan-Otto, and Olli Kangas. 2005. "Popular Support for Basic Income in Sweden and Finland." In Guy Standing, ed., *Promoting Income Security as a Right: Europe and North America*, 289–301. London: Anthem Press.

Andrews, Kate. 2015. "Reform Tax Credits with a Negative Income Tax, Says New Report." Press release, October 26, Adam Smith Institute, London. http://www.adamsmith.org /news/press-release-reform-tax-credits-with-a-negative-income-tax-says-new-report.

Anonymous. 1848/1963. "Project van eene Nieuwe Maetschappelijke Grondwet." In Hubert Wouters, ed., *Documenten betreffende de geschiedenis der arbeidersbeweging*, 963–966. Leuven and Paris: Nauwelaerts.

Arcarons, Jordi, Alex Boso, José Antonio Noguera, and Daniel Raventós. 2005. *Viabilitat i impacte d'una Renda Bàsica de Ciutadania per a Catalunya*. Barcelona: Fundació Bofill.

Arcarons, Jordi, Antoni Domènech, Daniel Raventós, and Lluís Torrens. 2014. "Un modelo de financiación de la Renta Básica para el conjunto del Reino de España: si, se puede y es racional." Sin Permiso, December 7. http://www.sinpermiso.info/sites/default/files /textos/rbuesp.pdf.

Arneson, Richard J. 1989. "Equality and Equal Opportunity for Welfare." *Philosophical Studies* 56(1): 77–93.

———. 1991. "A Defense of Equal Opportunity for Welfare." *Philosophical Studies* 62(2): 187–195.

Arnsperger, Christian. 2011. *L'homme économique et le sens de la vie*. Paris: Textuel.

Arnsperger, Christian, and Warren A. Johnson. 2011. "The Guaranteed Income as an Equal-Opportunity Tool in the Transition toward Sustainability." In Axel Gosseries and Yannick Vanderborght, eds., *Arguing about Justice: Essays for Philippe Van Parijs*, 61–70. Louvain-la-Neuve: Presses universitaires de Louvain.

Arrizabalaga, Jon. 1999. "Poor Relief in Counter-Reformation Castile: An Overview." In Ole Peter Grell, Andrew Cunningham, and Jon Arrizabalaga, eds., *Health Care and Poor Relief in Counter-Reformation Europe*, 151–176. London: Routledge.

Ashby, Peter. 1984. *Social Security after Beveridge—What Next?* London: National Council for Voluntary Organizations.

Atkinson, Anthony B. 1984. "The Cost of Social Dividend and Tax Credit Schemes." Working Paper 63, ESRC Programme on Taxation, Incentives and the Distribution of Income, London.

———. 1993a. "On Targeting Social Security: Theory and Western Experience with Family Benefits." STICERD Working Paper WSP/99, London School of Economics, London.

———. 1993b. "Participation Income." *Citizen's Income Bulletin* 16: 7–11.

———. 1993c. "Beveridge, the National Minimum, and Its Future in a European Context." STICERD Working Paper WSP/85, London School of Economics, London.

———. 1993d. "Comment." In Anthony Atkinson, ed., *Alternatives to Capitalism: The Economics of Partnership*. London: Macmillan and New York: St Martin's Press.

————. 1995. *Public Economics in Action: The Basic Income / Flat Tax Proposal.* Oxford: Oxford University Press.

————. 1996a. *Incomes and the Welfare State.* Oxford: Oxford University Press.

————. 1996b. "The Case for a Participation Income." *Political Quarterly* 67: 67–70.

————. 1996c. "James Meade's Vision: Full Employment and Social Justice." *National Institute Economic Review,* July, 90–96.

————. 1996d. "The Distribution of Income: Evidence, Theories and Policy." *De Economist* 144(1): 1–21.

————. 1998. *Poverty in Europe.* Oxford: Blackwell.

————. 2015. *Inequality: What Can Be Done?* Cambridge, MA: Harvard University Press.

Atkinson, Anthony B., and Joseph E. Stiglitz. 1980. "Production in the Firm." In Atkinson and Stiglitz, *Lectures in Public Economics.* New York: McGraw-Hill.

Australian Government Commission of Inquiry into Poverty. 1975. "Poverty in Australia: First Main Report." Canberra: Australian Government Publishing Service.

Babeuf, Gracchus. 1796. *Analyse de la doctrine de Babeuf, tribun du peuple, proscrit par le Directoire exéctutif pour avoir dit la vérité.*

Bachelot, Louis-Marie. 2011. "Contre l'Etat nounou, pour l'allocation universelle." Nouvelles de France, May 13. http://www.ndf.fr/la-une/13-05-2011/louis-marie-bachelot -contre-letat-nounou-pour-lallocation-universelle/.

Baker, John. 2008. "All Things Considered, Should Feminists Embrace Basic Income?" *Basic Income Studies* 3(3): 1–8.

Baldwin, Peter. 1990. *The Politics of Social Solidarity: Class Bases of the European Welfare State.* Cambridge: Cambridge University Press.

Balkenende, Jan Peter. 1985. "'Waarborgen voor zekerheid' en de verzorgingsmaatschappij." *Christen Democratische Verkenningen* 10: 473–484.

Banting, Keith, and Will Kymlicka, eds. 2006. *Multiculturalism and the Welfare State: Recognition and Redistribution in Contemporary Democracies.* Oxford: Oxford University Press.

————. 2016. *The Strains of Commitment: The Political Sources of Solidarity.* Oxford: Oxford University Press.

Bardhan, Pranab. 2016. "Could a Basic Income Help Poor Countries?" Project Syndicate, June 22. www.project-syndicate.org/commentary/developing-country-basic-income-by -pranab-bardhan-2016-06.

Bargain, Olivier, Mathias Dolls, Clemens Fuest, Dirk Neumann, Andreas Peichl, Nico Pestel, and Sebastian Siegloch. 2012. "Fiscal Union in Europe? Redistributive and Stabilizing Effects of an EU Tax-Benefit System." Discussion paper series, IZA DP No. 6585, May, Forschungsinstitut zur Zukunft der Arbeit / Institute for the Study of Labor, Bonn. http://ftp.iza.org/dp6585.pdf.

Barnes, Peter. 2014. *With Liberty and Dividends for All: How to Save Our Middle Class When Jobs Don't Pay Enough.* San Francisco: Berrett-Koehler.

Barrez, Dirk. 1999. "Tien frank per dag voor iedereen." *De Morgen* (Brussels), December 22.

Barry, Brian. 1992. "Equality Yes, Basic Income No." In Philippe Van Parijs, ed., *Arguing for Basic Income: Ethical Foundations for a Radical Reform*, 128–140. London: Verso.

———. 1994. "Justice, Freedom, and Basic Income." In Horst Siebert, ed., *The Ethical Foundations of the Market Economy*, 61–89. Tübingen: J. C. B. Mohr and Ann Arbor: University of Michigan Press.

———. 1996a. "Real Freedom and Basic Income." *Journal of Political Philosophy* 4(3): 242–276.

———. 1996b. "Surfers' Saviour." *Citizen's Income Bulletin* 22: 1–4.

———. 1997. "The Attractions of Basic Income." In Jane Franklin, ed., *Equality*, 157–171. London: Institute for Public Policy Research.

———. 2000. "Universal Basic Income and the Work Ethic." *Boston Review* 25(5): 14–15.

———. 2005. *Why Social Justice Matters*. New York: Wiley.

Bauer, Michael W., and Philippe Schmitter. 2001. "Dividend, Birth-Grant or Stipendium?" *Journal of European Social Policy* 11(4): 348–352.

Bauer, Péter Tamás. 1981. *Equality, the Third World and Economic Delusion*. London: Methuen.

Bauwens, Michel, and Rogier De Langhe. 2015. "Basisinkomen is geen vangnet maar een springplank." *De Morgen* (Brussels), June 2.

Bay, Ann-Helén, and Axel W. Pedersen. 2006. "The Limits of Social Solidarity: Basic Income, Immigration and the Legitimacy of the Universal Welfare State." *Acta Sociologica* 49(4): 419–436.

Bell, Edward. 1993. "The Rise of the Lougheed Conservatives and the Demise of Social Credit in Alberta: A Reconsideration." *Canadian Journal of Political Science* 26(3): 455–475.

Bellamy, Edward. 1888/1983. *Looking Backward, 2000–1887*. Harmondsworth: Penguin.

Belorgey, Jean-Michel, ed. 2000. *Minima sociaux, revenus d'activité, précarité*. Paris: La Documentation française.

Bentham, Jeremy. 1796/2001. "Essays on the Subject of the Poor Laws, Essay I and II." In *Writings on the Poor Laws*, ed. Michael Quinn, vol. 1, 3–65. Oxford: Oxford University Press.

Bergé, Pierre. 1991. *Liberté, j'écris ton nom*. Paris: Bernard Grasset.

Bergmann, Barbara R. 2008. "Basic Income Grants or the Welfare State: Which Better Promotes Gender Equality?" *Basic Income Studies* 3(3): 1–7.

Bernard, Michel, and Michel Chartrand. 1999. *Manifeste pour un revenu de citoyenneté*. Montréal: Editions du renouveau québécois.

Berzins, Baiba. 1969. "Douglas Credit and the A.L.P." *Labour History* 17: 148–160.

Bhargava, Saurabh, and Dayanand Manoli. 2015. "Psychological Frictions and the Incomplete Take-Up of Social Benefits: Evidence from an IRS Field Experiment." *American Economic Review* 105(11): 3489–3529.

Bidadanure, Juliana. 2014. "Treating Young People as Equals: Intergenerational Justice in Theory and Practice." PhD diss., University of York.

Birnbaum, Simon. 2012. *Basic Income Reconsidered: Social Justice, Liberalism, and the Demands of Equality*. New York: Palgrave Macmillan.

Blais, François. 1999. "Loisir, travail et réciprocité. Une justification 'rawlsienne' de l'allocation universelle est-elle possible?" *Loisir et société* 22(2): 337–353.

———. 2002. *Ending Poverty: A Basic Income for All Canadians.* Toronto: Lorimer.

Blaschke, Ronald, Adeline Otto, and Norbert Schepers, eds. 2010. *Grundeinkommen: Geschicht, Modelle, Debatten.* Berlin: Karl Dietz Verlag.

———. 2012. *Grundeinkommen. Von der Idee zu einer europäischen politischen Bewegung.* Hamburg: VSA Verlag.

Blaschke, Ronald, Ina Praetorius, and Antje Schrupp, eds. 2016. *Das Bedingungslose Grundeinkommen. Feministische und postpatriarchale Perspektiven.* Sulzbach: Ulrike Helmer Verlag.

Block, Fred, and Margaret Somers. 2003. "In the Shadow of Speenhamland: Social Policy and the Old Poor Law." *Politics & Society* 31(2): 283–323.

Boadway, Robin, Katherine Cuff, and Kourtney Koebel. 2016. "Designing a Basic Income Guarantee for Canada." September, Department of Economics, Queen's University.

Bond, Larry. 1997. "The Odds against Basic Income." Dublin: Irish National Organisation of the Unemployed.

Bonnett, Alastair, and Keith Armstrong, eds. 2014. *Thomas Spence: The Poor Man's Revolutionary.* London: Breviary Stuff.

Borjas, George J. 1999. "Immigration and Welfare Magnets." *Journal of Labor Economics* 17(4): 607–637.

Bouchet, Muriel. 2015. "Allocation universelle à la Luxembourgeoise: un cadeau empoisonné?" IDEA Foundation blog. http://www.fondation-idea.lu/2015/08/06/allocation-universelle-a-la-luxembourgeoise-un-cadeau-empoisonne/.

Bourdieu, Pierre. 1998. "Le mouvement des chômeurs, un miracle social." In Pierre Bourdieu, *Contre-Feux 2*, 102–104. Paris: Liber.

Boutin, Christine. 2003. *Pour sortir de l'isolement, Un nouveau projet de société.* Paris: Services du Premier Ministre.

Bovenberg, Lans, and Rick van der Ploeg. 1995. "Het basisinkomen is een utopie," *Economisch-Statistische Berichten* 3995: 100–104.

Bowles, Samuel. 1985. "The Production Process in a Competitive Economy: Walrasian, Neo-Hobbesian and Marxian Models." *American Economic Review* 75(1): 16–36.

Boyce, James K., and Matthew E. Riddle. 2007. "Cap and Dividend: How to Curb Global Warming While Protecting the Incomes of American Families." Working Paper 150, November, Political Economy Research Institute, University of Massachusetts Amherst. http://citeseerx.ist.psu.edu/viewdoc/download?doi=10.1.1.587.3768&rep=rep1&type=pdf.

———. 2010. "CLEAR Economics: State Level Impacts of the Carbon Limits and Energy for America's Renewal Act on Family Incomes and Jobs." March, Political Economy Research Institute, University of Massachussets Amherst. http://www.peri.umass.edu/fileadmin/pdf/other_publication_types/green_economics/CLEAR_Economics.pdf.

Boyer, George R. 1990. *An Economic History of the English Poor Law, 1750–1850.* Cambridge: Cambridge University Press.

Bradshaw, Jonathan. 2012. "The Case for Family Benefits." *Children and Youth Services Review* 34(3): 590–596.

Brady, David, and Amie Bostic. 2015. "Paradoxes of Social Policy: Welfare Transfers, Relative Poverty, and Redistribution Preferences." *American Sociological Review* 80(2): 268–298.

Bregman, Rutger. 2016. *Utopia for Realists. The Case for a Universal Basic Income, Open Borders and a 15-Hour Workweek.* Amsterdam: De Correspondent.

Bresson, Yoland. 1984. *L'Après-salariat. Une nouvelle approche de l'économie.* Paris: Economica.

———. 1994. *Le Partage du temps et des revenus.* Paris: Economica.

———. 1999. "Il faut libérer le travail du carcan de l'emploi." *Le Monde* (Paris), 16 mars.

———. 2000. *Le revenu d'existence ou la métamorphose de l'être social.* Paris: L'esprit frappeur.

Brinkley, Alan. 1981. "Huey Long, the Share Our Wealth Movement, and the Limits of Depression Dissidence." *Louisiana History* 22(2): 117–134.

Brittan, Samuel. 1973. *Capitalism and the Permissive Society.* London: Macmillan.

———. 1983. "Work Sharing: A Flawed, Dangerous Nostrum." *Financial Times,* October 6.

———. 1988. "The Never-Ending Quest. Postscript to the 1987–8 Edition." In Samuel Brittan, *A Restatement of Economic Liberalism,* 210–315. London: Macmillan.

———. 2001. "In Praise of Free Lunches." *Times Literary Supplement,* August 24.

Brown, Chris. 1992. "Marxism and the Transnational Migration of People." In Brian Barry and Robert E. Goodin, eds., *Free Movement: Ethical Issues in the Transnational Migration of People and of Money,* 127–144. University Park: Pennsylvania State University Press.

Brynjolfsson, Erik, and Andrew McAfee. 2014. *The Second Machine Age: Work, Progress, and Prosperity in a Time of Brilliant Technologies.* New York: W. W. Norton.

Büchele, Hervig, and Lieselotte Wohlgenannt. 1985. *Grundeinkommen ohne Arbeit. Auf dem Weg zu einer kommunikativen Gesellschaft.* Vienna: Europaverlag. Reprinted Vienna: ÖGB Verlag, 2016.

Bureau of Labor Statistics. 2015. "Women in the Labor Force: A Databook." December, BLS Report 1059.

———. 2016. "Union Members—2015." Economic News Release, January 28. http://www.bls.gov/news.release/union2.nro.htm.

Burke, Edmund. 1795. *Thoughts and Details on Scarcity Originally Presented to the Right Honourable William Pitt,* 250–280. First published in 1800. http://oll.libertyfund.org/title/659/20399.

Burns, Eveline M. 1965. "Social Security in Evolution: Towards What?" *Social Service Review* 39(2): 129–140.

Burtless, Gary. 1986. "The Work Response to a Guaranteed Income: A Survey of Experimental Evidence." In Alicia H. Munnell, ed., *Lessons from the Income Maintenance Experiments,* 22–52. Boston: Federal Reserve Bank of Boston.

———. 1990. "The Economist's Lament: Public Assistance in America." *Journal of Economic Perspectives* 4(1): 57–78.

Busilacchi, Gianluca. 2009. "Dagli rifiuti puó nascere un fiore: un reddito di base per salvare il pianeta." In BIN Italia, ed., *Reddito per tutti. Un'utopia concreta per l'era globale,* 167–176. Roma: Manifestolibri.

Caillé, Alain, ed. 1987. *Du revenu social: au-delà de l'aide, la citoyenneté?* Special issue of *Bulletin du MAUSS* (Paris) 23.

———. 1994. *Temps choisi et revenu de citoyenneté. Au-delà du salariat universel.* Caen: Démosthène.

———, ed. 1996. *Vers un revenu minimum inconditionnel?* Revue du MAUSS 7, Paris: La Découverte.

Cain, Glen G., and Douglas A. Wissoker. 1990a. "A Reanalysis of Marital Stability in the Seattle-Denver Income-Maintenance Experiment." *American Journal of Sociology* 95(5): 1235–1269.

———. 1990b. "Response to Hannan and Tuma." *American Journal of Sociology* 95(5): 1299–1314.

Callender, Rosheen. 1985. "The Economics of Basic Income: Response to Dr. Roberts' Paper." Paper presented at the Conference *Irish Future Societies,* Dublin, January 22.

———. 1986. "Basic Income in Ireland: The Debate to Date." In Anne G. Miller, ed., *Proceedings of the First International Conference on Basic Income,* 288–295. London: BIRG and Antwerp: BIEN.

Calnitsky, David. 2016. "'More Normal than Welfare': The Mincome Experiment, Stigma, and Community Experience." *Canadian Review of Sociology* 53(1): 26–71.

Calnitsky, David, and Jonathan Latner. 2015. "Basic Income in a Small Town: Understanding the Elusive Effects on Work." Paper presented at the conference The Future of Basic Income Research, European University Institute, Florence, June 26–27.

Canada. 2016. *Final Report of the House of Commons Standing Committee on Finance Regarding Its Consultations in Advance of the 2016 Budget,* March. Ottawa: House of Commons.

Caputo, Richard K. 2012. "United States of America: GAI Almost in the 1970s but Downhill Thereafter." In Richard K. Caputo, ed., *Basic Income Guarantee and Politics: International Experiences and Perspectives on the Viability of Income Guarantees,* 265–281. New York: Palgrave Macmillan.

Carens, Joseph H. 1981. *Equality, Moral Incentives and the Market: An Essay in Utopian Politico-Economic Theory.* Chicago: University of Chicago Press.

Casassas, David. 2007. "Basic Income and the Republican Ideal: Rethinking Material Independence in Contemporary Societies." *Basic Income Studies* 2(2): 1–7.

———. 2016. "Economic Sovereignty as the Democratization of Work: The Role of Basic Income." *Basic Income Studies* 11(1): 1–15.

Casassas, David, and Simon Birnbaum. 2008. "Social Republicanism and Basic Income: Building a Citizen Society." In Stuart White and Daniel Leighton, eds., *The Emerging Politics of Republican Democracy,* 75–82. London: Lawrence and Wishart.

Casassas, David, Daniel Raventós, and Julie Ward. 2012. "East Timor and Catalonia: Basic-Income Proposals for North and South." In Matthew C. Murray and Carole

Pateman, eds., *Basic Income Worldwide: Horizons of Reform*, 105–127. New York: Palgrave Macmillan.

Case, Anne, and Angus Deaton. 1998. "Large Cash Transfers to the Elderly in South Africa." *Economic Journal* 108(450): 1330–1361.

Castel, Robert. 1995. *Les métamorphoses de la question sociale. Une chronique du salariat.* Paris: Fayard.

———. 2009. *La montée des incertitudes. Travail, protection, statut de l'individu.* Paris: Le Seuil.

Castelein, Reinier. 2016. *Welzijn is de nieuwe welvaart.* Utrecht: Happy View.

Centre des Jeunes Dirigeants d'Entreprise. 2011. *Objectif Oikos. Changeons d'R. 12 propositions pour 2012.* Paris: CJD.

Charbonneau, Bernard, and Jacques Ellul. 1935/1999. "Directives pour un manifeste personnaliste," ed. Patrick Troude-Chastenet. *Revue Française d'Histoire des Idées Politiques* 9 (1999): 159–177.

Charlier, Joseph. 1848. *Solution du problème social ou constitution humanitaire. Basée sur la loi naturelle, et précédé de l'exposé des motifs.* Brussels: Chez tous les libraires du Royaume.

———. 1871. *Catéchisme populaire philosophique, politique et social.* Brussels: Vanderauwera.

———. 1894a. *La Question sociale résolue, précédée du testament philosophique d'un penseur.* Brussels: Weissenbruch.

———. 1894b. *L'Anarchie désarmée par l'équité. Corollaire à la question sociale résolue.* Brussels: Weissenbruch.

Christensen, Erik. 2000. *Borgerløn. Fortællinger om en politisk ide.* Højbjerg: Forlaget Hovedland.

Christensen, Erik, and Jørn Loftager. 2000. "Ups and Downs of Basic Income in Denmark." In Robert-Jan van der Veen and Loek Groot, eds., *Basic Income on the Agenda*, 257–267. Amsterdam: Amsterdam University Press.

City of Ypres. 1531/2010. *Forma Subventionis Pauperum.* In Paul Spicker, ed., *The Origins of Modern Welfare*, 101–140. Oxford: Peter Lang.

Clavet, Nicholas-James, Jean-Yves Duclos, and Guy Lacroix. 2013. "Fighting Poverty: Assessing the Effect of Guaranteed Minimum-Income Proposals in Québec." Discussion paper series, IZA DP No. 7283, March, Forschungsintitut für Zukunft der Arbeit/Institute for the Study of Labor, Bonn. http://ftp.iza.org/dp7283.pdf.

Clemons, Steven C. 2003. "Sharing, Alaska-Style." *New York Times*, April 9.

Clerc, Denis. 2003. "L'idée d'un revenu d'existence: une idée séduisante et . . . dangereuse." In Jean-Paul Fitoussi and Patrick Savidan, eds., *Comprendre les inégalités*, 201–207. Paris: PUF.

Cobbett, William. 1827/1977. *The Poor Man's Friend.* New York: Augustus M. Kelley.

Cohen, Nick. 2014. "Two Days, One Night—A Film That Illuminates the Despair of the Low Paid." *The Observer*, August 30.

Cole, George D. H. 1929. *The Next Ten Years in British Social and Economic Policy.* London: Macmillan.

———. 1935. *Principles of Economic Planning.* London: Macmillan.

———. 1944. *Money: Its Present and Future.* London: Cassel.

———. 1953. *A History of Socialist Thought.* London: Macmillan.

Collectif Charles Fourier. 1985. "L'allocation universelle." *La Revue Nouvelle* 81: 345–351. English translation: "The Universal Grant." *IFDA dossier* 48 (July/August): 32–37.

Colombino, Ugo. 2015. "Five Crossroads on the Way to Basic Income: An Italian Tour." *Italian Economic Journal* 1(3): 353–389.

Colombino, Ugo, Marilena Locatelli, Edlira Narazani, and Cathal O'Donoghue. 2010. "Alternative Basic Income Mechanisms: An Evaluation Exercise with a Microeconometric Model." *Basic Income Studies* 5(1): 1–31.

Colombino, Ugo, and Edlira Narazani. 2013. "Designing a Universal Income Support Mechanism for Italy: An Exploratory Tour." *Basic Income Studies* 8(1): 1–17.

Colombo, Céline, Thomas De Rocchi, Thomas Kurer, and Thomas Widmer. 2016. "Analyse der eidgenössischen Abstimmung vom 5. Juni 2016." Zürich: VOX.

Colombo, Giulia, Reinhold Schnabel, and Stefanie Schubert. 2008. "Basic Income Reform in Germany: A Microsimulation-Age Analysis." Unpublished ms. http://www.aiel.it /Old/bacheca/BRESCIA/papers/colombo.pdf.

Commission on Social Justice. 1994. *Social Justice. Strategies for National Renewal.* The Report of the Commission on Social Justice. London: Vintage.

Condorcet, Antoine Caritat Marquis de. 1795/1988. *Esquisse d'un tableau historique des progrès de l'esprit humain.* Paris: Garnier-Flammarion.

Considerant, Victor. 1845. *Exposition abrégée du système Phalanstérien de Fourier.* Paris: Librairie sociétaire.

Cook, Stephen L. 1979. "Can a Social Wage Solve Unemployment?" Working Paper 165, University of Aston Management Centre, Birmingham.

Coote, Anna, Jane Franklin, and Andrew Simms. 2010. *21 Hours: Why a Shorter Working Week Can Help Us All to Flourish in the 21st Century.* London: New Economics Foundation.

COSATU. 2010. *A Growth Path towards Full Employment: Policy Perspectives of the Congress of South African Trade Unions?* Johannesburg: COSATU.

Cournot, Antoine Augustin. 1838/1980. *Recherches sur les principes mathématiques de la théorie des richesses.* Paris: Vrin.

Crocker, Geoffrey. 2014. *The Economic Necessity of Basic Income.* Bristol: Technology Market Strategies.

CSC (Confédération des syndicats chrétiens). 2002. "Dans quelle mesure mon revenu est-il juste?" *Syndicaliste CSC* 560, January 25.

Cummine, Angela L. 2011. "Overcoming Dividend Skepticism: Why the World's Sovereign Wealth Funds Are Not Paying Basic Income Dividends." *Basic Income Studies* 6(1): 1–18.

Cunha, Jesse M. 2014. "Testing Paternalism: Cash versus In-Kind Transfers." *American Economic Journal: Applied Economics* 6(2): 195–230.

Cunliffe, John, and Guido Erreygers. 2001. "The Enigmatic Legacy of Charles Fourier: Joseph Charlier and Basic Income." *History of Political Economy* 33(3): 459–484.

————, eds. 2004. *The Origins of Universal Grants: An Anthology of Historical Writings on Basic Capital and Basic Income*. Basingstoke: Palgrave Macmillan.

Currie, Janet, and Firouz Gahvari. 2008. "Transfers in Cash and In-Kind: Theory Meets the Data." *Journal of Economic Literature* 46(2): 333–383.

Dalla Costa, Mariarosa, and Selma James. 1975. *The Power of Women and the Subversion of the Community*. Bristol: Falling Wall Press.

Danaher, John. 2014. "Feminism and the Basic Income. Parts I and II." Institute for Ethics and Emerging Technologies, blog post. Part 1, July 17: http://ieet.org/index.php/IEET /more/danaher20140717; Part 2, July 19: http://ieet.org/index.php/IEET/more/danaher 20140719.

Daniels, Norman. 1985. *Just Health Care*. Cambridge: Cambridge University Press.

Davala, Sarath, Renana Jhabvala, Soumya Kapoor Mehta, and Guy Standing. 2015. *Basic Income: A Transformative Policy for India*. London: Bloomsbury.

Davidson, Mark. 1995. "Liberale grondrechten en milieu. Het recht op milieugebruiksruimte als grondslag van een basisinkomen." *Milieu* 5: 246–249.

Davis, Michael. 1987. "Nozick's Argument for the Legitimacy of the Welfare State." *Ethics* 97(3): 576–594.

De Basquiat, Marc, and Gaspard Koenig. 2014. *LIBER, un revenu de liberté pour tous. Une proposition d'impôt négatif en France*. Paris: Génération Libre.

De Deken, Jeroen, and Dietrich Rueschemeyer. 1992. "Social Policy, Democratization and State Structure: Reflections on Late Nineteenth-Century Britain and Germany." In Rolf Torstendahl, ed., *State Theory and State History*, 93–117. London: Sage.

Defeyt, Philippe. 2016. *Un revenu de base pour chacun, une autonomie pour tous*. Namur: Institut pour le développement durable.

Defoe, Daniel. 1697/1999. *An Essay upon Projects*, New York: AMS Press.

————. 1704. *Giving Alms No Charity and Employing the Poor. A Grievance to the Nation*. London: Printed, and sold by the booksellers of London and Westminster.

De Jager, Nicole E. M., Johan J. Graafland, and George M. M. Gelauff. 1994. *A Negative Income Tax in a Mini Welfare State: A Simulation with MIMIC*. The Hague: Centraal Planbureau.

De Keyser, Napoleon. 1854/2004. *Het Natuer-regt, of de rechtveirdigheid tot nieuw bestuur als order der samenleving volgens de bestemming van den mensch*. Partial English translation as "Natural Law, or Justice as a New Governance for Society According to the Destiny of Man." In John Cunliffe and Guido Erreygers, eds., *The Origins of Universal Grants*, 56–72. Basingstoke: Palgrave Macmillan.

De Keyzer, Peter. 2013. *Growth Makes You Happy: An Optimist's View of Progress and the Free Market*. Tielt: Lannoo.

Dekkers, J. M., and Bart Nooteboom. 1988. *Het gedeeltelijk basisinkomen, de hervorming van de jaren negentig*. The Hague: Stichting Maatschappij en Onderneming.

Delvaux, Bernard, and Riccardo Cappi. 1990. *Les allocataires sociaux confrontés aux pièges financiers: Analyse des situations et des comportements*. Louvain: IRES.

De Paepe, César. 1889. "Des services publics." *La Revue socialiste* 10: 299–310. http://archive .org/stream/larevuesocialist10part/larevuesocialist10part_djvu.txt.

Deppe, Ina, and Lena Foerster. 2014. *1989–2014. 125 Jahren Rentenversicherung.* Berlin: August Dreesbach Verlag.

Desmet, Klaus, Ignacio Ortuño-Ortín, and Shlomo Weber. 2005. "Peripheral Linguistic Diversity and Redistribution." CORE Discussion Paper 2005/44, Université catholique de Louvain.

De Wispelaere, Jurgen. 2016. "The Struggle for Strategy: On the Politics of the Basic-Income Proposal." *Politics* 36(2): 131–141.

De Wispelaere, Jurgen, and Lindsay Stirton. 2007. "The Public Administration Case against Participation Income." *Social Service Review* 81(3): 523–549.

———. 2011. "The Administrative Efficiency of Basic Income." *Policy & Politics* 39(1): 115–132.

———. 2012. "A Disarmingly Simple Idea? Practical Bottlenecks in the Implementation of a Universal Basic Income." *International Social Security Review* 65(2): 103–121.

Dickens, Charles. 1838. *Oliver Twist, or the Parish Boy's Progress.* London: Richard Bentley.

Dilnot, Andrew, John A. Kay, and C. N. Morris. 1984. *The Reform of Social Security.* London: Institute of Fiscal Studies.

Dore, Ronald. 2001. "Dignity and Deprivation." In Philippe Van Parijs et al., *What's Wrong with a Free Lunch?* 80–84. Boston: Beacon Press.

Douglas, Clifford H. 1920. *Economic Democracy.* London: C. Palmer.

———. 1924. *Social Credit.* London: Eyre and Spottiswoode.

Dowding, Keith, Jurgen De Wispelaere, and Stuart White, eds. 2003. *The Ethics of Stakeholding.* Basingstoke: Palgrave Macmillan.

Duboin, Jacques. 1932. *La Grande Relève des hommes par la machine.* Paris: Fustier.

———. 1945. *Economie distributive de l'abondance.* Paris: OCIA.

———. 1998. *Le socialisme distributiste.* Paris: L'Harmattan.

Duboin, Marie-Louise. 1988. "Guaranteed Income as an Inheritance." In Anne G. Miller, ed., *Proceedings of the First International Conference on Basic Income,* 134–145. London: BIRG and Antwerp: BIEN.

Duchâtelet, Roland. 1994. "An Economic Model for Europe Based on Consumption Financing on the Tax Side and the Basic Income Principle on the Redistribution Side." Paper presented at the 5th BIEN Congress, London, September 8–10.

———. 2004. *De weg naar meer netto binnenlands geluk. Een toekomst voor alle Europeanen.* Leuven: Van Halewyck.

Dullien, Sebastian. 2014a. "The Macroeconomic Stabilisation Impact of a European Basic Unemployment Insurance Scheme." *Intereconomics* 49(4): 189–193.

———. 2014b. "Why a European Unemployment Insurance Would Help to Make EMU More Sustainable." *Social Europe,* October 3.

Dumont, Daniel. 2012. *La responsabilisation des personnes sans emploi en question.* Brussels: La Charte.

Durkheim, Emile. 1893/2007. *De la division du travail social.* Paris: P.U.F.

Dworkin, Ronald. 1981. "What Is Equality? Part II: Equality of Resources." *Philosophy and Public Affairs* 10/4: 283–345.

———. 1983. "Why Liberals Should Believe in Equality." *New York Review of Books,* February 3.

———. 2000. *Sovereign Virtue: The Theory and Practice of Equality.* Cambridge, MA: Harvard University Press.

———. 2002. "*Sovereign Virtue* Revisited." *Ethics* 113: 106–243.

———. 2004. "Ronald Dworkin Replies." In Justine Burley, ed., *Dworkin and His Critics,* 339–395. Oxford: Blackwell.

———. 2006. *Is Democracy Possible Now? Principles for a New Political Debate.* Princeton: Princeton University Press, 2006.

Dyer, Christopher. 2012. "Poverty and Its Relief in Late Medieval England." *Past and Present* 216(1): 41–78.

Easterlin, Richard A. 1974. "Does Economic Growth Improve the Human Lot? Some Empirical Evidence." In Paul A. David and Melvin W. Reder, eds., *Nations and Households in Economic Growth: Essays in Honor of Moses Abramovitz,* 89–125. New York: Academic Press.

———. 2010. *Happiness, Growth, and the Life Cycle.* Oxford: Oxford University Press.

Economiesuisse. 2012. "Bedingungsloses Grundeinkommen? Leider nein." *Dossiepolitik* 21, October 1.

Edin, Kathryn J., and H. Luke Shaefer. 2015. *$2.00 a Day: Living on Almost Nothing in America.* Boston: Houghton Mifflin Harcourt.

Einstein, Albert. 1955. "Introduction." In Henry H. Wachtel, *Security for All and Free Enterprise: A Summary of the Social Philosophy of Josef Popper-Lynkeus,* vii–viii. New York: Philosophical Library.

Elgarte, Julieta. 2008. "Basic Income and the Gender Division of Labour." *Basic Income Studies* 3(3).

Elster, Jon. 1986. "Comment on Van der Veen and Van Parijs." *Theory and Society* 15(5): 709–721.

———. 1988. "Is There (or Should There Be) a Right to Work?" In Amy Gutmann, ed., *Democracy and the Welfare State,* 53–78. Princeton: Princeton University Press.

Engels, Friedrich. 1845/2009. *The Condition of the Working-Class in England in 1844.* New York: Cosimo Classics.

———. 1880/2008. *Socialism: Utopian and Scientific.* New York: Cosimo Classics.

Engels, Wolfram, Joachim Mitschke, and Bernd Starkloff. 1973. *Staatsbürgersteuer. Vorschlag zur Reform der direkten Steuers und persönlichen Subventionen durch ein integriertes Personalsteuer- und Subventionssystem.* Wiesbaden: Karl Bräuer-Institut.

Erreygers, Guido, and John Cunliffe. 2006. "Basic Income in 1848." *Basic Income Studies* 1(2): 1–12.

Esping-Andersen, Gøsta. 1990. *The Three Worlds of Welfare Capitalism.* Princeton: Princeton University Press.

European Central Bank. 2013. "The Eurosystem Household Finance and Consumption Survey. Results from the First Wave." Statistics Paper Series no. 2, April.

European Commission. 2012. "Analysis of Options beyond 20% GHG Emission Reductions: Member State Results." Commission Staff Working Paper, Brussels, 1.2.2012, SWD (2012) 5.

———. 2014a. "Employment and Social Developments in Europe 2013." Luxembourg: Publications Office of the European Union.

———. 2014b. "National Student Fee and Support Systems in European Higher Education 2014/15." Eurydice-Facts and Figures, European Commission: Education and Training.

European Union. 2008. "European Union Public Finance," 4th ed. Luxembourg: Office for Official Publications of the European Communities.

———. 2011. "General Budget of the European Union for the Financial Year 2012: General Statement of Revenue." Brussels, June 15. http://eur-lex.europa.eu/budget/data/DB2012 /EN/SEC00.pdf.

Eydoux, Anne, and Rachel Silvera. 2000. "De l'allocation universelle au salaire maternel: il n'y a qu'un pas . . . à ne pas franchir." In Thomas Coutrot and Christophe Ramaux, eds., *Le bel avenir du contrat de travail*, 41–60. Paris: Syros.

Fantazzi, Charles. 2008. "Vives and the *Emarginati*." In Charles Fantazzi, ed., *A Companion to Juan Luis Vives*, 65–111. Leiden: Brill.

Faye, Michael, and Paul Niehaus. 2016. "What If We Just Gave Poor People a Basic Income for Life? That's What We're About to Test." Slate, April 14.

Federation of Claimants Union. 1985a. *On the Dole: A Claimant Union Guide for the Unemployed*. London: Federation of Claimants Union.

———. 1985b. *Women and Social Security*. London: Federation of Claimants Union.

Feige, Edgar L. 2000. "The Automated Payment Transaction Tax: Proposing a New Tax System for the 21st Century." *Economic Policy* 31: 473–511.

Feldstein, Martin. 1992. "The Case against EMU." *The Economist*, June 13.

———. 1997. "The Political Economy of the European Economic and Monetary Union: Political Sources of an Economic Liability." *Journal of Economic Perspectives* 11(4): 23–42.

———. 2012. "The Failure of the Euro: The Little Currency That Couldn't." *Foreign Affairs* 91(1): 105–116.

Fernández-Santamaria, J. A. 1998. *The Theater of Man: J. L. Vives on Society*. Philadelphia: American Philosophical Society.

Ferrarini, Tommy, Kenneth Nelson, and Helena Höög. 2013. "From Universalism to Selectivity: Old Wine in New Bottles for Child Benefits in Europe and Other Countries." In Ive Marx and Kenneth Nelson, eds., *Minimum Income Protection in Flux*, 137–160. New York: Palgrave Macmillan.

Ferry, Jean-Marc. 1985. "Robotisation, utilité sociale, justice sociale." *Esprit* 97: 19–29.

———. 1995. *L'Allocation universelle. Pour un revenu de citoyenneté*. Paris: Cerf.

———. 2000. *La Question de l'Etat européen*. Paris: Gallimard.

———. 2014. "Pour un socle social européen." *Cahiers philosophiques* 137: 7–14.

Fichte, Johann Gottlied. 1800/2012. *The Closed Commercial State*. Translation of *Der geschlossene Handelsstaat*. New York: SUNY Press.

Fitzpatrick, Tony. 1999a/2013. "Ecologism and Basic Income." In Karl Widerquist, Jose A. Noguera, Yannick Vanderborght, and Jurgen De Wispelaere, eds., *Basic Income: An Anthology of Contemporary Research*, 263–268. Chichester: Wiley-Blackwell.

———. 1999b/2013. "A Basic Income for Feminists?" In Karl Widerquist, Jose A. Noguera, Yannick Vanderborght, and Jurgen De Wispelaere, eds., *Basic Income: An Anthology of Contemporary Research*, 163–172. Chichester: Wiley-Blackwell.

———. 1999c. *Freedom and Security: An Introduction to the Basic Income Debate.* London: Macmillan.

Flomenhoft, Gary. 2013. "Applying the Alaska Model in a Resource Poor State: The Example of Vermont." In K. Widerquist and M. Howard, eds., *Exporting the Alaska Model: Adapting the Permanent Fund Dividend for Reform around the World*, 85–107. New York: Palgrave Macmillan.

Flora, Peter, ed. 1986. *Growth to Limits: The Western European Welfare States since World War II.* New York: De Gruyter.

Forget, Evelyn. 2011. "The Town with No Poverty: The Health Effects of a Canadian Guaranteed Annual Income Field Experiment." *Canadian Public Policy* 37(3): 283–305.

Foucault, Michel. 1961/2006. *History of Madness.* London: Routledge.

———. 1979/2008. *The Birth of Biopolitics, Lectures at the Collège de France 1978–79*, ed. M. Senellart. Basingstoke: Palgrave Macmillan.

Fourier, Charles. 1803/2004. "Letter to the High Judge." In John Cunliffe and Guido Erreygers, eds., *The Origins of Universal Grants*, 99–102. Basingstoke: Palgrave Macmillan.

———. 1822/1966. *Théorie de l'unité universelle*, vol. 3. Paris: Anthropos.

———. 1829. *Le nouveau monde industriel ou sociétaire ou invention du procédé d'industrie attrayante et naturelle distribuée en series passionnées.* Paris: Bossange.

———. 1836/1967. *La Fausse Industrie, morcelée, répugnante, mensongère, et l'antidote, l'industrie naturelle, combinée, attrayante, véridique, donnant quadruple produit et perfection extrême en toutes qualités.* Paris: Anthropos.

France Stratégie. 2014a. *Quelle France dans Dix Ans. Les chantiers de la décennie.* Paris: Commissariat général à la stratégie et à la prospective.

———. 2014b. *Quelle France dans Dix Ans. Repères pour 2025.* Paris: Commissariat général à la stratégie et à la prospective.

———. 2014c. *Quelle France dans Dix Ans. Réconcilier l'économique et le social.* Paris: Commissariat général à la stratégie et à la prospective.

Frank, Robert H. 2014. "Let's Try a Basic Income and Public Work." Response essay, Cato Unbound, August 11. http://www.cato-unbound.org/2014/08/11/robert-h-frank/lets-try-basic-income-public-work.

Frank, Robert H., and Philip J. Cook. 1995. *The Winner-Take-All Society: Why the Few at the Top Get So Much More Than the Rest of Us.* New York: Free Press.

Frankman, Myron J. 1998. "Planet-Wide Citizen's Income: Antidote to Global Apartheid." *Labour, Capital and Society* 31(1–2): 166–178.

————. 2004. *World Democratic Federalism: Peace and Justice Indivisible.* Basingstoke: Palgrave Macmillan.

Franzmann, Manuel, ed. 2010. *Bedingungsloses Grundeinkommen als Antwort auf die Krise der Arbeitsgesellschaft.* Weilerswist: Velbrück Wissenschaft.

Fraser, Nancy. 1997. "After the Family Wage: A Postindustrial Thought Experiment." In Fraser, *Justice Interruptus: Critical Reflections on the "Postsocialist" Condition,* 41–66. New York: Routledge.

Frazer, Hugh, and Eric Marlier. 2009. *Minimum-Income Schemes across EU Member States.* Brussels: European Commission and EU Network of National Independent Experts on Social Inclusion.

Frey, Carl Benedikt, and Michael Osborne. 2014. "Technological Change and New Work." Policy Network, May 15. http://www.policy-network.net/pno_detail.aspx?ID=4640&title =Technological-change-and-new-work.

Friedman, Milton. 1947. "Lerner on the Economics of Control." *Journal of Political Economy* 55(5): 405–416.

————. 1962. *Capitalism and Freedom.* Chicago: University of Chicago Press.

————. 1968. "The Case for the Negative Income Tax: A View from the Right." In John H. Bunzel, ed., *Issues of American Public Policy,* 111–120. Englewood Cliffs: Prentice-Hall.

————. 1972/1975. "Is Welfare a Basic Human Right?" In Milton Friedman, *There's No Such Thing as a Free Lunch,* 205–207. La Salle IL: Open Court, 1975.

————. 1973a/1975. "Playboy Interview." In Milton Friedman, *There's No Such Thing as a Free Lunch,* 1–38. La Salle IL: Open Court, 1975.

————. 1973b/1975. "Negative Income Tax." In Milton Friedman, *There's No Such Thing as a Free Lunch,* 198–201. La Salle IL: Open Court, 1975.

————. 1998. "The Government as Manager." Interview with Radio Australia, June 17. http://www.abc.net.au/money/vault/extras/extra5.htm.

————. 2000. "The Suplicy-Friedman Exchange." BIEN News Flash no. 3, May, 8–11. www .basicincome.org/bien/pdf/NewsFlash3.pdf.

Friedman, Yona. 2000. *Utopies réalisables,* 2nd ed. Paris: Editions de l'Eclat.

Friot, Bernard. 2012. *L'enjeu du salaire.* Paris: La Dispute.

Füllsack, Manfred. 2006. *Globale soziale Sicherheit: Grundeinkommen—weltweit?* Berlin: Avinus Verlag.

Fumagalli, Andrea, and Maurizio Lazzarotto, eds. 1999. *Tute bianche. Disoccupazione di massa e reddito di cittadinanza.* Rome: Derive Approdi.

Furukubo, Sakura. 2014. "Basic Income and Unpaid Care Work in Japan." In Yannick Vanderborght and Toru Yamamori, eds., *Basic Income in Japan: Prospects of a Radical Idea in a Transforming Welfare State,* 131–139. New York: Palgrave Macmillan.

Future of Work Commission. 2016. "Ten Big Ideas from Our Consultation: Snapshot of Work to Date." March, Labour Party, Wellington, New Zealand. https://d3n8a8pro7vhmx .cloudfront.net/nzlabour/pages/4237/attachments/original/1458691880/Future_of_Work _Ten_Big_Ideas_sm.pdf?1458691880.

Galbraith, John Kenneth. 1958. *The Affluent Society*. Boston: Houghton Mifflin.

―――. 1966. "The Starvation of the Cities." *The Progressive* 30 (12). Reprinted in J. K. Galbraith, *A View from the Stands: Of People, Politics, Military Power, and the Arts*. Houghton Mifflin, 1986.

―――. 1969. *The Affluent Society*, 2nd ed. London: Hamish Hamilton.

―――. 1972. "The Case for George McGovern." *Saturday Review of the Society*, July 1, 23–27.

―――. 1973. *Economics and the Public Purpose*. Boston: Houghton-Mifflin.

―――. 1975. *Money: Whence It Came, Where It Went*. New York: Houghton Mifflin.

―――. 1999a/2001. "The Unfinished Business of the Century." Lecture at the London School of Economics, June 1999. Reprinted in J. K. Galbraith, *The Essential Galbraith*, 307–314. Boston: Houghton Mifflin, 2001.

―――. 1999b. "The Speculative Bubble Always Comes to an End—And Never in a Pleasant or Peaceful Way." Interview with Elizabeth Mehren, *Los Angeles Times*, December 12. http://latimesblogs.latimes.com/thedailymirror/2008/10/voices―-john.html.

Garon, Sheldon M. 1997. *Molding Japanese Minds: The State in Everyday Life*. Princeton: Princeton University Press.

Gauthier, David. 1986. *Morals by Agreement*. Oxford: Oxford University Press.

Geffroy, Laurent. 2002. *Garantir le revenu. Histoire et actualité d'une utopie concrete*. Paris: La Découverte / MAUSS.

Gelders, Bjorn. 2015. "Universal Child Benefits: The Curious Case of Mongolia." Development Pathways, June 24. http://www.developmentpathways.co.uk/resources/universal-child-benefits-the-curious-case-of-mongolia/.

Genet, Michel, and Philippe Van Parijs. 1992. "Eurogrant." *Basic Income Research Group Bulletin* 15: 4–7.

Genschel, Philipp, and Peter Schwartz. 2011. "Tax Competition: A Literature Review." *Socio-Economic Review* 9(2): 339–370.

Genschel, Philipp, and Laura Seekopf. 2016. "Winners and Losers of Tax Competition." In Peter Dietsch and Thomas Rixen, eds., *Global Tax Governance: What's Wrong with It and How to Fix It*, 56–75. Colchester: ECPR Press.

George, Henry. 1879/1953. *Progress and Poverty*. London: Hogarth Press.

―――. 1881. *The Irish Land Question*. New York: D. Appleton & Company.

―――. 1887/2009. "Address at the Second Public Meeting of the Anti-Poverty Society." Reprinted in Kenneth C. Wenzer, ed., *Henry George, the Transatlantic Irish, and Their Times*, 267–282. Bingley: Emerald Group Publishing.

Gerhardt, Klaus Uwe, and Arnd Weber. 1983. "Garantiertes Mindesteinkommen." *Alemantschen* 3: 69–99.

GESOP. 2015. *L'Omnibus de GESOP. Informe de resultats Juliol de 2015*. Barcelona: GESOP.

Gheaus, Anca. 2008. "Basic Income, Gender Justice and the Costs of Gender-Symmetrical Lifestyles." *Basic Income Studies* 3(3): 1–8.

Gibran, Kahlil. 1923. *The Prophet*. New York: Knopf.

Gilain, Bruno, and Philippe Van Parijs. 1996. "L'allocation universelle: un scénario de court terme et son impact distributive." *Revue belge de Sécurité Sociale* 1996-1: 5–80.

Giraldo Ramirez, Jorge. 2003. *La renta básica, más allá de la sociedad salarial.* Medellin: Ediciones Escuela Nacional Sindical.

Glaeser, Edward. 2011. *The Triumph of the City.* New York: Penguin.

Glyn, Andrew, and David Miliband, eds. 1994. *The Cost of Inequality.* London: IPPR.

Godechot, Jacques. 1970. *Les Constitutions de la France depuis 1789.* Paris: Garnier-Flammarion.

Godino, Roger. 1999. "Pour la création d'une allocation compensatrice de revenu." In Robert Castel, Roger Godino, Michel Jalmain, and Thomas Piketty, eds., *Pour une réforme du RMI, Notes de la Fondation Saint Simon* 104: 7–20.

———. 2002. "Une alternative à la prime pour l'emploi: l'allocation compensatrice de revenu. Entretien avec Nicolas Gravel." *Economie publique* 2002(2): 9–14.

Goedemé, Tim. 2013. "Minimum Income Protection for Europe's Elderly: What and How Much Has Been Guaranteed during the 2000s?" In Ive Marx and Kenneth Nelson, eds., *Minimum Income Protection in Flux,* 108–133. New York: Palgrave Macmillan.

Goedemé, Tim, and Wim Van Lancker. 2009. "A Universal Basic Pension for Europe's Elderly: Options and Pitfalls." *Basic Income Studies* 4(1): 1–26.

Goldsmith, Scott. 2005. "The Alaska Permanent Fund Dividend: An Experiment in Wealth Distribution." In Guy Standing, ed., *Promoting Income Security as a Right: Europe and North America,* 553–566. London: Anthem Press.

Goodman, Paul, and Percival Goodman. 1947/1960. *Communitas: Means of Livelihood and Ways of Life.* New York: Random House.

Gorz, André. 1980. *Adieux au Prolétariat. Au-delà du socialisme.* Paris: Le Seuil.

———. 1983. *Les Chemins du Paradis. L'agonie du capital.* Paris: Galilée.

———. 1984. "Emploi et revenu: un divorce nécessaire?" Interview with Denis Clerc. *Alternatives Economiques* 23: 15–17.

———. 1985. "L'allocation universelle: version de droite et version de gauche." *La Revue nouvelle* 81(4): 419–428.

———. 1988. *Métamorphoses du Travail. Quête du sens.* Paris: Galilée.

———. 1992. "On the Difference between Society and Community, and Why Basic Income Cannot by Itself Confer Full Membership of Either." In Philippe Van Parijs, ed., *Arguing for Basic Income: Ethical Foundations for a Radical Reform,* 178–184. London: Verso.

———. 1997. *Misères du présent, Richesse du possible.* Paris: Galilée.

Goul Andersen, Jørgen. 1996. "Marginalization, Citizenship and the Economy: The Capacities of the Universalist Welfare State in Denmark." In E. O. Eriksen and J. Loftager, eds., *The Rationality of the Welfare State,* 155–202. Oslo: Scandinavian University Press.

Graeber, David. 2014a. "Why America's Favorite Anarchist Thinks Most American Workers Are Slaves." PBS News, April 17. http://www.pbs.org/newshour/making-sense/why -americas-favorite-anarchist-thinks-most-american-workers-are-slaves/.

———. 2014b. "Spotlight on the Financial Sector Did Make Apparent Just How Bizarrely Skewed Our Economy Is in Terms of Who Gets Rewarded." Salon, June 1. http://www

.salon.com/2014/06/01/help_us_thomas_piketty_the_1s_sick_and_twisted_new _scheme/.

Gratianus. 1140/1990. *Decretum.* Munich: Münchener Digitalisierungszentrum. http://geschichte.digitale-sammlungen.de/decretum-gratiani.

Greenberg, David H., and Mark Shroder. 2004. *The Digest of Social Experiments.* Washington DC: Urban Institute.

Green Party. 2015a. *For the Common Good. General Election Manifesto 2015.* London: The Green Party of England and Wales.

———. 2015b. *Basic Income: A Detailed Proposal.* London: The Green Party of England and Wales.

Green Party of New Zealand. 2014. *Income Support Policy.* Wellington: Green Party of Aotearoa New Zealand.

Greffe, Xavier. 1978. *L'Impôt des pauvres. Nouvelle stratégie de politique sociale.* Paris: Dunod.

Griffith, Jeremy. 2015. "Libertarian Perspectives on Basic Income." Unfettered Equality, January 15.

Groot, Loek, and Robert J. van der Veen. 2000. "Clues and Leads in the Debate on Basic Income in the Netherlands." In Robert J. van der Veen and Loek Groot, eds., *Basic Income on the Agenda,* 197–223. Amsterdam: Amsterdam University Press.

Gubian Alain, Stéphane Jugnot, Frédéric Lerais, and Vladimir Passeron. 2004. "Les effets de la RTT sur l'emploi: des simulations ex ante aux évaluations ex post." *Economie et statistique* 376: 25–54.

Guilloteau, Laurent, and Jeanne Revel, eds. 1999. "Revenu garanti pour tous." *Vacarme* 9: 9–22.

Gupta, Uttam. 2014. "Scrap the Food Security Act." May 28. www.thehindubusinessline .com.

Haarmann, Claudia, and Dirk Haarmann, eds., 2005. "The Basic Income Grant in Namibia. Resource Book." Windhoek: Evangelical Lutheran Church in the Republic of Namibia. http://base.socioeco.org/docs/big_resource_book.pdf.

———. 2007. "From Survival to Decent Employment: Basic Income Security in Namibia." *Basic Income Studies* 2(1): 1–7.

———. 2012. "Piloting Basic Income in Namibia—Critical Reflections on the Process and Possible Lessons." Paper presented at the 14th Congress of the Basic Income Earth Network (BIEN), Munich, September 14–16.

Hacker, Jacob S. 2002. *The Divided Welfare State: The Battle over Public and Private Social Benefits in the United States.* Cambridge: Cambridge University Press.

Haddow, Rodney S. 1993. *Poverty Reform in Canada, 1958–1978: State and Class Influences on Policy Making.* Montréal and Kingston: McGill-Queen's University Press.

———. 1994. "Canadian Organized Labour and the Guaranteed Annual Income." In Andrew F. Johnson et al., eds., *Continuities and Discontinuities: The Political Economy of Social Welfare and Labour Market Policy in Canada,* 350–366. Toronto: University of Toronto Press.

Hammond, Jay. 1994. *Tales of Alaska's Bush Rat Governor.* Alaska: Epicenter Press.

Handler, Joel F. 2004. *Social Citizenship and Workfare in the United States and Western Europe: The Paradox of Inclusion.* Cambridge: Cambridge University Press.

Häni, Daniel, and Philip Kovce. 2015. *Was fehlt wenn alles da ist? Warum das bedingungslose Einkommen die richtigen Fragen stellt.* Zürich: Orell Füssli.

Hanlon, Joseph, Armando Barrientos, and David Hulme. 2010. *Just Give Money to the Poor: The Development Revolution from the Global South.* Herndon VA: Kumarian Press.

Hannan, Michael T., and Nancy Brandon Tuma. 1990. "A Reassessment of the Effect of Income Maintenance on Marital Dissolution in the Seattle-Denver Experiment." *American Journal of Sociology* 95(5): 1270–1298.

Hannan, Michael T., Nancy Brandon Tuma, and Lyle P. Groeneveld. 1977. "Income and Marital Events: Evidence from an Income-Maintenance Experiment." *American Journal of Sociology* 82(6): 1186–1211.

———. 1983. "Marital Stability." In Gary Christophersen, ed., *Final Report of the Seattle-Denver Income Maintenance Experiment*, vol. 1, 257–387. Washington DC: U.S. Dept. of Health and Human Services.

Hansen, James. 2014. "Too Little, Too Late? Oops?" June 19, Earth Institute, Columbia University. http://www.columbia.edu/~jeh1/mailings/2014/20140619_TooLittle.pdf.

Harrington, Joel F. 1999. "Escape from the Great Confinement: The Genealogy of a German Workhouse." *Journal of Modern History* 71(2): 308–345.

Harvey, Philip L. 2006. "Funding a Job Guarantee." *International Journal of Environment, Workplace and Employment* 2(1): 114–132.

———. 2011. *Back to Work: A Public Jobs Proposal for Economic Recovery.* New York: Demos.

———. 2012. "More for Less: The Job Guarantee Strategy." *Basic Income Studies* 7(2): 3–18.

———. 2014. "Securing the Right to Work and Income Security." In Elise Dermine and Daniel Dumont, eds., *Activation Policies for the Unemployed, the Right to Work and the Duty to Work*, 223–254. Brussels: Peter Lang.

Hatzfeld, Henri. 1989. *Du paupérisme à la sécurité sociale 1850–1940. Essai sur les origines de la Sécurité sociale en France.* Nancy: Presses universitaires de Nancy. (First edition Paris: Armand Colin, 1971.)

Hattersley, Charles Marshall. 1922/2004. *The Community's Credit. A Consideration of the Principle and Proposals of the Social Credit Movement.* Excerpt in J. Cunliffe and G. Erreygers, eds., *The Origins of Universal Grants*, 141–148. Basingstoke: Palgrave Macmillan.

Haveman, Robert H. 1988. "The Changed Face of Poverty: A Call for New Policies." *Focus* 11(2): 10–14.

Hayek, Friedrich A. 1944/1986. *The Road to Serfdom.* London: Routledge and Kegan Paul, ARK ed.

———. 1945. "The Use of Knowledge in Society." *American Economic Review* 35(4): 519–530.

———. 1949/1967. "The Intellectuals and Socialism." In Hayek, *Studies in Philosophy, Politics and Economics*, 178–194. London: Routledge.

———. 1979. *Law, Legislation and Liberty*, vol. 3. Chicago: University of Chicago Press.

Healy, Seán, Michelle Murphy, and Brigid Reynolds. 2013. "Basic Income: An Instrument for Transformation in the Twenty-First Century." *Irish Journal of Sociology* 21(2): 116–130.

Healy, Seán, Michelle Murphy, Sean Ward, and Brigid Reynolds. 2012. "Basic Income—Why and How in Difficult Times: Financing a BI in Ireland." Paper presented at the BIEN Congress, Munich, September 14.

Healy, Seán, and Brigid Reynolds. 2000. "From Concept to Green Paper: Putting Basic Income on the Agenda in Ireland." In Robert-Jan van der Veen and Loek Groot, eds., *Basic Income on the Agenda,* 238–246. Amsterdam: Amsterdam University Press.

Hegel, Georg Wilhelm Friedrich. 1820/1991. *Elements of the Philosophy of Right.* Cambridge: Cambridge University Press.

Heineman, Ben, et al. 1969. *Poverty amid Plenty: The American Paradox. The Report of the President's Commission on Income Maintenance Programs.* Washington, DC: President's Commission on Income Maintenance Programs.

Hesketh, Bob. 1997. *Major Douglas and Alberta Social Credit Party.* Toronto: University of Toronto Press.

Heydorn, Oliver. 2014. *Social Credit Economics.* Ancaster: Createspace independent publishing platform.

Hildebrand, George H. 1967. *Poverty, Income Maintenance, and the Negative Income Tax.* Ithaca NY: New York State School of Industrial and Labor Relations, Cornell University.

Himmelfarb, Gertrude. 1970. "Bentham's Utopia: The National Charity Company." *Journal of British Studies* 10(1): 80–125.

———. 1997. "Introduction." In *Alexis de Tocqueville's Memoir on Pauperism,* 1–16. London: Civitas.

Hogenboom, Erik, and Raf Janssen. 1986. "Basic Income and the Claimants' Movement in the Netherlands." In Anne G. Miller, ed., *Proceedings of the First International Conference on Basic Income,* 237–255. London: BIRG and Antwerp: BIEN.

Holt, Steve. 2015. *Periodic Payment of the Earned Income Tax Revisited.* Washington DC: Brookings Institution.

Horne, Thomas A. 1988. "Welfare Rights as Property Rights." In J. Donald Moon, ed., *Responsibility, Rights and Welfare: The Theory of the Welfare State,* 107–132. Boulder: Westview Press.

Horstschräer, Julia, Markus Clauss, and Reinhold Schnabel. 2010. "An Unconditional Basic Income in the Family Context—Labor Supply and Distributional Effects." Discussion Paper No. 10–091, Zentrum für europäische Wirtschftforschung, Mannheim.

Hosang, Maik, ed. 2008. *Klimawandel und Grundeinkommen.* Munich: Andreas Mascha.

Howard, Christopher. 1997. *The Hidden Welfare State: Tax Expenditures and Social Policy in the United States.* Princeton: Princeton University Press.

Howard, Michael W. 2005. "Basic Income, Liberal Neutrality, Socialism, and Work." In Karl Widerquist, Michael Anthony Lewis, and Steven Pressman, eds., *The Ethics and Economics of the Basic Income Guarantee,* 122–137. New York: Ashgate.

———. 2006. "Basic Income and Migration Policy: A Moral Dilemma?" *Basic Income Studies* 1(1), article 4.

———. 2007. "A NAFTA Dividend: A Guaranteed Minimum Income for North America." *Basic Income Studies* 2(1), article 1.

———. 2012. "A Cap on Carbon and a Basic Income: A Defensible Combination in the United States?" In Karl Widerquist and Michael W. Howard, eds., *Exporting the Alaska Model*, 147–162. New York: Palgrave Macmillan.

———. 2015a. "Size of a Citizens' Dividend from Carbon Fees, Implications for Growth." BIEN News, September 14. www.basic income.org/news/2015/09/size-citizens-dividend -carbon-fees-implications-growth/.

———. 2015b. "Exploitation, Labor, and Basic Income." *Analyse & Kritik* 37(1/2): 281–303.

Howard, Michael W., and Robert Glover. 2014. "A Carrot, Not a Stick: Examining the Potential Role of Basic Income in US Immigration Policy." Paper presented at the 15th Congress of the Basic Income Earth Network (BIEN), Montreal, June.

Howard, Michael W., and Karl Widerquist, eds. 2012. *Alaska's Permanent Fund Dividend: Examining Its Suitability as a Model*. New York: Palgrave Macmillan.

Huber, Joseph. 1998. *Vollgeld. Beschäftigung, Grundsicherung und weniger Staatsquote durch eine modernisierte Geldordnung*. Berlin: Duncker & Humblot.

———. 1999. "Plain Money: A Proposal for Supplying the Nations with the Necessary Means in a Modern Monetary System." Forschungsberichte des Instituts für Soziologie 99–3, Martin-Luther-Universität Halle-Wittenberg.

Huber, Joseph, and James Robertson. 2000. *Creating New Money: A Monetary Reform for the Information Age*. London: New Economics Foundation.

Huet, François. 1853. *Le Règne social du christianisme*. Paris: Firmin Didot and Brussels: Decq.

Huff, Gerald. 2015. "Should We Be Afraid, Very Afraid? A Rebuttal of the Most Common Arguments against a Future of Technological Unemployment." Basic Income blogpost, May 25. https://medium.com/basic-income/should-we-be-afraid-very-afraid-4f7013a5137c.

Hum, Derek, and Wayne Simpson. 1991. *Income Maintenance, Work Effort, and the Canadian Mincome Experiment*. Ottawa: Economic Council of Canada.

———. 1993. "Economic Response to a Guaranteed Annual Income: Experience from Canada and the United States." *Journal of Labor Economics* 11(1): 263–296.

———. 2001. "A Guaranteed Annual Income? From Mincome to the Millenium." *Policy Options Politiques* 22(1): 78–82.

Hyafil, Jean-Eric, and Thibault Laurentjoye. 2016. *Revenu de base. Comment le financer?* Gap: Yves Michel.

IFOP. 2015. *Les Français et le libéralisme. Sondage IFOP pour l'Opinion / Génération libre / iTELE*. Paris: IFOP.

Iida, Fumio. 2014. "The Tensions between Multiculturalism and Basic Income in Japan." In Yannick Vanderborght and Toru Yamamori, eds., *Basic Income in Japan: Prospects of a Radical Idea in a Transforming Welfare State*, 157–168. New York: Palgrave Macmillan.

Ijdens, Teunis, Daniëlle de Laat-van Amelsfoort, and Marcel Quanjel. 2010. *Evaluatie van de Wet werk en inkomen kunstenaars (Wwik)*. Tilburg: IVA beleidsonderzoek en advies.

Internal Revenue Service (IRS). 2015. "EITC Participation Rate by States." https://www.eitc.irs.gov/EITC-Central/Participation-Rate.

International Monetary Fund. 2011. "IMF Executive Board Concludes 2011 Article IV Consultation with Kuwait." *Public Information Notice*, 11 / 93, July 19.

Ireland. 2002. *Basic Income: A Green Paper*. Dublin: Department of the Taoiseach.

Itaba, Yoshio. 2014. "What Do People Think about Basic Income in Japan?" In Yannick Vanderborght and Toru Yamamori, eds., *Basic Income in Japan: Prospects of a Radical Idea in a Transforming Welfare State*, 171–195. New York: Palgrave Macmillan.

Jackson, William A. 1999. "Basic Income and the Right to Work: A Keynesian Approach." *Journal of Post Keynesian Economics* 21(2): 639–662.

Jacobi, Dirk, and Wolfgang Strengmann-Kuhn, eds. 2012. *Wege zum Grundeinkommen*. Berlin: Heinrich Böll Stiftung.

Jauer, J., Thomas Liebig, John P. Martin, and Patrick Puhani. 2014. "Migration as an Adjustment Mechanism in the Crisis? A Comparison of Europe and the United States." OECD Social, Employment and Migration Working Papers, no. 155, OECD, Paris.

Jenkins, Davis. 2014. "Distribution and Disruption." *Basic Income Studies* 10(2): 257–279.

Jessen, Robin, Davud Rostam-Afschar, and Viktor Steiner. 2015. *Getting the Poor to Work: Three Welfare Increasing Reforms for a Busy Germany*. Discussion Paper 2015 / 22, School of Business and Economics, Freie Universität Berlin.

Johnson, Lyndon B. 1968. "Statement by the President upon Signing the Social Security Amendments and upon Appointing a Commission to Study the Nation's Welfare Programs." January 2. Online by Gerhard Peters and John T. Woolley, *The American Presidency Project*, http://www.presidency.ucsb.edu/ws/?pid=28915.

Johnson, Warren A. 1973. "The Guaranteed Income as an Environmental Measure." In Herman E. Daly, ed., *Toward a Steady-State Economy*, 175–189. San Francisco: Freeman.

Join-Lambert, Marie-Thérèse. 1998. *Chômage: mesures d'urgence et minima sociaux. Problèmes soulevés par les mouvements de chômeurs en France*. Paris: La Documentation française.

Jongen, Egbert, Henk-Wim de Boer, and Peter Dekker. 2014. *MICSIM—A Behavioural Microsimulation Model for the Analysis of Tax-Benefit Reform in the Netherlands*. Den Haag: Centraal Planbureau.

———. 2015. *Matwerk loont, Moeders prikkelbaar. De effectiviteit van fiscal participatiebeleid*. Den Haag: Centraal Planbureau.

Jordan, Bill. 1973. *Paupers: The Making of the New Claiming Class*. London: Routledge & Kegan Paul.

———. 1976. *Freedom and the Welfare State*. London: Routledge and Kegan.

———. 1986. "Basic Incomes and the Claimants' Movement." In Anne G. Miller, ed., *Proceedings of the First International Conference on Basic Income*, 257–268. London: BIRG and Antwerp: BIEN.

———. 1987. *Rethinking Welfare*. Oxford: Blackwell.

———. 1992. "Basic Income and the Common Good." In Philippe Van Parijs, ed., *Arguing for Basic Income: Ethical Foundations for a Radical Reform*, 155–177. London: Verso.

———. 1996. *A Theory of Poverty and Social Exclusion.* Cambridge, MA: Polity Press.

———. 2011. "The Perils of Basic Income: Ambiguous Opportunities for the Implementation of a Utopian Proposal." *Policy & Politics* 39(1): 101–114.

Jordan, Bill, Simon James, Helen Kay, and Marcus Redley. 1992. *Trapped in Poverty? Labour-Market Decisions in Low-Income Households.* London: Routledge.

Kaldor, Nicholas. 1955. *An Expenditure Tax.* London: George Allen and Unwin.

Kalliomaa-Puha, Laura, Anna-Kaisa Tuovinen, and Olli Kangas. 2016. "The Basic Income Experiment in Finland." *Journal of Social Security Law* 23(2): 75–88.

Kameeta, Zephania. 2009. "Foreword." In *Making the Difference: The BIG in Namibia*, vi–viii. Windhoek: Namibia NGO Forum.

Kangas, Olli, and Ville-Veikko Pulkka, eds. 2016. "Ideasta kokeiluun?—Esiselvitys perustulokokeilun" [From Idea to Experiment—Preliminary Report on a Universal Basic Income]. Prime Minister's Office, March 30, Helsinki.

Kant, Immanuel. 1797/1996. *Metaphysics of Morals.* Cambridge: Cambridge University Press.

Kaus, Mickey. 1992. *The End of Equality.* New York: Basic Books.

Kearl, James R. 1977. "Do Entitlements Imply That Taxation Is Theft?" *Philosophy and Public Affairs* 7(1): 74–81.

Kelly, Paul J. 1990. *Utilitarianism and Distributive Justice: Jeremy Bentham and the Civil Law.* Oxford: Clarendon Press.

Kershaw, David, and Jerilyn Fair. 1976. *The New Jersey Income-Maintenance Experiment*, vol. 1: *Operations, Surveys, and Administration.* New York: Academic Press.

Keynes, John Maynard. 1930a/1972. "Economic Possibilities for Our Grandchildren." In *Essays in Persuasion, The Collected Writings*, vol. 9: 321–332. London: Macmillan, for the Royal Economic Society.

———. 1930b/1981. "The Question of High Wages." In *Rethinking Employment and Unemployment Policies, The Collected Writings*, vol. 20, 2–16. London: Macmillan, for the Royal Economic Society.

King, Desmond. 1995. *Actively Seeking Work? The Politics of Unemployment and Welfare Policy in the United States and Great Britain.* Chicago: University of Chicago Press.

King, John E., and John Marangos. 2006. "Two Arguments for Basic Income: Thomas Paine (1737–1809) and Thomas Spence (1750–1814)." *History of Economic Ideas* 14(1): 55–71.

King, Martin Luther. 1967. *Where Do We Go From Here: Chaos or Community?* New York: Harper & Row.

Kipping, Katja. 2016a. "Ich streite schon über 15 Jahre für ein Grundeinkommen." Spreezeitung, February 8. www.spreezeitung.de/22398/katja-kipping-ich-streite-schon-ueber-15 -jahre-fuer-ein-grundeinkommen.

———. 2016b. "Grundeinkommen als Demokratiepauschale." Keynote speech at the Sixteenth Congress of the Basic Income Earth Network, Seoul, July. www.katja-kipping .de/de/article/1112.grundeinkommen-als-demokratiepauschale.html.

Klein, William A. 1977. "A Proposal for a Universal Personal Capital Account." Discussion Paper 422–77, Institute for Research on Poverty, University of Wisconsin–Madison.

Knott, John W. 1986. *Popular Opposition to the 1834 Poor Law.* London: Croom Helm.

Kobayashi, Hayato. 2014. "The Future of the Public Assistance Reform in Japan: Workfare versus Basic Income?" In Yannick Vanderborght and Toru Yamamori, eds., *Basic income in Japan: Prospects of a Radical Idea in a Transforming Welfare State,* 83–99. New York: Palgrave Macmillan.

Koistinen, Pertti, and Johanna Perkiö. 2014. "Good and Bad Times of Social Innovations: The Case of Universal Basic Income in Finland." *Basic Income Studies* 9(1–2): 25–57.

Kooistra, Pieter. 1983. *Voor.* Amsterdam: Stichting UNO-inkomen voor alle mensen.

———. 1994. *Het ideale eigenbelang, Een UNO–Marshallplan voor alle mensen.* Kampen: Kok Agora.

Kornbluh, Felicia. 2007. *The Battle for Welfare Rights: Politics and Poverty in Modern America.* Philadelphia: University of Pennsylvania Press.

Korpi, Walter, and Joakim Palme. 1998. "The Paradox of Redistribution and Strategies of Equality: Welfare State Institutions, Inequality, and Poverty in the Western Countries." *American Sociological Review* 63(5): 661–687.

Krätke, Michael. 1985. "Ist das Grundeinkommen für jedermann Weg zur Reform der sozialen Sicherheit?" In Michael Opielka and Georg Vobruba, eds., *Das Grundeinkommen.* Frankfurt: Campus.

Krause-Junk, Gerold. 1996. "Probleme einer Integration von Einkommensbesteuerung und steuerfinanzierten Sozialleistungen." *Wirtschaftsdienst* 7: 345–349.

Krebs, Angelika, ed. 2000. *Basic Income? A Symposium on Van Parijs.* Special Issue of *Analyse & Kritik* 22.

———. 2000. "Why Mothers Should Be Fed." In Angelika Krebs, ed., *Basic Income? A Symposium on Van Parijs.* Special Issue of *Analyse & Kritik* 22: 155–178.

Kropotkin, Peter. 1892/1985. *The Conquest of Bread.* London: Elephant Editions.

Krug, Leopold. 1810. *Die Armenassekuranz, das einzige Mittel zur Verbannung der Armuth aus unserer Kommune.* Berlin: Realschulbuchhandlung.

Krugman, Paul. 2011. "Boring Cruel Romantics." *New York Times,* November 20.

Kuiper, Jan Pieter. 1975. "Niet meer werken om den brode." In M. Van Gils, ed., *Werken en niet-werken in een veranderende omgeving.* Amsterdam: Swets & Zeitliger.

———. 1976. "Arbeid en Inkomen: twee plichten en twee rechten." *Sociaal Maandblad Arbeid* 9: 503–512.

———. 1977. "Samenhang verbreken tussen arbeid en levensonderhoud." *Bouw* 19: 507–515.

———. 1982. "Een samenleving met gegarandeerd inkomen." *Wending,* April, 278–283.

Kundig, Bernard. 2010. "Financement mixte d'un revenue de base en Suisse." In BIEN-Suisse, ed., *Le financement d'un revenu de base en Suisse,* 28–56. Geneva: Seismo.

Lampman, Robert J. 1965. "Approaches to the Reduction of Poverty." *American Economic Review* 55(1/2): 521–529.

Landelijk Beraad Uitkeringsgerechtigden. 1986. *Een basisinkomen van FL.1500,- per maand.* Nijmegen: LBU.

Lang, Kevin, and Andrew Weiss. 1990. "Tagging, Stigma, and Basic Income Guarantees." Paper presented at the Conference "Basic Income Guarantees: a New Welfare Strategy?" University of Wisconsin, Madison, April.

Lange, Oskar. 1937. "Mr Lerner's Note on Socialist Economics." *Review of Economic Studies* 4(2): 143–144.

Lavagne, Pierre, and Frédéric Naud. 1992. "Revenu d'existence: une solution à la crise agricole." In Gilles Gantelet and Jean-Paul Maréchal, eds., *Garantir le revenu: une des solutions a l'exclusion,* 95–106. Paris: Transversales Science Culture.

Lavinas, Lena. 2013. "Brazil: The Lost Road to Citizen's Income." In Ruben Lo Vuolo, ed. *Citizen's Income and Welfare Regimes in Latin America: From Cash Transfers to Rights,* 29–49. New York: Palgrave Macmillan.

Lechat, Benoît. 2014. *Ecolo. La démocratie comme projet 1970–1986.* Brussels: Etopia.

Le Grand, Julian. 2003. *Motivation, Agency and Public Policy.* Oxford: Oxford University Press.

Legum, Margaret. 2004. "An Economy of Our Own." SANE Views 4(8), July. The Hague: Centraal Planbureau.

Leman, Christopher. 1980. *The Collapse of Welfare Reform: Political Institutions, Policy and the Poor in Canada and the United States.* Cambridge, MA: MIT Press.

Lenkowsky, Leslie. 1986. *Politics, Economics, and Welfare Reform: The Failure of the Negative Income Tax in Britain and the United States.* New York: University Press of America.

Lerner, Abba P. 1936. "A Note on Socialist Economics." *Review of Economic Studies* 4(1): 72–76.

———. 1944. *Economics of Control: Principles of Welfare Economics.* New York: Macmillan.

Le Roux, Pieter. 2003. "Why a Universal Income Grant in South Africa Should Be Financed through VAT and Other Indirect Taxes." In Guy Standing and Michael Samson, eds., *A Basic Income Grant for South Africa,* 39–55. Cape Town: University of Cape Town Press.

Letlhokwa, George Mpedi. 2013. "Current Approaches to Social Protection in the Republic of South Africa." In James Midgley and David Piachaud, eds., *Social Protection, Economic Growth and Social Change,* 217–242. Cheltenham: Edward Elgar.

Levine, Robert A. et al. 2005. "A Retrospective on the Negative Income Tax Experiments: Looking Back at the Most Innovative Field Studies in Social Policy." In Karl Widerquist, Michael Anthony Lewis, and Steven Pressman, eds., *The Ethics and Economics of the Basic Income Guarantee,* 95–106. New York: Ashgate.

Lévi-Strauss, Claude. 1967. *Les Structures élementaires de la parenté.* Paris: Mouton.

Levy, Horacio, Christine Lietz, and Holly Sutherland. 2006. "A Basic Income for Europe's Children?" ISER Working Paper, 2006–47, Institute for Social and Economic Research, University of Essex.

Lewis, Michael. 2012. "Cost, Compensation, Freedom, and the Basic Income—Guaranteed Jobs Debate." *Basic Income Studies* 7(2): 41–51.

Locke, John. 1689. *First Treatise on Government.* London: Awnsham Churchill.

———. 1697. "On the Poor Law and Working Schools." http://la.utexas.edu/users/hcleaver /330T/350kPEELockePoorEdTable.pdf.

Long, Huey P. 1934. "Share Our Wealth: Every Man a King." In Robert C. Byrd, ed., *The Senate 1789–1989: Classic Speeches 1830–1993,* vol. 3, Bicentennial Edition, 587–593. Washington DC: U.S. Senate Historical Office, 1994. Radio address transcript: http://www .senate.gov/artandhistory/history/resources/pdf/EveryManKing.pdf.

———. 1935. "Statement of the Share Our Wealth Movement (May 23, 1935)." *Congressional Record,* 74th Congress, first session, vol. 79, 8040–43.

Longman, Phillip. 1987. *Born to Pay: The New Politics of Aging in America.* Boston: Houghton Mifflin.

Lubbers, Ruud F. M. 1985. "Standpunt met betrekking tot het WRR rapport 'Waarborgen voor zekerheid.'" The Hague: Kabinet van de Minister-President, 9 oktober.

Lubbi, Greetje. 1991. "Towards a Full Basic Income." *Basic Income Research Group Bulletin* (London) 12 (February 1991): 15–16.

Luxemburg, Rosa. 1918. "Die Sozialisierung der Gesellschaft." In *Gesammelte Werke,* Berlin 1970–1975, vol. 4, 431–434. English translation: "The Socialisation of Society." www .marxists.org/archive/luxemburg/1918/12/20.

Machiavelli, Niccoló. 1517/1969. *Discorsi sopra la prima deca di Tito Livio.* Reprinted in N. Machiavelli, *Opere,* 69–342. Milano: Mursia.

Malthus, Thomas Robert. 1798/1976. *An Essay on the Principle of Population.* New York: Norton.

Marc, Alexandre. 1972. "Redécouverte du minimum vital garanti." *L'Europe en formation* 143: 19–25.

———. 1988. "Minimum social garanti, faux ou vrai?" *L'Europe en formation* 272: 13–21.

Marcuse, Herbert. 1967. *Das Ende der Utopie und das Problem der Gewalt.* Berlin: Verlag Peter von Maikowski. English translation: Herbert Marcuse Home Page, May 2005.

Martz, Linda. 1983. *Poverty and Welfare in Habsburg Spain: The Example of Toledo.* Cambridge: Cambridge University Press.

Marx, Axel, and Hans Peeters. 2004. "Win for Life: An Empirical Exploration of the Social Consequences of Introducing a Basic Income." COMPASSS working paper WP2004–29.

Marx, Karl. 1867/1962. *Das Kapital,* vol. 1. Berlin: Dietz.

———. 1875/1962. "Randglossen zum Programm der deutschen Arbeiterpartei." In Karl Marx and Friedrich Engels, *Werke,* vol. 19, 13–32. Berlin: Dietz.

Mason, Paul. 2015. *PostCapitalism: A Guide to Our Future.* London: Allen Lane.

Matoba, Akihiro. 2006. "The Brussels Democratic Association and the Communist Manifesto." In Hiroshi Uchida, ed., *Marx for the 21st Century,* 165–178. London: Routledge.

Matthews, Dylan. 2014. "Mexico Tried Giving Poor People Cash Instead of Food. It Worked." Vox, June 26. http://www.vox.com/2014/6/26/5845258/mexico-tried-giving -poor-people-cash-instead-of-food-it-worked.

McGovern, George. 1974. *An American Journey: The Presidential Speeches of George McGovern.* New York: Random House.

———. 1977. *Grassroots: The Autobiography of George McGovern.* New York: Random House.

McGovern, George, and Wassily Leontief. 1972. "George McGovern: On Taxing and Redistributing Income." *New York Review of Books,* May 4.

McKay, Ailsa. 2001. "Rethinking Work and Income Maintenance Policy: Promoting Gender Equality through a Citizens Basic Income." *Feminist Economics* 7: 93–114.

———. 2005. *The Future of Social Security Policy: Women, Work and a Citizen's Basic Income.* London: Routledge.

———. 2007. "Why a Citizens' Basic Income? A Question of Gender Equality or Gender Bias." *Work, Employment & Society* 21: 337–348.

McLuhan, Marshall. 1967. "Guaranteed Income in the Electric Age." In Robert Theobald, ed., *The Guaranteed Income: Next Step in Socioeconomic Evolution?* 194–205. New York: Doubleday.

Meade, James E. 1935/1988. "Outline of an Economic Policy for a Labour Government." In Meade, *The Collected Papers of James Meade,* ed. Susan Howsen, vol. 1: *Employment and Inflation,* ch. 4. London: Unwin Hyman.

———. 1937. *An Introduction to Economic Analysis and Policy.* Oxford: Oxford University Press.

———. 1938. *Consumers' Credits and Unemployment.* Oxford: Oxford University Press.

———. 1948. *Planning and the Price Mechanism: The Liberal-Socialist Solution.* London: Allen and Unwin.

———. 1957. "The Balance of Payments Problems of a Free Trade Area." *Economic Journal* 67(3): 379–396.

———. 1971. *The Intelligent Radical's Guide to Economic Policy.* London: Allen and Unwin.

———. 1989. *Agathotopia: The Economics of Partnership.* Aberdeen: Aberdeen University Press.

———. 1993. *Liberty, Equality and Efficiency.* London: Macmillan.

———. 1995. *Full Employment Regained?* Cambridge: Cambridge University Press.

Meade, James E., ed. 1978. *The Structure and Reform of Direct Taxation. Report of a Committee Chaired by James E. Meade.* London: George Allen & Unwin.

———. 1991. "Basic Income in the New Europe." *BIRG Bulletin* 13: 4–6.

Meyer, Niels I. 1986. "Alternative National Budget for Denmark Including a Basic Income." Paper presented at the First International Conference on Basic Income, Louvain-la-Neuve, September.

Meyer, Niels I., Kristen Helveg Petersen, and Villy Sørensen. 1978. *Oprør fra midten,* Copenhague: Gyldendal. English translation: *Revolt from the Center.* London: Marion Boyars, 1981.

Milanovic, Branco. 2016. *Global Inequality: A New Approach for the Age of Globalization.* Cambridge, MA: Harvard University Press.

Mill, John Stuart. 1848/1904. *Principles of Political Economy.* London: Longmans, Green & Co.

———. 1861. *Considerations on Representative Government.* London: Parker, Son, and Bourn.

———. 1870/1969. *Autobiography*. Oxford: Oxford University Press.

———. 1879/1987. *On Socialism*. Buffalo NY: Prometheus Books.

Miller, Anne G. 1983. "In Praise of Social Dividends." Working Paper 83.1, Department of Economics, Heriot-Watt University, Edinburgh.

———. 1988. "Basic Income and Women." In Anne G. Miller, ed., *Proceedings of the First International Conference on Basic Income*, 11–23. London: BIRG and Antwerp: BIEN.

Miller, David. 1992. "Distributive Justice: What the People Think." *Ethics* 102: 555–593.

Miller, Raymond K. 1987. "Social Credit, an Analysis of New Zealand's Perennial Third Party." PhD diss., University of Auckland.

Milner, Dennis. 1920. *Higher Production by a Bonus on National Output: A Proposal for a Minimum Income for All Varying with National Productivity*. London: George Allen & Unwin.

Milner, Mabel, and Dennis Milner. 1918. *Scheme for a State Bonus*. London: Kent, Simpkin, Marshall & Co.

Mirrlees James A. 1971. "An Exploration in the Theory of Optimum Income Taxation." *Review of Economic Studies* 38(2): 175–208.

Mitschke, Joachim. 1985. *Steuer- und Transferordnung aus einem Guß. Entwurf einer Neugestaltung der direkten Steuern und Sozialtransfers in der Bundesrepublik Deutschland*. Baden-Baden: Nomos.

———. 1997. "Höhere Niedriglöhne durch Sozialhilfe oder Bürgergeld?" *Frankfurter Allgemeine*, September 28.

———. 2004. *Erneuerung des deutschen Einkommensteuerrechts*. Köln: Otto Schmidt Verlag.

Montesquieu, Charles-Louis de Secondat, baron de. 1748. *L'Esprit des Lois*, vol. 2. Paris: Flammarion.

More, Thomas. 1516/1978. *Utopia*. Harmondsworth: Penguin.

Morini, Cristina. 1999. "Alla ricerca della libertà: donne e reddito di cittadinanza." In Andrea Fumagalli and Maurizio Lazzarotto, eds., *Tute bianche. Disoccupazione di massa e reddito di cittadinanza*, 45–54. Rome: Derive Approdi.

Moynihan, Daniel Patrick. 1973. *The Politics of a Guaranteed Income: The Nixon Administration and the Family Assistance Plan*. New York: Random House.

Muellbauer, John. 2014. "Quantitative Easing for the People." Project Syndicate blog post, November 5. https://www.project-syndicate.org/commentary/helicopter-drops -eurozone-deflation-by-john-muellbauer-2014-11?barrier=true.

Müller, Christian, and Daniel Straub. 2016. *Die Befreing der Schweiz. Über das bedingungslose Grundeinkommen*. Zürich: Limmat Verlag.

Müller, Tobias. 2004. "Evaluating the Economic Effects of Income Security Reforms in Switzerland: An Integrated Microsimulation—Computable General Equilibrium Approach." June, Department of Econometrics, University of Geneva.

Mulvale, James P., and Yannick Vanderborght. 2012. "Canada: A Guaranteed Income Framework to Address Poverty and Inequality?" In Richard K. Caputo, ed., *Basic Income Guarantee and Politics: International Experiences and Perspectives on the Viability of Income Guarantees*, 177–201. New York: Palgrave Macmillan.

Murphy, Richard, and Howard Reed. 2013. "Financing the Social State: Towards a Full Employment Economy." Policy paper, April, Centre for Labour and Social Studies, London.

Murray, Charles. 2006. *In Our Hands: A Plan to Replace the Welfare State.* Washington, DC: AEI Press.

———. 2016. "A Guaranteed Income for Every American." *Wall Street Journal,* June 3. http://www.wsj.com/articles/a-guaranteed-income-for-every-american-1464969586.

Musgrave, Richard A. 1974. "Maximin, Uncertainty, and the Leisure Trade-Off." *Quarterly Journal of Economics* 88(4): 625–632.

Mylondo, Baptiste. 2010. *Un revenu pour tous! Précis d'utopie réaliste.* Paris: Utopia.

———. 2012. "Can a Basic Income Lead to Economic Degrowth?" Paper presented at the 14th Congress of the Basic Income Earth Network (BIEN), Munich, September 14–16.

Myrdal, Alva. 1945. "In Cash or In Kind." In Alva Myrdal, *Nation and Family: The Swedish Experiment in Democratic Family and Population Policy,* 133–153. London: Kegan Paul.

National Welfare Rights Organization. 1969/2003. "Proposals for a Guaranteed Adequate Income (1969)." In Gwendolyn Mink and Rickie Solinger, eds. *Welfare: A Documentary History of U.S. Policy and Politics,* 320–321. New York: New York University Press.

Nicholls, George. 1854. *A History of the English Poor Law in Connexion with the Legislation and Other Circumstances Affecting the Condition of the People,* vol. 1. London: John Murray.

Nichols, Austin, and Jesse Rothstein. 2015. "The Earned Income Tax Credit (EITC)." NBER Working Paper 21211, May. http://www.nber.org/papers/w21211.

Nixon, Richard. 1969. "Address to the Nation on Domestic Programs." August 8. Online by Gerhard Peters and John T. Woolley, *The American Presidency Project.* http://www.presidency.ucsb.edu/ws/?pid=2191.

Nobrega, Francisco. 2015. "Basic Income Alternative Reconsidered." Basic Income Earth Network blog post, June 12. http://basicincome.org/news/2015/06/basic-income-alternatives-reconsidered/.

Noguchi, Eri. 2012. "The Cost-Efficiency of a Guaranteed Jobs Program: Really? A Response to Harvey." *Basic Income Studies* 7(2): 52–65.

Nooteboom, Bart. 1986. "Basic Income as a Basis for Small Business." *International Small Business Journal* 5(3): 10–18.

Nozick, Robert. 1974. *Anarchy, State and Utopia.* Oxford: Blackwell.

———. 1989. *The Examined Life: Philosophical Meditation.* New York: Simon & Schuster.

Nyerere, Julius K. 1968. *Ujamaa: Essays on Socialism.* Oxford: Oxford University Press.

Nyland, Chris, Mingqiong Zhang, and Cherrie Jiuhua Zhu. 2014. "The Institution of Hukou-Based Social Exclusion: A Unique Institution Reshaping the Characteristics of Contemporary Urban China." *International Journal of Urban and Regional Research* 38(4): 1437–1457.

Nystrom, Scott, and Patrick Luckow. 2014. "The Economic, Climate, Fiscal, Power, and Demographic Impact of a National Fee-and-Dividend Carbon Tax." Prepared by Regional Economic Models, Inc., Washington DC, and Synapse Energy Economics, Inc., Cambridge, MA, for Citizens' Climate Lobby, Coronado CA. http://citizensclimatelobby.org/wp-content/uploads/2014/06/REMI-carbon-tax-report-62141.pdf.

Obinger, Julia. 2014. "Beyond the Paradigm of Labor: Everyday Activism and Unconditional Basic Income in Urban Japan." In Yannick Vanderborght and Toru Yamamori, eds., *Basic Income in Japan: Prospects of a Radical Idea in a Transforming Welfare State*, 141–155. New York: Palgrave Macmillan.

OECD. 2012. *OECD Economic Surveys: European Union 2012*. Paris: OECD Publishing.

Offe, Claus. 1985. "He Who Does Not Work Shall Nevertheless Eat." *Development* 2: 26–30.

———. 1992. "A Non-Productivist Design for Social Policies." In Philippe Van Parijs, ed., *Arguing for Basic Income: Ethical Foundations for a Radical Reform*, 61–78. London: Verso.

———. 1996a. "Full Employment: Asking the Wrong Question?" In Erik O. Eriksen and Jorn Loftager, eds., *The Rationality of the Welfare State*, 121–131. Oslo: Scandinavian University Press.

———. 1996b. "A Basic Income Guaranteed by the State: A Need of the Moment in Social Policy." In Offe, *Modernity and the State: East, West*, 201–221. Cambridge, MA: Polity.

Ontario. 2016. *Jobs for Today and Tomorrow. 2016 Ontario Budget: Budget Papers*. Ontario: Queen's Printer for Ontario. http://www.fin.gov.on.ca/en/budget/ontariobudgets/2016/papers_all.pdf.

Opielka, Michael, and Ilona Ostner, eds. 1987. *Umbau des Sozialstaats*. Essen: Klartext.

Opielka, Michael, and Georg Vobruba, eds. 1986. *Das garantierte Grundeinkommen. Entwicklung und Perspektiven einer Forderung*. Frankfurt: Fischer.

O'Reilly, Jacqueline. 2008. "Can a Basic Income Lead to a More Gender Equal Society?" *Basic Income Studies* 3(3): 1–7.

Orloff, Ann S. 1990/2013. "Why Basic Income Does Not Promote Gender Equality." In Karl Widerquist et al., eds., *Basic Income: An Anthology of Contemporary Research*, 149–152. New York: Wiley-Blackwell.

Ortiz, Isabel. 2015. "Social Protection for Children: Key Policy Trends and Statistics." Social Protection Policy Paper 14, December 6, International Labour Organization, Geneva. http://www.ilo.org/secsoc/information-resources/publications-and-tools/policy-papers/WCMS_366592/lang—en/index.htm.

Osterkamp, Rigmar. 2013a. "Lessons from Failure." Development and Cooperation blog post, March 5. www.dandc.eu/en/article/disappointing-basic-income-grant-project-namibia.

———. 2013b. "The Basic Income Grant Pilot Project in Namibia: A Critical Assessment." *Basic Income Studies* 8(1): 71–91.

Otsuka, Michael. 2003. *Libertarianism without Inequality*. Oxford: Oxford University Press.

Paine, Thomas. 1791/1974. "The Rights of Man." In Philip S. Foner, ed., *The Life and Major Writings of Thomas Paine*, 241–458. New York: Citadel Press.

———. 1796/1974. *Agrarian Justice*. In Philip S. Foner, ed., *The Life and Major Writings of Thomas Paine*, 605–623. New York: Citadel Press.

Painter, Anthony, and Chris Thoung. 2015. *Creative Citizen, Creative State: The Principled and Pragmatic Case for a Universal Basic Income.* London: Royal Society for the Encouragement of Arts.

Parker, Hermione. 1982. "Basic Income Guarantee Scheme: Synopsis." In *The Structure of Personal Income Taxation and Income Support* (House of Commons, Treasury and Civil Service Committee), 424–453. London: HMSO.

———. 1988. "Obituary: Sir Brandon Rhys-Williams." *BIRG Bulletin* 8: 21–22.

———. 1989. *Instead of the Dole: An Enquiry into the Integration of the Tax and Benefit Systems.* London: Routledge.

———. 1993. "Citizen's Income and Women." Discussion Paper no. 2, Citizens Income Study Centre, London.

Parti socialiste. 2016. "Entreprendre, travailler, s'accomplir. Les Cahiers de la Présidentielle." April, Parti socialiste, Paris. http://www.parti-socialiste.fr/wp-content/uploads/2016/04/CAHIER_n1_entreprendre_DEF2.pdf.

Pateman, Carole. 2004/2013. "Free-Riding and the Household." In Karl Widerquist, Jose A. Noguera, Yannick Vanderborght, and Jurgen De Wispelaere, eds., *Basic Income: An Anthology of Contemporary Research*, 173–177. New York: Wiley-Blackwell.

———. 2006. "Democratizing Citizenship: Some Advantages of a Basic Income." In Erik Olin Wright, ed., *Redesigning Distribution*, 101–119. London: Verso.

———. 2011. "Securing Women's Citizenship: Indifference and Other Obstacles." *Eurozine*, March 7. http://www.eurozine.com/articles/2011-03-07-pateman-en.html.

Pechman, Joseph A., and P. Michael Timpane, eds. 1975. *Work Incentives and Income Guarantees: The New Jersey Negative Income Tax Experiment.* Washington DC: Brookings Institution.

Peeters, Hans, and Axel Marx. 2006. "Lottery Games as a Tool for Empirical Basic Income Research." *Basic Income Studies* 1(2): 1–7.

Pelzer, Helmut. 1996. "Bürgergeld—Vergleich zweier Modelle." *Zeitschrift für Sozialreform* 42: 595–613.

Pen, Jan. 1971. *Income Distribution.* London: Alan Lane Penguin Press.

Peny, Christine. 2011. "Les dépôts de mendicité sous l'Ancien Régime et les débuts de l'assistance publique aux malades mentaux (1764–1790)." *Revue d'histoire de la protection sociale* 1(4): 9–23.

Permanent Fund Dividend Division. 2015. Annual report 2015, State of Alaska, Department of Revenue, Juneau.

Perrin, Guy. 1983. "L'assurance sociale—ses particularités—son rôle dans le passé, le présent et l'avenir." In Peter A. Köhler and Hans Friedrich Zacher, eds., *Beiträge zu Geschichte und aktueller Situation der Sozialversicherung*, 29–73. Berlin: Duncker & Humblot.

Petersen, Hans-Georg. 1997. "Pros and Cons of a Negative Income Tax." In Herbert Giersch, ed., *Reforming the Welfare State*, 53–82. Berlin: Springer.

Peterson, Paul E. 1995. *The Price of Federalism.* Washington DC: Brookings.

Peterson, Paul E., and Mark C. Rom. 1990. *Welfare Magnets: A New Case for National Standards.* Washington DC: Brookings Institution.

Pettit, Philip. 1999. *Republicanism: A Theory of Freedom and Government.* Oxford: Oxford University Press.

Phelps, Edmund S. 1994. "Low-Wage Employment Subsidies versus the Welfare State." *American Economic Review, Papers and Proceedings* 84(2): 54–58.

———. 1997. *Rewarding Work.* Cambridge, MA: Harvard University Press.

———. 2001. "Subsidize Wages." In Philippe Van Parijs et al., *What's Wrong with a Free Lunch?* 51–59. Boston: Beacon Press.

Pickard, Bertram. 1919. *A Reasonable Revolution. Being a Discussion of the State Bonus Scheme—A Proposal for a National Minimum Income.* London: George Allen & Unwin.

Pigou, Arthur Cecil. 1920/1932. *The Economics of Welfare.* London: MacMillan.

Piketty, Thomas. 1994. "Existence of Fair Allocations in Economies with Production." *Journal of Public Economics* 55: 391–405.

———. 1997. "La redistribution fiscale face au chômage." *Revue française d'économie* 12: 157–201.

———. 1999. "Allocation compensatrice de revenu ou revenu universel." In R. Godino et al., *Pour une réforme du RMI, Notes de la Fondation Saint Simon* 104, 21–29.

———. 2014. *Capital in the Twenty-First Century.* Cambridge, MA: Harvard University Press.

———. 2015a. *The Economics of Inequality.* Cambridge, MA: Harvard University Press.

———. 2015b. "Capital, Inequality and Justice: Reflections on *Capital in the 21st Century.*" *Basic Income Studies* 10(1): 141–156.

Piketty, Thomas, and Emmanuel Saez. 2012. "Optimal Labor Income Taxation." NBER Working Paper 18521, November, NBER, Cambridge, MA.

Pisani-Ferry, Jean, ed. 2000. *Plein emploi.* Paris: Conseil d'Analyse économique—La Documentation Française.

Pisani-Ferry, Jean, Erkki Vihriälä, and Guntram Wolff. 2013. "Options for an Euro-Area Fiscal Capacity." January, Bruegel Policy Contribution, Brussels.

Piven, Frances Fox, and Richard Cloward. 1993. *Regulating the Poor: The Functions of Public Welfare,* updated edition. New York: Vintage Books.

Pogge, Thomas. 1994. "An Egalitarian Law of Peoples." *Philosophy and Public Affairs* 23(3): 195–224.

———. 2001. "Eradicating Systemic Poverty: Brief for a Global Resources Dividend." *Journal of Human Development and Capabilities* 2(1): 59–77.

———. 2005. "Global Justice as Moral Issue: Interview with Alessandro Pinzani." *Ethic@* 4(1): 1–6.

Polanyi, Karl. 1944/1957. *The Great Transformation: The Political and Economic Origins of Our Time.* Boston: Beacon Press.

Popper, Karl. 1948/1963. "Utopia and Violence." In Popper, *Conjectures and Refutations,* 355–363. London: Routledge.

Popper-Lynkeus, Joseph. 1912. *Die allgemeine Nährpflicht als Lösung der sozialen Frage.* Dresden: Carl Reissner Verlag.

Prats, Magali. 1996. "L'allocation universelle à l'épreuve de la *Théorie de la justice*." *Documents pour l'enseignement économique et social* 106: 71–110.

Preiss, Joshua. 2015. "Milton Friedman on Freedom and the Negative Income Tax." *Basic Income Studies* 10(2): 169–191.

Quadagno, Jill. 1995. *The Color of Welfare: How Racism Undermined the War on Poverty*. New York: Oxford University Press.

Québec solidaire. 2014. *Plateforme électorale. Elections 2014*. Montréal: Québec solidaire.

Quinn, Michael. 1994. "Jeremy Bentham on the Relief of Indigence: An Exercise in Applied Philosophy." *Utilitas* 6(1): 81–96.

Raes, Koen. 1985. "Variaties op een thema. Kritiek op de loskoppeling." *Komma* 22: 21–32.

———. 1988/2013. "Basic Income and Social Power." In K. Widerquist Karl, J. A. Noguera, Y. Vanderborght, and J. De Wispelaere, eds., *Basic Income: An Anthology of Contemporary Research*, 246–254. New York: Wiley-Blackwell.

Rankin, Keith. 2016. "Basic Income as Public Equity: The New Zealand Case." In Jennifer Mays, Greg Marston, and John Tomlinson, eds., *Basic Income in Australia and New Zealand: Perspectives from the Neoliberal Frontier*, 29–51. New York: Palgrave Macmillan.

Rathke, Wade. 2001. "Falling in Love Again." In Philippe Van Parijs et al., *What's Wrong with a Free Lunch?* 39–42. Boston: Beacon Press.

Rätz, Werner, and Hardy Krampertz. 2011. *Bedingungsloses Grundeinkommen: woher, wozu und wohin?* Neu-Ulm: AG Spak.

Rätz, Werner, Dagmar Paternoga, and Werner Steinbach. 2005. *Grundeinkommen: bedingungslos*. Hamburg: VSA Verlag.

Raventos, Daniel. 1999. *El derecho a la existencia*, Barcelona: Ariel.

———. 2007. *Basic Income: The Material Conditions of Freedom*. London: Pluto Press.

Rawls, John. 1967. "Distributive Justice." In Rawls, *Collected Papers*, 130–153. Cambridge, MA: Harvard University Press.

———. 1971. *A Theory of Justice*. Cambridge, MA: Harvard University Press.

———. 1974. "Reply to Alexander and Musgrave." *Quarterly Journal of Economics* 88: 633–655. Reprinted in Rawls, *Collected Papers*, 232–253. Cambridge, MA: Harvard University Press.

———. 1988. "The Priority of Right and Ideas of the Good." *Philosophy and Public Affairs* 17: 251–276.

———. 1993. *Political Liberalism*. New York: Columbia University Press.

———. 1999. *The Law of Peoples*. Cambridge, MA: Harvard University Press.

———. 2001. *Justice as Fairness*. Cambridge, MA: Harvard University Press.

Rawls, John, and Philippe Van Parijs. 2003. "Three Letters on the Law of Peoples and the European Union." *Revue de philosophie économique* 8: 7–20.

Razin, Assaf, and Jackline Wahba. 2015. "Welfare Magnet Hypothesis, Fiscal Burden, and Immigration Skill Selectivity." *Scandinavian Journal of Economics* 117(2): 369–402.

Read, Samuel. 1829. *An Enquiry into the Natural Grounds of Right to Vendible Property or Wealth*. Edinburgh: Oliver and Boyd.

Reed, Howard, and Stewart Lansley. 2016. *Universal Basic Income: An Idea whose Time Has Come?* London: Compass.

Reeskens, Tim, and Wim van Oorschot. 2013. "Equity, Equality, or Need? A Study of Popular Preferences for Welfare Redistribution Principles across 24 European Countries." *Journal of European Public Policy* 20(8): 1174–1195.

Reeve, Andrew, and Andrew Williams, eds. 2003. *Real Libertarianism Assessed: Political Theory after Van Parijs.* Basingstoke: Palgrave Macmillan.

Reeves, Richard V. 2016. "Time to Take Basic Income Seriously." Brookings Opinion, February 23. http://www.brookings.edu/research/opinions/2016/02/23-time-to-take-basic-income-seriously-reeves.

Regnard, Albert. 1889. "Du droit à l'assistance." *La Revue socialiste* 10(September): 257–275. http://archive.org/stream/larevuesocialist10part/larevuesocialist10part_djvu.txt.

Reich, Robert. 2015. *Saving Capitalism: For the Many, Not the Few.* New York: Knopf.

Réseau Salariat. 2014. *Revenu inconditionnel ou salaire à vie?* Malzeville: Réseau Salariat.

Reynolds, Brigid, and Seán Healy, eds. 1995. *An Adequate Income Guarantee for All.* Dublin: CORI Justice Commission.

Rhys-Williams, Brandon. 1982. "The Reform of Personal Income Taxation and Income Support. Proposals for a Basic Income Guarantee." House of Commons, Sub-Committee on the Structure of Personal Income Taxation and Income Support, 420–424. London: HMSO.

Rhys-Williams, Juliet. 1943. *Something to Look Forward To: A Suggestion for a New Social Contract.* London: Macdonald.

Ricardo, David. 1817/1951. *Principles of Political Economy and Taxation.* In Piero Sraffa, ed., *The Works and Correspondence of David Ricardo,* vol. 1. Cambridge: Cambridge University Press.

Rignano, Eugenio. 1919. "A Plea for Greater Economic Democratization." *Economic Journal* 29: 302–308.

Ringen, Stein. 1997. *Citizens, Families and Reform.* Oxford: Oxford University Press.

Ritter, Gerhard A. 1904/1983. *Sozialversicherung in Deutschland und England.* München: Beck.

Roberts, Keith V. 1982. *Automation, Unemployment and the Distribution of Income.* Maastricht: European Centre for Work and Society.

Roberts, Yvonne. 2014. "Low-Paid Britain: 'People Have Had Enough. It's Soul Destroying.'" *The Observer,* August 30. http://www.theguardian.com/society/2014/aug/30/low-pay-britain-fightback-begins.

Robertson, James. 1989. *Future Wealth: A New Economics for the 21st Century.* London: Cassell.

———. 1994. *Benefits and Taxes: A Radical Strategy.* London: New Economics Foundation.

———, ed. 1998. *Sharing Our Common Heritage: Resource Taxes and Green Dividends.* Oxford: Oxford Centre for the Environment, Ethics and Society.

Robeyns, Ingrid. 2001a. "An Income of One's Own." *Gender and Development* 9: 82–89.

———. 2001b. "Will a Basic Income Do Justice to Women?" *Analyse und Kritik* 23: 88–105.

Roemer, John E. 1992. "The Morality and Efficiency of Market Socialism." *Ethics* 102: 448–464. Reprinted in J. E. Roemer, *Egalitarian Perspectives*, 287–302. Cambridge: Cambridge University Press, 1994.

———. 1996. *Equal Shares: Making Market Socialism Work*. London: Verso.

Roland, Gérard. 1988. "Why Socialism Needs Basic Income, Why Basic Income Needs Socialism." In Anne G. Miller, ed., *Proceedings of the First International Conference on Basic Income*, 94–105. London: BIRG.

Rosseels, David. 2009. *Implementation of a Tax on Electronic Transactions*. Université catholique de Louvain: Louvain School of Management.

Rossi, Peter H., and Katharine C. Lyall. 1976. *Reforming Public Welfare: A Critique of the Negative Income Tax Experiment*. New York: Russell Sage Foundation.

Rothbard, Murray N. 1982. *The Ethics of Liberty*. Atlantic Highlands NJ: Humanities Press.

Rothstein, Bo. 1998. *Just Institutions Matter: The Moral and Political Logic of the Universal Welfare State*. Cambridge: Cambridge University Press.

Rousseau, Jean-Jacques. 1754/1971. *Discours sur l'origine et les fondements de l'inégalité parmi les homes*. Paris: Flammarion.

———. 1762/2011. *Le Contrat social*. Paris: Le Livre de poche.

———. 1789/1996. *Les Confessions*, vol. 1. Paris: Pocket.

Russell, Bertrand. 1918/1966. *Roads to Freedom: Socialism, Anarchism and Syndicalism*. London: Unwin Books.

———. 1932/1976. "In Praise of Idleness." In Bertrand Russell, *In Praise of Idleness and Other Essays*, 11–25. London: Unwin Paperbacks.

Sala-i-Martin, Xavier, and Jeffrey Sachs. 1991. "Fiscal Federalism and Optimal Currency Areas: Evidence for Europe from the United States." NBER Working Paper no. 3855, October. http://www.nber.org/papers/w3855.

Sala-i-Martin, Xavier, and Arvind Subramanian. 2003. "Addressing the Natural Resource Curse: An Illustration from Nigeria." NBER Working Paper no. 9804, June. http://www.nber.org/papers/w9804.

Salam, Reihan. 2014. "Unconditional Basic Income? You're Kidding." Oregon Live, opinion, June 5. http://www.oregonlive.com/opinion/index.ssf/2014/06/one_great_welfare_mistake_slat.html.

Salehi-Isfahani, Djavad. 2014. "Iran's Subsidy Reform: From Promise to Disappointment." Policy Perspective no. 13, June, Economic Research Forum (ERF). http://erf.org.eg/wp-content/uploads/2015/12/PP13_2014.pdf.

Salverda, Wim. 1984. "Basisinkomen en inkomensverdeling. De financiële uitvoerbaarheid van het basisinkomen." *Tijdschrift voor Politieke Ekonomie* 8: 9–41.

Santens, Scott. 2014. "Why Should We Support the Idea of an Unconditional Basic Income: An Answer to a Growing Question of the 21st Century." Working Life blog, June 2, Medium Corporation. https://medium.com/working-life/why-should-we-support-the-idea-of-an-unconditional-basic-income-8a2680c73dd3.

Saraceno, Chiara. 1989. "Una persona, un reddito." *Politica ed Economi* 1: 27–32.

———. 2010. "Concepts and Practices of Social Citizenship in Europe: The Case of Poverty and Income Support for the Poor." In Jens Alber and Neil Gilbert, eds., *United in Diversity? Comparing Social Models in Europe and America*, 162–168. Oxford: Oxford University Press.

Sas, Willem, and Kevin Spiritus. 2015. "De Europese Centrale Bank kan de economie aanzwengelen met een beperkt monetair basisinkomen." *De Tijd*, April 9.

Schachtschneider, Ulrich. 2012. "Ökologisches Grundeinkommen—Ein Einstieg ist möglich." Paper presented at the 14th Congress of the Basic Income Earth Network (BIEN), Munich, September 14–16.

Scharpf, Fritz. 1993. "Von der Finanzierung der Arbeitslosigkeit zur Subventionierung niedriger Erwerbseinkommen." *Gewerkschaftliche Monatshefte* 7: 433–443.

———. 1994. "Negative Einkommensteuer—ein Programm gegen Ausgrenzung." *Die Mitbestimmung* 40(3): 27–32.

———. 1995. "Subventionierte Niedriglohn-Beschäftigung statt bezahlter Arbeitslosigkeit." *Zeitschrift für Sozialreform* 41(2): 65–82.

———. 2000. "Basic Income and Social Europe." In Robert J. van der Veen and Loek Groot, eds., *Basic Income on the Agenda*, 154–160. Amsterdam: Amsterdam University Press.

Schmähl, Winfried. 1992. "The Flat-Rate Public Pension in the German Social Policy Debate: From the Early 19th to the Late 20th Century." Arbeitspapier 6/92, Centre for Social Policy Research, Universität Bremen.

Schmid, Thomas, ed. 1984. *Befreiung von falscher Arbeit. Thesen zum garantierten Mindesteinkommen*. Berlin: Wagenbach.

Schmitt, Günther. 1980. "Vor einer Wende in der Agrarpolitik." *Agrarwitschaft* 29: 97–105.

Schmitter, Philippe, and Michael W. Bauer. 2001. "A (Modest) Proposal for Expanding Social Citizenship in the European Union." *Journal of European Social Policy* 11(1): 55–65.

Schor, Juliet B. 1993. *The Overworked American*. New York: Basic Books.

Schotter, Andrew. 1985. *Free Market Economics*. Cambridge: Cambridge University Press.

Schroeder, Wolfgang, Sascha Kristin Futh, and Bastian Jantz. 2015. "Change through Convergence? Reform Measures of European Welfare States in Comparison." Friedricht Ebert Stiftung Study, June.

Schulte-Basta, Dorotheee. 2010. *Ökonomische Nützlichkeit oder leistungsloser Selbstwert? Zur Kompatibilität von bedingungslosem Grundeinkommen und katholischer Soziallehre*. Freiberg: ZAS Verlag.

Scottish Green Party. 2014. "Citizen's Income." Green Yes, briefing note, August 10.

Scrope, George Julius Poulett. 1833. *Principles of Political Economy, deduced from the natural laws of social welfare, and applied to the present state of Britain*. London: Longman.

Scutella, Rosanna. 2004. "Moves to a Basic Income-Flat Tax System in Australia: Implications for the Distribution of Income and Supply of Labour." Melbourne Institute Working Paper No. 5/04, University of Melbourne.

Seekings, Jeremy, and Heidi Matisonn. 2013. "South Africa: The Continuing Politics of Basic Income." In Matthew C. Murray and Carole Pateman, eds., *Basic Income Worldwide: Horizons of Reform*, 128–150. New York: Palgrave Macmillan.

Segal, Hugh. 2012. "Scrapping Welfare: The Case for Guaranteeing All Canadians an Income above the Poverty Line." *Literary Review of Canada* 20(10): 8–10.

Sen, Amartya. 2009. *The Idea of Justice*. Cambridge, MA: Harvard University Press.

———. 2012. "What Happened to Europe? Democracy and the Decisions of Bankers." *The New Republic,* August 2. http://www.tnr.com/article/magazine/105657/sen-europe-democracy-keynes-social-justice.

Sennett, Richard. 2003. *Respect in a World of Inequality*. New York: Norton.

Shachar, Ayelet. 2009. *The Birthright Lottery: Citizenship and Global Inequality*. Cambridge, MA: Harvard University Press.

Shapiro, Carl, and Joseph Stiglitz. 1984. "Equilibrium Unemployment as a Worker Discipline Device." *American Economic Review* 74(3): 433–444.

Shaviro, Daniel. 1997. "The Minimum Wage, the Earned Income Tax Credit, and Optimal Subsidy Policy." *The University of Chicago Law Review* 64(2): 405–481.

Sheahen, Allan. 2012. *Basic Income Guarantee: Your Right to Economic Security*. New York: Palgrave Macmillan.

Shipler, David K. 2004. *The Working Poor: Invisible in America*. New York: Vintage Books.

Shirky, Ckay. 2008. *Here Comes Everybody: The Power of Organizing without Organizations*. New York: Penguin Books.

Shulevitz, Judith. 2016. "It's Payback Time for Women." *New York Times,* January 8.

Simon, Herbert A. 1998. "Letter to BIEN on the Flat Tax and Our Common Patrimony." *Basic Income* 29: 8. http://www.basic income.org/bien/pdf/BI29.pdf.

———. 2001. "UBI and the Flat Tax." In Philippe Van Parijs et al., *What's Wrong with a Free Lunch?* 34–38. Boston: Beacon Press.

Sirugue, Christophe. 2016. *Repenser les minima sociaux—Vers une couverture socle commune*. Paris: La Documentation française.

Skidelsky, Robert, and Edward Skidelsky. 2011. *How Much Is Enough? Money and the Good Life*. London: Penguin Books.

Skidmore, Felicity. 1975. "Operational Design of the Experiment." In Joseph A. Pechman and P. Michael Timpane, eds., *Work Incentives and Income Guarantees: The New Jersey Negative Income Tax Experiment,* 25–59. Washington DC: Brookings Institution.

Skidmore, Thomas. 1829. *The Rights of Man to Property*. New York: Burt Franklin.

Skocpol, Theda. 1991. "Targeting within Universalism: Politically Viable Policies to Combat Poverty in the United States." In Christopher Jencks and Paul E. Peterson, eds., *The Urban Underclass,* 411–436. Washington DC: The Brookings Institution.

Sloman, Peter. 2016. "Beveridge's Rival: Juliet Rhys-Williams and the Campaign for Basic Income, 1942–55." *Contemporary British History* 30(2): 203–223.

Smith, Adam. 1776/1977. *The Wealth of Nations,* Harmondsworth: Penguin Books.

Smith, Jeff. 2006. "Fund Basic Income Grants Not from Income but from Outgo." *Georgist Journal* 104. www.georgistjournal.org/104-spring-2006/.

Snowden, Edward. 2014. "A Nation Interview." *The Nation,* November 17. www.thenation.com/article/186129/snowden-exile-exclusive-interview.

Soboul, Albert. 1962. *Histoire de la revolution française 1. De la Bastille à la Gironde.* Paris: Gallimard.

Social Justice Ireland. 2010. *Building a Fairer Tax System: The Working Poor and the Cost of Refundable Tax Credits.* Dublin: Social Justice Ireland.

Sombart, Werner. 1896/1905. *Sozialismus und soziale Bewegung.* Jena: Gustav Fischer, 1905. English translation: *Socialism and the Social Movement.* London: Dent & Co. and New York: Dutton & Co., 1990.

Sommer, Maximilian. 2016. *A Feasible Basic-Income Scheme for Germany: Effects on Labor Supply, Poverty, and Income Inequality.* Cham: Springer.

Spafford, Jesse. 2013. "Reconciling Basic Income and Immigration." Metamorphoses and Deformations, blog post, December 8. http://jessespafford.tumblr.com/post/69381354548/reconciling-basic-income-and-immigration.

Spence, Thomas. 1775/1982. *The Real Rights of Man.* In Spence, *The Political Works of Thomas Spence,* ed. H. T. Dickinson. Newcastle Upon Tyne: Avero.

———. 1782/1982. "A Supplement to the History of Robinson Crusoe." In Spence, *The Political Works of Thomas Spence,* ed. H. T. Dickinson. Newcastle Upon Tyne: Avero.

———. 1797/2004. "The Rights of Infants." In Spence, *The Origins of Universal Grants,* ed. John Cunliffe and Guido Erreygers, 81–91. Basingstoke: Palgrave Macmillan, 2004. Also available from http://thomas-spence-society.co.uk/4.html.

Spicker, Paul. 2010. *The Origins of Modern Welfare: Juan Luis Vives, De Subventione Pauperum, and City of Ypres, Forma Subventionis Pauperum.* Oxford: Peter Lang.

Srnicek, Nick, and Alex Williams. 2015. *Inventing the Future: Postcapitalism and a World without Work.* London: Verso.

Standing, Guy, and Michael Samson, eds. 2003. *A Basic Income Grant for South Africa.* Cape Town: University of Cape Town Press.

Standing, Guy. 1986. "Meshing Labour Flexibility with Security: An Answer to Mass Unemployment?" *International Labour Review* 125(1): 87–106.

———. 1999. *Global Labour Flexibility: Seeking Distributive Justice.* Basingstoke: Macmillan.

———. 2011. *The Precariat: The New Dangerous Class.* London: Bloomsbury.

———. 2012. "Why a Basic Income Is Necessary for a Right to Work." *Basic Income Studies* 7(2): 19–40.

———. 2014a. *A Precariat Charter: From Denizens to Citizens.* London: Bloomsbury.

———. 2014b. "Cash Transfers Can Work Better than Subsidies." *The Hindu,* December 6. www.thehindu.com/article6666913.ece.

Steensland, Brian. 2008. *The Failed Welfare Revolution: America's Struggle over Guaranteed Income Policy.* Princeton: Princeton University Press.

Steiber, Nadia, and Barbara Haas. 2012. "Advances in Explaining Women's Employment Patterns." *Socioeconomic Review* 10(2): 343–367.

Steiner, Hillel. 1992. "Three Just Taxes." In Philippe Van Parijs, ed., *Arguing for Basic Income: Ethical Foundations for a Radical Reform,* 81–92. London: Verso.

———. 1994. *An Essay on Rights.* Oxford: Blackwell.

———. 2003. "Compatriot Solidarity and Justice among Thieves." In Andrew Reeve and Andrew Williams, eds., *Real Libertarianism Assessed: Political Theory after Van Parijs*, 161–171. Basingstoke: Palgrave Macmillan.

Stern, Andy. 2016. *Raising the Floor: How a Universal Basic Income Can Renew Our Economy and Rebuild the American Dream*. New York: Public Affairs.

Stigler, George. 1946. "The Economics of Minimum Wage Legislation." *American Economic Review* 36: 358–365.

Stiglitz, Joseph. 2012. *The Price of Inequality*. New York: Columbia University Press.

St John, Susan. 2016. "Can Older Citizens Lead the Way to a Universal Basic Income?" In Jennifer Mays, Greg Marston, and John Tomlinson, eds., *Basic Income in Australia and New Zealand: Perspectives from the Neoliberal Frontier*, 95–114. New York: Palgrave Macmillan.

St John, Susan, and Larry Willmore. 2001. "Two Legs are Better than Three: New Zealand as a Model for Old Age Pensions." *World Development* 29(8): 1291–1305.

Stoffaës, Christian. 1974. *Rapport du groupe d'étude de l'impôt négatif*. Paris: Commissariat du Plan.

Stoleru, Lionel. 1973. "Politique sociale et garantie des revenus." *Futuribles* 16: 47–68.

———. 1974a. *Vaincre la Pauvreté dans les pays riches*. Paris: Flammarion.

———. 1974b. "Coût et efficacité de l'impôt négatif." *Revue Economique* 5: 745–761.

Story, Michael. 2015. *Free Market Welfare: The Case for a Negative Income Tax*. London: Adam Smith Institute.

Sturn, Richard, and Dujmovits, Rudi. 2000. "Basic Income in Complex Worlds: Individual Freedom and Social Interdependencies." *Analyse und Kritik* 22(2): 198–222.

Summers, Lawrence H. 2016. "The Age of Secular Stagnation." *Foreign Affairs* 95(2): 2–9.

Suplicy, Eduardo M. 2006. *Renda de Cidadania. A saída é pela porta*, 4th ed. Sao Paulo: Cortez Editora.

———. 2011. "Towards an Unconditional Basic Income in Brazil?" In Axel Gosseries and Yannick Vanderborght, eds., *Arguing about Justice: Essays for Philippe Van Parijs*, 337–346. Louvain-la-Neuve: Presses Universitaires de Louvain.

Surrender, Rebecca. 2015. "South Africa: A Different Welfare and Development Paradigm?" In Reza Hasmath, ed., *Inclusive Growth, Development and Welfare Policy: A Critical Assessment*, 161–178. Oxford: Oxford University Press.

Sutter, John D. 2015. "The Argument for a Basic Income." CNN online, March 15. http://edition.cnn.com/2015/03/01/opinion/sutter-basic-income/index.html.

Sykes, Jennifer, Katrin Križ, Kathryn Edin, and Sarah Halpern-Meekin. 2015. "Dignity and Dreams: What the Earned Income Tax Credit (EITC) Means to Low-Income Families." *American Sociological Review* 80(2): 243–267.

Tabatabai, Hamid. 2011. "The Basic Income Road to Reforming Iran's Price Subsidies." *Basic Income Studies* 6(1), 1–24.

———. 2012. "From Price Subsidies to Basic Income: The Iran Model and Its Lessons." In Karl Widerquist and Michael Howard, eds., *Exporting the Alaska Model*, 17–32. New York: Palgrave Macmillan.

Takamatsu, Rie, and Toshiaki Tachibanaki. 2014. "What Needs to Be Considered When Introducing a New Welfare System: Who Supports Basic Income in Japan?" In Yannick Vanderborght and Toru Yamamori, eds., *Basic Income in Japan: Prospects of a Radical Idea in a Transforming Welfare State*, 197–218. New York: Palgrave Macmillan.

Tanghe, Fernand. 1989. *Le Droit au travail entre histoire et utopie: de la répression de la mendicité à l'allocation universelle.* Florence: European University Institute.

———. 2014. "1848 and the Question of the *droit au travail:* A Historical Retrospective." In Elise Dermine and Daniel Dumont, eds., *Activation Policies for the Unemployed, the Right to Work and the Duty to Work,* 23–32. Brussels: Peter Lang.

Taylor-Gooby, Peter. 2013. "Why Do People Stigmatise the Poor at a Time of Rapidly Increasing Inequality, and What Can Be Done about It?" *Political Quarterly* 84(1): 31–42.

Theobald, Robert. 1961. *The Challenge of Abundance.* New York: Clarkson N. Potter.

———. 1963/1965. *Free Men and Free Markets.* New York: Anchor Books.

———. 1966. "The Guaranteed Income: What and Why." In John H. Bunzel, ed., *Issues of American Public Policy,* 99–108. Englewood Cliffs: Prentice-Hall.

———, ed. 1967. *The Guaranteed Income: Next Step in Socioeconomic Evolution?* New York: Doubleday.

Thornhill, John, and Ralph Atkins. 2016. "Basic Income: Money for Nothing." *Financial Times,* May 26. http://www.ft.com/intl/cms/s/0/7c7ba87e-229f-11e6-9d4d-c11776a5124d.html#axzz49pivjtkE.

Thurow, Lester C. 1974. "Cash versus In-Kind Transfers." *American Economic Review* 64(2): 190–195.

———. 1977. "Government Expenditures: Cash or In-Kind Aid?" In Gerald Dworkin, Gordon Bermant, and Peter G. Brown, eds., *Markets and Morals,* 85–106. New York: Wiley.

Tinbergen, Jan. 1956. *Economic Policy: Principles and Design.* Amsterdam: North Holland.

Tobin, James, Joseph A. Pechman, and Peter M. Mieszkowski. 1967. "Is a Negative Income Tax Practical?" *The Yale Law Journal* 77(1): 1–27.

Tobin, James. 1965. "On the Economic Status of the Negro." *Daedalus* 94: 878–898.

———. 1966. "The Case for an Income Guarantee." *The Public Interest* 4: 31–41.

———. 1968. "Raising the Incomes of the Poor." In Kermit Gordon, ed., *Agenda for the Nation,* 77–116. Washington DC: The Brookings Institution.

———. 1978. "A Proposal for International Monetary Reform." *Eastern Economic Journal* 4: 153–159.

———. 2001. "The Suplicy-Tobin Exchange." BIEN News Flash 11, September. www.basicincome.org/bien/pdf/NewsFlash3.pdf.

Tocqueville, Alexis de. 1833/1967. "Voyage en Angleterre de 1833." In Tocqueville, *Voyages en Angleterre et en Irlande,* ed. Jacob Peter Mayer, 3–120. Paris: Gallimard.

———. 1835/1997. *Memoir on Pauperism.* London: Civitas.

Tomlinson, John. 2012. "Australia: Will Basic Income Have a Second Coming?" In Richard K. Caputo, ed., *Basic Income Guarantee and Politics: International Experiences and Perspectives on the Viability of Income Guarantees,* 153–175. New York: Palgrave Macmillan.

Torry, Malcolm. 2012. "The United Kingdom: Only for Children?" In Richard K. Caputo, ed., *Basic Income Guarantee and Politics: International Experiences and Perspectives on the Viability of Income Guarantees,* 235–263. New York: Palgrave Macmillan.

———. 2013. *Money for Everyone: Why We Need a Citizen's Income.* Bristol: Policy Press.

———. 2015. *101 Reasons for a Citizen's Income: Arguments for Giving Everyone Some Money.* Bristol: Policy Press.

———. 2016. *The Feasibility of Citizen's Income.* London: Palgrave Macmillan.

Townsend, Peter B. 1968. "The Difficulties of Negative Income Tax." In Townsend, *Social Services for All?* London: Fabian Society.

Tremblay, Robert. 1984. Lettre à Michel Rochon, Secrétaire de la Commission [Macdonald], Fédération québécoise anti-pauvreté, Québec, August 10.

Trudeau Foundation. 2013. *Backgrounder. Responsible Citizenship: A National Survey of Canadians.* Montreal: Trudeau Foundation.

Turgot, Anne-Robert Jacques. 1757. "Fondation." In *Encyclopédie,* tome 7, 72–77.

Unemployed Workers Movement. 1979. "The Guaranteed Minimum Income." Paper presented at the State Conference of UWU, Perth, Australia, July 28–29.

UNISON. 2016. Record of Decisions, 2016 Unison National Women's Conference, March 8, London. https://www.unison.org.uk/content/uploads/2016/03/2016-National-Womens -Conference-Decisions-Booklet.docx.

United Kingdom. 2015. "2010 to 2015 Government Policy: Welfare Reform. Appendix 1: Government Policy on Universal Credit, an Introduction." Policy paper, updated May 2015. Department for Work and Pensions, London. www.dwp.gov.uk/universal-credit.

Vallentyne, Peter. 2000. "Introduction: Left-Libertarianism—A Primer." In Peter Vallentyne and Hillel Steiner, eds., *Left-Libertarianism and Its Critics,* 1–20. Basingstoke: Palgrave Macmillan.

Vallentyne, Peter, and Hillel Steiner, eds. 2000a. *The Origins of Left-Libertarianism.* Basingstoke: Palgrave Macmillan.

———, eds. 2000b. *Left-Libertarianism and Its Critics.* Basingstoke: Palgrave Macmillan.

Van Berkel, Rik et al. 1993. *Met z'n allen zwijgen in de woestijn. Een onderzoek naar het basisinkomen binnen de Voedingsbond FNV.* University of Utrecht: Vakgroep Algemene Sociale Wetenschappen.

Vandenbroucke, Frank. 1997. "A propos de l'instauration pragmatique d'une allocation universelle." *La Revue nouvelle* 105: 161–166.

Vanden Heuvel, Katrina, and Stephen F. Cohen. 2014. "Edward Snowden: A 'Nation' Interview." *Nation,* October 20.

Vanderborght, Yannick. 2001. "La France sur la voie d'un 'revenu minimum inconditionnel'?" *Mouvements* 15–16: 157–165.

———. 2002. "Belgique: VIVANT ou l'allocation universelle pour seul programme electoral." *Multitudes* 8: 135–145.

———. 2004a. "La faisabilité politique d'un revenu inconditionnel." PhD diss., Université catholique de Louvain.

———. 2004b. "Universal Basic Income in Belgium and the Netherlands: Implementation through the Back Door?" EUI Working Paper SPS No. 2004/4, European University Institute, Florence.

———. 2006. "Why Trade Unions Oppose Basic Income." *Basic Income Studies* 1(1): 1–20.

Vanderborght, Yannick, and Yuki Sekine. 2014. "A Comparative Look at the Feasibility of Basic Income in the Japanese Welfare State." In Yannick Vanderborght and Toru Yamamori, eds., *Basic Income in Japan: Prospects for a Radical Reform in a Transforming Welfare State*, 15–34. New York: Palgrave Macmillan.

Vanderborght, Yannick, and Philippe Van Parijs. 2001. "Assurance participation et revenu de participation. Deux manières d'infléchir l'état social actif." *Reflets et perspectives de la vie économique* 40: 183–196.

———. 2005. *L'Allocation universelle.* Paris: La Découverte.

Van der Veen, Robert J., and Philippe Van Parijs. 1986a. "A Capitalist Road to Communism." *Theory and Society* 15: 635–655.

———. 1986b. "Universal Grants versus Socialism. Reply to Six Critics." *Theory and Society* 15: 723–757.

———. 2006. "A Capitalist Road to Global Justice. Reply to Another Six Critics." *Basic Income Studies* 1(1): 1–15.

Van Donselaar, Gijs. 2009. *The Right to Exploit: Parasitism, Scarcity, and Basic Income.* Oxford: Oxford University Press.

———. 2015. "In Company of the Funny Sunny Surfer off Malibu." *Analyse & Kritik* 2: 305–317.

Van Hove, Hildegard et al. 2011. *Femmes et hommes en Belgique. Statistiques et indicateurs de genre*, 2e édition. Bruxelles: Institut pour l'égalité des femmes et des hommes.

Van Keirsbilck, Felipe. 2015. "Un horizon peut-être, un chemin sûrement pas." In *Allocation universelle: miroir aux alouettes*, special issue of *Ensemble!* 89: 23–24.

Van Lancker, Wim, and Natascha Van Mechelen. 2015. "Universalism under Siege? Exploring the Association between Targeting, Child Benefits and Child Poverty across 26 Countries." *Social Science Research* 5: 60–75.

Van Male, Patrick. 2003. "A Basic Income Funded by the EU?" BIEN NewsFlash 22, July.

Van Mechelen, Natascha, and Jonathan Bradshaw. 2013. "Child Poverty as a Government Priority: Child Benefit Packages for Working Families, 1992–2009." In Ive Marx and Kenneth Nelson, eds., *Minimum Income Protection in Flux*, 81–105. New York: Palgrave Macmillan.

Van Middelaar, Luuk. 2013. *The Passage to Europe: How a Continent Became a Union.* New Haven: Yale University Press.

Van Ojik, Bram. 1982. *Basisinkomen.* Amsterdam: Politieke Partij Radikalen Studiestichting.

———. 1983. "Basisinkomen en arbeidstijdverkorting." *Socialisme en Democratie* 10: 25–30.

———. 1985. *Basisinkomen. Over arbeidsethos, inkomen en emancipatie.* Amsterdam: PPR Studiestichting.

———. 1989. *Basisinkomen. Van veenbrand naar gidsland.* Amsterdam: Politieke Partij Radikalen.

Van Ojik, Bram, and Bart Teulings. 1990. *De band tussen arbeid en inkomen: losser of vaster?* Amsterdam: Wetenschappelijk Bureau GroenLinks.

Van Parijs, Philippe. 1983. "L'allocation universelle." *Ecolo-Infos* (Namur) 16(7 February): 4–7.

———. 1985. "Marx, l'écologisme et la transition directe du capitalisme au communism." In Bernard Chavance, ed., *Marx en perspective,* 135–155. Paris: Ecole des Hautes Etudes en Sciences Sociales.

———. 1987a / 2013. "A Green Case for Basic Income?" In K. Widerquist, J. A. Noguera, Y. Vanderborght, and J. De Wispelaere, eds., *Basic Income: An Anthology of Contemporary Research,* 269–274. Chichester: Wiley-Blackwell.

———. 1987b. "A Revolution in Class Theory." *Politics and Society* 15: 453–482.

———. 1988. "Rawls face aux libertariens." In Catherine Audard et al., *Individu et justice sociale. Autour de John Rawls,* 193–218. Paris: Le Seuil.

———. 1990. "The Second Marriage of Justice and Efficiency." *Journal of Social Policy* 19: 1–25.

———. 1991. "Why Surfers Should Be Fed: The Liberal Case for an Unconditional Basic Income." *Philosophy and Public Affairs* 20: 101–131.

———. 1992. "Competing Justifications of Basic Income." In Philippe van Parijs, ed., *Arguing for Basic Income: Ethical Foundations for a Radical Reform,* 3–43. London: Verso.

———. 1995. *Real Freedom for All: What (If Anything) Can Justify Capitalism?* Oxford: Oxford University Press.

———. 1997. "Reciprocity and the Justification of an Unconditional Basic Income. Reply to Stuart White." *Political Studies* 45: 327–330.

———. 1998. "James Tobin, the Demogrant and the Future of US Social Policy." *Basic Income* 29: 6–7. http://www.basic income.org/bien/pdf/BI29.pdf

———. 2001. "Real Freedom, the Market and the Family. Reply to Seven Critics." *Analyse & Kritik* 23: 106–131.

———. 2002. "Difference Principles." In Samuel Freeman, ed., *The Cambridge Companion to John Rawls,* 200–240. Cambridge: Cambridge University Press.

———, ed. 2003a. *Cultural Diversity versus Economic Solidarity.* Brussels: De Boeck Université. http://www.uclouvain.be/en-12569.html.

———. 2003b. "Hybrid Justice, Patriotism and Democracy: A Selective Reply." In Andrew Reeve and Andrew Williams, eds., *Real Libertarianism Assessed: Political Theory after Van Parijs,* 201–216. London: Palgrave Macmillan.

———. 2006. "Basic Income versus Stakeholder Grants: Some Afterthoughts on How Best to Redesign Distribution." In Erik Olin Wright, ed., *Redesigning Distribution: Basic Income and Stakeholder Grants as Cornerstones of a More Egalitarian Capitalism,* 199–208. London: Verso.

————. 2007. "International Distributive Justice." *The Blackwell's Companion to Political Philosophy*, ed. Robert E. Goodin, Philip Pettit, and Thomas Pogge, vol. 2, 638–652. Oxford: Blackwell.

————. 2009. "Political Ecology: From Autonomous Sphere to Basic Income." *Basic Income Studies* 4(2): 1–9.

————. 2011. *Linguistic Justice for Europe and for the World*. Oxford: Oxford University Press.

————. 2015a. "Epilogue: Justifying Europe." In Luuk van Middelaar and Philippe Van Parijs eds., *After the Storm: How to Save Democracy in Europe*, 247–261. Tielt: Lannoo.

————. 2015b. "Real Freedom for All Women (and Men). A Reply." *Law, Ethics and Philosophy* 3: 161–175.

Van Parijs, Philippe, Laurence Jacquet, and Claudio Salinas. 2000. "Basic Income and Its Cognates." In Robert J. van der Veen and Loek Groot, eds., *Basic Income on the Agenda*, 53–84. Amsterdam: Amsterdam University Press.

Van Parijs, Philippe, and Yannick Vanderborght. 2001. "From Euro-Stipendium to Euro-Dividend." *Journal of European Social Policy* 11(4): 342–346.

Van Rie, Tim, Ive Marx, and Jeroen Horemans. 2011. "Ghent Revisited: Unemployment Insurance and Union Membership in Belgium and the Nordic Countries." *European Journal of Industrial Relations* 17(2): 125–139.

Van Trier, Walter. 1992. "Het basisinkomen als derde weg?" *Streven* 59(9): 779–801.

————. 1995. "Everyone a King: An Investigation into the Meaning and Significance of the Debate on Basic Incomes." PhD diss., Katholieke Universiteit Leuven.

Varian, Hal. 1975/1979. "Distributive Justice, Welfare Economics and the Theory of Fairness." In F. Hahn and M. Hollis, eds., *Philosophy and Economic Theory*, 135–164. Oxford: Oxford University Press.

Varoufakis, Yanis. 2016. "The Universal Right to Capital Income." Project Syndicate, October 31. www.project-syndicate.org/commentary/basic-income-funded-by-capital-income-by-yanis-varoufakis-2016-10.

Ventry, Dennis J. 2000. "The Collision of Tax and Welfare Politics: The Political History of the Earned Income Tax Credit, 1969–99." *National Tax Journal* 53(4): 983–1026.

Vielle, Pascale, and Philippe Van Parijs. 2001. "La prime de virilité." *Le Soir,* December 1.

Vives, Jan Loys. 1533/1943. *Secours van den Aermen*. Brussels: Valero & Fils.

Vives, Johannes Ludovicus. 1526/2010. *De Subventione Pauperum. On the Relief of the Poor, or of Human Needs*. In Paul Spicker, ed., *The Origins of Modern Welfare*, 1–100. Oxford: Peter Lang.

Voedingsbond FNV. 1981. *Met z'n allen roepen in de woestijn. Een tussenrapport over het losser maken van de band tussen arbeid en inkomen*. Utrecht: Voedingsbond FNV.

Von Schmoller, Gustav. 1890. *Zur Social- und Gewerbepolitik der Gegenwart*. Leipzig: Duncker & Humblot.

Wachtel, Henry H. 1955. *Security for All and Free Enterprise: A Summary of the Social Philosophy of Josef Popper-Lynkeus*. New York: Philosophical Library.

Wagner, Adolf. 1881. *Der Staat und das Versicherungswesen*. Tübingen: Laupp.

Walker, Mark. 2016. *Free Money for All: A Basic Income Guarantee Solution for the Twenty-First Century*. New York: Palgrave Macmillan.

Waltenberg, Fabio. 2013. "Are Latin Americans—Brazilians in Particular—Willing to Support an Unconditional Citizen's Income?" In Ruben Lo Vuolo, ed., *Citizen's Income and Welfare Regimes in Latin America: From Cash Transfers to Rights*, 141–167. New York: Palgrave Macmillan.

Warin, Philippe. 2012. "Non-Demand for Social Rights: A New Challenge for Social Action in France." *Journal of Poverty and Social Justice* 20(1): 41–55.

Weitling, Wilhelm. 1845. *Garantien der Harmonie und Freiheit*, 2nd ed. Hamburg: Im Verlage des Verfassers.

Weitzman, Martin L. 1984. *The Share Economy: Conquering Stagflation*. Cambridge, MA: Harvard University Press.

Wenger, Albert. 2016. "World after Capital." Self-published essay. https://www.gitbook .com/book/worldaftercapital/worldaftercapital/details.

Werner, Götz. 2006. *Ein Grund für die Zukunft. Das Grundeinkommen*. Stuttgart: Verlag freies Geistesleben.

———. 2007. *Einkommen für alle*. Köln: Kiepenheuer & Witsch.

Werner, Götz, and Adrienne Goehler. 2010. *1000 € für jeden. Freiheit, Gleichheit, Grundeinkommen*. Berlin: Econ.

Werner, Götz, and Benediktus Hardorp. 2005. "Wir würden gewaltig reich warden." Der Spiegel Online, November 30.

Werner, Götz, and André Presse, eds. 2007. *Grundeinkommen und Konsumsteuer*. Karlsruhe: Universitätsverlag Karlsruhe.

Wernerus, Sabine. 2004. "Les syndicats contre l'allocation universelle? Mise en perspective des points de vue belges et québecois." Master's thesis, Université catholique de Louvain.

White, Stuart. 1996. "Reciprocity Arguments for Basic Income." Paper presented at the 6th Congress of the Basic Income European Network, Vienna, September 12–14.

———. 1997. "Liberal Equality, Exploitation, and the Case for an Unconditional Basic Income." *Political Studies* 45(2): 312–326.

———. 2003a. *The Civic Minimum*. Oxford: Clarendon Press.

———. 2003b. "Fair Reciprocity and Basic Income." In Andrew Reeve and Andrew Williams, eds., *Real Libertarianism Assessed: Political Theory after Van Parijs*, 136–160. London: Palgrave Macmillan.

———. 2015. "Basic Capital in the Egalitarian Toolkit?" *Journal of Applied Philosophy* 32(4): 417–431.

Widerquist, Karl. 1999. "Reciprocity and the Guaranteed Income." *Politics and Society* 33(3): 386–401.

———. 2005. "A Failure to Communicate: What (If Anything) Can We Learn from the Negative Income Tax Experiments." *Journal of Socioeconomics* 34(1): 49–81.

———. 2011. "Why We Demand an Unconditional Basic Income: The ECSO Freedom Case." In Axel Gosseries and Yannick Vanderborght, eds., *Arguing about Justice: Essays for Philippe Van Parijs*, 387–394. Louvain-la-Neuve: Presses Universitaires de Louvain.

———. 2012. "Citizens' Capital Accounts: A Proposal." In Karl Widerquist and Michael Howard, eds., *Exporting the Alaska Model: Adapting the Permanent Fund Dividend for Reform around the World*, 183–203. New York: Palgrave Macmillan.

———. 2013. *Independence, Propertylessness and Basic Income: A Theory of Freedom as the Power to Say No*. New York: Palgrave Macmillan.

Widerquist, Karl, and Michael Howard, eds. 2012a. *Alaska's Permanent Fund Dividend: Examining Its Suitability as a Model*. New York: Palgrave Macmillan.

———. 2012b. *Exporting the Alaska Model: Adapting the Permanent Fund Dividend for Reform around the World*. New York: Palgrave Macmillan.

Widerquist, Karl, Jose A. Noguera, Yannick Vanderborght, and Jurgen De Wispelaere, eds. 2013. *Basic Income: An Anthology of Contemporary Research*. New York: Wiley-Blackwell.

Widerstrom, Klaus. 2010. "Erich Fromm and His Proposal for a Basic Income." Indybay, July 6. http://www.indybay.org/newsitems/2010/07/06/18652754.php.

Wilkinson, Richard G., and Kate Pickett. 2009. *The Spirit Level: Why More Equal Societies Almost Always Do Better*. London: Allen Lane.

Willmore, Larry. 2007. Universal Pensions for Developing Countries. *World Development* 35(1): 24–51.

Withorn, Ann. 1993/2013. "Is One Man's Ceiling Another Woman's Floor?" In Karl Widerquist et al., eds., *Basic Income: An Anthology of Contemporary Research*, 145–148. New York: Wiley-Blackwell.

Wogaman, P. 1968. *Guaranteed Annual Income: The Moral Issues*. Nashville: Abingdon Press.

Wood, Adrian. 1994. *North-South Trade, Employment and Inequality*. Oxford: Oxford University Press.

Woolf, Virginia. 1929/1977. *A Room of One's Own*. St Albans: Panther Books.

Woolley, Frances. 2004. "Why Pay Child Benefits to Mothers?" *Canadian Public Policy* 30(1): 47–69.

Workers Party. 1985. *Social Welfare for All*. Dublin: The Workers Party.

Wright, Erik O. 1986. "Why Something Like Socialism Is Necessary for the Transition to Something Like Communism." *Theory and Society* 15(5): 657–672.

———, ed. 2006. *Redesigning Distribution: Basic Income and Stakeholder Grants as Cornerstones of a More Egalitarian Capitalism*. London: Verso.

———. 2015. "Eroding Capitalism: A Comment on Stuart White's 'Basic Capital in the Egalitarian Toolkit.'" *Journal of Applied Philosophy* 32(4): 432–439.

WRR (Wetenschappelijke Raad voor het Regeringsbeleid). 1985. *Safeguarding Social Security*. The Hague: Netherlands Scientific Council for Government Policy.

Yamamori, Toru. 2014. "A Feminist Way to Unconditional Basic Income: Claimants Unions and Women's Liberation Movements in 1970s Britain." *Basic Income Studies* 9(1–2): 1–24.

Yamamori, Toru, and Yannick Vanderborght. 2014. "Income Security and the 'Right to Subsistence' in Japan." In Yannick Vanderborght and Toru Yamamori, eds., *Basic Income in Japan: Prospects for a Radical Reform in a Transforming Welfare State*, 1–11. New York: Palgrave Macmillan.

Yamashita, Junko. 2014. "The Impact of Basic Income on the Gendered Division of Paid Care Work." In Yannick Vanderborght and Toru Yamamori, eds. *Basic Income in Japan: Prospects for a Radical Reform in a Transforming Welfare State*, 117–130. New York: Palgrave Macmillan.

Yunker, James A. 1977. "The Social Dividend under Market Socialism." *Annals of Public and Cooperative Economy* 48(1): 91–133.

———. 2013. "The Basic Income Guarantee: A General Equilibrium Evaluation." *Basic Income Studies* 8(2): 203–233.

Zwolinski, Matt. 2011. "Classical Liberalism and the Basic Income." *Basic Income Studies* 6(2): 1–14.

———. 2013. "Why Did Hayek Support a Basic Income?" Libertarianism.org, December 23. http://www.libertarianism.org/columns/why-did-hayek-support-basic-income.

———. 2014. "The Pragmatic Libertarian Case for a Basic Income Guarantee." Cato Unbound blog, August 4. http://www.cato-unbound.org/2014/08/04/matt-zwolinski /pragmatic-libertarian-case-basic-income-guarantee.

Zylberman, Ariel. Forthcoming. "Bread as Freedom: Kant on the State's Duties to the Poor." In Dai Heide and Evan Tiffany, eds., *Kantian Freedom*.

Acknowledgments

This book grew out of a short introductory book published in French in 2005 under the title *L'allocation universelle* and subsequently translated into several other European languages. Our initial plan was to prepare an English version better suited for a non-European audience. Due to other commitments, we could not implement this plan straightaway and turned to it only years later. In the meantime, so much had happened in connection with the topic in the world and in our minds that we felt we had a very different and much bigger book to write. Obviously, some of the core ideas were already present in the 2005 book and indeed in many of our other publications on the topic. In particular, earlier versions of the first and last chapters appear in two collective volumes: *The Good Life Beyond Growth* (H. Rosa and C. Henning eds., Palgrave Macmillan) and *Inclusive Growth, Development and Welfare Policy* (R. Hasmath ed., Oxford University Press).

During the many years of indirect and direct preparation of this book, we benefited immensely from information and insights gathered from fellow life-members of BIEN, the (now worldwide) basic-income network founded in Louvain-la-Neuve in 1986, and from participants in its sixteen congresses so far. We owe very special thanks to John Baker, Sue Black, Laurent de Briey, Michael Howard, Jonathan Van Parys, and two anonymous readers for comments on large parts of an earlier draft, and to Juliana Bidadanure and Robert Lepenies for masterminding an exceedingly fruitful workshop about our manuscript at the European University Institute in June 2015.

For providing us with stimulating feedback, useful tips, and reliable information on specific matters—from the most exact translation of "proventus vitae" in More's *Utopia* to the most accurate estimates of the maximum yield of carbon taxes—we are most grateful to many colleagues next door and far away: Randall Akee, Kaoru Ando, Richard Bellamy, Ronald Blaschke,

David Calnitsky, Valérie Cayouette-Guilloteau, Ugo Colombino, John Cunliffe, Marc de Basquiat, Alexander de Roo, Jurgen De Wispelaere, André Decoster, Paul-Augustin Deproost, Guido Erreygers, Evelyn Forget, Tim Goedemé, Loek Groot, Sjir Hoeijmakers, Derek Hum, Dirk Jacobi, Markus Kanerva, Yoonkyung Lee, Otto Lehto, Catharina Lis, Télémaque Masson, Philippe Maystadt, Liam McHugh-Russell, Caitlin McLean, Claus Offe, Elena Pribytkova, Michael Quinn, Andrea Robiglio, Philippe Schmitter, Paul Spicker, Brian Steensland, Kevin Spiritus, Hillel Steiner, Nenad Stojanović, Lluis Torrens Mèlich, Jonathan Rée, Wayne Simpson, Hamid Tabatabai, Pierre-Etienne Vandamme, Bruno Van der Linden, Toon Vanheukelom, Vincent Van Steenberghe, Walter Van Trier, Juri Viehoff, Mehrdad Yousefian, and Ariel Zylberman.

Finally, we want to thank Michael Aronson, who persuaded us to write this book as early as 2006, Ian Malcolm, who took over from him and steered the book towards completion, Julia Kirby, who greatly improved the manuscript at the final stage, and the other members of the staff of Harvard University Press involved in the production of this book. It has been a pleasure to work with them.

This book is dedicated to our respective spouses. We have countless reasons for being grateful to them. One of these reasons is that they did not resent too much the time we spent working on this book. With their kind blessings, all royalties earned from it will be paid into a fund to be used in support of further discussion and action around the radical yet sensible proposal to which it is devoted.

Index

Pages numbers followed by f and t indicate figures and tables. Pages numbers followed by n and nn indicate notes.